Cubed

Cubed

A Secret History of the Workplace

Nikil Saval

Doubleday

NEW YORK   LONDON   TORONTO   SYDNEY   AUCKLAND

www.doubleday.com

DOUBLEDAY and the portrayal of an anchor with a dolphin are registered
trademarks of Random House LLC.

Portions of this book appeared in different form as
"Birth of the Office" in *n +1,* issue 6 (Winter 2008).

Jacket design by Oliver Munday

Library of Congress Cataloging-in-Publication Data
Saval, Nikil.
Cubed : a secret history of the workplace / Nikil Saval.
pages cm
Includes bibliographical references and index.
1. Offices—History.
2. Clerks—History.   3. Office management—History.
4. Office layout—History.   5. Office buildings—History.   I. Title.
HF5547.S336 2014
651.09—dc23   2013037635

ISBN 978-0-385-53657-8 (hardcover)
ISBN 978-0-385-53658-5 (eBook)

MANUFACTURED IN THE UNITED STATES OF AMERICA

1 3 5 7 9 10 8 6 4 2

First Edition

| For Shannon |

I have known the inexorable sadness of pencils . . .

—*Theodore Roethke, "Dolor"*

ESTEEMED GENTLEMEN,

I am a poor, young, unemployed person in the business field, my name is Wenzel, I am seeking a suitable position, and I take the liberty of asking you, nicely and politely, if perhaps in your airy, bright, amiable rooms such a position might be free. I know that your good firm is large, proud, old, and rich, thus I may yield to the pleasing supposition that a nice, easy, pretty little place would be available, into which, as into a kind of warm cubbyhole, I can slip . . .

—*Robert Walser, "The Job Application"*

Contents

Introduction   *1*

1
The Clerking Class   9

2
The Birth of the Office   *33*

3
The White-Blouse Revolution   *72*

4
Up the Skyscraper   *96*

5
Organization Men and Women   *143*

6
Open Plans   *183*

7
Space Invaders   *221*

8
The Office of the Future   *256*

9
The Office and Its Ends   *278*

Acknowledgments   313
Notes   315
Index   333

Cubed

INTRODUCTION

Because the footage comes from a security cam, the images are grainy and silent, the perspective fixed. We are in a recognizable scene: a cubicle farm, with workers crammed next to each other, all staring at their computers, in a tiny, fluorescent-lit space. A man in a shirt and tie sits at his desk while a co-worker crouching next to him collects papers from a file cabinet. Time passes with little else happening until the crouching man suddenly grabs the sheaf of papers and hurls it at his colleague. The colleague backs away as the man lifts up his hulking computer monitor—a cathode ray behemoth from another time—to send it careening to the next cubicle over, where it crashes into the corner of a desk before tumbling to the floor, exhaling smoke. With self-possession and eerie calm, the man collects more papers from the floor before aiming and snapping his arm as he slingshots them at transfixed colleagues farther away, the pile fluttering into the air like oversized confetti. He gets up on a desk and begins kicking at the thin partitions that grid the room, bending them out of shape. Two co-workers hiding behind a corner record the scene with cell phone cameras as the man, prowling the room, lithe and balletic in his rage, secures a large stick from behind a desk and quickly lights into the copy machine. At last one of the other employees works up the temerity to grab the stick from him and wrestle him down to the ground. Disarmed, pinned to the carpet, he is incapacitated by a Taser. In the last images, we see him fetal, writhing, clawing at his stomach, his collar, his tie.

"Security Cam Footage of Cubicle Rage to the Extreme Is Every

Cube Dweller's Fantasy," read the *Gizmodo* post from June 2008 linking to the video. Over time, as the original footage went viral, one of the cell phone cameramen would post his video too: with sound and color, it better conveyed the sickly, toothpaste green of the walls, the shrieks of the onlookers amid the flurry of white papers, and the pain and exhilaration of the man in the last minutes of his revolt. Yet nothing could top the original security-cam video for its panoptic view of the office from above: how recognizably cramped it looked; how obvious were the conditions and potential for this rage. "This dude rocks," ran the first comment. "He really knows how to live. His cellmates should've joined in the rebellion." Inevitably, after it had been viewed millions of times, some would charge that the video was fake (who doesn't have a flat-screen LCD monitor these days?), but, authentic or not, the video struck a nerve. Common among the sentiments, whether pro or con, was this, from a blogger: "Deep down every employee wants it to be real."

☐

In 1997 Steelcase surveyed cube dwellers and found that 93 percent of them would prefer a different workspace. A 2013 study from two University of Sydney researchers indicates that little has changed: the cube-ists (about 60 percent of office workers) expressed the highest rates of unhappiness with their work setup. (People with closed doors were unsurprisingly the most satisfied of the bunch.) This dissatisfaction with office spaces and office life more generally— the myriad aggravations, small ironies, larger defeats, and modest victories—has been seeping into the broader culture for years. In the film *Office Space*, a trio of disgruntled tech employees take out their frustration at their company's downsizing by annihilating the office printer with baseball bats and dropkicks. (You can find dozens of amateur remakes on YouTube.) In the novels *Personal Days* by Ed Park and *Then We Came to the End* by Joshua Ferris, proper e-mail etiquette becomes the subject of quasi-academic debate, and the highlight of a typical day is discovering that free bagels have been left over from a breakfast meeting. Both novels are narrated by an impersonal "we," the better to capture the passive conform-

Destroying the printer of oppression in *Office Space* (1999). *Photofest*

ism and bland anonymity of the contemporary white-collar landscape. The original British version of *The Office* (now remade in the United States, France, Germany, Quebec, Israel, and Chile, with Swedish and Chinese versions in the works) had one character torment the other by encasing his stapler in a Jell-O mold. Meanwhile, the Danish author Christian Jungersen's worldwide best seller *The Exception* took the concept of "office politics" to the extreme by having office workers seem to plot against and murder each other.

Above all, of course, we've had *Dilbert*, a comic strip that converted fungible dullness into concise, portable office satire. Appropriately enough, the original *Dilbert* comic grew into a small franchise, which soon became a cliché fixture of the very office environment that it satirized so well, with ubiquitous desk calendars, coffee mugs, mouse pads, and plush toys (all available in the online store's "Cubeware" section). As bleak as *Dilbert* sometimes was, running through all of it was a simple, even humanist sentiment, most succinctly expressed by one of the characters in *Office Space*: "Human beings were not meant to sit in little cubicles staring at computer screens all day."

Or you might take a cue from Rousseau: *Man is born free, but he is everywhere in cubicles.*

□

Happiness has no history, says Balzac; neither does the office. "The white-collar people crept silently into this world," wrote the sociologist C. Wright Mills, and the office that housed them appeared with reticence as well. Other workplaces, like the factory, entered clanging and whistling; the office was typically demure. By the middle of the twentieth century, when Mills was writing his book *White Collar*—to this day, the only comprehensive treatment of the subject—men and women who worked in offices were on the verge of constituting a majority of the American population. But where the office came from has remained a mystery—too banal, perhaps, to be felt worthy of serious inquiry.

People first began to notice offices in the middle of the nineteenth century, when such spaces were first called countinghouses— virtually indistinguishable from the Italian merchants' offices of centuries ago. These were small, cozy—or certainly small. "The door of Scrooge's counting-house was open that he might keep his eye upon his clerk, who in a dismal little cell beyond, a sort of tank, was copying letters." *A sort of tank*, where men entered in the prime of health and exited shrunken and phthisic; where so much activity took place, but only paper seemed to be produced. From the outset, the office was considered unworthy of its own appointed tasks. Business was noble, exciting even: one could risk, venture, thrive, and grow prosperous.

The office, meanwhile, was weak, empty, and above all boring. If business took place in the office, it was a dry, husky business. And yet it was this boredom, this tedious respectability, that made the office the forging ground for a twentieth-century discourse that has proved indispensable: the rhetoric of the middle class, and the promise of upward mobility. The clerk in his dismal cell might one day rise up to the top; the accountant marooned out in the snake pit of the data-processing pool could, with pluck, become the president of his company; the drone in the cubicle could code his way into the boardroom. No other workplace, no matter how degraded, has been such a constant source of hope about the future of work and the guarantee of a stable, respectable life.

In other words, offices were never meant to be icons of tedium. In fact, since the early twentieth century, the office has been the source of some of the most utopian ideas and sentiments about American working life. From their very origins at the beginning of the twentieth century, when they began to expand as administrative centers to ever larger Gilded Age businesses, offices offered a potential refuge from that other icon of tedium, the factory. Visionary architects like Louis Sullivan and Frank Lloyd Wright designed offices that hummed with the efficiency and regularity of an assembly line but with less physical danger and manual hardship and, therefore, more social prestige. By the 1950s, it was possible for an entry-level employee to imagine himself (and, considerably less often, herself) rising through the ranks, taking on more tasks and counting beneath him ever more subordinates.

Few jobs rivaled in prestige and symbolic power that of white-collar workers in mid-twentieth-century America. The structures that housed them—like the Lever House and the Seagram Building—would be among the most iconic buildings of the century. In the 1960s, management theorists began to imagine new kinds of office workers who, aided by technological advances in computing, would become "knowledge workers"—highly educated, creative white-collar professionals who would be paid to *think*. Office design theorists tried to house this new kind of worker with a bewildering number of designs, from the German *Bürolandschaft* ("office landscape"), which tried to make indoor offices cohere with the ebb and flow of paperwork, to Robert Propst's Action Office, which consisted of shiftable, modular walls for the active, hard-thinking office worker of the future. The 1990s witnessed yet more office utopianism, fueled by the perfervid fantasies of the dot-com bubble: offices that were miniature cities, offices equipped with bowling alleys, offices as big as college campuses, offices as small and as comfortable as your tricked-up garage or rec room. With better telecommuting technologies in the first decade of the twenty-first century and beyond, designers and theorists began to glimpse the end of the physical office itself, to be replaced by an invisible and ubiquitous office of networkers in cafés and living rooms who attend the virtual meetings of a company nominally based in Bombay while they lounge in New Canaan in their pajamas.

Look closer, though, and the picture gets grimmer. Transposing the factory model to the office turned white-collar work into numbing, repetitive labor. The mid-century middle manager began to feel himself as spiritually trapped—an "organization man," his soul made captive to his company. Soon after joining the workforce, women were often assigned to administrative or secretarial roles from which it was impossible to rise, and they faced a double subordination in sexual harassment. The offices themselves began to be reproduced endlessly: for every elegant Seagram Building, there were ten more soulless modular knockoffs, their interiors lacking in human warmth. Honest attempts to fix these problems produced more problems: the German "office landscape" was chaotic and inhospitable to concentration. Robert Propst's Action Office would be perverted over the years into the most notorious symbol of the American office world: the cubicle. Even the crazy dot-com offices would be remembered not for their architectural utopianism but for the crazy hours their denizens worked: "white-collar sweatshops," many began to call them. Meanwhile, the burgeoning café life of the freelancer is a reality for many, but it comes with persistent financial insecurity, no benefits, and a relatively asocial work environment. In short, the story of white-collar work hinges on promises of freedom and uplift that have routinely been betrayed.

Why have the best intentions of planners and architects, designers and executives, fallen short of producing a happy environment for the American worker? And among the rare instances of successful offices, what about them works so well? Why has the allure of office life (so prestigious on the face of it) consistently proved to be so elusive or disappointing, from the earliest days of "Bartleby, the Scrivener" to the baseball-bat-wielding dudes from *Office Space*? How have the compromises and changes made inside the office come to affect the world outside it?

Cubed talks about design and history, and it speaks through faceless, unnamed workers, and sometimes the typewriters and file cabinets they used and the chairs they sat in. But it also chronicles the history of individuals who sought to shape the office, whether physically or socially—often with the aim of bettering the lives of individuals within it and usually achieving something far from what they intended. It is a history from the perspective of the people who felt these changes from their desks.

□

This book is inspired by and is an homage to C. Wright Mills's *White Collar*, a dyspeptic and classic work about the nonmanual worker at mid-century. Though I don't discuss this book in detail, its influence and ideas are everywhere. There are differences, of course, in the method: Mills's work was sociology, or at least his own, highly subjective brand of it. This book is a social history, mixed with some journalism and, toward the end, some stabs at futurology. Moreover, Mills's term "white collar" is at once more expansive and more vague than "the office," referring, as he does, to professors and salesmen, doctors and military generals, alongside clerks and stenographers. By restricting my view to the office, I omit many of the larger questions about professionals and politics that he describes; or those questions come up more indirectly. Here history is glimpsed through the office—through the feelings and attitudes of those who worked in offices over the decades, as well as those who tried to impose a vision on what office workers could do, and what their work should be like.[1]

White Collar came out in 1951, when white-collar workers constituted just under half of the workforce. They were an emerging group whom most observers saw as replacing the old middle class of artisans and small shopkeepers—their salient characteristics had to be defined, and their politics and outlook on life remained amorphous. Mills's portrait was scathing: he saw white-collar people as "little men," or autonomous followers, people who felt themselves to be independent, entrepreneurial, even when they were enslaved to large companies. Though their work was becoming just as routinized as factory labor, the intangible aspects of their job—prestige, high status—rendered them immune to the idea that they belonged to a particular class with particular interests. Their politics were up for grabs. "Of what bloc or movement will they be most likely to stay at the tail?" he wrote. "And the answer is, The bloc or movement that most obviously seems to be winning."[2] He was right to see the self-understanding of white-collar workers as highly subject to vague categories like prestige. And the social features of the workplace he described have remained: the office as a place of glad-handing and vacuous sociability, alongside tedious, numbing work and individual isolation.

Mills argued his case as if the entire white-collar workforce could be seen as a new middle class, and therefore could be viewed as constituting a single bloc. But the history of office work betrays less solidity than that. Few things ever remained fixed about the office, or outside the realm of contestation, least of all the understanding that office workers had of themselves, and what their life chances were. Subjecting Mills's synoptic portrait of the office to the claims of history reveals ideologies and classes being made and unmade, along with fundamental notions of how and why we work.

Nor could Mills have quite realized what the world would look like when the office was not just another workplace, alongside the store and the factory, but the signature of an advanced industrial society. When the German journalist Siegfried Kracauer visited Berlin in the 1920s, he was astonished by how much the city seemed to be characterized by an "employee culture," how overrun it was by salaried office workers. In what American city now—or indeed any European city—would this be a startling observation? The culture of the office has become the dominant workplace culture of the country; the United States is a nation of clerks. *Cubed* is the history of how this came to be, and an analysis of what it has meant and might mean in the future.

THE CLERKING CLASS

The torn coat sleeve to the table. The steel pen to the
ink. Write! Write! Be it truth or fable. Words! Words!
Clerks never think.

—BENJAMIN BROWNE FOSTER, *Down East Diary* (1849)[1]

They labored in poorly lit, smoky single rooms, attached to merchants and lawyers, to insurance concerns and banks. They had sharp penmanship and bad eyes, extravagant clothes but shrunken, unused bodies, backs cramped from poor posture, fingers callused by constant writing. When they were not thin, angular, and sallow, they were ruddy and soft; their paunches sagged onto their thighs.

Clerks were once a rare subject in literature. Their lives were considered unworthy of comment, their workplaces hemmed in and small, their work indescribably dull. And yet one of the greatest of short stories is about a clerk. In "Bartleby, the Scrivener" (1853), Herman Melville, who had become famous for writing memoirs and novels about spectacular sea voyages to exotic islands—gaining a readership he eventually lost with that strange, long book about a whaling voyage—decided to turn inward, to the snug, suffocating world of the office. The titanic hunt for the white whale was exchanged for the hunt for the right-sized pen. And for finding the right position to sit at a desk: "If, for the sake of easing his back, he brought the table lid at a sharp angle well up towards his chin, and wrote there like a man using the steep roof of a Dutch house for his desk, then he declared that it stopped the circulation in his arms. If now he lowered the table to his waistbands, and stooped over it in writing, then there was a sore aching in his back."[2]

Melville himself had worked as a clerk for a merchant in Albany before he—as Ishmael put it—took to the ship. He knew from the inside the peculiar emptiness that office work could often have, its atmosphere of purposeless labor and dead-endedness. Even in *Moby-Dick* he speaks of the thousands in Manhattan who idle along the Battery, lost in "sea-reverie," avoiding returning to their work lives "pent up in lath and plaster—tied to counters, nailed to benches, clinched to desks."[3] Appropriately, the few windows in the Bartleby office look out onto nothing but more walls. "On one end," the unnamed narrator writes, the window faced "the white wall of the interior of a spacious sky-light shaft, penetrating the building from top to bottom."[4] And on the other side, "an unobstructed view of a lofty brick wall, black by age and everlasting shade." This wall, the narrator adds, wryly, "required no spy-glass to bring out its lurking beauties, but, for the benefit of all near-sighted spectators, was pushed to within ten feet of my window panes."[5] On two sides, then, two walls: one, the white wall of the light shaft; the other, a soot-black brick wall hemming in vision and light. A walled-in window: a room with no view.

But the office of "Bartleby," like the *Pequod* of Ishmael and Ahab, is also a place of male bonding, cheery with camaraderie and bonhomie. The narrator, a lawyer, initially employs three clerks with absurd nicknames—Turkey, Nippers, and Ginger Nut—that he uses affectionately. Each of them behaves with exact predictability the same way every day; for example, Turkey, an old man, always ceases to get work done after his noontime dinner, which he takes with an inordinate quantity of wine, causing his face to "blaze like a grate full of Christmas coals."[6] But the boss is too kind to do anything Trump-like, and the distempered workers never challenge their boss.

The entire order dissolves, however, when a sudden increase in the volume of business pushes the narrator into hiring a new scrivener—the eponymous Bartleby. He arrives looking "pallidly neat, pitiably respectable," and, mysteriously enough, "incurably forlorn."[7] The narrator gives him a desk next to a window, but like the other windows it offers little to look at, "having originally afforded a lateral view of certain grimy backyards and bricks, but which, owing to subsequent erections, commanded at present no view at all, though," the narrator concedes, "it gave some light."[8]

At first Bartleby works diligently, his thinness inversely proportional to his ravenousness for writing: "As if long famishing for something to copy, he seemed to gorge himself on my documents. There was no pause for digestion. He ran a day and night line, copying by sun-light and by candle-light. I should have been quite delighted with his application, had he been cheerfully industrious. But he wrote on, silently, palely, mechanically."[9] The trouble comes when this routine is interrupted. The lawyer-narrator calls Bartleby in for assistance in comparing two copies of a document. After outlining the duty, the narrator is stunned by Bartleby's infamous reply—"I would prefer not to." Repeating the maddening phrase at the narrator's every spluttering attempt to get him to work, Bartleby plunges the calm predictability of the office into thunderous irregularity. In the end, the lawyer, baffled by Bartleby's intransigence, his passive resistance, is forced to leave his office altogether; Bartleby himself is taken off to prison, where, bereft of his sustenance of documents, he starves to death.

What "Bartleby" *means* has been a subject of endless debate. Office workers have always taken it to be a mirror of their condition, with Bartleby's "I would prefer not to" an encapsulation of how the office reduces all titanic conflicts to petty grievances and simmering resentments. But in 1853, when the story was written, the term "office"—and the sort of labor that was performed there—had nowhere near the universal significance it has now. In those tense years before the Civil War, clerks were a small but unusual phenomenon, a subject of anxious scrutiny; their workplaces were at once significant centers of American business and breeding grounds for a kind of work that nobody recognized as work. Clerks were a kind of worker that seemed, like Bartleby, at once harmless and ominous. "Bartleby" was evidence that the office had just begun to blot its inky mark on the consciousness of the world.

□

When does the office begin? It's a question without an easy answer. One can associate the origins with the beginning of paperwork itself—until recently, the most common mental association with office work (think of the derogatory phrase "paper pusher"). In other words, since the invention of writing and the corresponding ability to keep records in a systematic manner, there have always been places that resemble offices: monasteries, libraries, scholars' studies. Banking furnished an especially large amount of paperwork; the Uffizi, an incomparable gallery of Renaissance art in Florence, was also one of the first office buildings—the bookkeeping offices of the Medici family's groundbreaking financial operations. Clerks, too, have existed for ages, many of them unclinching themselves from their desks to become quite famous: from Samuel Pepys, the British government diarist who reported on the gossipy world of seventeenth-century England, to Alexander Hamilton, who had cut his teeth as a merchants' clerk before he became the first secretary of the Treasury of the United States; Benjamin Franklin, paragon of pecuniary restraint and bourgeois self-abnegation, started out as a dry goods clerk in 1727. Perhaps some of the tediousness of Franklin's own writing was honed in the conditions of his first job: since clerks have had the opportunity to keep diaries, they have bemoaned the sheer boredom of their tasks—the endless copying, the awkward postures, the meaninglessness of their work. When not doing writing for the job, clerks have cultivated the habit of writing about the job—or literally around it, as in the case of some infamous marginalia from medieval scribes. "Writing is excessive drudgery," one such jotting reads. "It crooks your back, it dims your sight, it twists your stomach and your sides." "Oh, my hand," goes another—even though writing out that sentence would have only magnified the problem it described.[10]

The notion of the office as the quintessential location of alienated work, or simple drudgery, is far from the etymological root of the word. "Office" itself comes from the Latin for "duty." One of the more famous philosophical works of Cicero, long-winded scold of the latter days of the Roman Republic, is a treatise called *De officiis*, usually translated as "Of Duty" or "On Duty," though it might just as well be "Of Office." For Cicero's understanding of duty isn't far from our contemporary sense of "holding office" or the "office of the president": "office" as connoting a specific set of responsibilities. For Cicero, "office" was what was proper to you, what fitted you as your natural duty. This, too, seems far from any understanding of the office as workplace: few people have ever considered office work to be natural, proper, or fitting.

To find the emergence of the office in history—the workplace that prefigures the offices of today—one has to look at a peculiar confluence of new sorts of buildings, deep economic changes, as well as (most slippery of all) new kinds of feelings and mass awareness of one another among particular strata of the workforce. Industrialization in Britain and America was producing more and more administrative work, and alongside it a need for a rational approach to managing accounts, bills, ledgers: in short, paperwork. Rising to take these positions were clerks, who, looking around, began to see themselves growing in number, and to feel themselves as belonging vaguely to a special group. One finds the evolution of the office coinciding, then, with a change in the position of the clerks themselves—a new restiveness on their part, a new sense of power. They were not quite sure of themselves, but they were no longer isolated. By the middle of the nineteenth century, clerks and their workplaces begin to appear with a new regularity in the literature and journalism. "Bartleby," with its simultaneously assertive and retiring protagonist, nicely captures this ambivalence in the early world of the office.

What "Bartleby" also captured, as other descriptions of office life at the time did, was the sense that office work was *unnatural*. In a world in which shipping and farming, building and assembling, were the order of work, the early clerical worker didn't seem to fit. The office clerk in America at the high noon of the nineteenth century was a curious creature, an unfamiliar figure, an inexplicable phenomenon. Even by 1880, less than 5 percent of the total workforce, or 186,000 people, was in the clerical profession, but in cities, where the nation's commentariat was concentrated (who themselves tended to work in office-like places), clerks had become the fastest-growing population.[11] In some heavily mercantile cities, such as New York, they had already become ubiquitous: the 1855 census recorded clerks as the city's third largest occupational group, just behind servants and laborers.[12]

For many, this was a terrible development. Nothing about clerical labor was congenial to the way most Americans thought of work. Clerks didn't work the land, lay railroad tracks, make ammunitions in factories, let alone hide away in a cabin by a small pond to raise beans and live deep. Unlike farming or factory work, office work didn't produce anything. At best, it seemed to *reproduce* things. Clerks copied endlessly, bookkeepers added up numbers to create more numbers, and insurance men literally made more paper. For the tobacco farmer or miner, it barely constituted work at all. He (and at that point it was invariably a he) was a parasite on the work of others, who literally did the heavy lifting. Thus the bodies of real workers were sinewy, tanned by the relentless sun or blackened by smokestack soot; the bodies of clerks were slim, almost feminine in their untested delicacy.

The lively (and unscrupulous) American press occasionally took time to level invectives against the clerk. "We venture the assertion that there is not a more dependent or subservient set of men in this country than are the genteel, dry goods clerks in this and other large cities," the editors of the *American Whig Review* held. Meanwhile, the *American Phrenological Journal* had stronger advice for young men facing the prospect of a clerical career. "Be men, therefore, and with true courage and manliness dash into the wilderness with your axe and make an opening for the sunlight and for an independent home." *Vanity Fair* had the strongest language of all: clerks were "vain, mean, selfish, greedy, sensual and sly, talkative and cowardly" and spent all their minimal strength attempting to dress better than "*real* men who did *real* work."[13] Somehow it was never questioned that journalism, also conducted in offices and with pen and paper, constituted "*real* work."

Clerks' attire was a glaring target for the barbs of the press, since the very concept of business attire (not to speak of business casual) came into being with the mass appearance of clerks in American cities. "In the counting-room and the office," wrote Samuel Wells, the author of a "manual of republican etiquette" from 1856, "gentlemen wear frock coats or sack coats. They need not be of very fine material, and should not be of any garish pattern."[14] Other fashion advisers pointed to a whole host of "business coats," "business surtouts," and "business paletots," which you could find at new stores like Brooks Brothers. Working-class Americans would be seen in straw hats or green blouses; what distinguished the clerk was his collar: usually bleached an immaculate white and starched into an imposing stiffness. But collared business shirts were expensive, so stores catering to the business customer began to sell collars by themselves, half a dozen collars running to under half of what a cheap shirt would cost. The white collar, detachable and yet an essential status marker, was the perfect symbol of the pseudo-genteel, dual nature of office work.

The self-regarding clerk in his white collar became a stock subject of satire. Edgar Allan Poe, in his story "The Man of the Crowd," saw the "tribe of clerks" as being composed entirely of overdressed dandies, imitating aristocratic styles already several years old:

> There were the junior clerks of flash houses—young gentlemen with tight coats, bright boots, well-oiled hair, and supercilious lips. Setting aside a certain dapperness of carriage, which may be termed *deskism* for want of a better word, the manner of these persons seemed to me an exact fac-simile of what had been the perfection of *bon ton* about twelve or eighteen months before. They wore the cast-off graces of the gentry;—and this, I believe, involves the best definition of the class.
>
> The division of the upper clerks of staunch firms, or of the "steady old fellows," it was not possible to mistake. These were known by their coats and pantaloons of black or brown, made to sit comfortably, with cravats and waistcoats, broad solid-looking shoes, and thick hose or gaiters.—They all had slightly bald heads, from which the right ears, long used to pen-holding, had an odd habit of standing off on end. I observed that they always removed or settled their hats with both hands, and wore watches, with short gold chains of a substantial and ancient pattern. Theirs was the affectation of respectability;—if indeed there be an affectation so honorable.[15]

It fell to the poet Walt Whitman, bard of the masculine professions—the farmer, the builder, even the loafer and layabout—to establish that clerking was antithetical to manly American democracy. In a journalistic piece called "Broadway," the poet turns up his nose at a "jaunty" group of "down-town clerks" sauntering down the great avenue toward their cramped rooms in lower Manhattan. "A slender and round-shouldered generation, of minute leg, chalky face, and hollow chest." Again, what distinguished the clerks was their dandyishness, "trig and prim in great glow of shiny boots, clean shirts—sometimes, just now, of extraordinary patterns, as if overrun with bugs!—tight pantaloons, straps, which seem coming little into fashion again, startling cravats, and hair all soaked and 'slickery' with sickening oils." But their sparkling clothes merely hid the truth of their bodies: "What wretched, spindling, 'forked radishes' would they be, and how ridiculously would their natty demeanor appear if suddenly they could all be stript naked!"[16]

But the fantasy of exposing the clerk to his own inadequacy only concealed a deeper fear about the changing world of American business. Under the pressures of growing industrialization in the North of the United States, the Jeffersonian democracy of farmers was heading toward the same fate as the buffalo. More important, the old eighteenth-century world of businessmen who were also craftsmen—white-collar types who worked with their hands—began to suffer a slow decline as merchants and their groups of clerks started to exploit their superior knowledge of distant markets, and industries began to require more and more bookkeepers to maintain their ever more complicated accounts. New York was a case in point: by 1818, a packet line had begun to carry goods from the East River docks and Liverpool (which had one of the highest concentrations of clerks in England); by 1825, the completion of the Erie Canal had connected the city with western New York; importers in lower Manhattan had set up shop to get goods from markets in the Caribbean and Asia as well as from Europe. The growth of manufacturing led to myriad urban retail and wholesale establishments, which in turn required people to do the paperwork. The "Basis of Prosperity," *Hunt's Merchants' Magazine* held in 1839, lay in "the vast modern increase of the facilities for diffusing and obtaining full and correct information on everything pertaining to trade."[17] The people who handled this were clerks. Cities began to acquire ever more sizable numbers of clerks ambling down their broad avenues for men like Whitman to gawk at and fret over. By 1860, 25 percent of Philadelphians were working in nonmanual occupations; in the brand-new city of San Francisco it was already 36 percent; in Boston it was nearly 40 percent. Not all of these were clerks exactly, but the trend was clear: more and more people had ceased to work with their hands and were now working with their heads. The journals of opinion in the United States might have hated the "wretched, spindling" office worker, but the hatred refracted the intense ambivalence over the nature of business—and the possibility that clerks might be not an aberration but the future.[18]

□

Despite the furor over their aggressive unmanliness, clerks, and with them the office, crept silently into the world of nineteenth-century America. Moral philosophers were mostly preoccupied with the clang of industrialization and its satanic mills, and most regarded as negligible the barely audible scratch of pens across ledgers and receipts that characterized the new world of clerical work. It was only a "dry, husky business," as the narrator of "Bartleby" had it. Yet the expansion of the clerking force heralded a change as great as that of industry, and the humble clerk in the white collar would be as significant a figure as the factory hand in blue.

Part of what made the office so unworthy of notice was the fact that clerks in the mid-nineteenth century seemed to do business in exactly the same way as clerks decades before, in colonial and revolutionary America. The typical structure of a merchants' firm was still the partnership of two or three people, often in the same family, with the venture secured by a contract. The standard method of accounting, double-entry bookkeeping, had been developed in Italy in the fourteenth century. And the offices, too, resembled the banking and merchants' offices of Renaissance Italy—called in America, as they had been in the Renaissance, countinghouses. In these office spaces, a door from the street would open into darkness, perhaps graced by a single window streaked with dust from the outside, glommed over on the inside with soot from the potbellied stove in the middle of the room. A high rolltop desk was where one of the partners sat; a higher desk in the corner was reserved for his small staff of clerks. The partners themselves were often absent from this scene, making personal calls to conduct their business transactions while the clerks stayed behind and copied documents, endlessly. The other signal figure of this office was the bookkeeper: the patient, sallow-faced pen-and-ink man regarding the ledger carefully through his pince-nez, whose chief source of pride was his ability to conjure the sum of a column of numbers quickly and efficiently.

A former employee of the Jones and Laughlin Steel Company in Pittsburgh in 1869, whose office had all of six men (three of them partners, three others doing bookkeeping and clerical work), recalled the office life at the time some seventy years later: "There were no telephones, stenographers, or typewriters, and business was done face to face. A man would travel hundreds of miles to buy a carload of iron (15 tons), rather than write because he could see all the iron manufacturers, and felt he could more than save his expenses in getting the lowest price. There were probably more callers at our office than there are today . . . Business hours began at seven in the morning and six in the evening was recognized as quitting time only if the day's work was finished, and it was not unusual to continue work after supper."[19] Even if the workday was long, the pace of business was almost enviably slow, as one partner's account of a "busy" day had it. "To rise early in the morning, to get breakfast, to go down town to the counting house of the firm, to open and read letters—to go out and do some business, either at the Custom house, bank or elsewhere, until twelve, then to take a lunch and glass of wine at Delmonico's; or a few raw oysters at Downing's; to sign checks and attend to the finances until half past one . . . to return to the counting house, and remain until time to go to dinner, and in the old time, when such things as 'packet nights' existed [when packet ships came in], to stay down town until ten or eleven at night, and then go home and go to bed."[20]

The offices themselves were crowded and characterized above all by face-to-face interactions, as was industry in general. One exemplary office, of a New York commission house that sold western and southern produce, was only twenty-five square feet in size but managed to house four partners and six clerical workers, all men. One was an office manager; two clerks handled the major accounts, while a fourth handled the smaller ones. A fifth acted as secretary to the senior partner; a sixth was a receiving and delivery clerk who worked "from early in the morning until eight to ten o'clock at night" handling freight and storage. There was a group of salesmen who went in and out of the office to arrange transactions and a collector who processed bills and handled bank deposits.[21]

But the surface continuities in the lives of office clerks masked a deeper, momentous series of changes in the structure of office work

The General Business Office of the Stratton Commercial School, Boston (1884). *Early Office Museum*

itself, which subtly began to reshape American cities and the working worlds they contained.

One such change was the increasing specialization of business. The previous century had seen a host of mercantile activities united in one figure, the merchant, who was "exporter, wholesaler, importer, retailer, shipowner, banker and insurer" all at once (in the words of the business historian Alfred Chandler). By mid-century, all these tasks were divided. There were banks to handle the money, insurance firms to minimize risk, and shippers to carry goods, while merchants themselves ceased to handle multiple products, focusing on just one or two, and only on one aspect of the business (importing or exporting), while the day-to-day business was increasingly being handled by subordinate staff.[22] In retail, the growth of manufacturing meant that the goods being sold (clothes, say) were made off-site, and stores simply took on the function of selling—again, with a host of underlings to record the day's transactions. In other words, manual work was being separated from nonmanual work.[23]

The separation of tasks, and the making of things from their selling, crystallized in the development of offices with clerks, sometimes completely separated from the dirty, noisy, and smelly world of "*real*" work." In city directories of the time, one notices for the first time companies that have factories in or near a city, with a separate listing for an office in what increasingly began to be called, and exclusively in American English, "down-town" (the first usage is recorded in 1836). At the same time, the customary word "countinghouse" began to give way to the word "office." Even where administrative offices remained on factory property, they were often separated from the shop floor itself so that factory managers and clerks had entrances to their places of work physically distinct from that of the manual workers (and the office entrances were often prettier as well, distinguished by lintels and columns framing the doorway, rather than the warehouse atmosphere of the factory). Office buildings began to acquire their own architectural idiom, a "Greek Revival" style replete with Doric pilasters and large display windows for retail. It was a sign that the work being done within was noble, dignified, and important.[24]

Another, otherwise invisible but significant distinction adhered to the split of income between manual and nonmanual workers. Most married skilled laborers barely earned enough off one job to support their families, with the average running to about $500 a year. Meanwhile, *Hunt's Merchants' Magazine* estimated that the average annual expenses of a family of four, living frugally, amounted to $1,500—*three times* the average income of a manual laborer. While clerks usually faced dismal incomes their first year clerking, with an entry-level salary of about $50, their earning power could rise well above the low ceiling of a manual laborer's salary, and there are plenty of reports of clerks in their late twenties and early thirties, often single men, earning as much as $1,500 or $2,000. Above all, the income difference lay in how these incomes, whether small or large, were paid out. Manual workers received hourly or piece-rate wages, while nonmanual workers earned annual salaries. What this meant for white-collar workers, in an American economy beset by intense fluctuation in prices and frequent financial panics, was a measure of stability that manual workers never enjoyed.[25] A small shift in power had begun to take place. If people who "worked with their hands" still assumed their possession of the world of things, clerical workers, those working "with their heads," were now at the heart of capitalism's growing world of administration and direction—close to power, if not exactly in control of it.

And so unlike "solidarity," the key word of the European industrial labor movement that had made its way to England and America, the ethic that began to take hold among clerks was that of "self-improvement." Clerical workers were uprooted from the close-knit world of families and farms, where knowledge was passed down from father to son. Other clerks were merely their competition; they had no one to rely on but themselves. "The man who does not at least propose to himself to be better this year than he was last must be very good or bad indeed," wrote the merchant's clerk Edward Tailer in his diary entry on New Year's Day 1850. There is, he continued, "no such thing as a stationary point in human endeavors; he who is not worse to day than he was yesterday is better; and he who is not better is worse."[26]

Self-education became a key component separating the office world from the rest of the world of work. Entire schools—a parallel academy for clerks—sprang up in cities everywhere to assist young people with the new knowledge they needed to succeed in business. The loftiest of the heads in the countinghouses of America was the bookkeeper, who was the closest to true knowledge in the white-collar workplace. Accounting courses proliferated—usually $25 a pop, a sum that only more stable families could afford—and some offered to "watch over your work as you advance step by step, from book to book, entry to entry, and transaction to transaction." Accounting books like S. W. Crittenden's *Elementary Treatise on Book-Keeping* became widely known, thanks to their promise to "bring the subject within the grasp of any boy or girl." Though copy clerks had to acquire their own special skills in these schools, such as the ability to write thirty words in sixty seconds—the measure of good penmanship—bookkeepers were the source of fundamental truth in American business. The numbers, after all, had to add up. So pervasive was the bookkeeping impulse in American life that Thoreau made it a chief object of parody in the "Economy" chapter of *Walden*, where, in order to argue the superiority of his frugal, simplified life, he ostentatiously added up his food expenses in a ledger.

□

Unlike the anonymous, wide, deep, air-conditioned warrens that most workers around the world experience as their offices today, the early offices of the Western world—particularly those of England and America—were intimate, almost suffocatingly cozy spheres, characterized by unctuous male bonding between business partners and their clerks. Because of the close proximity of clerks to their bosses, they were sometimes considered by their bosses, as the great historian of the workplace Harry Braverman had it, "assistant manager, retainer, confidant, management trainee, and prospective son-in-law."[27] Or, as *Hunt's Merchants' Magazine* had it, the merchant's clerk "is to business what the wife is to the order and success of the home—the genius that gives form and fashion to the materials for prosperity which are furnished by another"—a comparison that could hardly give comfort to those who worried about the "femininity" of American clerical work.[28] At the same time, the closeness belied a deeply competitive streak in the American clerk. Unlike their brothers in the factory, who had begun to see organizing on the shop floors as a way to counter the foul moods and arbitrary whims of their bosses, clerks saw themselves as potential bosses. What appeared to be an exemplary "middle-class" patience, a willingness to endure anything in order to rise to the top, went hand in hand with utter impatience. Indeed, their whininess was proverbial. As America's finest moralist, Ralph Waldo Emerson, wrote in his canonical essay "Self-Reliance": "If the finest genius studies at one of our colleges, and is not installed in an office within one year afterwards in the cities or suburbs of Boston or New York, it seems to his friends and to himself that he is right in being disheartened, and in complaining the rest of his life."[29] But the complaint derived from the proximity to power that a seat in an office guaranteed them. Virtually no space separated clerks from their superiors; between their position and that of the partners of their firms lay only time.

Edward Tailer, a New York merchant's clerk who kept a steady diary throughout his years in business, gives a vivid picture of the working world of clerks. He sounds the proper, Uriah Heep–ish tone for the early white-collar worker as well: humility masking greed, whininess masking confidence. The son of a rich lawyer, in 1848, at age eighteen, Tailer managed, largely through the efforts of his well-connected family, to procure a clerkship in the merchants' firm of Little, Alden & Co., which was an importer of British, French, and German dry goods. Aside from the partners (Mr. Little and Mr. Alden), the small dark office consisted of a single bookkeeper, Frederick Haynes. When not delivering bills to dry goods houses owing money to Little, Alden & Co. or depositing said money in the bank, Tailer was employed in an endless monotony of filing receipts. In one entry he writes with satisfaction that his day consisted of filing three hundred freight and receipt bills. Highly self-conscious of the stereotypes of spindling weakness associated with members of his profession, Tailer became an exhausting propagandist for regular exercise and wrote several newspaper articles praising the gym he went to. In a piece for the *New-York Enquirer* in 1848, he wrote, "It is particularly recommended to those of sedentary habits, to undergo the training which is to be found [on Crosby near Bleecker]." As if responding to the satire of people like Walt Whitman, Tailer argued that after regular exercise "narrow and contracted chests are soon turned into broad and expansive ones, and the puny limbs of him who is not accustomed to exercise are soon changed into well developed and finely formed ones, and he imperceptibly finds himself re-established in health and strength."[30] The idea of a manly, ripped clerk has its contemporary counterpart in the health-crazed office workers of today, whose biceps stiffen and shift like packs through their shirtsleeves, though they rarely lift more than boxes of files or a planter of ferns at their workplace. The office—and the fears of physical degradation it engendered—might in fact have given birth to our modern idea of the gym.

At the same time, the obscurity of the poorly lit office drives him to complain about the worsening of his eyesight: "My eyes felt, when the labors of the day were finished, as if I was to become blind, a cloud appeared to hover over them, which prevented my seeing distinctly those minute objects which would be presented for admission to be portrayed upon the retina. The reason which I assigned to account for this singular occurrence was that they had been strained

Thomas O'Brien, notary public, sitting at his Wooton desk (c. 1900).
Early Office Museum

and sorely tried by the miserable light which finds its way into our counting room."[31] The darkening of Tailer's vision might have had less to do with the light and more to do with complaints about his position. Earlier in the same diary entry, Tailer complains that he has yet to hear from his boss over a request he had made, three days earlier, for a raise: "The answer which I have been daily expecting from Mr Alden, whether he will furnish me to draw for one hundred fifty or not, has not yet made its appearance. It strikes me most forcibly as exhibiting a mean trait of character, that a man, who has made thousands of dollars, should refuse the paltry sum to a faithful and hard working clerk, which would make him feel happy and independent, and inwardly bless the bountiful hand which could thus place him above want."[32] Tailer's request was for a yearly salary of $150—a raise of $100 from his $50 starting salary, after less than a year of employment. Such was the salary he deserved, he argued, and moreover it was the only salary that would allow him to support himself and relieve his (wealthy) father of the burden. Alden's response at the time, measured and calm, was that Tailer was asking too much for his position: Boston clerks, he argued, received only $50 their first year, with a $50 raise every subsequent year.

With Alden stalling on the raise month after month, Tailer's list of affronts began to multiply. In several entries he testifies to the strain on his eyesight. He also complains about the manual labor he is often forced to perform—an affront to his status as a clerk who works with his head: "It often occurs to me, that it is time Little Alden & Co had a young man to carry out bundles and parcels of pattern cards, as I have now been with them over a year, and it is not creditable to myself that this kind of awkward and clumsy work should still devolve upon me."[33] Tailer, a "young man" himself, didn't mean that he wanted someone younger; rather, he wanted a porter to do the work, which he would eventually get. The distinction that Tailer drew between clerking and portering was both class based and race based; most porters tended to be immigrants or minorities of some stripe—at least 66 percent in New York City, according to the 1855 census, while 6 percent were African American—giving the work an especially low cast in the minds of clerks. The whiteness of their collars was about more than just attire.

Tailer's worries over his position were common in a clerking world where the distance between junior clerk and partner was seen as both enormous and easily surmountable. No other profession was so status conscious and anxiety-driven and yet also so straightforward seeming. No matter how dull their work might be at any given moment, there was little doubt that clerks saw themselves, and were seen by their bosses, as apprentice managers—businessmen in training. Few people thought they would languish as clerks, in the way that it became proverbial to imagine people spending their lives in a cubicle, or how for decades becoming a secretary was the highest position a woman office worker could aspire to. Part of the prestige of clerking lay in the vagueness of the job description. The nature of the dry goods business meant that clerks often spent time in the stores where their goods were sold, acting as salesmen and having to be personable to customers. In other words, the duties of clerks were vast enough to allow them to be tasked with anything, which meant that so much of their work depended upon so many unmeasurable factors besides a clerk's productivity: his attitude, good manners, even his suitability as a future husband for the boss's daughter. A good clerk besieged his bosses' emotions the way he did customers—flattering them to the point of obsequiousness, until the bosses were assured that they had a good man on their hands. These personal abilities were part of the skill set of a clerk—something we know today as office politics—and though they couldn't be notched on a résumé, they were the secret of the supposed illustriousness of business life. The work might dehumanize you, but whatever part of you that remained human was your key to moving up in the job.

This was also the reason clerks felt superior to manual laborers. Young men entering a factory job had no illusions about running the factory, which is why a few of them began to join the nascent American labor movement. But clerks were different from people who "worked with their hands," and they knew it—a consciousness that Tailer registers when he declares the "awkward and clumsy work" of a porter unworthy of him. Young men who wanted to get into business knew they had to clerk, and they also knew that clerks could and often did eventually become partners in their firms. "Time alone will suffice to place him in the same situation as those his illustrious predecessors now hold!" Tailer wrote in one entry, loftily referring to himself in the third person. But though patience was the signal virtue of clerking—to write on, as Bartleby did, "silently, palely, mechanically"—impatience was its most signal marker. From the shop floor, the top of the Pittsburgh steel mill looked far off indeed. But in the six-person office, it was right next to you, in the demystified person of the fat and mutton-chopped figure asleep at the rolltop desk, ringed with faint wisps of cigar smoke.

Tailer was momentarily gratified when he at last received the raise he asked for—including the potential of a $50 bonus. Then the firm's profits began to skyrocket, and Tailer, in full possession of the details of these profits (after all, he was the one depositing and withdrawing the checks), began once again to feel agitated over his compensation, the mere hundreds he received compared with the "thousands" pocketed by Alden. Two and a half years later, Tailer found a position with another firm as a salesman; upon leaving, he was told by Alden that his "greatest failing was too strong an anxiety to force myself ahead." Yet the anxiety paid off. Only a few years later, at age twenty-five, Tailer would count himself a merchant; later in life he would have the money to travel extensively in Cuba and western Europe, and he had meetings with the Mormon pioneer Brigham Young, President Franklin Pierce, and Pope Pius IX.

□

The simultaneous impatience and obsequiousness of a figure like Tailer would become a leitmotif of white-collar workers in the century and a half since the clerk first rose to prominence. As such, offices became highly ambiguous spaces in the fast-developing world of American capitalism. Were clerks part of the growing industrial working class, replacing the artisans and small farmers of the old-world economy? Or were they merely stopping points on the way to becoming part of the "ruling class"? The answer appears to be that they were somewhere uncomfortably in between: not "middle class" exactly, or not yet—the phrase was never used, and the concept hadn't yet sprung up among nineteenth-century Americans—but somehow neither of the working class nor of the elite holders of capital. White-collar workers rarely knew where they were, whom they should identify with. It was an enduring dilemma, rooted in what might be called a class *un*consciousness, that would characterize the world of the office worker until the present day.

In one sense, early office workers were definitely part of an elite. For one thing, immigrants were virtually barred from becoming clerks; overt racism of course played a role, but more pertinent was the fact that clerking required an exceptional command of English, and specifically business English, which meant that it was comparatively easier for immigrants to slip into factories or other kinds of manual labor that hardly required speaking or writing at all. In their pay structure, appearance, and style of dress, early office workers seemed to be elite as well. Clerks were salaried, not waged; they often dressed to the nines; and they had the thin wrists and creamily pale complexions of aristocrats unused to hard labor, in a country born in a revolt against an aristocracy.

Politically and culturally, clerks began to form their own caste institutions. While most recoiled from the brutal, backslapping world of mid-century urban politics—with its ward bosses, gangsters, canned soapbox speeches, and blatant corruption, all of which clerks like Tailer dismissed as "electioneering"—they developed their own, semi-genteel spaces in which to pursue political and intellectual questions. They joined debating societies and subscription libraries, forming the core constituencies of lyceums and athenaeums all over the country's cities. The Mercantile Library Association, a private library formed in 1820, counted among its members a sizable number of clerks, Tailer among them, who argued in his diary that the "cherished institution" was "destined to perform a great deal of infinite good for some of the more unenlightened members of the mercantile community." This was all part of the dogma of "self-improvement" that young clerks could count as their collective contribution to society.

It also signified a commitment to gentility and honor, when many in the media were contending that young effete clerks were ruining the morals of their customers in retail stores, or, worse, dissipating in brothels and public houses.[34] Some clerks, like Tailer, went out of their way to affirm their own virtuousness. Tramping around the city, as he often did for work and pleasure alike, Tailer would come across scenes like one recorded in his diary, where Broadway "litterally [sic] swarmed with the most depraved of women."[35] But many other clerks succumbed, with considerably less sanctimony, to the "vices" offered in abundance by the antebellum city. Clerks' barrooms—called "porterhouses"—often became the preserve of low-level clerks who were about to set out for a "spree" with prostitutes. Magazines with titles like *Whip, Rake,* and *Flash,* as well as a host of erotic novels, offered gossip about especially enterprising clerks who exhibited impressive powers of seduction—tales that might have helped clerks manage their own identities in the face of repeated charges against their manliness.[36]

The one collective movement that clerks engaged in might have turned into a confrontation, in which the status of clerks might have been posed in the open and contested (if not resolved), but clerks made every effort to keep it civil and friendly to their employers, leaving things ambiguous—where, it seemed, clerks wanted them to be. This was their movement to regulate the closing hours of the retail stores where their firms sold goods. In the early nineteenth century, these stores had arbitrary hours, and merchants and retailers were thereby able to keep their clerks at the stores late into the night, usually until 10:00—preventing them from the few hours of leisure available to them, in which they could have gone to the gym or the library. By 1841, enough of them had banded together to form a demand to close the stores significantly earlier, at 8:00 p.m. But these demands were couched in the countinghouse language of friendship and bonhomie: they sought a "solicitation" of merchants' goodwill and argued that a few hours of rest would make more "willingly devoted servants" in the store.[37] They earned the enmity of a few owners and newspaper editors, who muttered imprecations over the moral lassitude of brothel-going clerks in one breath and more deep-seated fears over a labor revolt in another. The clerks responded agilely, arguing in petitions and letters that they merely wanted to devote themselves to study; as for a labor revolt, they had no plans of striking, instead hoping to win over their owners by softly voiced requests.

The powerfully influential editor of the *New-York Tribune,*

Horace Greeley, welcomed the movement as a sign that the clerks were at last moving toward becoming true citizens of the Republic. "The ignorance, emptiness and foppery of Clerks have been the theme of popular ridicule long enough," he wrote in his first editorial. But if the satire were true, he argued, then naturally "means should be taken to improve [the clerks'] condition."[38] After the passage of the early closing petition in the clerks' association, the editor wrote again, urging the adoption of the act, arguing that with their new freedom the clerks could take advantage of moral education: "Under the old system the time of the Clerks was so incessantly occupied as to deprive them entirely of that leisure for mental, moral and social improvement which should be enjoyed by every one just entering upon the duties and responsibilities of active life."[39] He hoped ardently that the newly "emancipated" clerks would take it upon themselves to enjoy their new liberty in hallowed sanctuaries, like the "New-York Lyceum" and other debating and education societies.

But most merchants continued to resist. It didn't help that the clerks were making requests rather than demands and forming associations rather than unions. A strike would have utterly crippled the commercial life of New York; a petition merely made most of the merchants chuckle. The clerks were determined, however, to minimize any similarities between their meek and courteous requests for more time and the violent means usually employed by striking manual laborers. When unsigned members of the Committee of the Dry Goods Clerks wrote in to the *Tribune* to threaten a particular merchant who refused to close early ("you had better look out for your glass if you want to save them [*sic*] from being smashed"), the chairman of the early-closing committee went out of his way to disassociate his body from the more radical sentiments, claiming the letter as sabotage by "some malicious person" attempting to "thwart our measures."[40] Despite several larger associations, and even a concession to forming an alliance with the Industrial Congress of trade unions, by 1852 the early-closing movement had run out of steam, dissipating in failure.

Did the clerks want to win? Or, in winning, would they have compromised their own position—as junior businessmen rather than workers? By their own lights, clerks were not a threat to anything. In the varied world of American work, they portrayed themselves as baby workers, always on the verge of tears but stunned into passivity at the offer of a symbolic pacifier. "Bartleby," which exploited the ambiguous nature of clerical work that Melville had known firsthand, is a story of the only kind of resistance a clerk could offer: *passive* resistance. "You *will* not?" the fatherly narrator asks. "I *prefer* not," Bartleby corrects—stumping his boss by substituting a mild preference for a stubborn desire. One clerk put their situation thus:

> The interest which clerks generally feel in the business and success of their employers, is, I believe, estimated too cheaply and that many feel so little, is, perhaps, as often the fault of their employers as their own. The majority of clerks are young men who have hopes and prospects of business before them. They have not yet thrown off that trusting confidence and generous friendship peculiar to youth—they are disposed to think well of themselves and the world, and they feel it deeply when too great a distance is maintained between themselves and their superiors . . .
>
> A good clerk feels that he has an interest in the credit and success of his employer beyond the amount of his salary; and with the close of every successful year, he feels that he too, by his assiduity and fidelity, has added something to his capital— something to his future prospects, and something to his support if overtaken with adversity; and a good merchant encourages and reciprocates all these feelings.[41]

Years before the rise of the clerk, American economists had worried over a growing distinction between producing classes, who did all the work, and consuming classes, who simply enjoyed the products. But from the 1830s to the 1850s, when clerks conducted their inauspicious rise into the lower frequencies of the American imagination, the discourse shifted away from this distinction toward discussing the possibility of a "harmony of interests" between employers and workers.[42] Prompted most obviously by the threats from socialists in Europe and America—people like Charles Fourier and Karl Marx, Robert Owen and Henry George—who proclaimed an irreconcilable conflict between capital and labor, these writers were also describing, perhaps inadvertently, the world that the office world was giving harbor to: one where workers were in harmony with their employers. To be sure, the office, from its earliest days, was rich in antagonisms, petty grievances, and outright hostility. But in the mind of the typical office worker, there never appeared to be a contradiction in pursuing his own interests alongside those of his employer. The Civil War would puncture the national harmony engendered in American workplaces—especially the southern cotton fields that were the most unequal workplaces of all. But the office, which grew to prominence in the years that followed, expanding to rows upon rows of desks and engulfing American cities in skyscrapers, admitted little of the strife clamoring outside its walls. With reformers promising a utopia of one kind, the office promised another, which would prove more enduring: an endless, placid shaking of hands.

2

THE BIRTH OF THE OFFICE

In every city, town, and farmhouse, were myriads
of new types,—or type-writers,—telephone and
telegraph girls, shop clerks . . . running into millions
on millions, and, as classes, unknown to themselves
as to historians.

—HENRY ADAMS, *The Education of Henry Adams* (1907)[1]

Imagine a bookkeeper pausing to look down at his ledger in 1860, only to look back up in 1920. He might be surprised to see that his familiar small surroundings had melted away entirely, converted into a space whose high ceilings and tall columns resembled nothing so much as a cave swollen with stalactites. His lone colleague and brother-in-arms, the clerk, was gone, replaced by dozens of unfamiliar faces surrounding him in neat serried rows of desks. The cigar-chomping partner at the nearby rolltop desk would be gone too, having multiplied into a small squadron of bosses locked away in snug executive suites high up in the stratosphere.

His work is now harried, insistent, relentless. Farewell the tranquil, languorous days of the countinghouse; greetings to the factory-like labor of the office. The texture of time has grown rougher, tighter—a moment as difficult to pinpoint as it is decisive. Men with stopwatches record the motions of his pencil, his filing habits, when and whether he goes to the bathroom, how long he lingers at the watercooler, how many minutes he wastes. The viscous silence of the old office is sliced through with the high-pitched metal clack of the typewriter, the adding machine, the sliding and slamming of file cabinets. He clocks in and out; shrill bells ring in his workday and push him out squinting into the early evening darkness, shoved and jostled by the black-coated thousands following him, out of his office, in an endless, dark stream.

Between 1860 and 1920, business became big business, and the number and kinds of positions in the office ballooned. The change in the work environment reflected a change in work itself. Administration and bureaucracy had taken over the world of business. *Walden* was a powerful protest against the tedium of pointless labor in the antebellum era, but its quiet, sturdy aperçus were rendered inaudible by the clang of a new, aggressive industriousness. The postbellum era gave figures like Thoreau one riposte after another; the new tone of the world of work was sounded by one of the best-selling pamphlets of the 1880s, *Blessed Be Drudgery*, written by the Christian evangelist William Gannett. Rather than preaching the importance of the contemplative life against the evils of a new, greedy age, as one might have expected from a religious man, Gannett created an improbable—and improbably intoxicating—reconciliation. He acknowledged the awfulness of work, the way it intervened between ourselves and our ideals—he noted how one might "crave an outdoor life" and yet still have to "walk down town of mornings to perch on a high stool [in an office] till supper-time."[2] But our desire for culture and leisure, Gannett argued, could only be guaranteed by "our own plod, our plod in the rut, our drill of habit." "In one word," he said, it "depends upon our 'drudgery.' "[3] Drudgery wasn't antithetical to culture; on the contrary, drudgery was the source of *all* culture. The argument reversed the entire history of Western thought since the Bible, which held that labor was the curse of man since the expulsion from paradise. Work was not a burden; it was freedom—the road back to paradise.

The place that was supposed to guarantee this freedom most was the office. In a series of tremendously popular novels, Horatio Alger Jr., the greatest ideologue of self-reliance since Emerson, depicted again and again the improbable rise of a street urchin to white-collar respectability. Not just statistics but much personal and anecdotal evidence suggested this sort of trajectory wasn't very likely; even Alger's own protagonists always depended on the sudden intervention of a wealthy patron. Despite that, a "Horatio Alger story" became shorthand for ascending from the bottom of the heap to the top. The belief that little lay in a poor urchin's way not only took root; it persisted and grew. "Why should he not rise to a position of importance like the men whom he had heard of and seen, whose beginning had been as humble as his own?" one of the eponymous heroes of *Rough and Ready; or, Life Among the New York Newsboys* wonders.[4] The sentiment had once captured thousands; by 1920, it held millions.

In 1889, inspired by Alger's books, the board game company Parker Brothers (which would eventually become famous for Monopoly) created a fantasy for children called Office Boy. Cleverly fashioned as a spiraling series of honeycomb cells representing way stations of the office boy's progress, the simple dice-based game showed how, with patience and fortitude, a young office minion could rise to the top of his company. Starting as "office boy" and moving through "porter" and "stock boy," the steadfast office worker, as long as he steered clear of the cells marked "careless," "inattentive," and "dishonest" and landed instead on the classic bourgeois virtues—"capable," "earnest," and "ambitious"—might eventually reach the center of the board, and become "Head of the Firm."

Yet these were old fantasies—powerful and apparently indelible, given their staying power—which had little application to the world of the office at the turn of the century. Their persistence helped workers cope with, rather than understand, the changes of the world around them. For whatever heroic, quixotic air still attended the cheery countinghouse and dandyish dry goods clerks, sequestered in unmarked little rooms along quaintly narrow urban streets, had dissipated by 1900. No longer earthbound, they worked by the hundreds in office buildings numberless to man, which spun upward from the ground, flouted the horizon, and cut jaggedly into the skyline. Church spires were humbled by the gargoyles and finials crowning the new office buildings, which, hundreds of feet high, appeared from the pavement like masters of their cold stratosphere, as much affronts to nature and scale as testaments to human power and inventiveness. The wide, free shop floors of the steel mills that circled Ohio and Pennsylvania, Youngstown and Pittsburgh, were rivaled by row after row of typists machine-gunning pages high above them in New York and Chicago—indeed, so much American steel was going into *building* these office towers, from which a steel executive might direct his empire of industry. In this historic ferment, untold millions who might otherwise have been small entrepreneurs steadily became employees of newly enormous corporations, in which only a few could ascend. But in the discourse of office work, the potential for upward mobility and respectability was ritually affirmed. This dissonance between the perceived potential of the office and its actual nature would remain unresolved. It challenged, and was fundamental to, the idea of white-collar work as middle class.

Enormous technological advances aided the growth of offices. By 1860, iron frames permitted the construction of taller buildings; by 1870, elevators assisted the climb. The Remington typewriter entered the office in 1874; Bell's telephone was patented two years later; Morse telegraphs had been in use for several years earlier.[5]

In 1860, the census recorded the existence of 750,000 people engaged in "professional service" work; by 1890, this number had more than doubled to 2,160,000; twenty years later, the census registered the same leap: by 1910 there were 4,420,000 office workers in America.[6] And—most startling of all, for the observers who lived through it—nearly half of them were women.[7]

What had befallen America that it suddenly needed so many offices?

□

The small world of the countinghouse had corresponded to the small, disconnected world of the United States, which had innumerable towns but was mostly made up of a patchwork of farms. But

Facing page: Parker Brothers' Office Boy (1889). *Courtesy of the Carson Collection of the Rare Book Division of the Library of Congress*

by the late nineteenth century, a burgeoning system of railroads had scythed through this pastoral landscape. The Pennsylvania Railroad; Michigan Central; Union Pacific; Chicago, Burlington & Quincy—these names overlaid an entirely new geography of the American imagination. The railroads lowered transportation costs, expanded markets and therefore the cost of goods and products. Telegraphs and telegraph companies had made instant communication across hitherto unfathomable masses of land possible for the first time. By connecting the eastern and western halves of the continent, they had—in one colossal, world-bestriding stroke—annihilated the old concepts of space and time.

In the analysis of Alfred Chandler, the railroads precipitated an organizational change which proved as consequential as the technological revolution that had powered the trains. To coordinate a network of trains required managers who could control the activities of disparate units, who would have to be housed in their own structures across the country. Partnerships that were adequate to manage shipping, a plantation, or a textile mill couldn't handle a railroad. Even the speculators and capitalists whose names otherwise fill the headlines and polemics of the period did little to change the form of companies; instead, it was a new stratum of managers, who began to occupy the "middle" between workers and the top executives, that determined the changes in organizational form—which in turn formed the core of the offices that would soon dominate the American landscape.[8]

The railroads adopted a seemingly simple but in fact pathbreaking organizational form, based on the division of a company into departments. At the top, a board of directors held sway; under them lay the president. But beneath him, the chart of responsibilities begins to spread, in the classic M-form. Finance, freight, and construction were divided, and these in turn split into separate divisions with managers helming various departments—purchasing, machinery, accounting—spread across the various regional offices that coordinated the activities throughout the country. The state had a significant role to play in the organizing of American life: the legal fiction of the "corporation" famously made the ownership of a firm separate from its management. Gone were the multifarious responsibilities that attended clerks and partners; in their place came career managers, who spent years ascending a now highly articulated ladder, themselves hiring and directing employees picked to ascend the very same ladder. (In fact, the use of the word "ladder" to indicate the levels of a company came into use around this time.)

The change between the latter years of the cozy world of "Bartleby" and the vast, cavernous halls of the new office can be seen in the career of a single person. Like Edward Tailer, E. P. Ripley got a job working as a dry goods clerk in Boston immediately after high school, at age seventeen. Four years later, in 1866, he joined the Union Railroad as a contracting agent in its Boston office. In 1870 he was hired by a different railroad, Chicago, Burlington & Quincy, as general freight agent in its Chicago office. In Chicago he became traffic manager. The next year he became general manager and helped to crush the railroad strike of 1888. In 1890, he became a vice president of yet another railroad company, rising to the presidency of the Santa Fe Railway in 1896, at age fifty-one. In the place of two positions—clerk and partner—there were now seven. And this picture doesn't even indicate how much clerks had become differentiated: file clerks, shipping clerks, billing clerks, among other "semiskilled" laborers (as the census classification had it). Many other railroad executives followed similar trajectories—even if most dry goods clerks didn't become railroad executives.[9]

In fact, as companies expanded, it became less and less likely that clerks would "apprentice" themselves in anything like the manner that their forebears did. The specialization of clerical work meant that most workers only knew one thing—be it accounting or filing or billing—and had little incentive or opportunity to learn the entire business. The bottom of a vast and impersonal machinery, the clerk who entered the world of business as E. P. Ripley had was more likely to have seen his intimate world dismantled and reapportioned among hundreds of desks.

What the trains had also destroyed were the old merchants' networks that had sustained the small partnerships of the counting-houses. Merchants had depended upon their special knowledge of isolated regions and markets, which, when opened by quick access to other regions and markets with rail access, lost their isolation and therefore their dependence on merchant oligarchies. Depression hit the United States, first in the 1870s, and then once again in the 1890s; this prompted manufacturers to consolidate, and to integrate vertically, in order to lower prices.[10] The only way to keep earning money in this new system of competition—what really felt, in the Gilded Age, like open warfare—was to merge. A wave of mergers swept through business in the 1890s, consolidating industries in steel, oil, tobacco, food, and meatpacking. Between 1897 and 1904 alone more than 4,000 firms collapsed into 257 combinations, trusts, and corporations.[11]

The invention of telecommunications allowed offices to be separated from factories and warehouses and in turn expanded the range of jobs available to office workers. Consider a mail-order company and its warehouse. Bosses and errand boys no longer had to conduct transactions in person; aside from the occasional messenger, it was now possible to send and receive information from your warehouse, or factory, or printing house, using Morse code or by picking up the phone. Within the office itself, the use of pneumatic tubes made it possible to run material between levels of a company, while Dictaphones, which could carry a smoke- and bourbon-ragged voice from a snug top-floor executive suite down to a harried typist marooned in the steno pool, made transcription rational and smoothly impersonal.

Paradoxically, this new capacity to communicate speedily and efficiently resulted in more and more work for workers to push through—more physical products, but also more paperwork (invoices, receipts, contracts, memos, profit-and-loss statements), which meant more typewriters, which meant more typists, which in turn meant more messages and therefore more messengers.

Things that were heralded as "laborsaving" devices gave rise to a whole new industry, and to more labor. As the great theorist of technology Marshall McLuhan put it in *Understanding Media*, "It was the telephone, paradoxically, that sped the commercial adoption of the typewriter. The phrase 'Send me a memo on that,' repeated into millions of phones daily, helped to create the huge expansion of the typist function."[12] In Sinclair Lewis's office novel *The Job* (1917), his protagonist, Una Golden, suffers a sublime kind of dread when she confronts the expanse of supposedly laborsaving machines:

"machines for opening letters and sealing them, automatic typewriters, dictation phonographs, pneumatic chutes." But she's surprised to discover that "the girls worked just as hard and long and hopelessly after their introduction as before; and she suspected that there was something wrong with a social system in which time-saving devices didn't save time for anybody but the owners."[13]

Less heralded than the typewriter and the telegraph, though no less consequential, was the invention of the vertical file cabinet. Though filing, as in organizing company papers, was as old as the office itself, file cabinets only began to appear in the 1880s. Initially, these were wooden and wardrobe-like, with drawers that stored box files or held loose papers with a metal clamp. Before that, files were stored in pigeonholes in a clerk's desk, making them largely inaccessible. Incredible as it seems now, it took many years until the notion of storing papers flat—first horizontally and then on edge—became widely accepted. Once it became apparent that the immense volume of internal correspondence could be stored more easily in a vertical file, the system became ubiquitous.[14] As office buildings grew taller, and flammability became a problem, steel file cabinets replaced wooden ones—the tall cabinets mimicking the shape of the skyscraper, such that the "file" seemed to be a metaphorical stand-in for the office itself. "Each office within the skyscraper," C. Wright Mills would argue some years later, "is a segment of the enormous file, a part of the symbolic factory that produces the billion slips of paper that gear modern society into its daily shape."[15] Aldous Huxley, in his dystopian novel *Brave New World*, could imagine no more powerful symbol of a totally bureaucratized world than the idea of each person having his or her name on a file:

> No longer anonymous, but named, identified, the procession [of test tubes] marched slowly on; on through an opening in the wall, slowly on into the Social Predestination Room.
>
> "Eighty-eight cubic metres of card-index," said Mr. Foster with relish, as they entered . . .
>
> "Brought up to date every morning," added the Director [of hatcheries].
>
> "And co-ordinated every afternoon."[16]

A more subtle requirement that changed the form of the office, however, was the new need to design spaces that could distinguish between the now-multiple levels of management. The informal, easy consensus of the countinghouse had meant that a clerk could sit just a few feet away from his partner, who might have only bettered his clerk in visible prestige because his desk was of marginally better quality. But the proliferation of senior managers and vice presidents suddenly meant that power relationships were at once plainly hierarchical and confusingly similar. How much separated a manager from a senior manager, besides a few hundred dollars in their salaries? The office, ever more refined in its distribution of status rewards, would make the difference plain as daylight—giving desks to some and private spaces to others; mass-produced metal chairs competed with the chocolate richness of hand-carved mahogany; even the quality of carpeting or the finish on a table leg could distinguish one kind of worker from another.

The most obvious difference lay in the clerical desk. The classic desk of the old countinghouse was the Wooton—a massive, high-backed, grandiose affair riddled with cubbyholes and with foldout wings that seemed to reach around and clasp the sitter in warm embrace. This was a desk you could burrow into, a desk you could lose yourself in—one that truly signified a home. And at the end of the day, you could shut it up and lock it closed. All your papers would be waiting there expectantly for you the next morning.

But once the clerk was no longer the omnicompetent handyman of the office, relegated instead to the wide expanse of the floor, it seemed a touch expensive to give him such a fancy desk. The executives who essentially did no work—or hardly any paperwork, anyway—got to keep the wood-trimmed Second Empire furniture, while the clerks were handed the Modern Efficiency Desk. Invented in 1915 by the Steelcase Corporation (then called the Metal Office Furniture Company), it was a flat metal table, occasionally outfitted with file drawers. The key was that it gave clerks and their papers nowhere to hide. The new class of managers loved it: as they passed slowly and ominously down the long aisles it was easy to watch what clerks were doing.

□

The expansion in the range and scope of the office, in the specialization and refinement of its activities, happened so quickly, netting so many new workers eager to get in on the managerial binge, that at a certain point a problem became obvious and ineluctable. The problem was people didn't know what to do with offices. "The old slipshod way of our forefathers," as one writer in the 1890s had it, prevailed in office design; in other words, there was no design at all.[17]

By the turn of the century, the question had acquired a particular urgency. Institutions, both public and private, were considered by many to be seriously out of control. It started on the shop floor. Factories were not running at their best: rising labor strife was leading to frequent equipment sabotage, walkouts, and massive strikes; even on a daily level, managers complained, workers tended to malinger and dawdle, deliberately slowing down operations, a practice that became known as soldiering. A common feature of any workplace, workers especially liked to deploy it when managers would red-facedly scream for more speed.

Not that management had any idea what it was doing either. The adoption of organizational hierarchies hadn't always resulted in greater efficiency, as Chandler had argued; companies often merged out of expediency, and they imitated organizational forms that weren't always appropriate. The size of organizations had gotten so unwieldy that it wasn't clear who was responsible for what. Before World War I, General Motors had tons of disparate factories and distribution facilities, but it hadn't diversified its management properly; a single executive, William C. Durant, made virtually all the decisions. In an example of his infinite wisdom, he had decided that since automobiles were a growth industry, there was no need for cash reserves. When a downturn hit the economy in 1910, the company nearly went bankrupt. Meanwhile, Standard Oil had tons of cash but didn't know what to do with it, because the company didn't know how much it had. It hadn't standardized its accounting practices over its long existence; none of the books matched up. The American states, too, had lost track of themselves. One California legislator described his state's finances (apparently a problem since time immemorial) in 1909: "There was little short of chaos as far as any orderly provisions for state expenditures were concerned. There had been no audit of the state finances for over twenty years. The finance committees of the two houses were scenes of a blind scramble on the part of the various institutions and departments of the state in an endeavor to secure as large a portion as possible of whatever money might happen to be in the treasury . . . Logrolling and trading of votes on appropriation bills was the common practice among members of the legislature."[18]

It didn't help that the offices where everything was done were, by and large, dismal. One worker in 1894 asked readers to descend with him into the depths:

> Imagine a room with its floor some steps below the level of the sidewalk; a small and dusty room, ill-lighted by an abortive skylight, and two windows upon one side; worse ventilated by one door opening into an equally dismal office, and another communicating directly with the foundry, whence drifted in a dull and heavy air, laden with smoke and evil odors, ornamented with graceful festoons of cobwebs, thrice magnified by accumulated grime and soot. The side windows, facing the west, opened upon a narrow driveway, on the opposite side of which were a dirty boiler-room and a noisy engine . . . This unattractive picture, far from being overdrawn, really serves to give but a faint idea of the . . . office of a large and famous establishment in New York city.[19]

Clerical workers, no longer enjoying the easy rapport with their two or three fellow workers and their bosses, were now massed together in highly regimented rows, to mimic—for lack of another precedent—the factory floor. From any viewpoint in the room, the world appeared to be an endless and innumerable sea of desks. Their bosses were usually out of sight, on a floor above them—the one that contained the sole bathroom, which workers had to take several flights of stairs to get to.

To the Gilded Age's reputation for nonchalant corruption at every level of government, literally murderous corporations, and a yawning black gap of inequity between the classes should be added the sense that sheer chaos was taking hold over the country's organs of administration, public and private. From an elite perspective, America could seem a hopeless, even dangerous case: revolutionaries seemed to be crawling out from every corner of the Republic, sometimes rushing into executive offices with guns trained, other times lobbing bombs at presidents, all in the hopes of inspiring those restless and uneasy masses of laboring men in fields and factories; the offices from which they were supposed to be directed were sinking under mounds of paperwork—lost orders, missing receipts, smudged and totally faked accounts, which added up to millions of dollars that would, when checked, be found missing. Managers didn't know how to manage. If industrial life in America were to be kept alive, the salvation would have to come from the controlling heart of the American economy—the office, and its new class of managers. To rationalize the office, and improve the efficiency of American business, management would have to become a science.

☐

In 1898, the Bethlehem Iron Company, a supplier of domestic armaments to the U.S. Navy and, despite its name, a steel producer, hired Frederick Taylor as a consultant. Taylor was a member of the American Society of Mechanical Engineers, and he had quietly begun to distinguish himself with a series of papers addressing common problems of incentives and the efficiency of the manufacturing process, which had earned the attention of a few executives who happened to get their hands on them.

He had also distinguished himself, among friends, as something of an odd duck. Less generous observers might have called him a maniac. Throughout his life, he displayed an obsession with measurements and with ensuring that every physical activity was being performed with the maximum possible level of efficiency. The young Taylor insisted on measuring out a square for a game of rounders (an ancestor of baseball) in exact feet and inches.[20] In adulthood Taylor would show up at recreational tennis games with a patented racket he had designed, bent in the middle, claiming it increased the productivity of his swing; he had also taken out patents for new, more efficient nets and net supports. Odd, too, was his golf game: his driver was ten inches longer than the standard; he used a homemade two-handed putter, which he swung croquet-style. He had developed an unusual swing based on amateur motion studies: bending one leg and raising one shoulder, he would spring as he struck the ball, managing nonetheless to achieve an incredibly long drive. Responding in a letter to a friend who poked fun at his swing, he wrote, coolly,

> Your mind seems to run entirely to implements, while mine has been working rather in the direction of motion study. I wish it were possible to convey to you an adequate impression of some of the beautiful movements that I have been working up during the past year. The only possible drawback to them is that the ball still refuses to settle down quietly into the cup, as it ought to, and also in most cases declines to go either in the direction that I wish or the required distance. Aside from these few drawbacks, the theories are perfect.[21]

Many of his obsessions can be traced back to his youth. He was born in 1856—the same year as Freud—to a successful and wealthy Philadelphia family, who brought him up in a culturally rich household and schooled him for three years in Europe, where Taylor acquired fluency in French and German. But Taylor displayed little interest in cultural pursuits. Though he was sent to the prestigious Phillips Exeter Academy, where he was groomed for Harvard, his grades were mediocre. After beginning to study harder and improve his performance, Taylor started to suffer from frequent eyesight problems and painful headaches. Physiologically, this probably represented a lack of medical attention (he simply needed to wear glasses), but Taylor's parents took his medical problems to mean that he had worked too hard and needed to reconsider college altogether. One of Taylor's biographers, the psychiatrist Sudhir Kakar, has argued, somewhat outlandishly, that Taylor's headaches were in fact psychosomatic manifestations of an existential crisis: Taylor was crippled by his desire to reject Harvard, a symbol of his father's elite inheritance, for real manly work.

Whatever his reasons, it was in fact a little strange that Taylor, rather than securing a safe and unstrenuous job as a clerk in a manner appropriate to his class, decided to slum it and work instead as an apprentice machinist in a hydraulic works (where, rather than payment from the factory, he received an allowance from his father). He would later claim that his apprenticeship had made him deeply aware of the attitudes of workmen.[22] Yet his understanding of the workers' point of view, rather than making him sympathetic to concerns on the shop floor, instead hardened his opinion against them. Workers didn't work very hard in his opinion and spent extravagant amounts of time chatting, taking smoke breaks, and slowing down their pace when they needed to rest. At the same time he began to turn against the habitual attitudes of executives and capitalists, who, it seemed to him, had an equal misunderstanding of what was necessary to make work more efficient. After his apprenticeship, he became an executive trainee at the Midvale Steel Works, where, as he tells it, he became acquainted with soldiering, the practice that would preoccupy and enrage him for the rest of his life.

At Midvale, Taylor became the demon of the workplace. He was constantly berating workers for their deliberate dawdling, their refusal to take or follow orders as he outlined them. And of course they responded with choice words of their own. "I was a young man in years," he would say later, testifying before Congress, "but I give you my word I was a great deal older than I am now with worry, meanness, and contemptibleness of the whole damn thing. It is a horrid life for any man to live, not to be able to look any workman in the face all day long without seeing hostility there."[23] After moving from Midvale to Bethlehem, he decided he would break the hostility once and for all. The key, he would discover, was to take knowledge away from the workers and install it in a separate class of people.

There is not a single worker, Taylor would repeat, "who does not devote a considerable part of his time to studying just how slowly he can work and still convince his employer that he is going at a good pace."[24] But it was the lackadaisical management styles that prevailed in one factory office after another that were to blame. There wasn't a single manager who knew how long each task was ideally

Frederick "Speedy" Taylor
(1856–1915). *Frederick Winslow
Taylor Collection, Samuel C. Williams
Library, Stevens Institute of Technology,
Hoboken, N.J.*

supposed to take. No one had studied the kinds of motions involved in completing a task. No one knew whether the tools were designed to create the most efficiency in making the particular product. As on the tennis court, so in the office: in Bethlehem, Taylor insisted on the creation of teams of people to draw up an entire diagram of the labor process, to see where lacunae and inefficiencies existed and to see where workers doing needless tasks could be disposed of.

"Dealing with every workman as a separate individual in this way involved the building of a labor office for the superintendent and clerks who were in charge of this section of the work," Taylor wrote of one factory example. "In this office every laborer's work was planned out well in advance, and the workmen were all moved from place to place by the clerks with elaborate diagrams or maps of the yard before them, very much as chessmen are moved on a chess-board, a telephone and messenger system having been installed for this purpose."[25] He demanded the separate observation, study, and encouragement of each individual worker. And, most notoriously of all, he ensured that all workers were doing their jobs as quickly and efficiently as possible by having hired experts time their every motion with a stopwatch. After observation, Taylor would divide up each job into a series of pieces and assign each segment a rate. This "piece-rate" system also corresponded to a system of incentives: rather than being paid a single wage, workers would be paid based on the completion of particular segments of their work; if they managed to increase their speed, they would get a raise. Fans of the book and subsequent film *Moneyball*, where a form of Taylorism is applied to the baseball dugout and diamond, will recognize the broad fundamentals of the approach: The old stubborn insistence on guts and instinct has to be disposed of. Instead, one must uphold the sanctity of measurable results: diagrams, metrics—"science."

But what Taylor was arguing for was much bigger than the pursuit of mere efficiency. Taylorism implied a wholesale change in the nature and understanding of work itself.

Dividing up labor and tasks wasn't itself new. The increasing technical division of labor into separable, minute activities had been foreseen at least as early as Adam Smith, with his imaginary pin factory in *The Wealth of Nations*; industrial machinery was already making most work homogeneous and automatic, such that what was once a complex object crafted by at most two or three hands would increasingly be divided up among dozens of workers, who contributed to the final product simply by pulling a crank at the right time. Workers who might have initially taken pride from their work were now reduced to, as the phrase went, "cogs in a machine," indistinguishable from each other, no longer possessed of any particular skills or abilities that they could hold as points of pride. Many would see—and have seen—Taylorism as arguing for an even deeper kind of degradation, since it divided up work even further, into the smallest units possible.

Strangely enough, Taylorism was pitched as an attempt to redeem the division of labor and emancipate the individual worker. Taylor hated unions, which claimed that workers could get together to protect their collective interests; he argued the opposite, that each individual worker had his own interests and that a worker could and should be responsible for his own rise. Workers had no common interests; they competed with each other. The system of incentives he established showed how a worker could improve his own working abilities and how he could visibly measure the results of his improvement, with improving marks on his time card. If the early-twentieth-century workplace seemed to be destroying the individual, Taylor's system would attempt to restore it.

Of course, the pitch was patently false. Taylor's come-hither comments to American workers belied some of his more aggressive statements on behalf of his vision, a fact lost on very few actual workers. "In the past the man has been first," Taylor wrote. "In the future, the system must be first."[26] Taylorism was a way of thinking that came at the expense of workers' own knowledge of their system. Whatever mental components went into manual labor had to be stripped and given to specially trained foremen, who would reorganize the job in such a way that it became impossible for any group of workers to take control of the process. And the Taylorists would do it by any means necessary. With impressively crazed clarity, Taylor summed up his philosophy thus:

> It is only through *enforced* standardization of methods, *enforced* adoption of the best implements and working conditions, and *enforced* cooperation that this faster work can be assured. And the duty of enforcing the adoption of standards and enforcing this cooperation rests with the *management* alone.[27]

(Emphasis in the original.)

Though slow to gain acceptance in the world of business, Taylor's system steadily gained repute. He gradually accrued a circle of acolytes, who propagated his system in various workplaces as freelance consultants. The Society to Promote the Science of Management held its first meeting at Keens Chophouse in New York, in the hopes that one day the principles would catch on.

In November 1910, the breakthrough came. Railroads were seeking to raise their freight rates by $27 million. Along with the executives, railroad workers and insurance companies (representing investors holding railroad bonds) supported the move; the shippers who would have borne the brunt of the costs opposed it. Louis Brandeis, a middle-aged lawyer from Boston who had gained some repute for drawing on socioeconomic factors in his legal briefs, decided to fight the railroads for no fee. In early arguments he repeat-

edly questioned the railroad executives about their accounting rationale for raising costs. No one could give Brandeis a straight answer.
During a recess in the trial, Brandeis sought more information to
bolster his case; one of his friends—Harrington Emerson, an efficiency expert with the Santa Fe Railway (not part of the suit)—told
him to seek out Frederick Taylor. "I quickly recognized," he would
later say, "that in Mr. Taylor I had met a really great man." Staying in close touch with the circle, Brandeis became more and more
convinced that the movement for scientific management was greater
than all others "in its importance and hopefulness." When the trial
resumed, Brandeis proclaimed that more efficiency was possible:
"We offer cooperation to reduce costs and hence to lower prices.
This can be done through the introduction of scientific management." All of Taylor's associates testified. On November 10, 1910,
the *New York Times* headline read,

ROADS COULD SAVE
$1,000,000 A DAY

———

Brandeis Says Scientific Management
Would Do It—Calls
Rate Increases Unnecessary

Over the next two months, the papers tried to find the man behind
this new "scientific management." The morning the *New-York Tribune* profile appeared—"Weeding Waste out of Business Is This
Man's Special Joy: Perhaps Our Railways Might Save One Million
Dollars a Day by Listening to Him"—Taylor woke up famous.[28]

With Taylor's articles now finding a home in more popular journals, the obscure Taylorists, embracing each other and their love
of efficiency like members of a persecuted religious sect, suddenly
burst into the limelight.[29] Even Lenin, soon after the Bolshevik Revolution, could be found arguing in *Pravda* for the usefulness of Taylorism in the development of Soviet industry:

> The Taylor system ... like all capitalist progress, is a com-
> bination of the refined brutality of bourgeois exploitation and

a number of the greatest scientific achievements in the field of analyzing mechanical motions during work, the elimination of superfluous and awkward motions, the elaboration of correct methods of work, the introduction of the best system of accounting and control, etc. The Soviet Republic must at all costs adopt all that is valuable in the achievements of science and technology in this field.[30]

Taylor and the figure of the "efficiency expert" became subjects of caricature throughout the country, with every unnecessary motion, even whistling, considered an impediment to pure efficiency. He distilled his theories into the book *The Principles of Scientific Management*, which was influential as far afield as Japan, where many executives attributed his influence to the country's successful recovery from the war. When Taylor's son Robert visited a Toshiba factory in 1961, executives clamored for a picture or even a pencil— anything that his great father might have touched with his hands.

The Taylorist triumph that had taken over the news would spread on the shop floor more surreptitiously, like a virus. Factory workers on the shop floor began to report sudden appearances of "white shirts" in their midst, creeping in at first one by one, before suddenly they were everywhere in a blinding white swarm. Motion-capture cameras, which had been developed first by the revolutionary photographer Eadweard Muybridge, were soon deployed by white shirts in factories to ensure that the motion of every laborer was efficient. A group of machinists from the New England Bolt Company of Everett, Massachusetts, testified to their comrades being surrounded: "Cameras to the front of them. Cameras to the rear of them. Cameras to the right of them. Cameras to the left of them . . . If the 'Taylorisers' only had an apparatus that could tell what the mind of the worker was thinking, they would probably develop a greater 'efficiency' by making them 'cut out' all thoughts of their being men."[31]

But the most infamous element of the Taylorist model was the man with the stopwatch. It would start with one white shirt with a watch. The only line in the May 28, 1915, diary entry of Will Poyfair Jr., an autoworker for Buick, reads, "Stop watched today." The

THE EFFICIENCY EXPERT DISCOVERS THAT IT COSTS THE FIRM THOUSANDS OF DOLLARS EVERY TIME EDDIE THE OFFICE BOY GOES WHISTLING DISTURBING JAZZ AIRS THROUGH THE ACCOUNTING DEPARTMENT.

A cartoon in *Life* magazine (1925).

terseness is ominous. One week later, he notes that his four-man
drip-pan gang has been split up, their work divided into separate
tasks, each assigned a quota and a piece rate. At the Watertown
Arsenal, a group of molders walked out when one worker refused
to labor under the stopwatch and his fellow workers followed; the
strike led to a five-month congressional hearing into the nature of
Taylorism.[32]

Taylor died in 1915 of pneumonia. He was already becoming a
cult figure, drawing acolytes, each of whom attempted to outdo the
other in faithfulness to the master's ideas. It's no wonder he exerted
such a tremendous influence on his contemporaries: through sheer
compulsion he had become a titan, channeling the entire spirit of
his age to lend his name to a new way of working and of managing work. The management theorist Peter Drucker would class him
alongside Freud and Darwin (with Taylor replacing the usual Marx)
as the three progenitors of the modern age. Few writers about management or the division of labor or the history of work have failed
to pay homage—either in admiration or in scorn—to Taylor. But it
was the novelist John Dos Passos, in his trilogy of experimental novels, *U.S.A.*, who offered perhaps the most quietly sardonic portrait,
drawing on the legend that Taylor wound up his watch first thing in
the morning: "He couldn't stand to see an idle lathe or an idle man.
Production went to his head and thrilled his sleepless nerves like
liquor or women on a Saturday night . . . on the morning of his fif-
tyninth birthday, when the nurse went into his room to look at him
at fourthirty, he was dead with his watch in his hand."[33]

☐

Taylor's animus was lodged entirely against the laziness of the
industrial shop floor. But his greatest influence lay elsewhere. For
in divesting workers of their own ways of handling work—what
one union organizer, "Big Bill" Haywood, had called "the manager's brains . . . under the worker's cap"—he had simply trans-
ferred the work of management elsewhere: into the office. Offices
became massive overheads for Taylorist operations, with organizational charts to designate, down to the minutest detail, the labor

process that workers once carried within their own heads. Offices grew enormously simply to house all the new white shirts, with their stopwatches and cameras. Even where Taylorism in its strictest form wasn't adopted—and, indeed, this was true of most offices—the spirit of management itself spread far and wide.

To adopt scientific management therefore required an enormous expansion of office bureaucracies. "All of this [that is, scientific management] requires the kindly cooperation of the management, and involves a much more elaborate organization and system than the old-fashioned herding of men in large gangs," Taylor wrote. "This organization consisted, in this case [that is, Bethlehem Steel], of one set of men, who were engaged in the development of the science of laboring through time study, such as has been described above; another set of men, mostly skilled laborers themselves, who were teachers, and who helped and guided the men in their work; another set of toolroom men who provided them with the proper implements and kept them in perfect order, and another set of clerks who planned the work well in advance, moved the men with the least loss of time from one place to another, and properly recorded each man's earnings, etc." This simplified model of the Taylor system indicated what a profound increase in hierarchy, in terms of levels and departments, scientific management required. For all the costs that the system saved on the factory floor, it was likely that it reproduced them within the company offices with all the new hired hands.

Had Taylor been the only one bitten with the efficiency bug in his time, his system might have died as a peculiar monomania. After the Watertown Arsenal strike, workers and labor unions were on the lookout for white shirts, and as a result may have ultimately prevented the purest form of scientific management from taking hold on the shop floor. But Taylorism was only one—and the most famous and influential—school attempting to systematize the workplace. The Pennsylvania Railroad had introduced a piece-rate system well before Taylor rationalized it, and efficiency had become a watchword as soon as American industry began to fall into its Gilded Age chaos and lassitude. In 1900, a group of efficiency-obsessed managers seized the spirit of the age and started a magazine, called—inevitably, perhaps—*System*. Subtitled *A Monthly Magazine for the Man of Affairs*, each volume had articles proposing new models for the minutiae of office life, whether a new system of filing or a more efficient mode of envelope licking. In the section "Successful Through System," quotations from successful, whiskered, and white-haired executives confirmed the importance and necessity of systems in business organization. "A technical knowledge of and training in systematic methods and organization is the prime requisite in the education of the modern business man," claimed Thomas Phillips, president of the Federal Trust and Savings Bank in Chicago; meanwhile, Edward Lacey, president of the Bankers' National Bank, affirmed that business had changed such that systems were now vital to the functioning of business: "While the business world was a mass of smaller units, the necessity for system was not so apparent, but as business units increased in size, necessity soon brought about the adoption of systematic principles and methods."[34] The relationship of systematic thinking to the office was also made explicit. Each issue of *System* contained a special section of photographs, titled "Battlefields of Business," where various methods and forms of office layout were held up as examples to emulate. (*System*'s popularity ballooned in the Roaring Twenties, and in 1929 it was changed to a weekly and relaunched under the name it carried until 2009—*BusinessWeek*.)

In the spirit of the master, Taylor's associates and acolytes soon began systematizing everything they saw: medicine, bricklaying, sports—you name it, the Taylorists tried to make it more efficient. A husband-and-wife team, Frank and Lillian Gilbreth, became famous for Taylorizing their own large family of twelve children—portrayed in the popular book and film *Cheaper by the Dozen*. After Frank's death, Lillian carried on the mission, bringing the principles of scientific management into the hiring and firing of employees. Lillian believed strongly that Taylor's version of scientific management neglected the "human element," attempted to force itself on workers without ensuring that the workers consented to the imposition. Developing personality and psychological testing for the hiring of employees, her "personnel management" system soon became as famous and popular as scientific management. Supposedly a more humanizing version of Taylor's system, it in fact performed exactly what workers had sarcastically joked about before: it was an apparatus for getting inside the minds of the workers and ensuring that they submit docilely to management's demands. The department of personnel management has been one of scientific management's most lasting achievements, having come down to us under a different but familiar name: human resources.

With this flurry of activity surrounding the office, it was only a matter of time, of course, before the office itself—where scientific management was being fomented—became the object of systematization. In the introduction to Frank Gilbreth's treatise on reducing inefficient body movements, *Motion Study*, the author Robert Thurston Kent notes how, inspired by Gilbreth's descriptions of faster bricklaying, he began to scrutinize the circulation of outgoing mail in the office of his trade engineering publication. Applying motion study to the stamping of envelopes, he notes, began to improve the speed of output, to 100–120 envelopes a minute. It took only a minute's reflection to recognize that the office could stand to be much more systematized.[35]

Taylor's disciple W. H. Leffingwell conducted the most far-reaching experiments in organizing offices, publishing his first findings in *System*, later organizing his research into two long-winded and sententious books, *Scientific Office Management* (1917) and the eight-hundred-page textbook *Office Management* (1925). Like the Taylorist works on the factory (there were also pamphlets for housewives on home management), *Scientific Office Management* touts the importance of individual observation and the results of time and motion study: only rather than pulleys and lathes, the means of production to be rationalized in the office are pens and envelopes, typewriters and receipt forms, file cabinets and desks. In an inimitable tone, at once loftily knowing and completely oblivious, Leffingwell details the horrors of the inefficient, underobserved office:

> There are millions of unnecessary motions, and when one begins to investigate an office with an eye for these alone, one comes to believe that most of them are in the office. Watch a

girl jogging paper or cards. Long after the work is done she goes on calmly patting them here and there. Watch a clerk rushing through his work, throwing the papers in a disorderly heap as he goes and then when he has finished, watch him spend a few minutes straightening things up. It never occurs to him to pile them in an orderly manner in the beginning. Watch him when there are a few letters to be sealed or stamped. First he carefully moistens the gummed end, then presses it down, then pounds each stamp with his fist. Watch clerks enclosing printed matter in envelopes. A trained expert will do as much as four or more untrained workers, yet only half of the difference is in the speed, the other half being in the elimination of waste motions.[36]

Photograph captions indicate how the scientifically managed office earns savings of 20 percent in envelope stuffing, through the elimination of useless motions and the deployment of more salubrious furniture. "This 'motion-studied' mail opening table made possible a 20% increase in the output," Leffingwell writes in one caption. "This girl takes out money and letters and pins and sorts them at the rate of 310 an hour. Note the sunken baskets and the footrest."[37] Observation also reduces fatigue and inefficiency in typing: "A typist who could write very rapidly had the habit of continually twisting her head to read the copy, often as many as four or five times for each sentence. It was only a habit, since there was nothing the matter with her memory, as was proved by asking her to repeat a sentence of the copy which she had only read once. When it was pointed out to her that she was twisting her head eight or ten times a minute, over 500 times an hour, the habit was stopped, resulting in an immediate increase of speed and a decrease in fatigue."[38] At the same time, Leffingwell notes the difficulty of instituting time study and management techniques on the office floor and suggests manipulative forms of games to encourage workers to participate in the study: "One manager who has had considerable success in introducing the use of the stop watch in his office, casually remarks to his subject: 'I wonder how long it takes you to do that job?' After two or three employees have been timed and nothing has happened, the rest of the office force is usually not only willing but anxious to be 'time studied.' "[39]

Yet for the most part, besides demonstrating the mania of the Taylorists for infinite subdivision of tasks and time study, Leffingwell's treatise unconsciously reveals the sheer novelty of office life itself—the fact that managers were mostly unsure of how to organize and run offices. When not discussing time and motion study, Leffingwell covers fundamentals in office life in a superficial, basic way. "In many offices little attention is given to the selection of pencils," he writes, alarmed. "In some kinds of work a soft lead pencil is required, in others a medium, and in still others a hard lead. Sometimes an eraser is necessary."[40] Discussing lighting in an office, Leffingwell writes, in a mixed tone of discovery and authoritativeness, that "some kinds of work require much better light than others—see that those workers who require the most light get their preference."[41] As for office layout, his "scientific" inclination is to reproduce the assembly-line model of the factory floor. He suggests that departments which depend on each other be placed near each other. And his recommendation on water fountains, with its exceedingly precise calculations, can read like a satire on Taylorism itself: "The average person should drink water at least five or six times a day. If each of one hundred clerks in an office were compelled to walk fifty feet to, and fifty feet from, the fountain, five times a day, each one would walk five hundred feet a day. Multiplied by one hundred clerks the distance traveled would be fifty thousand feet, or nearly ten miles! Multiplied by three hundred working days, the clerks would be walking three thousand miles for water in a year."[42] Elsewhere in his book, Leffingwell emphasized the importance of what was called "welfare work"—which today we would class as the amenities offered by a particular office (recreational facilities, adequately potable coffee, the occasional leftover bagel from a breakfast meeting). In the mechanized world of the Taylorist office, the amenities were different: a "rest room," where women could lie down on couches or congregate around a phonograph to dance, or one where men could retreat during fifteen-minute breaks to smoke.

All these were the signs of an office world that was only just coming into its own; the notion of "the office" itself, as a separate world, with its own rules and atmosphere and culture, was being justified under the rubric of management. The office was no longer merely an administrative holding tank, parasitic on the "real work" done in factories and fields, but the place where the real work was in fact getting done. Lee Galloway, another Taylor disciple, addressed this very misconception in the opening to his manual, *Office Management*: "When it is seen that the activities of production and distribution are made possible only through the operations covered by the term 'office work,' then we approach the truer appraisal of the office as a necessary economic factor. The office managers and employees cease to be passive agents in the promotion of business and their labor is no longer charged to a non-productive account. They at once rise to the dignity of active forces which furnish constructive ideas, and co-ordinate the activities of the business into smoothly working units of enormous size and power."[43] The office, in other words, was becoming the real workplace, and scientific management attempted to view it as the site of a potential utopia: where buzzing managers proliferated like cicadas in summer, where impeccably ordered rows of desks receded into the vanishing point of the horizon, where American business became inexorable, honed, and proud.

□

It's worth dwelling on what Taylorism and other contemporary theories of efficiency must have done to the world of the office worker. The effects were no doubt felt unequally among generations. Much like contemporary office workers who witnessed the last throes of the typewriter and the Dictaphone and learned to embrace the personal computer and the photocopier, office workers in the twenty years following the turn of the century experienced a profound shift in the pace, nature, and volume of work. Offices with only a few clerks suddenly had hundreds; bosses who were once as near to you as the length of your arm were suddenly insulated in posh executive suites. The small merchants' offices had metastasized into a paperwork empire, spanning not only dense cities but entire continents. Offices were segregated into departments, and the departments split hierarchically into managers and clerks. Work had, for most people, gotten more specialized and less interesting. *Blessed be drudgery!*

Office workers were forced to become aware of their bodies and their motions in time beyond anything that they had known before. Taylorism, whether applied in its most ruthless form or not, ensured constant supervision. Pictures of offices from the time show foreman-like workers pacing the floors over sitting clerks with their heads bowed—no one seeming to make light conversation, no one daring to turn their eyes from their work. In many offices, the wrong motion would earn demerits. Thanks to the spread of Taylorism, managers believed almost dogmatically that slight shifts in office arrangements could change behavior as well as allegiances and work habits. And in fact they were right. The early management theorist R. H. Goodell described an example where clerical workers were constantly disrupted by visitors passing in a corridor. He decided to turn the desks away from the door, and also from their supervisor's desk. This meant that they were no longer disrupted but also no longer saw their supervisor observing them—even though they knew he was constantly watching.[44] In other words, it was easier for workers to continue working if they internalized the watchful eye of their boss. No doubt, still other offices observed the more casual nature of the old countinghouses, but these were usually smaller firms. The unscripted practices of the old offices would remain, but as a kind of subterfuge: in the future, a leisurely pace wouldn't be the norm; time would not be given, but stolen.

Taylorism succeeded not just because of the force of its founder's personality; it also harmonized with a broader cultural shift toward anatomizing the movements of people's bodies in time. From Cubist painters like Braque and Picasso to photographers like Eadweard Muybridge, the late nineteenth and early twentieth centuries witnessed an obsession with breaking down objects, moments, and bodies—one that corresponded to a breaking down of the features of the mind itself. The strict movements of classical ballet were giving way to the seemingly more free but no less planned motions of modern dance. And finally, the birth of the cinema meant that motion could be captured in a continuous stream and then slowed down—viewed in its component parts. Among the most fervent moviegoers, of course, were clerks themselves. The workers who labored under Taylorism saw themselves as swept up in a tremendous current in which hitherto unacknowledged aspects of their lives were being scrutinized.[45]

The sense of being watched was part of a larger change in the process of work, in which segments of the office workforce felt themselves turned into objects rather than agents of capitalism. Until the turn of the century, it was easier to draw distinctions along what has only half jokingly been called the "collar line," the separation between manual and nonmanual labor that made most clerks feel that they belonged naturally to the upper stratum of society. Indeed, the very phrase "white-collar" to designate a certain kind of worker was coined when the socialist writer Upton Sinclair deployed it in his polemic against the mainstream press, *The Brass Check* (1920), to describe conservative journalists who looked down on the industrial working class. "Because they are allowed to wear a white collar," he sneered, "[they] regard themselves as members of the capitalist class."[46] Cartoon images of the Taylor system depicted snooty, pale, vested men directing begrimed and sweaty industrial workers: here was the office taking precedence over the factory, the white collar over the blue, and the skilled, knowledgeable worker over the drone he has forcibly de-skilled.

But this image of superiority was no longer the experience of many workers. Even the office had been fractured by the forceful separation of ownership from management and the construction of a new, elaborate system of hierarchies in the modern American corporation. "The clerical employee is no longer as intimate as he used to be," *BusinessWeek* (née *System*) noted in 1929. "He is anybody at all, a worker, almost a number, like a mill hand."[47] There was no longer the easy correlation to be made between clean labor and being middle-class. The connection that a man like Edward Tailer once drew between his low position as a clerk and that of his boss became separated by a gulf. By separating knowledge from the basic work process ("the separation of conception from execution," as Harry Braverman once put it), in the factory as well as in the office, the ideology of Taylorism all but ensured a workplace divided against itself, both in space and in practice, with a group of manag-

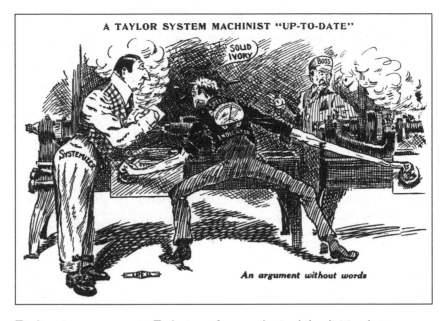

Trade union responses to Taylorism often emphasized the division between genteel white-collar managers and the work they forcibly (mis)directed.
Smithsonian Institution

ers controlling how work was done and their workers merely performing that work. Somewhat more dangerously, this division put into serious doubt the notion that office workers were, as a whole, on the way up. Some of them were closer in income, status, and life chances to the grimy manual workers they were supposed to be directing. It became increasingly clear from the shape of the offices themselves, and from the distance between the top and the bottom rungs of the "ladder," that some workers were never going to join the upper layers of management. For some, work was always, frankly, going to suck. How they would react to these changes would shape the course of the office for generations to come.

□

In 1906, some years before Taylor had achieved his fame, an office building appeared whose concerted, unified conception of architecture, layout, design, and management seemed to anticipate and solve all the problems of management and office labor. On the outside, the Larkin Administration Building in Buffalo, New York, designed by the young Frank Lloyd Wright for the Larkin Soap Company, looked heavy and undistinguished: a stern pile of brick piers, guarded at the corners by pylon-like stair towers, seemingly at one with the smoke-ringed, snow-walled surroundings of turn-of-the-century upstate New York. But visitors entering the building were astounded by the airiness and light of the interior court, where under a lofty ceiling orderly rows of clerks diligently handled the piles of correspondence pouring into the building with implacable speed. Unusual for any office building was the coolness of the air, maintained at a temperate level even as the midsummer heat asphyxiated Buffalo's residents outside. The lives of all the workers were at once supervised and organized, with Larkin offering lunchrooms, a bathhouse, hospital clinics, safety training, a gym, thrift clubs, benefit funds, picnics, weekly concerts, and a profit-sharing plan.[48] Striving at once to be the acme of a progressive company and the model office, Larkin anticipated the familial and all-enveloping nature of many corporations to come.

The Larkin Company started out in 1875 as a manufacturer of soap, which its traveling salesmen sold on the road, later branching into various perfumes and powders. But in 1881 it began to experiment with soliciting storekeepers by mail, which unexpectedly resulted in a boom in orders. Soon Larkin began, in what seemed like a natural leap, to provide general luxury items, like a fine handkerchief or a small art photograph, and to select orders as a sales incentive. It worked: gradually Larkin began to buy mass quantities of all kinds of products—bicycles, silverware, baby carriages, clothing, guns—directly from manufacturers and sell them through its newly expanded mail-order business.[49] Much like Amazon.com a century later, Larkin was forced to expand enormously from its original raison d'être to focus on managing the sheer volume of mail orders coming through. Twelve new soap factory buildings were constructed in the 1890s, but it quickly became clear that the mail-order business was no longer secondary. By 1903, the company was receiving five thousand orders a day.[50] Darwin D. Martin, one of the accounting secretaries, developed a highly efficient account-filing system for tracking orders, but the innovation couldn't compensate for the lack of space. The company administration decided that it could no longer have its clerks working in hot, dirty, noisy environs surrounded by soap vats. The thirty-five-year-old Wright was young for an architect and mostly known for his houses, which were already famous. "His houses are called 'freak' houses," wrote Darwin Martin in a letter to John Larkin, reassuring him that "the owners, whom we met, were not freaks."[51] In person, Wright impressed the Larkin managers with his evangelism for clean air and well-lit spaces. On the strength of his near-messianic fervor, he was hired.

The challenges in designing the Larkin Building were many. It needed to accommodate eighteen hundred office workers processing their six daily shipments of mail orders while nonetheless maintaining a comfortable, spacious environment. Part of the problem was the location: Buffalo was not a hospitable city for a clean, well-lit office. Surrounding the site for the company, near the already built factories, were railroad lines, forges, foundries, coal yards, and other heavy industry—a grimy, dusty environment for a soap company. Without atmospheric control, soot was bound to accumulate along the walls and on the desktops. The original factory buildings where the office workers were housed had nothing in the way of air-conditioning (it hadn't been invented yet), and no example existed of an office building that had successfully managed the circulation of air and still maintained an adequate quantity of light. Wright's design would meet all of these challenges and in the process raise the status of office design to an art. "In-so-far as it is simple and true it will live," Wright would intone some months after its completion, "a blessing to its occupants, fulfilling in a measure on behalf of the men who planted it there their two great reciprocal duties, duty to the Past and duty to the Future—duties self imposed upon all right thinking men."[52]

Wright had promised his commissioners that the offices would be as "light as out doors"—this despite the plans to seal the interior with solid slabs of brick massing. And yet the most immediately obvious achievement in the building was the gleaming ubiquity of natural light—something that workers in supposedly progressive offices today sometimes go an entire day without. The basement received natural illumination from windows in the foundation wall and from skylights. Otherwise densely packed stairways were leavened by both skylights and slits of windows along the climb. The entrance to the lobby was opened up by large sheets of clear glass, framed as doors; this was an unusual move at the time, but following Larkin it became a commonplace of all building lobbies. But Larkin's most famous feature was its central light court. Filtered by a metal-and-glass roof, the skylight cascaded downward through a vast cavern of space carved by balconies, flooding and reflecting off the white walls. A light court was a common feature of skyscrapers in Chicago, but unlike those buildings, where retail stores filled the periphery spaces, Larkin used its court as office space—indeed, the central administrative space, where Darwin Martin and William Heath sat alongside an orderly row of administrative assistants.

Yet such plentiful daylight, and Buffalo's general predilection for viciously humid summers, made ventilation and temperature control a big problem. Wright's solution appears to have come to him in a burst of inspiration: "The solution that had hung fire came in a flash. I took the next train to Buffalo to try and get the Larkin Company to see that it was worth thirty thousand dollars more to build the stair-towers free of the central block, not only as independent stair-towers for communication and escape, but also as air-intakes for the ventilating system."[53] The pylon-like towers on the outside were therefore kept exterior to the building itself precisely to make the interior more habitable. In other words, it was the needs of office and the mechanical structure of the ventilation system that determined the shape of the building, a rare instance of form truly following function. Air came in through the ducts in the walls of the corner towers; entering the basement, the air was filtered and either heated or, after the installation of a new refrigeration system, cooled. This "conditioned" air was then distributed on each floor of the building. Though less advanced than the systems that would follow the mass adoption of cooling systems, Larkin's innovative environment made it very nearly the first air-conditioned building in the country.

The arrangement of the desks and offices themselves appeared traditional at first. On either side of the chest-high walls flanking the central gallery lay modular file cabinets and row after row of custom-designed desks, grouped in packs of four, each equipped with a fancy metal cantilevered folding chair that swung in and out (which despite its fanciness was apparently rather uncomfortable to sit in for the whole day).[54] The general pleasantness of the conditions smoothed the impressively organized flow of paperwork, which sped from the low-level receiving area up to the top of the building and then trickled down through several departments until it could safely be expedited to the factory floor. Correspondents would dictate responses to mail-order inquiries into gramophones; these recordings were pressed onto wax disks that were taken by messengers to a typing pool; the typed-up responses were checked; then they were sent to the warehouse. (Wright would revisit this slow downward curve some fifty years later in designing the interior spiral of the Solomon R. Guggenheim Museum in New York City.) A number of rooms were devoted to relief and enjoyment. A YWCA was available in the building chiefly for therapy and counsel (there were not enough young male employees to justify a YMCA). A library provided four hundred circulating titles and the latest magazines, while a "rest room" was equipped with leather chairs and a player piano. Tiled roof gardens offered escape in spring and autumn.[55]

Though employee testimonials are few, the ones that survive affirm a special pride in the warm nature of the business. "A class place to work in Buffalo," a former secretary reported. "They took *care* of you."[56] One visitor claimed that hundreds of thousands of visitors came to marvel at the building—including several Russian aristocrats and various engineers and designers from around the world—which was somewhat strange for what was, after all, merely an office.

But more was at stake in the thoroughness of the Larkin Building's design than mere problem solving or taking good care of its workers, as the thousands of visitors would indicate. Wright and the Larkin people had created a total office environment, every detail of which was intended to exude the enlightened attitude of the company itself. Again, like the offices of Google, the Larkin Building was an advertisement for the company; its reputed attention to the work process helped sell the company's products. It inscribed the walls with inspirational buzzwords, goads to the collective productive spirit:

GENEROSITY ALTRUISM SACRIFICE
INTEGRITY LOYALTY FIDELITY
IMAGINATION JUDGMENT INITIATIVE
CO-OPERATION ECONOMY INDUSTRY
INTELLIGENCE ENTHUSIASM CONTROL

The building was also an advertisement, for the staff as much as for visiting foreign dignitaries, for the health and fortitude of American business. "It is enterprise, American enterprise, that drives the wheels," wrote the observer George Twitmyer in the *Business Man's Magazine*, "carefully organized systems and methods are the jewel bearings; good will, the lubricant."[57] Wright, too, would proclaim the ineluctable Americanness of the building. "The American flag is the only flag that would look well on or in this building; the only flag with its simple stars and bars that wouldn't look incongruous and out of place with the simple rectangular masses of the exterior and the straightforward rectilinear treatment of the interior." In tones reminiscent of Ralph Waldo Emerson, he proclaimed the building's independence from malign European influences: "I think our building is wholly American in its directness and freshness of treatment. It wears no badge of servitude to foreign 'styles' yet it avails itself gratefully of the treasures and the wisdom bequeathed to it by its ancestors."[58]

At the same time, though it was infinitely more advanced and considered than the dingy, gloomy offices that were beginning to climb undeservedly high above American cities, there was a danger in the Larkin Building's totalizing nature that would appear again and again in the history of the office. For what passed for workers' welfare could with a little imagination also be seen as social control. Look at the photograph of the light court: a row of identically attired and coiffured women together in a visual line, guarded at the desk corners by four male executives. Was this a communal, team-focused environment? Or was it one designed for easy supervision and surveillance, a way to enforce discipline and adherence to unity? Even the recreational activities stressed cooperation and commitment. The theme of a "masque" held for executives and secretaries in 1916 was described in a pamphlet with the mock language of

The light court of Frank Lloyd Wright's Larkin Building (1904).
Buffalo Historical Society

seventeenth-century allegory, spiced with a few choice words from twentieth-century management theory: "That when Industry is mastered by Ignorance, and all the qualities that go with Ignorance, like Disorder, Sloth, Greed, Inefficiency, and Strife, Industry becomes useless and unable to serve mankind. When, however, Industry is freed from Ignorance by Imagination, and the spirits which accompany Imagination, like Service, Co-operation, Order, System, and Ambition, then Industry becomes the true servant of mankind and indispensable to its happiness."[59]

"System," "Order," "Inefficiency": these were also the shibboleths and scare words of the scientific managers, potentially making a major bummer out of what was otherwise a company party designed for relaxation. "Relaxation," however, was not a neutral fact; it was rather the other half of the managerial equation—evidence of the Larkin Company's commitment to what was known at the time as "industrial betterment." A loose movement of reformers and visionaries, alarmed by the rising tide of strikes and sabotage committed by restless, unmotivated workers, they didn't feel that the solution lay in reducing the monotony of the work—say, by rotating workers from job to job or offering workers more control over the pace of their labor. On the contrary, for the reformers, monotony was in fact the *good* part about industrialized work. The intellectual historian Daniel Rodgers puts it elegantly: "Borrowing the concept of habit from late nineteenth-century psychologists, they insisted that routine emancipated the worker by wearing deep and comfortable tracks in the nervous system that set his mind free for thought. Hence, if industrial employees chafed at their tasks, effective cures concentrated not on the work but on the worker's mental state."[60] The task was therefore to offer amenities on and off the job. The Larkin Building corresponded precisely to this ideal: the work process was as regimented as a Taylorist office, but the workers had, by way of compensation, noonday lectures to attend; classes to frequent; a company newspaper, *Ourselves*, which the workers could help put out or at least read. The numbing work remained the same. Though the Larkin Building had elevated the process and environment for working, it did little to change the nature of how work was organized or how hierarchies were rationalized—in short, how the office could offer better work, not just a better working environment. The Larkin Building would remain the best office building on offer for years to come. But its design could only refract, not solve, the growing problem of office work and its discontents in the early twentieth century.

3

THE WHITE-BLOUSE REVOLUTION

The offices of our grandfathers were without steel
frames and files, without elevators and radiators,
without telephones,—and without skirts.

—CHARLES LORING, ARCHITECT[1]

In his early novel *The Job*, Sinclair Lewis, America's first writer to win the Nobel Prize for Literature, set himself the task of depicting a phenomenon that was simultaneously new and extraordinarily common: the ascendancy of a woman from the provinces who finds a big-city job in an office. Before the figure became a stereotype—the "w.c.g.," or "white-collar girl"—Lewis had set her essential outlines. His heroine, Una Golden, grows up in Panama, Pennsylvania, its smug isolation somewhere out in the lonely green middle west of the state belying the exoticism of its name. "Not pretty, not noisy, not particularly articulate, but instinctively on the inside of things," Una has an innate aptitude for manners and etiquette—"a natural executive," who ensures that her father, Captain Lew Golden, never eats with his knife and that her mother doesn't lose her mind reading too many drugstore dime novels.[2]

Ambitious but untrained, desiring freedom without any idea what it would look like, she reads widely and haphazardly in high school, preparing herself for a local, Panamanian existence: securing a local husband from among the few available males and contenting herself with the sparse amenities of private life, snatched from in between hours of daily domestic labor. That is, until her father dies—leaving her, at age twenty-four, and her hapless mother, at a much more advanced and unusable age, weighed down with what had been hidden debts. And so Una follows the path that untold millions like her will take: she enrolls in a local commercial college, which teaches her stenography, typing, filing, and minor bookkeeping, and takes her newfound skills to an office in New York, from which she draws a meager salary that might keep the bill collectors at bay.

"They are a new generation of their sex, cool, assured, even capable," wrote the popular novelist Christopher Morley in a newspaper column in 1921, describing seeing a scrum of w.c.g.'s in the subway. "They are happy, because they are so perishable, because (despite their naive assumption of certainty) one knows them so delightfully only as an innocent ornament of this business world of which they are so ignorant."[3] Lewis would sound the note of the white-collar girl's alienation in a tone of greater disaffection, even genuine hatred. It was a "vast, competent, largely useless cosmos of offices," a "world whose crises you cannot comprehend unless you have learned that the difference between a 2-A pencil and a 2-B pencil is at least equal to the contrast between London and Tibet; unless you understand why a normally self-controlled young woman may have a week of tragic discomfort because she is using a billing-machine instead of her ordinary correspondence typewriter."[4] Lewis knew that his (somewhat overwrought) satire only masked something essential about office life: that it had taken an outsized place in the mental life of an entire generation of people all over the world. "Not through wolf-haunted forests nor purple canyons, but through tiled hallways and elevators move our heroes of today," he wrote. "An unreasonable world, sacrificing bird-song and tranquil dusk and high golden noons to selling junk—yet it rules us." The office was nevertheless not to be discounted, Lewis wrote, because "life lives there." "The office is filled with thrills of love and distrust and ambition," he continues. "Each alley between desks quivers with secret romance as ceaselessly as a battle-trench, or a lane in Normandy." He neglected to add (though he no doubt recognized) that the rules governing the sexes were being rewritten there as nowhere else. Few social transformations in the twentieth century have been as quietly revolutionary.

□

The American government began to hire female clerical workers in the 1860s, when a sizable chunk of the literate male labor force had exchanged crisp white collars for bloodstained blue Union uniforms. The U.S. treasurer Francis Elias Spinner led the way, overcoming opposition from the men in his office who foresaw the sanctity of their male preserve being compromised. Spinner kept the dangerous new hires away from any sensitive work, assigning them light, thoughtless tasks instead—like sorting and packaging bonds and currency—as a kind of experiment. To his pleasant surprise, the women did an excellent job. The plus: you didn't have to pay them as much as the men. So he continued to hire women after the war had concluded, while federal legislators stepped in to ensure that they didn't cost too much: a maximum salary for women of $900 a year was established in 1866, whereas maximum salaries for men ranged between $1,200 and $1,800.[5] "Some of the females are doing more and better work for $900 per annum than many male clerks who were paid double that amount," Spinner declared with satisfaction in 1869.[6]

Once it became apparent that women were perfectly capable office workers—and often accounted better than men—they began to enter the office world en masse, completely upending the male enclaves that had been dominant until the Civil War. The changes in proportion were enormous, accompanying the growth of the clerical workforce itself. In 1870, there were eighty thousand clerical workers in America; only 3 percent were women. Fifty years later, there were three million clerical workers, of whom women made up nearly 50 percent.[7]

The extraordinary growth in women's employment was contingent on their being limited to particular positions, where they practically established a monopoly—if the kind of monopoly that indicated widespread subjection and nonchalant discrimination rather than unchecked power. Stenography was one of these fields.

Office stenographers mostly took longhand dictation, especially important since handwritten notes—even if composed by a third party—were still considered more respectful than typed ones. As a result they were slightly higher in status and salary than typists but below private secretaries, who at least enjoyed personal proximity to executive power (nonetheless out of their grasp). Like so much of the office world, much of the stability of the workforce—its relative freedom from labor-management strife otherwise taking hold in other workplaces throughout the world—depended on this simple ambiguity of what status a stenographer held. Regardless of status, however, there was no question about the quality or interest of the work itself: Whether handwritten dictation or mechanical typing, the work didn't involve much in the way of imagination or initiative, since women were seen as being better able to handle thankless work.

With hiring practices tilting toward women in typing and steno functions, these jobs became so associated with them that the workers themselves were often referred to simply as "type-girls"; sometimes, dispensing with the need to distinguish humans from machines, women were just called "typewriters."[8] Advertisements for the Remington typewriter—the first widely adopted typewriter in the office—were populated almost exclusively by stereotypically supple-wristed female angels, their delicate, elongated piano fingers hovering expectantly over the keys. Christopher Sholes, the designer of the first commercially produced typewriter in 1867, called it "obviously a blessing to mankind, and especially to womankind."[9] One advertisement for the Remington typewriter, appearing in the depths of the depression of the 1870s in the *Nation* magazine, suggested it would be a way for the genteel to help some young woman make her way out of poverty:

> No invention has opened for women so broad and easy an avenue to profitable and suitable employment as the "Type-Writer," and it merits the careful consideration of all thoughtful and charitable persons interested in the subject of work for woman.
>
> Mere girls are now earning from $10 to $20 per week with

the "Type-Writer," and we can at once secure good situations for one hundred expert writers on it in court-rooms in this city.

The public is cordially invited to call and inspect the working of the machine, and obtain all information at our show-rooms.[10]

The private secretary, too, gradually became identified as wholly female. Unlike the tediousness of stenography and typing, it was the dead-endedness of secretarial work that supposedly made it appropriate for women. "A woman is to be preferred to the secretarial position," wrote W. H. Leffingwell, Taylor's disciple in office design, "for she is not averse to doing minor tasks, work involving the handling of petty details, which would irk and irritate ambitious young men, who usually feel that the work they are doing is of no importance if it can be performed by some person with a lower salary."[11] "They are steadier than boys," a railroad official said, when discussing his preference for hiring women clerks. "They are not so damn anxious to get out and rustle around . . . They never think of themselves as General Managers of a railroad and are content to work along."[12]

By 1926, 88 percent of secretarial positions were held by women. Women were nearly 100 percent of typists, stenographers, file clerks, and switchboard operators.[13] The lowest positions in any office were likely to be occupied by women. Even the term "office boy," meaning the lowest-paid and most menial job in the workplace, came to designate someone of either sex: one employment ad from the 1920s said, "Wanted—a boy, either sex."[14]

Though it was obviously beneficial for companies to have cheap labor, there was nothing new about unequal pay for women at the turn of the century that made them instantly more preferable. Nor did men begin to consider women more suited for menial and repetitive labor overnight. The oversupply of women for the office, at least, was furnished by the convulsions in the economy. Before and immediately after the Civil War, family farms provided plenty of work for women—much of it unremunerated work, to be sure, but productive work nonetheless. Fathers and mothers were less likely to let their daughters pack up for the cities when they were needed at home. But as industries began to consolidate, many of the goods formerly produced locally by farms were now being manufactured in cities and placed in stores across the country. Factory-spun clothing, canned goods, and bakery-made bread replaced the handwoven, self-farmed, and home-cooked goods that women were supposed to provide in the home as a matter of course. Independent farmers themselves were being subsumed by larger farms; farmland by cities and industry. Here, again, was the large story of the old middle class dying out and a "new" middle class coming into being—but one whose specific consequences for the gendered division of labor would be profound. With money for small-business men drying up and less productive work for women to do in the home, the office proved to be an opportunity that women couldn't turn down. The new supply of labor coincided marvelously with the new needs of management. On the industrial shop floor teams of skilled laborers were, with unskilled laborers, subject to managers. The office did the factory one better. For the "unskilled" segment of the force, there was a supply of women, who were doubly subordinated: they could be set up at machines that kept them doing monotonous work, and there was no chance of their ever becoming managers. The widespread acceptance of forms of scientific management in fact depended on women being in the office.

When Upton Sinclair had coined the term "white collar," it was to sneer at those lowly paper pushers who believed that they, unlike their poor, dirty factory brethren, were filing and copying their way into the ranks of the ruling class. As we've already observed, this distinction had become increasingly untenable (if nonetheless vigorously asserted) in the age of the massive factory-style office. But now all the lowly work was increasingly taken up by women; the pay for these jobs was also degraded (and degrading); and there was never a question that women would be able to move up the company ladder in the way men could, since it remained unfathomable for male executives to place women alongside them in managerial roles. So within the office itself, a class division sprang up that fell neatly along gender lines. Men were allowed to think of themselves as middle-class so long as women, from their perspective, remained something like the office proletariat, took office jobs to help their families until they married or, in the retrograde words of *The Job*, were kept "so busy that they change[d] from dewy girls into tight-lipped spinsters before they discover[ed] life."

□

Yet the office offered a sense of freedom to many women that shouldn't be underestimated. The office chose women, but women also chose the office. Nor was it the case, among women in the office, that the workers perceived themselves as wholly and universally degraded. For many children of working-class men and women, the office offered an escape route into an arena of middle-class respectability that also paid more than most other opportunities; for children of the middle class, especially those whose parents couldn't afford a more expensive college education, commercial training and a clerical job were ways to get into business (and away from what had become habitual "women's professions," such as teaching). The testimony of Rose Chernin, a Russian Jew, is exemplary. She had spent World War I working in a factory making ammunition shells—while also attending high school continuation classes, so as not to forsake her education for work. She clung to the hope that education would at last allow her a chance to escape the factory and make it into an office:

> Do you know what it's like, ten hours a day, looking at shells in a noisy, dirty plant? You turn over a shell, this way, that way, until your mind goes blank. And always you're waiting for the break, the five-minute break to go to the toilet. This became the one meaningful thing in the ten hours of the day. You felt that there had to be another way. I thought, with the naïveté of a child, that to get an education, a high-school education, would give me a job in an office. In an office! When we crossed the yard into the factory, we passed the offices. I looked at those girls, sitting there, cleanly dressed at their desks. And I thought, There is another world.[15]

The paths and opportunities for working-class women differed greatly from those of the middle class. Much of the difference came from education. Until 1900, hardly any Americans, men or women, stayed in school through to high school; a good number of fourteen-year-olds, particularly the children of immigrants and the working class, didn't make it past fourth grade.[16] Of course, the decision to drop out had a certain rationality to it: the few jobs open to the lower classes usually didn't require special training, and in any case the public schools didn't offer any commercial education. But industry had a growing hunger for competent clerical labor that wasn't being satisfied. So business leaders turned to the schools. Progressive school reformers and executives united to devise a program to keep children in school—and to turn them into potential clerks. Since most city school boards contained a preponderance of business leaders and professionals, it was relatively easy to add vocational programs to the curriculum of high schools. And it worked: high school dropout rates fell as children stayed in school to study the arts of bookkeeping and stenography, the promise of a job lying just beyond graduation becoming more realizable. If they wanted to continue their studies, they could go on to a commercial college. It was a major moment in the history not just of the office but of the system of education, for it had become the avowed goal of American public schools to train people for work in an office. The country was fast becoming a nation of clerks.

The schools trained women and men, however, in considerably divergent ways. They constantly encouraged men to study bookkeeping and accounting, for the purposes of developing "business leadership" skills in them. By contrast, women were seen as naturally suited for stenography. Though this arbitrary division between the harder, numbers-driven executive commanding the subordinate secretary or stenographer—and the corresponding thinking that women were innately better suited for light, mechanical work and incapable of handling math—would stubbornly persist, even into the present day, some women, even more stubbornly, refused to uphold the division. Despite a plethora of guidebooks that proclaimed the joys of the steno pool and the proximity it offered to business, the few women who went into the business side of things found that they were the best-paid women in the office (though still paid less than men doing the same job). For middle-class women, by contrast, it was considered a particularly low form of employment to take on stenographic work. More suitable was working as a private secretary, which brought one closer to power. Secretarial guidebooks promised a fun and exciting rise up the corporate ladder that was nowhere borne out in the statistics on secretarial mobility. They were encouraged to be enchanted by the notion of their work being "professional" and by working in the upper-class, highly stylized parlors of banks and executive suites—many of which resembled homes. In a strange way, it was considered higher class to be essentially a domestic servant to a boss, attending to moods and whims, than to be a stenographer with demonstrable skills. The business historian and management theorist Rosabeth Moss Kanter would later describe this phenomenon—the way the prestige of the secretarial profession derived less from work satisfaction than from one's proximity to (usually masculine) power and prestige—as "status contingency." Stories were told of secretaries who gained the trust of their bosses and began earning enough to acquire offices with mahogany and carpet; in one instance, a secretary had an "office on the seventeenth floor of one of the buildings owned by [her] corporation with a magnificent view over the city."[17] She was in charge of the office anytime the boss was out. Such stories were extremely rare but nonetheless powerful inducements for secretaries.

□

It was only natural that with so many unwritten rules governing the new world of the office, a substantial amount of confusion, panic, and ostentatious hand-wringing would circle male discussion of the presence of women, and the attendant problem of sex. Victorian America's stern observance of the separation of spheres for women and men suddenly no longer held, and it remained an open question what kind of influence women would bring to the male preserves of the workplace. Would women, who were held to be innately superior moral beings, bring civilization and order, as well as a sense of manly purpose, to the lazy and effeminate clerks? Or would women, who were also held to be tempting and thereby destructive to the coolly ascetic male work ethic, orchestrate sexual chaos in the office and bring down the world of business? The urgency of these questions was exacerbated by the common observance of the "marriage bar" for women—that is, the convention that women would remain in the office only as long as they were unmarried, domestic servitude presumably being its own profession, incompatible with a seat in the steno pool.

Though the proportion of women office workers who were married, or who got married and continued working, would increase over the early twentieth century, the fact that most of them were single made their presence potentially troubling to the largely single men and to the married ones as well. In a pamphlet about the relationship between the stenographer and her boss, put together by the writer Fessenden Chase, stenographers were branded, predictably, as prostitutes in waiting. "In the cozy den or private 'studio' of her employer, temptations and opportunities are constantly arising, and the susceptible employer is easy picking for the girl of brilliant plumage with tender glances that fascinate and lure," Chase wrote, quietly amping up the lurid voyeurism of the scene. "It is only a step from the tender glances to the satisfying kiss, and we cannot escape that the 'private-office' girl is generally quite willing to kiss and to be kissed, in order to secure special favors and perhaps an increase in her salary from her susceptible employer."[18]

The entry of women into the office overlapped—not coincidentally—with the growth of the cause of women's suffrage. Growing independence in the sphere of work naturally corresponded to claims for rights and freedom in that of citizenship. As a result, there was considerable discussion among women—in a burgeoning progressive female public sphere that sought to judge, at every moment—of the dangers and possibilities that the office offered women. Jane Addams, progenitor of the industrial betterment movement (the spirit presiding over the welfare policies of the Larkin Building), worried that the open environment of the office was teeming with irresistible temptation and that women would be forced to take money and gifts from their bosses in exchange for sexual favors; women of their own accord, she wrote, given the unbearable free-

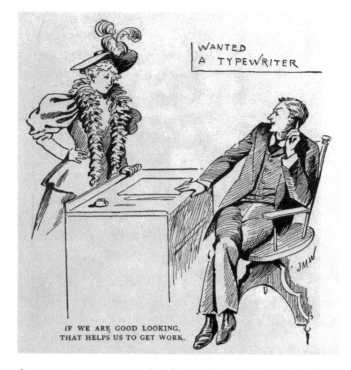

WANTED
A TYPEWRITER

IF WE ARE GOOD LOOKING,
THAT HELPS US TO GET WORK.

A cartoon in a stenographers' journal, capturing early office sexual politics (May 1895). *General Research Division, The New York Public Library, Astor, Lenox and Tilden Foundations*

dom of the workplace, would "fall into a vicious life from the sheer lack of social restraint." Slightly more realistic were the fears that women would have to navigate an impossible path—between, as Janette Egmont wrote in one of the stenography trade journals, "the Scylla of prudery and the Charybdis of familiarity, to raise the standard (and in this generation, even establish the standard) by which men will judge [their] sex in this profession."[19] In the end, for writers like Egmont, the problem seemed inescapable: the specter of sex was simply irresistible; the business of the office would inevitably be compromised; and the solution was nowhere in sight. In the meantime, there would always be scenes where "there are two or three girls, the male clerks will compare the blonde with the brunette, and the discussion is apt to last too long."[20]

But naturally much of the fear of women's power over men was expressed by men. And when men imputed the dangerousness of life in the office to women, they were likely to be rebuffed by the women office workers on whose behalf they presumed to speak. In 1900, Len G. Broughton, a popular evangelical pastor of Atlanta's Tabernacle Baptist Church, traveled to Brooklyn, New York, where, speaking to an all-male audience at the YMCA, he proceeded to deliver a series of invective-laden perorations against the growing lewdness of the white-collar workplace. He claimed that stenographers' diplomas were not tickets to business success, nor even to finding a successful mate, but rather "so many licenses to a life of lewdness. I'd rather put a through passport to hell direct in a young woman's hands than that certificate which admits her to the upper office of her employer, behind closed doors." Many female clerks got wind of his message; they were not inclined silently to suffer any implications about their weakness in the face of men. Their responses were not, however, always as politically salubrious as a modern reader might hope. A stenographer who identified herself as "Miss Ware" wrote in to the *Atlanta Constitution* to decry his suggestion that stenographers were "vicious and impure." She insisted that at least "ninety and nine" percent of the stenographers who entered and exited the office were virtuous Christians; only those who were poor, desperate, and without religion would give in to aggressive employers. New York commentators went even further in separating office workers from what they saw as lower orders, arguing that Broughton seemed to forget that "he is not dealing with the colored race of the South" but rather women of "a higher type of intellectual development."[21]

Whether women office workers were virtuous Christians or not (though, at least until the postwar era, they were almost all white), the workplace they entered was indeed without virtually any protections when it came to sexual harassment—a phrase that was itself unknown until late in the twentieth century. The responses that guidebooks and organizations offered were equivocal. Women were expected to respond to come-ons with patient silence or cheerful unawareness. One secretarial guidebook from 1919 argued, "She must learn not to see that his glance is too fervid, not to feel that hand that rests on hers or the arm that slips around the back of the chair." And she was supposed to do so with "tact and politeness, for it is not the rebuff that counts so much as the way in which it is done."[22] One sees in the guidebooks a presumption that men were not to be challenged unless women wanted to lose their jobs. And they did lose their jobs: a survey of twelve thousand fired secretaries from 1937 indicated that at least two-thirds of them were let go because of their or their bosses' "personality and character defects." These included, according to some, "an unwillingness [on the part of the secretary] to go night-clubbing with the boss."[23] Like other office workers, white-collar women had to act as professionals, each responsible for her own work and her own success.

The fears about sexuality in the workplace played deeply on the status anxieties of male office workers as well, anxieties that went as far back as the countinghouse era, when white-collar men were seen as unmasculine. The presence of women in the workplace might have given men—managers particularly—a confirmation of their own middle-class superiority and power. But over the first decades of the twentieth century, as their failure to organize unions started to result in wage stagnation, costing them their economic advantages over blue-collar workers, their manliness once again came into question. In the 1920s, a scandalous and nationally publicized murder case managed to refract all these workplace fears at once.

At the offices of Chase National Bank in New York City, a woman in the steno pool, Shirley McIntyre, met Walter Mayer, an accounting clerk—in other words, someone not much higher up the totem pole. Mayer fell hard for McIntyre and impetuously asked for her hand. Initially she agreed; later, after she apparently had been taken out by superiors in the office who had given her a "taste of the high life" (Mayer's words), she decided against the marriage. Mayer pleaded, threatening suicide; McIntyre responded by calling him an "inferior" whom she could no longer marry. Mayer's response was brutal: he found McIntyre in her apartment and shot her to death before shooting himself. But Mayer survived. A few years later, sufficiently recovered, he was put on trial for murder. Mayer argued bathetically to an extraordinarily receptive jury that his fiancée had become materialistic, placing "things" over love. McIntyre's mother was summoned, and even she testified to Mayer's good sense and her daughter's ill manners. It worked. The jury convicted him on a lesser charge than murder, adding a plea for leniency.[24]

What had intervened between the murder and the trial was a burst of sympathetic coverage in the newspapers. There was plenty of evidence for a conviction of first-degree murder; Mayer had clearly planned McIntyre's murder well in advance (as some unambiguous letters he had written proved). Yet in the papers, Mayer was held up as a symbol of ailing white-collar manhood. McIntyre actually had a higher salary than Mayer did—she earned $60 a week and he earned $10 less. He had therefore only acted as any man in his situation would. In the nineteenth century, the papers adduced, Mayer and McIntyre would have easily settled into blandly contented matrimony. But now the tables had turned. Unlike women who were gaining financial independence, men like Mayer were marooned in dead-end clerical jobs. "There are big jobs for a few men but oars in the galley for all the rest of the slaves," the papers reported Mayer saying to a friend. What might have been seen as sheer loserdom was converted into a story about the pathos of the white-collar man—which working women were expected to accept, or at least rebuff in a kinder manner.[25]

In the years following the Great Depression, which put a sizable dent in the confidence of businessmen and their not so upwardly mobile clerks, insinuating that women were ruining the office became a sport of popular culture. The film *Baby Face* (1933), made before the Hays Code put a swift end to Hollywood's appetite for frank salaciousness, not only had the virtue of bringing a still-unknown Barbara Stanwyck to a starring role but also solidified the "gold digger" as a cultural archetype in the growing population of office women whom office men were supposed to desire and fear. Stanwyck's Lily Powers comes from a mill town where she works at her father's impressively grimy speakeasy, haunted by physically broken and socially desperate working-class men, from whom she fends off constant groping. She receives advice from a fatherly German émigré cobbler to settle down and tap her natural powers. "You don't understand your *potentialities*," he cries. "Didn't you read that Nietzsche I gave you?" Later in the film, alone with Lily in his workshop, he leaps into a surpassingly strange, pseudo-philosophical oration on the nature of the female will to power: "A woman, young, beautiful like you, can do anything she wants. You have power over men. But you have to use them, not let them use you . . . Exploit yourself! Use men! Be strong, defiant—use men, to get the things you want!" When her father dies in a freak accident, she flees to New York, along with an African American friend, Chico (Theresa Harris), who worked in the speakeasy, to better understand her "potentialities."

Thanks to sleeping with the hiring officer, Lily ends up establishing herself at the bottom rung of a bank, the fictional Gotham Trust Company, housed in an Art Deco skyscraper. (Chico becomes

Barbara Stanwyck as Lily Powers in *Baby Face* (1933), using her "potentialities." *Photofest*

her maidservant, occasionally punctuating the film with blues renditions. Though Harris shares a good deal of time on-screen with Stanwyck, *Baby Face* takes for granted that her character would never be accepted as a white-collar worker.) In an ingenious and grotesque motif, the film pans up from window to window as Lily sleeps her way upward through the bank, from foreign exchanges to filing to the mortgage department to escrow to accounting, all the way to the highest ranks of the company. She even ditches a young John Wayne for his higher-up. "Wake up, kid," a female clerk says to him when he gives a winningly jilted look, "Baby Face is moving out of your class." Every time she seems to be trapped, she simply turns on the charm—something the film represents by focusing in on her glittering, smiling face, deliberately blurred by the camera to seem even more ethereal. But her desire is nothing but material: we keep returning to her apartment, and with each step she climbs, the larger and more luxurious her lodgings get. Finally caught in a scandal when one former lover shoots her latest beau, the president of the company, and kills himself, she ends up getting sent to Gotham Trust's branch in Paris—where she's back at the bottom. There, the new president, Courtland Trenholm, visits her and succumbs to her charms.

But it's the Depression, we're meant to remember, and banks aren't as stable as they used to be. The bank suffers a panic, and Trenholm has to put up a million dollars of his own money to save it. He begs Lily to sell all her things. "No, I can't do it," she concludes. "I have to think of myself. I've gone through a lot to get those things. My life has been bitter and hard. I'm not like other women. All the gentleness and kindness in me has been killed. All I've got are those things, without them I'd be nothing. I'd have to go back to what I was. No, I won't give them up." It's a startling, revealing speech, the first time that Lily forthrightly admits her motives. Unfortunately, it's all undercut by a lame, moralizing ending: Trenholm tries to kill himself, and Lily finally admits in the ambulance carrying him off to the hospital that she, in fact, loves him. She gives up her money to return to her class. *Baby Face* might be commended for at least giving the Lily character some agency—Stanwyck labors mightily to convey this—if only to suggest that in the end she's like any other woman: looking for marriage, not power. *Baby Face*, like a number of films of its era, refracts the unconscious fears of an entire class of men, who saw their lack of willpower as being the cause of their ultimate failure in business. So, too, did the film—like many at the time—reassure classless America that its class boundaries were not being transgressed: though Lily sought to escape the working class, she marries a poor Trenholm.

Possessed by these deep-seated terrors, not all offices waited around to see if more male clerks would murder unreceptive women, or to have gold diggers destroy their companies. The generalized fear of what men and women working together might do to both sexes in the office, and to society outside it, led some companies to cleanse their work spaces of any vestiges of male privilege while simultaneously segregating their work environments by sex. In the Metropolitan Life Insurance Building, one of the largest and most iconic Manhattan skyscrapers of the early twentieth century, the cuspidors of the old merchants' clerks offices were forbidden, alongside smoking, except in certain permitted areas. The office itself, unlike most, was kept spotless—"a model of domestic cleanliness," as the historian Olivier Zunz has written. Meanwhile, men and women had separate entrances, hallways, elevators, and stairways; rest areas were also segregated by sex. In the Taylorist fashion, work was distributed in such a way as to keep people busy during their entire working day, and electric clocks kept rigorous time, while supervisors ensured that no quiet conversation, let alone loud talking or laughing, took place.[26]

At the same time, mirroring their less segregated social world of theaters, cinemas, nightclubs, and amusement parks, men and women found ways to interact within their office environs that prepared them for the more open sexual world outside the office. At the very least, women had to interact with men as subordinates, whether stenographers taking dictation or in the typing pool supervised by a male clerk. But more important were the recreational programs established by Met Life. One such program was dance instruction—inspired by the jazz dancing craze (the jitterbug, the Charleston) that was overtaking American urban centers everywhere. Though Met Life's women—advertised in their brochures

The "Belles" of the Metropolitan Life Building. *Museum of the History of New York*

as the "Metropolitan Belles"—were permitted to learn only among themselves, groups of male and female clerks often gathered on the roof of the building to practice dancing.

Even the relationship between a female secretary and her employer, as compromised as it was, could lead to new kinds of interactions between men and women. The term "office wife" began to enter the vernacular to describe the secretary who was closer to her boss than he was to his own wife. The novelist Faith Baldwin, an extremely popular documenter of the sexual life of the office, explored the idea in her bestseller *The Office Wife* (1929): "She felt very near her employer in the rather garrulous boyish moods which always followed a victory or the promise of one. She thought . . . how well she had grown to know him. She had learned to tell in the instant of their meeting if he was tired or out of sorts, if the day was going well or badly, if he looked forward to a battle or simply wearily girded himself for it without much enthusiasm."[27] In Baldwin's novel, the secretary, privileged by occupying the inner sanctum of his office suite, rather than being stuck out on the steno pool floor, soon begins to accompany her boss everywhere, replacing all the comforts that his wife might otherwise offer. She becomes passionately good at her job, a model employee; then, in a fairy-tale ending, the office wife marries her boss—seeming to prove that the office is a place not of unwanted advances and harassment but of potential happiness. The other side of this, of course, is that the novel offers marriage to one's boss as a consolation prize, in the place of career advancement. You're good at your job, but you can't move up in the world; your reward is that you can marry someone who can. It was a way of managing what now seems like an intolerable situation, of plausibly resolving what was a genuine and debilitating social contradiction.

These seem like trivial features of office life to us now, even unpleasant ones. But these kinds of interactions were new. For better or for worse, the office engineered so much of the sexual world we now inhabit. It made it possible for men and women to meet—if certainly not as equals, then at least on a terrain outside the fraught, unobserved world of the home. Though women remained a minority in office work for some years more, and among managerial ranks they were virtually excluded altogether, they became the chief source of common stereotypes about office life.

It also became true of media: the "white-collar girl" became the subject of an impressive number of popular novels throughout the second and third decades of the twentieth century. There was a certain congruence between the types of women depicted in these novels and the women who read them. Though women had worked in factories for decades, the difference was that these were almost exclusively working-class, immigrant women, without access to English media. But the middle-class women who worked in the office were often in the same class as the audience for novels, which was mostly female to begin with. This continued a trend with office novels and cinema, where the people depicted in particular media held jobs very similar to the consumers of the media.

Novels about white-collar girls were remarkable in their similarity, perhaps because for many years they tended to be written by men. In Lewis's *The Job*, and the roughly contemporaneous *Alice Adams* by Booth Tarkington and the massive Depression-era best seller *Kitty Foyle* by Christopher Morley, the female protagonist is forced to take a white-collar job after the death of the male breadwinner—the protagonist's father—who wasn't doing too well to begin with. The commonplace of a woman thrown into work masks the whole history, in which many women were choosing, of their own will and desire, to enter the workplace. But Lewis and his contemporaries were indebted to the naturalist novels of the time, by Theodore Dreiser and Jack London, themselves following Émile Zola, in which inherited biological traits and massive social forces narrowly constricted and determined choices.

Only Lewis among them conceived of a feminist novel in which, however improbably, a woman achieves professional success. Una Golden, like her sisters in the office, expects only to suffer through its drudgery until she can find a marriageable office husband. She sees women much older struggling with the office machines and then breaking down over the meaninglessness of their work: "Epidemics of hysteria would spring up sometimes, and women of thirty-five or forty—normally well content—would join the old ladies in sobbing. Una would wonder if she would be crying like that at thirty-five—and at sixty-five, with thirty barren, weeping years in between." She falls in love with a young co-worker, Walter Babson, a restless, fast-talking, slangily charming editor, who occasionally voices support for labor unions and socialism. But unable to advance up the company ladder and lacking money for a wedding, he goes west, leaving Una contemplating a future of single life. When Una's mother dies, and in grief and a fit of uselessness, she marries a salesman, Eddie Schwirtz. A heavy-drinking habit causes him to lose his job, and he begins to leech off Una.

After years of abuse, she leaves him, takes another, better office job, and moves into an all-female residence. It is at this point that the novel begins to take a strange, even radical turn. Listening to the stories of other women's lives gives Una a new confidence; she manages to talk herself into a low-level managerial position at White Line Hotels. Her skill moves her up through the ranks, leading her to hire an assistant—who turns out to be her old lover, Walter Babson. Una becomes an executive at White Line and marries Walter. At the end of the novel, she imagines having a child while staying in her position: "I will keep my job—if I've had this world of offices wished on to me, at least I'll conquer it, and give my clerks a decent time." This was an unusual, and strictly implausible, fantasy of individual achievement, no less hopeful than the Horatio Alger stories that were popular at the time. Yet the fantasy was a feminist one—one that imagined the "marriage bar" as no bar at all. It was one that virtually no woman at the time could realize. Yet the office managed to produce the fantasy nonetheless. The years that followed would witness the struggle to make it true.

□

If offices weren't hospitable to women as equals, despite what secretarial manuals seemed to suggest, then, some others argued, at least they could be made as hospitable as possible. They had to be made home-like, efficient, and clean. Sexualizing the workplace endangered the middle-class virtues that the office was supposed to exude. Some women therefore took it upon themselves to ensure that at least the female office workers themselves would never compromise the sanctity of this milieu.

In 1909, a middle-aged Providence housewife, Katharine Gibbs, found herself suddenly adrift after her husband died in a yachting accident, leaving her widowed and having to care for two sons. Untrained in anything beyond housework, Gibbs desperately threw herself into entrepreneurial life. She first tried dressmaking, a venture that quickly failed. Gibbs eventually followed the path that millions like her at the time were taking: she enrolled in a stenography class at Boston's Simmons College. Simmons was a different kind of secretarial school, one that taught foreign languages alongside stenography, imbuing the women who left it with both skills and an educated, cosmopolitan air that made them professionally attractive to companies that wanted their secretarial pool to exude braininess along with sheer physical magnetism. It was a lesson that Gibbs would take to heart.

Selling all her jewelry for $1,000, she used the money to start her own training institute, buying the Providence School for Secretaries in 1911. What became known informally as the "Katie Gibbs" schools were seen as the choice for smart women who only needed a little finishing. And the Gibbs schools did the finishing, and much more. They focused on turning out what they deemed were appropriate office personalities: demure, intelligent, efficient women who responded to their bosses without challenging them or making them feel ill at ease. Besides typing and shorthand, office procedures and telephone techniques, the curriculum consisted of law, math, and English.[28] Later, it would come to include production management, labor relations, finance, accounting essentials, and current events.[29] And the training naturally included tips on dressing and appearance. Katie Gibbs girls were to aim not for beauty but for "prestige appearance"—which reflected good judgment rather than sex appeal. In a *BusinessWeek* profile of the school on its fiftieth anniversary, "businesslike touches" included "street dresses rather than skirts and blouses; light use of cosmetics and jewelry; high heels and stockings; and for outdoors, hat and gloves."[30] Especially wealthy and particularly concerned parents were welcome to send their children to Bermuda for early spring classes.[31] Only one man ever enrolled full-time.[32] At Gibbs and competitive schools like it, the workload was strenuous: fifty hours a week, half spent in class, the other half on homework. And the discipline was equally intense: one student recalled a typing test where a woman made a mistake at the beginning, restarted by inserting another piece of paper—and was accordingly expelled.[33]

A "Katie Gibbs" type became proverbial in the culture at large. Gibbs herself was the perfect symbol of the delicate sternness that she wanted to cultivate in her students. In Judith Krantz's soapy-dirty roman à clef *Scruples*—published in the late 1970s but set in the early 1960s on the cusp of the sexual revolution—her protagonist, Billy, recalls stepping off the elevator at the entrance to the Gibbs school for the first time: "The first thing that met her eyes was the gaze of the late Mrs. Gibbs, preserved with all its stern implacable presence in the portrait that hung over the receptionist's desk. She did not look mean, thought Billy, only as if she knew all about you and had not decided whether to actively disapprove—yet."[34] Her vivid description of the school's rigorous educational program jibes with many other accounts:

> Why had people been so cruel as to invent shorthand, she wondered, as the infernal, eternal hourly buzzers went off and she moved hurriedly, but with the required precision, from the steno room to the typing room and then back to the steno room again. Many of her classmates had some knowledge of typing before they entered Katie Gibbs, but even those who thought they had a leg up on the system were swiftly disillusioned about their skills. Being "Gibbs Material" meant that you were expected to reach certain degrees of proficiency that struck Billy as outrageous. Were they seriously expecting her to be able to take one hundred words a minute in shorthand and type faultlessly at a minimum of sixty words a minute by the time she had completed her course? They were indeed.[35]

Nothing about the school's famous discipline prevents Billy from indulging in her first experiments in casual sex—in fact, the discipline and her sexual life seem to complement and encourage each other: "Billy could feel her strong obsessive drives finally coming to her aid, helping her to bite into the work with the confidence that she would master it, make it her own . . . She became so sexually charged that sometimes, between classes at Katie Gibbs, she had to duck into the ladies' room, lock herself in a stall, thrust a finger up between her thighs, and, rubbing hastily, have a quick, silent, necessary orgasm."[36] Becoming "Gibbs material" helps her to become adult, confident, assured. "Although Billy was five months short of her twenty-first birthday," Krantz writes of her postgraduation, "she looked and sounded a superbly balanced twenty-five." She swiftly lands a secretarial position at Ikehorn Enterprises, on the upper echelons of the new Pan Am Building towering above Grand Central Terminal and Park Avenue.

Gibbs girls, writes Lynn Peril in her rich history of the secretarial world, were trained to be "no less than office geishas." They were taught how to make small talk on the telephone and also to discourse sparklingly about current affairs at cocktail parties. They were, in other words, consummately *finished*—unembarrassed accessories for bosses looking to embellish their offices. But also, as Krantz and others showed, office women had to prepare themselves for a world thick as any Jane Austen novel with subtle codes and systems of manners. They wouldn't subvert the order they entered; they would simply master it. Gibbs herself recognized the injustice of the world for which she was preparing her students: "A woman's career is blocked by lack of openings, by unjust male competition, by prejudice and, not least, by inadequate salary and recognition."[37] Yet aside from the question of finding a job, being a Gibbs student remedied hardly any of these problems. Gibbs might have been a businesswoman, but her students were merely supposed to work for businessmen. Much as earlier generations of guidebooks and organizations had taught women to shrug off the unwanted advances of rapacious businessmen, Gibbs taught her trainees to deal with the office world with a certain measure of aplomb. That was the best, it seemed, that they could ask for.

4

UP THE SKYSCRAPER

If your eyes could penetrate the opaque masses of
the façades, they would see an incredible spectacle:
three hundred thousand, five hundred thousand men
and women—perhaps more—at work in a pool of
space at the same time. A humanity having broken
its millenary destiny which was to be attached to
the ground, which is suspended between heaven and
earth, going up and down at high speed in clusters
of twenty and in sheaves of two hundred. Is it a new
scene in purgatory?

—LE CORBUSIER, *When the Cathedrals Were White*[1]

By mid-century, with the United States hunkering down for the first frigid decade of the Cold War, nothing signaled the dynamism of American business more than the skylines of its cities. The Communists might have touted the equality of their peoples, but in terms of the jagged inequality of their skylines Moscow and East Berlin, let alone Beijing and Hanoi, had nothing on New York and Chicago, whose silhouettes looked a lot like the wild spikes and dives of a GDP chart. Photographs of the time of lower Manhattan from across the Brooklyn Bridge show a mountainous cluster of ridges, some of them sleek and glassy, others stern shafts of masonry and steel, ornamented by spires and finials, while the Loop in Chicago was a tour through a flatter and more elegant skyscraper plateau, placidly regarding the smooth curve of Lake Michigan. Skyscrapers were the birth and growth of the office made visible.

Until the resurgence of globalization after the Cold War, when tall buildings began to bloom along the coastline of southern China and on the Arabian Peninsula, the skyscraper would remain one of the most peculiarly American of white-collar institutions, much more a symbol of the prowess, even ruthlessness, of American-style capitalism than what it equally was: an especially tall collection of boring offices. Abroad they were viewed as objects of aspiration for men and women of business; it's no wonder that the signal image of the growth of contemporary China is Shanghai's Pudong district, burgeoning with weird and futuristic skyscrapers. As Taylorism and other related managerial ideas spread throughout the world, the administrative branches of industry, along with financial institutions, grew enormously throughout the Western world (if not quite to the same extent as in the United States). But European cities didn't exhibit the same pattern of development. They were older, denser, constrained by centuries of building tradition as well as the sheer thickness of their urban fabric. European cities imposed height restrictions well before skyscrapers even became popular in the United States. The London Building Act of 1894 limited heights to 30 meters; in Berlin for many years the maximum was 22. Wartime devastation cleared spaces to build higher, and restrictions were loosened, but a certain resistance remained—enabled by strong welfare states where property developers were tacitly seen as enemies of social democracy. By 1950, the tallest building in the United States was 373.5 meters (the Empire State Building). Fifteen years later, London's tallest buildings were the Shell Centre and Portland House, which were 107 meters and 100 meters, respectively. The next three tallest were below 70 meters.[2]

The relentless pace of skyscraper building in the United States meant that the character of its cities changed drastically. The transformation was so enormous, powerful, and lasting that for contemporary city dwellers and visitors it can be hard to imagine what urban life might otherwise have been like, without so many offices around. Places like Chicago and New York, once known as much for their industries (the stockyards in Chicago, shipping in New York) as for their financial districts, became full to the brim with offices. Small, low-density residential areas were rezoned and demolished, replaced by buildings that housed thousands of office workers. Between 1871 and 1923, New York built about seventy-four million square feet of office space; from the 1920s through the early 1930s, the city added more than thirty-eight million more—thirteen million built from 1930 to 1933, the first years of the Great Depression. Even the collapse of the world economy could not stop the building; it was the endless capacity to build that seemed, on the ground, at once the most exhilarating and the most frightening fact of all: that all the short houses and apartments could be leveled for more offices; that one could simply build higher and higher. And the infinity of the skyscraper corresponded to the deepening and widening of the offices inside. The experience of the man on the street, alienated by the towers around him, became a classic trope of American literature. "What sphinx of cement and aluminum bashed open their skulls and ate up their brains and imagination?" Allen Ginsberg wailed in *Howl* (1955). It was "Moloch," the god of child sacrifice, "whose buildings are judgment! . . . whose eyes are a thousand blind windows! / Moloch whose skyscrapers stand in the long streets like endless Jehovahs!" And Ginsberg testified only to the presence of the skyscrapers; some years later the poet James Merrill, in "An Urban Convalescence" (1962), would conjure the absence caused by the process of destruction, the thousands of buildings cleared in the "urban renewal" plans to make way for the new buildings. "You would think the simple fact of having lasted / Threatened our cities like mysterious fires." By the middle of the century, it had become a source of worry to many that the jagged skyline might only be a mirage of variety; that any beautiful skyscraper was actually filled story after story with identical-looking white-collar workers; that the city glinting over the river at night consisted of little more than millions of square feet of office space.

The rise of the skyscraper is one of the most well-documented aspects of the history of the office, the subject of countless works of architectural history. But they almost exclusively fasten onto the exterior of the buildings, their scale and power and imposing bulk. You might never know from the books on skyscrapers that people

The office zombies of King Vidor's *The Crowd* (1920). *Photofest*

actually work in these buildings. ("What our critics have learned to admire in our great buildings is their photographs," Lewis Mumford lamented in *Sticks and Stones* in 1924.) But during their implacable ascent over the cities of the United States, the life inside the skyscrapers was as much a subject of interest as the gargoyles springing from the tops of the towers. And much of how the skyscraper would be shaped drew upon the struggles going on within them. The most famous shot of King Vidor's film *The Crowd* (1928) makes this point dramatically: the camera approaches a conventional Art Deco skyscraper and begins to scale up along a column of windows, until it enters one, and we hover above a waste and empty sea of desks, with countless clerks minutely filling in columns of ledgers. Later, we see the same figures exiting en masse and meeting friends who work in other skyscrapers. More and more people who looked up to the skyscrapers from the street in dread eventually went to work in them. These were the new figures who made up the lives of the skyscrapers, who were at the heart of American business. What did they see?

□

As with the interior expansion of the office, technological advances once again aided the skyward growth of the office building. Until the 1870s, a six-story building was about as high as things got, thanks—as the architectural historian Hugh Morrison has written—"to a universal human disinclination to walk up more than five flights of stairs."[3] Passenger elevators propelled by steam were developed in the 1850s but not used in an office building until 1871; the hydraulic elevator was patented in 1872 and used in the New York Tribune Building, lifting it to ten stories off the ground. Meanwhile, the other key ingredient—a skeleton steel frame to support the exterior wall—was first used in the Home Insurance Building in Chicago in 1884–85, a building often cited as the first skyscraper. After Louis Sullivan and Dankmar Adler's genre-defining Wainwright Building went up in St. Louis in 1891, the rage for skyscraper building proceeded unabated, the most significant of them going up in Chicago. The names of skyscraper architects have entered the canon of American architecture, often referred to informally as the Chicago school: Sullivan and Adler, Daniel Burnham and John Wellborn Root. Now that their buildings have passed into art history, it's hard to recall the terror and fear these marvels aroused. In his classic *The Protestant Ethic and the Spirit of Capitalism*, Max Weber made recourse to a skyscraper-inspired metaphor when he argued that modern bureaucratic administration was tightening around humanity with a "shell as hard as steel."[4]

But, of course, the steel was only in the interior, visible to the gawking, fascinated public when the giant things were going up. For modern viewers inured even to the most hyperbolic deployments of glass and concrete, the old skyscrapers of New York and Chicago, with their exotic brickwork, refined masonry, and spectacular lobbies done up in patins of gold and arching ironwork, exude an especially refined, even rococo attention to ornamental detail that one associates with the buildings of the more distant past. But, despite the modernity of their construction materials and the power of their sheer immensity, the skyscrapers were deliberately cast as antimodern when they were built, designed to mitigate their potential appearance as cold, cruel paeans to efficiency and greed. Sullivan's towers were infamously divided just like columns: a base of large windows and high ceilings allowed for courtyards or street-facing businesses; an unbroken stretch of office floors constituted the shaft; and a square roof capped the affair—the cornice of which, from the street, seemed to point outward and upward, continuing the sense, as your eye wandered up the building, of soaring thrust. Showy ornamentation, engaged columns and pilasters interrupting the upward flow of the building, reduced and tamed their bulk. In New York, the drive to festoon skyscrapers was even more relentless. The neo-Gothic Woolworth tower, the Venetian bell-tower shape of Metropolitan Life: these were modern buildings that shamelessly conjured styles and notions from the past.

Ensuring that the skyscraper preserved the aristocratic heroism of modern life while also conveying the power of American business remained a constant preoccupation of figures like Sullivan and his contemporaries. "How shall we impart to this sterile pile, this crude, harsh, brutal agglomeration, this stark, staring exclamation of eternal strife, the graciousness of those higher forms of sensibility and culture that rest on the lower and fiercer passions?" Sullivan wrote in "The Tall Office Building Artistically Considered," from 1896. "How shall we proclaim from the dizzy height of this strange, weird, modern housetop the peaceful evangel of sentiment, of beauty, the cult of a higher life?"[5] Why this intensely florid preoccupation with the "cult of a higher life" for buildings that were about progress and the creative-destructive power of business? Why, in other words, were the titans of commerce seemingly so afraid of the implications of modern life?

For an answer, there's no better place to look than Chicago. The home of the skyscraper was also the home of a business district constructed essentially from scratch, perhaps the purest "downtown" of any American city: namely, "the Loop," a place devoted entirely to the consecration of white-collar work. Before the fire of 1871 tore through the area, the Loop was already the cause of worry for many of the city's more traditional residents. It was filling up with office buildings, but also with warehouses and workshops; though low-rise, these commercial structures had already begun to overshadow the churches and residences of the midwestern city.[6] After the fire, the chance to reshape the district forcefully emerged. Part of the district had originally been home to a working-class neighborhood that was illegible to the city's middle classes. In the words of Mahlon D. Ogden, a real estate investor, it was "covered with countless old rookeries and miserable shanties, occupied, for the past twenty years, as dens of infamy and low gambling dives, the resort and rendezvous of thieves, burglars, robbers, and murderers of all grades and colors, to the exclusion of all decency, or business purposes."[7] The fire cleared out this entire section, making land available and the character of the neighborhood more appealing to speculative real estate developers. To drive up rents, business moved out warehouses and factories northwest of the area.

Besides maintaining high real estate prices, in those years there was another reason to keep the factories and stockyards away from the centers of administration. For the spectacular, relentless development of industry in Chicago hadn't come without social costs, which took the form of the city's increasingly restive labor movement. As industry increased, so did the level and tenor of the impulse to organize. In the 1860s, Chicago was home of the campaign for the eight-hour day; by the 1880s, the city government had become sympathetic to the union efforts, and city police often refused to cooperate with business when the latter attempted to hire nonunion labor or replace striking workers with scabs. Skyscraper development itself, dependent on wage labor, was halted by frequent strikes: three of the greatest examples of the Chicago school—Richardson's Marshall Field Wholesale Store, Burnham and Root's Rookery, and Adler and Sullivan's Auditorium—were beset by strikes from carpenters, masons, and bricklayers.[8] The local architecture journals covered the growth of the movement with alarm; they usually advocated on behalf of strikebreakers.

Especially terrifying to the city's business leaders and the skyscraper architects they employed, as well as less welcome to the city's political establishment, were the radical anarchist factions of the labor unions. Besides the world-leveling scope of their ideas, it didn't help that the anarchists took special care to organize immigrants whom many other labor unions left out: many of the union leaders and members—though by no means as many as their xeno-phobic opponents alleged—were German immigrants, bearing with them the vigorous debates and ideas animating the socialist and anarchist Left in their home country. They advocated a radical solution to the growing gulf between capitalists and workers—"the establishment of a free society based on co-operative organization of production"—which of course implied the elimination of a capitalist class altogether. Rather than on the fringes of society, the offices of the anarchist journal *Alarm* were located very close to the Loop; not just a few of the anarchists despised the skyscrapers that were rising all around them. In one article written for *Alarm* in 1885, Lucy Parsons, a former slave who had come north with her husband and who was one of the leading anarchist figures, interpreted the sky-scraper precisely as architects and executives might have hoped—as a consummation of American business—only to invert the moral of the story:

> We build magnificent piles of architecture whose dizzy heights dazzle us, as we attempt to follow with our eye along the towering walls of solid brick, granite, and iron, where tier after tier is broken only by wondrous panels of plate glass. And as we gradually bring the eye down story after story, until it reaches the ground, we discover within the very shadow of these magnificent abodes the homeless man, the homeless child, the young girl offering her virtue for a few paltry dollars to hire a little room way up in the garret of one of them . . . Yet it was their labor that erected these evidences of civilization.[9]

In another article, Parsons went on to advocate a particular form of direct action: "Each of you hungry tramps who read these lines, avail yourselves of those little methods of warfare which Science has placed in the hands of the poor man, and you will become a power in this or any other land. Learn the use of explosives!" The threat of a violent action against the city—bombs planted in a skyscraper—seized a city still traumatized by the fire of 1871. In January 1885, someone planted an explosive device in the Chicago, Burlington & Quincy Railroad offices in the heart of the Loop, housed in a new skyscraper built by Burnham and Root. It was defused before it could go off. On May 4, 1886, however, at a gathering of labor union activists and members in Haymarket Square, a bomb did go off—no one knows who set it—killing seven police officers and wounding many more. In the hysteria that followed, thirty-one anarchists were rounded up and put on trial, and four were sentenced to death and hanged. The entire period of the 1880s began to be remembered as the anarchist era, and it was a story of national interest. "During the anarchist time," says one of the characters in Henry Blake Fuller's *Cliff-Dwellers* (1893), a novel set in a skyscraper, "folks down East were a good deal more scared than we were."[10]

The Haymarket bombing and the trial dampened—momentarily, at least—the more radical side of the labor movement. But the sense of terror they had sown among the planners and builders of Chicago's Loop had lasted. "Architecture and massive masonry are symbols of law and order, and the iconoclast longs to pull them down," ran one typical editorial in the architecture trade journal *Building Budget*. "When society becomes unsettled, and property is rendered insecure, men are not disposed to launch out in beautiful and substantial structures . . . The anarchist is the plain and practical foe of the architect and builder. Art, indeed, and anarchy cannot exist together. They are as antagonistic as light and darkness, cosmos and chaos, order and confusion."[11] In other words, commercial architecture and radical change were opposed: if the labor movement won, the skyscraper would lose. The working classes were a source of lurking danger to the ideals of business.

For the business leaders of Chicago and their architects, the solution—more fortuitously arrived at than actively planned—was to separate factory labor from business administration: to divide, as forcibly and thoroughly as possible, blue-collar work from the office. The net result was a white-collar district of special purity: as one observer wrote, "The customs of the city have crystallized the tendency towards centralization to an unusual degree."[12]

Architects designed these buildings for clients who wanted to place the accent on the elevated nature of office work, its aristocratic placement above the dangerous world of the factory. As the architectural historian Daniel Bluestone has argued, they were fashioned in an "aesthetic that created a necessary connection between commerce and culture, denying their incompatibility and suggesting instead that refinement might emanate from tasteful workplaces."[13] Though many architectural critics and other like-minded observers complained that skyscrapers were bereft of aesthetic beauty and ornament—"a welter of objects in which relief, detachment, dignity, meaning, perished utterly,"[14] wrote the American novelist Henry James, revisiting his country after several decades abroad—architects were in fact at pains to enhance the aesthetic power of their otherwise utilitarian objects. Rather than covering their buildings with tracery and other efflorescences, they deployed ornament in areas that would benefit the clients entering the building and the higher-up managers and executives in their offices (themselves often having to entertain clients). The entrances, for example, were usually decked out in a profusion of competing styles from the past to indicate the high-toned nature of the work within. One contemporary city guidebook entry for the Unity Building (1892), designed by Clinton J. Warren, captured the experience of coming into one of these buildings:

> Entering through the great arch of the portal, rising to the height of a story and a half, the walls of the outer vestibule are composed of Numidian, Alps, Green and Sienna marbles. Over the inner door is an artistic screen of glass and bronze. Passing through the rotunda the eye is dazzled by its surprisingly brilliant beauty, designed in the style of the Italian renaissance. From the floor of the marble mosaic whose graceful design and harmonious color combinations are taken from the best example of the renaissance in the Old World, rises the first story by a marble balcony with marble balusters and balustrades.[15]

As anyone who has taken a tour of an older building knows, elevators, too, were often enclosed in beautifully patterned wrought iron and bronze.

The offices themselves were often less extraordinary. Workers on the bottom rung tended to work in bland rooms that followed the spirit, if not the letter, of broadly Taylorist conceptions of efficiency.

And among office workers themselves, there were class divisions as stark as any in early-twentieth-century society, belying the entirely "middle class" nature of their employment. But the importance of maintaining an office workforce that could otherwise imagine itself to be above and beyond factory work had been exacerbated by the "anarchist time"; even where the offices were drab, the architects were often asked to make provisions for ensuring dozens of amenities that would make workers feel that they were part of a grand, middle-class enterprise. This included their being within some proximity of the executive class and being given the possibility of aspiring to their position. Lynn Harding, the entry-level clerical worker protagonist of Faith Baldwin's novel *Skyscraper* (1931), describes her own office as "a strictly utilitarian room. There were no splendid draperies, no massive furniture, no murals, no inches-thick carpet in this room . . . row upon row of green metal files."[16] But when she enters her boss's, she becomes filled with "subdued excitement. The room was enormous, it was pillared. Heavy velvet carpeting lay upon the floor. The walls were treated with costly and beautiful simplicity. The flat-topped desks, mahogany, were less businesslike in appearance than Lynn's own."[17] Even if most office workers were stuck outside the pillared and velvet-carpeted rooms, it seemed to be significant that one could approach them, go into them, even one day command them. One of the attractions of training to be a professional secretary, guidebooks used to suggest, would be the comfort and classiness of the surroundings, suggesting that to be a "confidential secretary to a captain of industry" meant that your "office hours are spent amid mahogany or walnut furniture, richly-toned leather upholstery and handsome rugs."[18] Much of the special conditions for office work drew upon the abundance of natural light that the best buildings received. To be sure, light was important for the kind of work being done—typing, filing, adding, and the rest—but there was no reason why gas or electrical lighting couldn't accomplish the same. Large windows and natural light were also crucial in elevating the work in a *cultural* sense, suggesting that office workers were indeed performing a kind of special labor for which light, airy conditions were de rigueur.

When looking for entertainment, Chicago office workers rarely even had to leave their buildings. Roof gardens were available on several buildings, and in the warmer months they hosted theatrical productions, concerts, and vaudeville shows. Barbershops, newsstands, banking services, dry cleaners and tailors, doctors' and dentists' offices, libraries, restaurants, recreational rooms—all of these were available in the best of the Chicago office buildings, aspects that assiduous architects and building managers emulated all over the country.[19] Some buildings became miniature cities; it was nearly possible for some office workers to avoid city life altogether. Contemporary reviewers of the Solon S. Beman–designed Pullman Building (1883–84) suggested that the building's "palatial" air—it had a restaurant, library, and sitting room for employees and employee families, as well as model apartments for the office staff—made it "much more extensive and elaborate than required for the purposes of office accommodations."[20] Pullman himself had hoped that a grand building would be "productive of harmony and good feelings, while it will interest [the employees] more in the work for which they are employed."[21]

These sentiments (from 1873) would prove ominous. Pullman had made his fortune manufacturing sleeping cars in the 1860s for the fast-growing railroads. After Abraham Lincoln's assassination, the president's body was carried from Washington, D.C., to Springfield, Illinois, in a Pullman sleeping car. In 1880, troubled by the wave of labor unrest beginning to sweep Chicago and its environs, Pullman decided to set up a manufacturing plant just south of Chicago, with a town surrounding it, hoping that it would have an "ennobling and refining" effect on the workers—much as the skyscraper would on its inhabitants. The town was self-sufficient. Built entirely of brick, it contained many detached homes and ten larger tenement buildings; the Arcade Building, which had thirty retail stores, a thousand-seat theater, a bank, and a library (its six thousand volumes donated by Pullman himself); a hotel and hotel bar; a school; and several parks and fields.

Workers did not own their homes, however; they rented them, generating profits directly for the company. And the rents continued to go up, while their own wages stagnated. In 1894, Pullman's workers organized, affiliating with the American Railway Union,

The other company town: the Pullman Car Company's Chicago headquarters. *New York Public Library*

led by the future Socialist presidential candidate Eugene V. Debs. The workers demanded lower rents or higher wages. When the company refused to negotiate, they went on strike; the four thousand workers in the town were eventually joined by fifty thousand others. Eventually, the federal government intervened to break the strike, but in the process Pullman's own hopes for a workers' utopia had been dashed.[22] The only place where he had succeeded, it seemed, alongside many others like him, was in the business district of the Loop. When railroad workers struck, the velvet-carpeted cells of his office building were quiet. For these reasons, it had become normal for guidebooks to Chicago to recommend that visitors to the city skip over visits to the North Side manufacturing and warehouse district and instead obtain a "comprehensive view" from the top of the Masonic Temple building—then the tallest office building in the world.[23]

Yet the utopia of the Loop was difficult to replicate in cities elsewhere; and even within the Loop, buildings began to spring up that were less enlightened—and literally less well lit—than places like the Pullman Building. Especially in New York, skyscrapers seemed to be littered about with delirious abandon, few of them obeying the dictates of any aesthetic theory. Looking at the skyline of New York as early as 1893, the great American novelist William Dean Howells commented that, "architecturally," it resembled "nothing so much as a horse's jaw-bone, with the teeth broken or dislodged at intervals." Yet the architects were not at fault, in Howells's opinion.[24] "I can blame nothing so much for the hideous effect," he went on, "as the rapacity of the land-owner holding on for a rise, as it is called. It is he who most spoils the sky-line, and keeps the street, mean and poor at the best in design, a defeated purpose, and a chaos come again."[25] Complaints about skyscraper heights were recurring features of urban life; so, too, did the density of occupants in one area begin to provoke anxiety over the ever more congested downtown streets. In one famous *Chicago Tribune* editorial cartoon from the period, an artist imagined what it would be like if the six thousand workers of the Monadnock Building exited at one time: his image depicted regiment after regiment of black-coated, hatted workers, piled on top of each other, blocking out an entire street. The synthesis of naked commerce and organic architecture, so ardently desired by Louis Sullivan, had no sooner been achieved than it began, under steady skepticism, to unravel.

Looking at Sullivan's classic text "The Tall Office Building Artistically Considered" already reveals the problem. Trying to understand the skyscraper from the inside out, Sullivan had argued that the most basic unit of the skyscraper was the "cell," at once the building block of the body and, in Sullivan's particular imaginary, the single hexagon that makes up a beehive. (The beehive has long been a common metaphor for the office tower: it was the shape of the Parker Brothers game Office Boy, and in more recent years it has served as the logo for Freelancers Union, with the bees—that is, freelancers—hovering outside it.)[26] The shaft of the tower, Sullivan argues, is based on an "indefinite number of stories of offices piled tier upon tier, one tier just like another tier, one office just like all the other offices—an office being similar to a cell in a honeycomb." Meanwhile, the size of the office itself determines the size of everything else: "We take our cue from the individual cell, which requires a window with its separating pier, its sill and lintel, and we, without more ado, make them look all alike because they are all alike." Everything else is standardized in turn: "The practical horizontal and vertical division or office unit is naturally based on a room of comfortable area and height, and the size of this standard office room as naturally predetermines the standard structural unit, and, approximately, the size of window openings."

Scaling the sublime height of the building into the banal warrens of the office reveals the paradox at the heart of the skyscraper, even in Sullivan's "artistically considered" version. For the skyscraper is based on the standardization of office units ("cells")—each of these multiplied out to fill the space offered by the building site, in the process creating a floor plan that constitutes the basic shape of the building itself—which are made to "look all alike because they are all alike." Multiplied "indefinite[ly]" up and down the height of the building, the floors, too, are simply all alike. The pinnacle of creation, one of the greatest "opportunities" that God has ever offered man, becomes a mechanism for producing cookie-cutter offices, all of them looking, inevitably, alike. The formula that Sullivan coined to explain this individualist-conformist principle has become a commonplace of architectural history: "Form follows function."[27] The envelope of the building was to reflect no particular style, no empty ideal, but rather, with as pure a transparency as possible, the shape and feel of the interior. It was the office that determined the skyscraper—a fact that might have had a beneficial effect on the form of the office itself.

But the result was the opposite: few conceptions of the office have had a more deleterious effect on the human work environment than this—one, ironically enough, claiming to be artistic. By the early twentieth century, the standard office unit—the cell, in Sullivan's imaginary—also tended toward standardization. Small offices were usually partitioned off from the corridor with a wall of framed translucent glass; larger offices would be divided into a T shape, with a reception area for a stenographer and files and two private offices behind of about 120 square feet each. So powerful was the impetus to make offices uniform that this plan became adopted for private offices in American skyscrapers almost universally. If Sullivan's motto can't account for the wild kitsch that began to overrun

American skyscraper design, and the sheer amount of it that got built, then perhaps a variation on it can. The title of an influential work by the architectural historian Carol Willis gives us a better, if less palatable, explanation: *Form Follows Finance*. For by and large, making an office "functional" had less to do with making it serve the needs of a particular corporation and much more with serving *any* corporation. The point was not to make an office building per specification of a given company (although this was intermittently the case for some companies) but rather to build for an economy in which an organization could move in and out of a space without any difficulty. The space had to be eminently *rentable*. Offices therefore could only partly be about art and work; the winners in this new American model weren't office workers or architects, not even executives or captains of industry, but real estate speculators. The skylines of American cities, more than human ingenuity and entrepreneurial prowess, came simply to represent dollars per square foot.

☐

After the garish ornamentation of the skyscrapers of the 1920s, something seemed to intervene in the advance of the skyscraper toward ever more absurdity. The open competition from the *Chicago Tribune* to design its newest office building resulted in hundreds of bizarre entries from around the world—including one from Europe that outlined the building in the shape of a cigar-store "Red Indian." Adolf Loos, an Austrian modernist who had become infamous for an essay which argued that ornament on architecture should be considered a criminal offense, just submitted a parody of Sullivan's ideals: a giant column festooned with windows. The winning building, by Raymond Hood (who later was responsible for Rockefeller Center), was a safe neo-Gothic structure. The runner-up, Eliel Saarinen (father of the more famous Eero, who became a distinguished office architect), proposed a slim, unadorned modernist slab, something as yet unseen in the West. In later years, when glass slabs became de rigueur, this would be seen as the real winner. Yet the *Tribune* competition—often cited in architectural histories of the period as a peak of public fascination over the skyscraper—seemed actually to be the point of decline for the first phase of skyscraper architecture. Having been built in terrible abundance, skyscrapers were no longer functioning as efficiently as they should, nor housing their workers in adequate conditions. Deep changes from within the office would gradually transform their outward conditions.

The 1920s began inauspiciously for office workers. During the war, they had lost ground on bread-and-butter issues. Unions had cemented industrial privileges—the eight-hour day, pro-labor arbitration boards, the practice of collective bargaining—and as a result organized manual laborers started reducing the wage differential between themselves and office workers. In 1915, the average white-collar employee in industry earned over twice as much as the average factory worker; by 1920, this had decreased to less than one and a half times as much. In the same period, the cost of living nearly doubled.[28]

A brief but grim recession followed World War I, and it affected office workers in particular. Unemployment, reduced wages, and diminished chances for upward mobility had dented the middle-class dreams of many. With the distance between themselves and skilled laborers closing, the idea of organizing a union became more appealing. During the war and especially afterward, the white-collar labor movement in the United States began to grow. The Retail Clerks International Protective Association (RCIPA) grew from 15,000 members before the war to 21,000 in 1920. RCIPA began to organize women clerical workers, and their house magazine, *The Advocate*, adopted a radical tone, speaking of white-collar workers as members of the larger "toiling masses" of the country.[29] The bookkeepers', stenographers', and accountants' unions increased in size as well: from eight cities with locals before the war to forty cities afterward. The railway clerks' union grew from 5,000 to 186,000 between 1915 and 1920.[30]

The "return to normalcy" of the 1920s, and the consequent upsurge in prosperity (if also inequality), destroyed these gains almost as quickly as they had been made. Though much of the income was paid out in dividends and interest—in other words, to people playing the finance game—real wages still increased continuously from 1920 to 1929. The white-collar unions lost numbers relatively as well as absolutely: the number of workers had grown, but the unions had failed to organize them, and many of their own members drifted away. A conservative turn in the country more generally also meant a turn against organized labor. The Industrial Workers of the World (IWW)—the most radical, anarcho-syndicalist movement of the previous two decades—was by 1924 a spent force. But even considerably less intransigent unions were in retreat.

The net result was a hardening of attitudes regarding white-collar workers on both the Left and Right. Office workers were of course a heterogeneous mass, cleaved by class and gender. But they became the subject of mass appeals, as if anyone who wore a white collar, no matter what his or her education or life chances or abilities, would have the same basic mental attitudes and outlook on life. For business more generally, the office employee was naturally the most loyal of figures, the deepest believer in the likelihood and rightness of upward mobility. Professional schools for aspiring business managers and executives, such as the Harvard Business School, promoted the idea that the higher rungs of the office world needed specialized training in the arts of management. Popular culture directed at office workers—film, light fiction, advertising—flattered the concept of self-improvement, often through the new resources of pop Freudianism. The French psychologist and public speaker Émile Coué electrified the country on his speaking tours, urging people to believe that the practice of "autosuggestion" would lead them to success. "Day by day, in every way, I am getting better and better," he urged his white-collar audiences to repeat.[31]

The business caricature of the white-collar worker as the perfect picture of American individualism was arguably less cartoonish than the one that came to be offered by radicals in the 1920s. In what were years of defeat for the American Left, the figure of the lower-middle-class office worker, spellbound by false consciousness, became a pervasive scapegoat. The "white-collar man" became the standard image of the harried American, losing ground when lesser people everywhere seemed to be gaining. When cartoonists wanted to depict John Q. Public, they showed a white-collar worker: as one contemporary account had it, "a frail man, timid, retiring, a tiny derby seated atop a worried brow."[32] Films like *The Crowd* showed offices as machines for producing conformity, churning out thousands of drones in cavernous spaces dressing in the same standard attire, working at the same kind of desk, talking in the same tired mannerisms. The phrase "white-collar slave" became a popular one in the press, particularly to describe the stereotype of the office worker who failed to recognize the fact of his own exploitation.

The office worker had become what the gum-chewing, racist "hard hat" would be for the 1970s: the symbol of a backlash. Like the hard hat, the stereotypical frustrated white-collar man avoided dealing with his own problems by lashing out at minorities stealing his job. In Elmer L. Rice's critical, hallucinatory play *The Adding Machine* (1923), the protagonist, Mr. Zero, is a frustrated book-keeper who sits on a stool in a room with an assistant adding num-bers all day. At the same time we see him daydreaming about his managers praising him, or fantasizing about really sticking it to his boss. "I'll say, 'I ain't quite satisfied. I been on the job twenty-five years now and if I'm gonna stay I gotta see a future ahead of me,' " he imagines himself saying. We discover that in fact he's stayed in the same job for twenty-five years, never advancing or raising his voice. By the middle of the play, he is slated to be replaced by an adding machine. In frustration, he and his white-collar friends get drunk and launch into an impassioned peroration against various groups: "Damn Catholics! Damn sheenies! Damn niggers! Hang 'em! Burn 'em! Lynch 'em! Shoot 'em!" He eventually kills his boss and is executed for the crime. At the end of the play, we see Mr. Zero in the afterlife, discovering that he is going to be reincarnated as the operator of a "super-adding machine."

Union organizers lamented their inability to make inroads into the ranks of office workers, tending to chide the white-collar slaves for their false consciousness. In an article from August 1929, noting the increasing similarities between office work and factory work, the editors of *American Federationist*, the magazine of the Ameri-can Federation of Labor (AFL), implored the office workers to "be wise" and "lose no time in providing for their future protection and welfare." "You cannot stop progress," they counseled. "You should be ready to have an intelligent part in progress."[33] But this politely urgent tone didn't last. Confronted with the growing mass of unor-ganized white-collar workers, Samuel Gompers, the powerful head of the AFL at the time, is alleged to have shouted in frustration, "Show me two white-collar workers on a picket line, and I'll organize the entire working-class."[34] Gompers's (possibly apocryphal) line captured the contradictory understanding of the office worker, who was *of* the working class but refused to believe it or participate in any of its activities, political ("a picket line") or otherwise. And not only that: the office workers' resistance to unions was in fact preventing the entire working class from getting organized. They were acting as a buffer between capital and labor.

□

Though the class nature of the office worker was becoming an obsession in the United States, analysis tended to fall into predictable patterns of confirmation of American business prowess on the one hand, and the sign of political idiocy on the other. But contemporary political changes in Europe would resonate at home, and transform the nature of the American conversation irrevocably. This was above all the case in Germany, the country most obviously convulsed by changes after the war.

German scholarship on the growth of employment in the office is easily the richest body of work on white-collar workers anywhere in the world. German sociologists had been interested in the rise of what they had been calling the "new middle class" (*der neue Mittelstand*) for generations; the best work on American white-collar workers before World War II is by a German (Jürgen Kocka), and the theoretical apparatus of C. Wright Mills's *White Collar* depends heavily on German sources. The main impetus for this efflorescence of thinking had been an arcane but unusually intense debate that took place around the turn of the century within the ranks of German socialists and their newly formed Social Democratic Party (SPD) over the nature of class divisions in society. Following the usual interpretation of *The Communist Manifesto*, one faction of so-called orthodox Marxists had argued that society was broadly dividing into two opposed groups, capitalists and proletarians, and politics had to shore up working-class power particularly. Another "revisionist" group (who, had they looked, might have found writings by the mature Marx noting this class diversity) pointed out that classes in society weren't simplifying into a schema, but rather growing more complex. One had only to look, they said, at the growing mass of white-collar workers—themselves split into various class fractions. What side of the orthodox schema did they fall into? For the orthodox, the answer was simple enough: they were by and large members of the working class, a "stiff-collar working class" (*Stehkragenproletariat*), who, under the pressure of the gradually unraveling contradictions of capitalism, would eventually recognize their place in the mass of toiling people. For many of the revisionists, the answer was considerably less clear.

These questions gained particular urgency in the Weimar Republic of the 1920s, when the stability of the buffer supposedly offered by white-collar workers was beginning to shake uncontrollably. The old question that had attended the clerks in the mid-nineteenth century—who were they? where did their loyalties lie?—became unignorable. The reason lay in political crisis. Inflation and depression hit Weimar Germany earlier than elsewhere, thanks to the fallout from the war, and office workers were thrown into unemployment. Economic crisis threw salt on already festering political wounds, opened by the German defeat in World War I. Pitched street fights between far-right and far-left groups became common throughout the country. Seeing that Germany's Communist Party largely focused on uniting the industrial working class, journalists and social scientists worried that the driftless and disorganized office workers—the *Angestellte*, or "salaried employees," in German—would be up for grabs by the rising Nazis.

In the midst of this turmoil, the German sociologist Emil Lederer began to explore the notion that white-collar workers belonged to a "new middle class." Despite the repeated appeals by politicians to small business, the old middle class of shopkeepers and entrepreneurs was disappearing; salaried employees—office workers—had emerged in their place. There was a time, Lederer noted, when salaried employees were strong in number and could imagine themselves as "mediators"—again, a buffer—in the growing strife between capital and labor. Indeed, Lederer had himself endorsed this position when he made his first inquiry into the problem in 1912. But the war and economic stress had made the salaried employee's middle status precarious:

> . . . his permanent dependence on an employer; the fact that he is at the mercy of the labor market; the development of a remunerative system based on the prevailing economic and financial situation; finally, the ever growing practice of compensation in proportion to one's efficiency—which means that the employee's pay decreases the older he grows—all these factors help to undermine the social and economic status of the salaried employee, who thus finds himself exposed to the danger of proletarization."[35]

In other words, the employee became exposed to the idea that he might, without too much trouble, fall into the ranks of the working classes. The salaried employee would have to take sides. Channeling the apocalyptic mood of 1920s Germany, Lederer suggested that the coming years would indicate which side the office worker was on. His prediction was that the salaried masses would join the stratum of the working class in a union of all who were employed.

Others were skeptical. Around the same time, the left-wing journalist and early film theorist Siegfried Kracauer took up the same theme, but with a different method: in what he called "more of an adventure than any film trip to Africa," he set out to spend time among the "salariat," as a reporter. He interviewed them at and around their places of work or traveled to the pleasure palaces that kept them distracted after hours—bars that doubled as brothels, sports arenas, massive upscale restaurants. Berlin, where he did his reporting, seemed to him to be "a city with a pronounced employee culture: i.e. a culture made by employees for employees and seen by most employees as a culture."[36] The sentiment should strike us as odd, living as most of us do in cities largely characterized by white-collar and service labor. But in the industrial 1920s this was absolutely strange; it was alienating enough that Kracauer could see the office worker from a distance. He found in the "salariat" a generation and a class that he declared to be "spiritually homeless." "They are living at present without a doctrine to look up at or a goal they might ascertain," he wrote. "So they live in fear of looking up and asking their way to the destination."[37]

He found them stratified, distinguished from blue-collar workers by their places of work and their styles of life. German firms, following American customs, insisted on elaborate tests of personality and aptitude (and sometimes handwriting and phrenology) to ensure that their office workers fit properly into their organization—standards no one used for blue-collar workers. The rigors of the test, the total view that they demanded, meant that "a salaried type" was beginning to develop in Berlin: "Speech, clothes, gestures and countenances become assimilated and the result of the process is that very same pleasant appearance, which with the help of photographs can be widely reproduced."[38] The children of the former middle class were seeing their bourgeois skills put to new uses: "Many girls who now punch cards used to stumble through *études* at home on the pianoforte." He compared the feel of the office hierarchy to the atmosphere of modernist novels: "If literature usually imitates reality, here it precedes reality. The works of Franz Kafka give a definitive portrait of the labyrinthine human big firm—as awesome as the pasteboard models of intricate robber-baron castles made for children—and the inaccessibility of the supreme authority."[39] And he recognized that the employee unions were doing little to nothing to stop the tedious mechanization of the workplace. "The machine," one union official tells him, "must be an instrument of liberation."[40] Employee unions for salaried workers in Germany existed and represented many thousands of workers, yet many of them tended to dissociate themselves from the blue-collar unions affiliated with the Social Democratic and Communist Parties; many employee unions were essentially close to business. White-collar unions insisted on their difference, both from each other and above all from the blue-collar workers they saw as socially beneath them. "The distinct mania in bourgeois Germany to raise oneself from the crowd by means of some rank, be it only an imaginary one, hampers solidarity among salaried employees themselves," Kracauer wrote, contradicting Lederer's prediction of a gradual "proletarianization" of white-collar workers.[41]

As the German economy and Weimar Republic staggered from one crisis to another, culminating in the blowup of 1929, a vague anxiety that the lower stratum of white-collar workers was beginning to form a reactionary mass, and a natural base for the growing Nazi party, became a fixation among left-wing writers. The socialist Theodor Geiger argued that lower-middle-class office workers were uniquely susceptible to claims of prestige and status; to him, it was a matter of political logic that their sliding economic position would come into conflict with their elevated sense of being middle class—a phenomenon that came to be known in sociology as "status panic"—and they would naturally vote for the Nazis.[42]

The problem with this position, as with the analogous Left caricature of the "white-collar slave" in the United States, was that it lacked an empirical basis. Though a portion of white-collar workers did move rightward in their voting patterns over the course of the 1920s, these tended to be the richer and more secure of the white-collar workers. The Nazis themselves made no specific appeal to white-collar workers, and received only a small proportion of their votes. Even after 1929, when unemployment scythed the ranks of white-collar workers, the great mass of white-collar votes went to the other parties (the socialist Social Democrats, the nationalist German National People's Party, and the liberal German Democratic Party). Still, in the wake of the Nazi victory, the caricature not only persisted, but grew in stature and acceptance. The roots of fascism were complex; the Nazis' rise to power did not depend on a single class or stratum. But part of the party's success derived from the fracturing of the country's Left, alongside the failure of the more traditional parties. An inability to completely acknowledge this led to the construction of the lower-middle-class white-collar worker as natural reactionary, a scapegoat for much deeper failures. The desire to locate the failures or success of a political movement by looking at a country's office workers was irrepressible. In the United States the unusual struggle over the soul of the office worker had only just begun.

□

It didn't take long for the news of the white-collar Nazis to make it over to America. The United States had its own worries about creeping fascism—as Sinclair Lewis, author of *The Job*, demonstrated in his counterfactual story of authoritarian America, *It Can't Happen Here* (1935)—and more than a few of them involved office workers. The specter of fascism in America produced, with considerable speed and aplomb, the same basic outlines of the debate taking place in Germany.

To catch the tone with which office workers were figured as agents of fascism, there's no better place to look than *New Masses*, a lively and surprisingly popular magazine for American Marxists, which, alongside publishing Theodore Dreiser and John Dos Passos, as well as the early work of Richard Wright and Ralph Ellison, reported widely on the reactionary tendencies of the gray-flannel-suited stooges. One writer described his memory of watching office drones on Wall Street joining cops in beating up a group of radical protesters. "The sight of a group of radicals being beaten up was something in the nature of a circus to these white-collar workers," wrote the author. "Up on the Treasury Building steps, out of the windows of office buildings, skyscrapers, twenty dollars-a-week clerks in striped collegiate cravats howled with delight as the police swung their clubs at the hapless heads of the manifestants."[43] A long poem in clumsy blank verse, "White Collar Slaves," imagined a host of technicians, "movers of pencils," singing woozily about their sinister craft of transforming hard labor into figures on a soft ledger:

> *We are three hundred strong, and every day*
> *Over the tables where our bodies bend,*
> *Our pencils juggle numbers, numbers, numbers,*
> *Whether it be a heap of rusting iron,*
> *Cutting of wages, or a newfound treasure,*
> *We are the ones who mark it in our numbers—*
> *We whom the workers scorn as "glossy pants*
> *Who sit all day playing with pencils" while they*
> *Sweat and bend for their little stack of pay:*
> *Yet whom they know as the stronger, since we keep*
> *Numbers that hold strange meanings: numbers that tell*
> *Secret tales that they may never know.*[44]

The nasty tone was relentless. Office workers were the "most unstable and deluded class in our social system." The *New Masses* literary

In the 1930s, white-collar unions urged office workers
to mimic the "manliness" of their blue-collar brethren.
Tamiment and Robert F. Wagner Library, New York University

critic, Michael Gold, went so far as to locate the 1920s vogue for
Ernest Hemingway in the way the writer expressed "the soul of the
harried white-collar class." "I know a hundred gay, haggard, witty,
hard-drinking, woman-chasing advertising men, press agents, dentists, doctors, engineers, technical men, lawyers, office executives,"
wrote Gold, describing what he saw as the white-collar source of
the typical Hemingway hero. "They go to work every morning, and
plough their weary brains eight hours a day in the fiercest scramble for
a living the world has ever known . . . [they] become nervous wrecks
under the strain of American business competition."[45] Hemingway's aggressively wounded masculinity deriving from the travails

of white-collar life: as literary analysis, it was ingenious. But the dis-ingenuousness of the attacks on office workers was plain enough; despite their proletarian sympathies, the highly educated magazine staff of *New Masses* was white-collar through and through, their vituperations as much signs of self-loathing as a genuine exhorta-tion to action. The fact that the left-wing writers of the country were engaged in "mental labor" themselves led to considerable contortions over their need to deny this fact in their own writing.

But the stock-market crash and the Depression, with impressive speed, changed the tune of the Left. Rather than denying the fig-ures in the mirror, the cultural workers of the Left began to see the white-collar workers as budding proletarians. "It is clear that the masses of lower salaried employees (including salaried profession-als) are *not* members of the middle class," wrote the Marxist Lewis Corey in his surprise best seller *The Crisis of the Middle Class* (1935), with the unflappable certainty common in those days, before launching into a fit of messianic italics: *"They are economically and functionally a part of the working class: a 'new' proletariat."*[46] The new, inclusive political awareness that came over organizers regard-ing office workers was ascribed to a new militancy from the workers themselves, but it seems just as likely that the desperation engen-dered by the financial crisis led organizers and writers to "discover" the new white-collar class consciousness. "White Collar Workers and Students Swing into Action" and "Technicians in Revolt," pro-claimed the headlines in *New Masses*, describing violent strikes and confrontations with police by the movers of pencils. "On the White Collar Front" covered a strike in the book publishing industry, where conditions were generally supposed to be grim. "Like horse breeding, a snob-and-specialty industry," according to *New Masses*, book publishing was worse than most office environments for hav-ing cultivated "an aura of gentility which leads to self-deception on the part of many workers in it." This was despite the fact that in publishing "the majority of office workers are miserably paid" and "unpaid overtime work is general." (*Plus ça change . . .*) Nonethe-less, it was surprising when the workers of Macaulay Company, members of the Office Workers Union, went on strike for improved working conditions—creating the "first labor trouble in the history of book-publishing." Famous writers and editors such as Dashiell Hammett and Malcolm Cowley joined the strikers in support, with other authors withdrawing their books until the strike was settled—as, eventually, it was, and in favor of the workers. Some magazines were organized as well: Cowley's own *New Republic* came to be represented by the United Office and Professional Workers of America, an affiliate of the Communist Party of America.[47]

This increasing politicization of mental labor—what the historian Michael Denning has called "the cultural front"—became an essential part of left-wing strategy in the era of the New Deal.[48] The new class consciousness running through the office started to affect popular culture as well. Faith Baldwin, last seen purveying narratives of upward mobility in which secretaries married their bosses, wrote a post-crash novel, *Skyscraper* (1931), in which the upper-class professional heartthrob was figured as a malign influence on the economy, and the skyscraper as a symbol of speculation and excess. The ingenue secretary, Lynn Harding, though initially tempted by the wealth and power of lawyer David Dwight, comes to be disgusted with him for attempting to make money off an insider trading deal; she eventually realizes that her proper place is with her own right-thinking, moral class. After several spells of indecision, she marries the lower-middle-class clerk who has been courting her the entire novel. Meanwhile a linocut "graphic novel," *White Collar* (1940), by the Italian

The protagonist of Giacomo Patri's linocut novel, *White Collar*, trapped inside his class illusions.

immigrant Giacomo Patri (which bore an afterword by the power-ful United Mine Workers president and New Deal architect John L. Lewis), told the wordless story of an advertising man who conspicu-ously ignores the rising tide of labor activism all around him, even though he gets laid off and begins to suffer deprivation. At the end of the novel, he becomes a convert to the cause of labor. The final image depicts a multitude of workers marching alongside their brothers and sisters in white collars.

The unrest in the air alarmed the denizens of executive suites. They were also panicking over the first worker-friendly measures of the New Deal, such as the Social Security Act, guaranteeing pen-sions to the aged partly through levying taxes on employers, and the National Labor Relations Act of 1935, which legalized the right of workers to bargain collectively. Amid all the turmoil, the office bull pens remained quiet. Despite pockets of successful unionization, office workers had resisted labor's increasingly strident calls to orga-nize. But was it the calm before the storm? Would they now, in a fit of inspiration proffered by their restive blue-collar brethren, break their pencils over their thighs, smash their counting machines and Dictaphones, and barricade their boss inside his glass-partitioned office until they got what they wanted? Had the paper pushers sit-ting quietly at the flat metal desks been revolutionaries all along?

The annual conference of the National Office Management Association, a group founded in 1919 by the Taylor-trained special-ist on office space W. H. Leffingwell, began to turn its attention away from the usual fascinating discussions of filing methods and the latest communications technology, devoting more and more time to the task of countering a labor menace that might rear its head any day. An industrial "consultant" who had spent time spying on work-ers in hot spots around the world, from Welsh mines to midwestern railroad offices, reassured the management association that all the office workers he had seen were "individualists" in the true Ameri-can tradition. Only when the rungs of the company ladder began to rise out of reach, and the possibility of moving up appeared to vanish, would the office worker lose faith in the dream and begin to band together with his fellow paper pushers. Factory workers feared joblessness, the consultant argued, and therefore sought help in unions for job security; office workers by contrast feared that some-one might not give them sufficient credit for their work—which in turn raised the specter that their promotion might be tied not to spe-cial ability or accomplishment but to some bureaucratic factor like seniority. In workplaces ruled by the norms of bureaucracy, rather than individual achievement, then, lurked the threat of a union.[49]

The way to counter the threat, the managers decided, was to design better offices.

Year after year during the Great Depression, the National Office Management Association affirmed, as it never had before, the impor-tance of a good, clean, well-lit place for work. Under the spreading influence of Freud and theories of human psychology, the idea of the office worker as a figure who could be disciplined into productivity through proper incentives started to give way, making more room for theories of the "subconscious" (as the language of pop psychology had it). "The effect of clean offices . . . is more or less subconscious," one human resources director said. "Nevertheless, unsatisfactory conditions are often the start of a complaining attitude of mind, that eventually leads up to the more serious grievances."[50] The ten-dency of offices to centralize all their operations—resulting in the vast caverns of bull pens and steno pools that the Taylorists had rationalized into spectacles of pure efficiency—was now faulted for giving workers the impression that their jobs were routine and dead-end. Where, the newly skeptical managers wondered, would future executives come from, if entry-level work had been pooled, parceled out, and de-skilled to within an inch of its life? How could anyone learn the mental habits for management if his work had been entirely stripped of mental activity?[51] Another motivation for the change in managerial attitudes was the entry of women into the office. This meant for them that any whiff of the dirty frat-house atmosphere lingering from the nineteenth-century office had to be flushed out. Offices, managers now believed, had to have a good "matrimonial rating"—more cleanliness signifying, apparently, the wider availability of potential life partners.[52]

The transformation in the rhetoric of office management res-onated with broader changes in American business. The Great Depression had stripped business of its Gilded Age swagger; union confidence, and the ever-present alternative of a "workers' state" in the Soviet Union (which seemed from the outside to have survived the Depression better than the capitalist countries), produced a corporate ethos of being willing to bargain and compromise, in order to forestall more radical demands. The ruthless supervision and fiat solutions of the Taylorists survived in part, but they would be mollified with a veneer of pop Freudianism. The growing popularity of behavioral sciences—sociology, anthropology, psychology—led managers to try to discover how workers *actually* behaved rather than how they *should* behave. In turn, better workplaces more suited to workers' actual needs would—the theory went—obviate any grievance that might snowball into a full-blown strike.

The new, kinder, gentler American workplace took shape under the auspices of what came to be called the "human relations" movement. Its sources lay in the failure of one kind of social science experiment, based on faulty assumptions, which ironically enough would give rise to new kinds of speculation based on equally questionable methods. From the late 1920s through the early 1930s, a series of lighting experiments were conducted by researchers in behavioral psychology at Western Electric's Hawthorne Works in Cicero, Illinois. The researchers were trying to discover the effect of changes in lighting on factory productivity. According to the premises of the experiment, there would have been an easy cause and effect to measure: raise the lights, raise productivity—or, potentially, vice versa. Frustratingly, there appeared to be no relationship at all between lighting and workers' productivity. Sometimes more lighting did the trick; sometimes less. After endless soul-searching, the researchers deduced their conclusion: it was the fact of *being watched* that affected how much the workers worked, not the intensity of the lighting.

The findings were disturbing enough to the complacency of social scientists; it took another turn of the intellectual screw for the deductions to be applied to the workplace. In the early 1930s, Elton Mayo, a professor of business at Harvard, began work on a pamphlet meditating on the meaning of the Hawthorne experiments. The resulting conspectus, *The Human Problems of an Industrial Civilization*, became the founding document of human relations.

Mixing accounts of Hawthorne and other social science experiments with somber exegeses of Freud's and Émile Durkheim's studies on suicide, Mayo concluded his exploration with the doom-laden sentiment that human beings were lost in a state of anomie, which they neither understood nor desired. Mayo argued that it was an impoverished view of man which held that he was only *Homo economicus*, blindly pursuing his own self-interest. Unintentionally echoing the ideas of the anarchist Peter Kropotkin, he affirmed that cooperation was as much part of nature as competition. Only human collaboration on the widest scale, fostered by a corporate world more attuned to the needs of its employees, could save the earth from otherwise inevitable chaos. Administrators needed to become "listeners," he said; they needed to become anthropologists, even biologists of their own workplaces.[53] Human beings needed to feel a sense of belonging, of togetherness. Only then would workers feel at peace in their organizations—and managers feel at peace with their workers.

Architects, like managers, saw themselves as confronting a revolutionary situation—one in which agitation meant that what was needed was a new style of building entirely. For architects, as for others, it was an age of polemics, with contending schools rising one after the other, each devoted to attacking the problem of finding a proper home for man in an industrial age. But where "modernism" in the arts often found itself allied to mass movements, left and right, the fantasies of architects were opposed to turmoil; because built environments were meant to last, architects more often than not wanted to reestablish quiet and harmony—even if this meant revolutionizing all hitherto existing styles to find a new, safe middle ground.

The Swiss-French architect Le Corbusier, whose penchant for strikingly large glass panes might have been his most widely followed contribution to the discipline, was paradigmatic. He posed the problem starkly in his vatic, mirthless, brilliant little book from 1923, *Towards a New Architecture*. After several sections of justly famous (if also dubious) aphorisms ("There is no such thing as primitive man, there are only primitive resources"; "The house is a machine for living in") outlining the technological means (chiefly, concrete) now available for the "new spirit" taking over the globe, he wrote his most directly political material. "It is a question of building which is at the root of social unrest today," he argued.[54] He meant that building had failed to keep pace with technological progress, which had accelerated with such rapidity at the end of the nineteenth century and the beginning of the twentieth that man was left both exhilarated and bewildered. Le Corbusier charged architects with signally failing to understand the "deep chasm" existing between previous eras and the modern age. A transformation in means had to result in a transformation in ends. The transcendental homelessness of man would be solved by architecture—or it would be solved in the streets: "Society is filled with a violent desire for something which it may obtain or may not. Everything lies in that: everything depends on the effort made and the attention paid to these alarming symptoms."[55]

The choice was clear: "architecture or revolution." He concluded, laconically, "Revolution can be avoided."[56]

□

Le Corbusier—the nom de plume of Charles-Édouard Jeanneret—was an autodidact who insisted constantly on his professionalism, a deeply political thinker who considered himself above politics. The most influential architect of the twentieth century, he spent much of his career devising plans that were never built, and fomenting committees and organizations to transmit ideas that few accepted. In his zeal to plan, to corral, and to reshape the living and working arrangements of humankind, he resembled Frederick Taylor—another prophet-like figure who achieved prominence (and vilification) late in life. The resemblance isn't entirely coincidental. Le Corbusier was one of the earliest advocates for Taylorist thinking in France. He seems to have become familiar with scientific management, and the writings of its founder, during World War I. In the wake of the war's devastation, he, like many of his contemporaries, came to propound Taylorism as a source of social renewal, a productivity miracle for a ruined and needy continent. Though his chief concern was mass-producing homes—a genuine social concern in the 1920s, when thousands of Parisians died from inadequate provision of housing—he eventually came to conceive of technocratic, centrally planned solutions for organizing work, as well.

In the 1930s, Le Corbusier made a much-publicized visit to the land of Taylor, and to New York, recorded in his travelogue *When the Cathedrals Were White*. New York thrilled him, but not just for its architecture: pages and pages of his memoir record the powerful effect that jazz had on him—its long, improvised musical lines floating on swift-moving currents of chords, at once atavistic and incomparably modern. (Around the same time, the Dutch painter Piet Mondrian would try to give his dancing red-and-yellow abstract streetscape of Manhattan the imagistic feel of jazz, calling it *Broadway Boogie-Woogie*.) But jazz seemed to Le Corbusier to outpace the actual quality of Manhattan architecture. Something about the coolness of jazz exposed what was so square about the stiff, classical tones of New York's fat, shuffle-footed towers.

"The skyscrapers are too small, and there are too many of them," Le Corbusier concluded, dumbfounding the press that followed him. "The reasoning is clear and the supporting proofs abundant, streets full of them, a complete urban disaster," he continued.[57] In his eyes Manhattan had made the mistake of seeing skyscrapers as "plumes" rising from the face of the city rather than as functional forms for organizing and controlling populations, "a prodigious means of improving the conditions of work, a creator of economies and, through that, a dispenser of wealth."[58] But they were marred by unnatural functions, such as generating money for real estate developers. They rose in steps like Mesopotamian ziggurats, thanks to ineffective zoning laws. Worst of all, they were unable to provide the calm, quiet conditions of work that were within our grasp but nowhere realized. Le Corbusier began to imagine what it would be like to have truly perfect offices. "Office life, made intensely productive through mechanical rationalization: post office, telephone, telegraph, radio, pneumatic tubes, etc. . . . thus the benefit of excellent psycho-physiological conditions: luxury, perfection, quality in the whole building—halls, elevators, the offices themselves (quiet and pure air)," he intoned, before launching into an attack on the still unrationalized Parisian office: "Ah! wretched, mediocre and miserable offices, an unsuspected degradation of the spirit of work—those

Le Corbusier's office design for a project in Algiers (1938–1942).

entrances, those grotesque, ridiculous, idiotic elevators, those dark and bleak vestibules, and the series of dim rooms open on the hubbub of the street or on the dreariness of courts."[59]

New York was on the verge of breaking away, of showing the world what it could do with the organization of offices through skyscrapers; it had only to complete the revolution it had begun. Le Corbusier's vision went under different names: *Ville radieuse* ("radiant city"), Le Corbusier sometimes called it, or *cité d'affaires* ("business district"), or *ville contemporaine* ("contemporary city"). Though the plans differed from year to year, in essence he imagined a flat cityscape punctuated by massive towers, rising as high as 720 feet, spaced evenly across a radiating web of streets, in which the offices rested atop foundations of shops designed to serve the towers ("the common services of the skyscraper restaurants, bars, showrooms, barber shops, dry-goods stores, etc"). In a way, Le Corbusier's dreams had already been realized in Raymond Hood's Rockefeller Center, an entirely self-sufficient white-collar island. But following Le Corbusier, architects around the world would come to imagine urban utopias that consisted entirely of office workers: the influential Japanese architect Kenzo Tange's plan for Tokyo, in 1960, was a design to centralize the "tertiary industrial population" (that is, white-collar workers).

The penchant for conglomerating business functions in single spaces had been a hallmark of progressive office design, from the Pullman Building on. But perhaps Le Corbusier's most lasting gift to the future of the office was his ideological embrace of glass. "The exterior of the skyscraper, the façade—the façades—can be a film of glass, a skin of glass. Why repudiate richness itself: floods of light coming in."[60] It would be a keynote of the new style of architecture coming to American cities, soon to be dubbed the "International Style"—thanks to the promotion of American architects Philip Johnson and Henry-Russell Hitchcock, and an exhibit they mounted with that title at the Museum of Modern Art in 1932. Associated with European architects, such as Le Corbusier, Walter Gropius, and Ludwig Mies van der Rohe, the International Style was essentially the name for architectural modernism, which was initially formed in order to solve urban problems (such as workers' housing) with new materials (concrete), free from the modes and concerns of the past; it ended up being the style that Americans used to express corporate power. Whatever had initially been "international" about the International Style soon became identified with the United States and, through it, the architecture of corporate globalization.

Along with concrete, glass was the ideal expression of austere architectural modernism, and its use has persisted into the wilder forays of our postmodernist times. As Mies van der Rohe (or simply Mies, as he preferred to be called) would show with his Barcelona Pavilion in 1929, and his American acolyte Philip Johnson would repeat with his marvelous Glass House in New Canaan, Connecticut, glass was an extraordinary medium for facilitating light, elegant spaces within domestic-scaled interiors—a perfect, airy complement to the flat slabs of modernist roofs and walls. Cut into varying shapes and occasionally colored, it could resemble a miniature by Mondrian. Scaled to the size of an office building, however, it could transform a tower into a shimmering thing, a mass of living light, reflecting the low brick buildings of an older skyline or the slow amble of a cloud. As early as 1921, Mies, then in Weimar Germany, had sketched his dream of a glass-and-steel skyscraper; he had dared to imagine a pure sheet of glass seemingly unimpeded by climbing mullions or cinching spandrels. As any city dweller anywhere in the world knows, his dream has been realized in extraordinary, even obscene abundance, with latter-day crystal palaces cresting every skyline.

Glass had always been a potential replacement for stone exteriors, ever since steel frames had eliminated the need for load-bearing exteriors. But a fully glass "curtain wall"—that is, an exterior sheath protruding and masking the building, much as a curtain shielded a window—presented problems for the interior environment. For no one needed as much light as a glass "skin" would create in a building; in fact, a glass exterior would allow in inordinate quantities of warmth, producing a greenhouse effect that would fry the inhabitants—something Le Corbusier found out the hard way with his Cité de Refuge, a Salvation Army hostel and one of the earliest large glass-walled buildings, which was impressively temperate during the winter that it first opened but embarrassingly broiling by the ensuing summer.[61]

Luckily for modernists, technology swept in to sanction their worship of the god of glass. Willis Carrier, a man as important in some ways as Thomas Edison but nowhere near as hallowed, began his experiments with controlling interior humidity around the turn of the century. He spent years with trial-and-error attempts to use spray nozzles and filter out airborne water drops from saturated air. But soon a number of patents came together to allow the automatic filtration of air and its thermal control. "Man-made weather," the Carrier Corporation haughtily called it, well into the decades when others were content to use the more commonplace and easily understood term "air-conditioning."[62] It took several decades to become widespread, initially being adopted in large auditoriums and other amphitheater-like spaces and later being deployed in office buildings. The first American office building in the International Style, the Philadelphia Savings Fund Society building (1933), outfitted with a stylish glass curtain wall traversed by glinting mullions, was also the second fully air-conditioned office building in the country. (The first was the Milam, built in San Antonio in 1928.) Observers began to record the new and startling phenomenon of seeing office workers huddling in thick sweaters in the middle of summer, shielding themselves from the blasts of frigid air.

Two other inventions coincided with the rise of air-conditioning: the fluorescent lightbulb, which consumed vastly less energy than bulbs of traditional wattage; and the suspended ceiling, which, like the curtain wall protruding from the frame, hung down from the actual load-bearing ceiling, opening up a space in between the two levels. It was suddenly possible to hide the wiring for light fixtures and the tubes for air-conditioning—they could be sequestered between the two ceiling levels. The ceiling heights were reduced, leading to the compressed, boxed-in floors we know today. Though glass was intended to bring light in, air-conditioning and fluorescent light made it possible to push people farther and farther into the depths of the building, where they might get no natural light at all, let alone air (with powerful winds buffeting the top floors of the skyscraper, it was impossible to keep the windows open). From the 1950s to early 1960s, the depth of office floors grew exponentially: in 1962, the average tenant occupied 2,622 square feet, double the number from 1952, the first year such a number was recorded.[63] In roughly the same span, the number of white-collar workers had also doubled.[64]

With the completion of the UN Secretariat Building in 1952 and its enormous sea-green sheath of glass—its design partly by the hand of Le Corbusier—the signal was given to go wild. Glass boxes began popping up all over the country, inspired by the same "form follows finance" principle that had sanctioned the previous building binge. Only seven years later, the New Yorker's architecture critic Lewis Mumford would enumerate a depressing catalog of the new office building landscape: "greedy buildings, hogging every cubic foot of space the law allows; flashy buildings, with murals in the lobby whose winking leer at art has something less than honorable intentions; gaudy buildings, whose unpleasant colors resemble Detroit's recent favourite hues and in a few years will look similarly old-fashioned; buildings slickly covered with sheets of pressed metal, which are cheaper than stone or brick and which, despite all the decorative embossments, look just that—magnificently cheap; and corner-cutting buildings often with ceilings so low that their claims to being adequately air-conditioned must be considered brazen effrontery, as their inmates have doubtless been discovering."[65]

Mumford, a polymathic student of urban history and stern critic of the excesses of architecture, was one of the most widely read and conspicuously ignored writers of his day. He would be an inspiration to Jane Jacobs (author of the classic *The Death and Life of Great American Cities*) in his criticisms of urban renewal. And he would be satirized as a "collectivist" in Ayn Rand's paean to lone architectural genius, *The Fountainhead*, whose architecture critic character Ellsworth Toohey, the "collectivist," was partly modeled on Mumford. Yet, somewhat like Rand, Mumford worried over the homogenizing tendencies of postwar life and feared that beneath the flashy technological advances of consumer society lay bland anonymity and spiritual homelessness. Architecture was failing to house people in more practical ways as well. His repeated charge against modernism was that it didn't accommodate "human functions and human needs"—the barest requirement, one would think, of architecture. He was a "sidewalk critic," posing not as an expert insider architect but as a city dweller concerned with how architecture affected the inhabitants of a city as well.

In his view even the most startling and powerful architectural symbol, the skyscraper, merited the charge. "At no point in the evolution of the skyscraper was the efficient dispatch of business under conditions that maintained health and working capacity the controlling element in the design," he wrote in the 1950s. It came from a review of the UN Secretariat Building, which he would hold up for particular censure. It exemplified the chief defect of the form: disregard for the needs of the workers inside. Fundamental aspects of the design had unintended, miserable consequences. The building had been built running north to south, which meant that the windows faced east and west. In the mornings, the sun rising over the East River had an unimpeded penetration into the building's glass facade, meaning that the workers on the perimeter of the building had to draw shades to keep themselves from being fried. On the other hand, not everyone enjoyed the benefits of the abundance of light. For the offices themselves, the architects had simply adopted the standard T formation. This meant that the secretaries' offices were separated by opaque glass partitions; whatever seeped through was their only natural light, in a building that otherwise had it in abundance. Such obvious disregard for the building's workers reminded Mumford of tougher times: "New York's tenements of the eighteen-fifties had exactly the same kind of partition, a pitiful effort to atone for the fact that no daylight or ventilation was provided for the inner bed-rooms. To see this symbolic substitute for light and air reappearing in a building that prides itself on its aesthetic modernity is like seeing Typhoid Mary pose as a health inspector."[66] Small amenities were missing, like cafés on each floor where workers in different depart-ments could socialize. Mumford was one of the earliest writers to recognize the importance of random interaction and collaboration in workplaces. Isolated workers in austere conditions, utopian plans leading to dystopian spaces: these critiques would constitute a leit-motif in complaints about offices in the decades to come.

Despite his disdain for the skyscraper—he considered it an "obso-lete" form—one emerged on Park Avenue that managed to satisfy nearly all the strictures Mumford held. Indeed, the headquarters for the Lever Brothers company—affectionately called Lever House by most—became one of the great office buildings of the time. Designed on the outside by Skidmore, Owings and Merrill (SOM), coordinat-ing with Raymond Loewy Associates for the inside, it was a model for countless other glass skyscrapers to follow and a likely source for the Sterling Cooper advertising agency offices in *Mad Men*. A dramatically thin slab of green glass rising from a flat base, it took up only 46 percent of the buildable floor area for the site and broke with the skyline of Park Avenue by having its principal face directed south rather than east, toward the street. In the richness of its mate-rials and the lovely, tactile glass skin, the Lever House seemed to embody all the futuristic ambitions of 1950s America, as well as its unexampled prosperity and guileless optimism. Three out of its four sides were covered in a sheer skin of glass, divided only by the horizontal blue-green stainless steel spandrels that indicated the divi-sion of floors, accentuating the fresh image that Lever, which sold soap and cleaning products, was naturally trying to promote. To add an exclamation point to this congruence of building and corporate image, a mechanical cleaning apparatus was designed especially for the building; cleaners in their window-washing gondola scaled the tower every day, keeping the glass smoothly reflective.

When it opened, Lever House was an instant hit. *Life* observed that pedestrians and taxi drivers slowed down to a near halt when they passed by. Remarking on the open forecourt of its lobby, with

The shimmering curtain wall of Lever House. *Ezra Stoller, ESTO*

Lever House's thin, light-filled interior. *Ezra Stoller, ESTO*

its sleek marble and steel-encased columns, *BusinessWeek* reported the pleasure of not knowing whether one was in an office building or a resort hotel.[67] After it opened, a building designed for only twelve hundred workers was burdened by thousands of visitors, demanding entrance "as if this was the eighth wonder of the world," Mumford wrote. Yet Lever House was successful not simply because of the outward show it made before the public (although this was extraordinary enough). It was also thoroughly designed in its interior to give maximum comfort to its employees. Rather than taking the standard office unit as the building block, or (in Sullivan's words) "cell," for the building, the interior designers designed their space around the desk. In other words, the offices were designed with the open steno pool in mind, not the executive suite.[68] The desks themselves were old-fashioned, with rounded corners ("to reduce the number of nylon snags," according to Mumford), and had adjustable heights. Though offices lined part of the perimeter as usual, the building was only sixty feet wide, meaning that most desks were never more than twenty-five feet from a window. Amenities abounded: the second floor had an employees' lounge, colored a dark green and mustard yellow; the third story had a luxuriously fitted kitchen and cafeteria; the roof of the building's base had a garden for outdoor seating. The only flaw in Mumford's eyes was a retro-styled and garish executive floor, which broke from the new practice of having executives and employees seated "democratically" in similar spaces, on the same floor.

There was, however, a danger contained in the success of Lever House. "Standing by itself, reflecting the nearby buildings in its mirror surface, Lever House presents a startling contrast to the old-fashioned buildings of Park Avenue," Mumford wrote approvingly, before sounding an ominous note: "But if its planning innovations prove sound, it may become just one unit in a repeating pattern of buildings and open spaces." By 1958, the pattern was beginning to emerge. The Colgate-Palmolive Building three blocks south (by Emery Roth & Sons), and the Davies Building (by the same) at 57th Street, were among the half dozen imitations that had sprung up just a few years after the appearance of SOM's dazzling slab. And when Park Avenue had already been glutted with slick curtain walls, Sixth Avenue offered a fresh chance to repeat the same dismal success. The grid of the curtain wall and the grid of the city streets began to converge with uncanny precision. Where the earlier skyscrapers had pointed up their aloof, ornamental dignity, the new glass slabs emphasized corporate organizational form, and irremediable rationality. The curtain wall had become a simple, neutral technology, endlessly reproducible. It was a potentially nightmarish vision that director Alfred Hitchcock nicely turned into a joke in the Saul Bass–designed title sequence for *North by Northwest,* slotting actors' names into a grid that gradually revealed itself as the Secretariat's immense curtain wall: so human beings do have a place in this world.

Only one of Lever's neighbors equaled, if not surpassed, its triumph. This was of course the topaz-tinted wall of Mies van der Rohe's Seagram Building. Having opened just a few years after Lever, Seagram's dark glass facade and bronze mullions immediately presented a contrast: a rich, bracing whiskey to Lever's sudsy

The Seagram Building—the original "black box." *Ezra Stoller, ESTO*

sea green. Like the Lever House, the Seagram Building ostentatiously disdained the buildable area, the central tower seeming to float on a handful of columns, set back amid a gleaming, almost blindingly white travertine plaza graced with two reflecting pools. Unlike Lever, which broke the sight lines of Park Avenue by orienting its central tower east–west, the thirty-five-story Seagram faced, with a kind of solemn forthrightness, the city it delicately belonged to. Across the street, it engaged in dignified, urbane dialogue with McKim, Mead & White's neoclassical racquet club from 1911. The marbled plaza encircling Seagram seemed at once capacious and austere. It was designed to encourage gawking—the ceiling lights were shaped like panels and when lit up at night mimicked the exterior curtain wall—if not necessarily lingering. (In contrast, the brilliant, iconoclastic Italian architecture critic Manfredo Tafuri saw Seagram as adopting "a perfect and disquieting silence" in the midst of an urban "chaos." It was the "void as symbolic form"—pure negation of the urban setting.)[69] It became a pop culture icon in the film *The Best of Everything* (1959), set in a fictional publishing house in the building. One of the early shots of the film, in which the character Caroline Bender (Hope Lange) is seen looking up at the building, became reproduced as Cindy Sherman's *Untitled Film Still #14*, one of her most famous images.

The interiors of the building had been designed chiefly by Philip Johnson, one of Mies's greatest promoters in the United States (he had helped Mies secure the commission by speaking with Phyllis Lambert, the architecturally astute and informed daughter of Seagram's president). Johnson had followed a curious trajectory since mounting the International Style exhibit in 1932. He had quit his job and attempted to become a populist opponent of the New Deal; he also indulged a fondness for Nazism to an extraordinary degree, traveling to Germany and following the Wehrmacht to Poland. "We saw Warsaw burn," he wrote in a cheerful letter. "It was a stirring spectacle."[70] Returning to architecture after the United States entered the war, he was publicly sorry for his actions, as of course he had to be. He retained, however, a unique attitude toward the style he had promoted, his rebellious sense of taste imbuing Mies's classical modernism with emotional force and theatricality. An art collector, Johnson had designed reception and conference areas to display priceless art: Mirós, Picassos, Rodins.[71] He had conceived of the spectacular lighting for the building, and had insisted on a venetian-blind system that permitted only three positions, in order to display the blazing interior at night. Johnson also designed the Four Seasons restaurant that occupied one of the building's wings: rich with wood walls and overhung with shimmering Richard Lippold sculptures, it instantly became the city's premier spot for power brokers—the theater of corporate power at the base of American business's architectural expression.

Though the building had used inordinately expensive materials, making it still richer and statelier than any of its rivals (its bronze mullions could be polished only with lemon oil), Seagram brought to completion the possibilities of standardization inherent in the modernist skyscraper. Somewhat inadvertently it spawned the first of the innumerable "black boxes" that would take over the business districts of American cities everywhere. "What makes Mies such a great architect is that he is so easy to copy," Johnson is supposed to

A middle manager's office in the Seagram Building (1958). *Ezra Stoller, ESTO*

have quipped some years after Seagram. Critics would claim a special place for buildings like Lever and Seagram, arguing that their breakthroughs had little to do with the inferiority of the copies built by speculators and designed by engineers rather than architects. But for the sidewalk viewer, these "original" buildings often look the same as all the rest, like icebergs melting into an undifferentiated sea of glass. Seagram was a monument, a technical masterpiece, and an aestheticizing of what was fundamentally an architecture of corporate bureaucracy. Ultimately, it was an office building, and it spawned office buildings like it—the speculative returns on offices along Park Avenue promising more revenue than apartments. "New York's midtown has many places with intensive daytime use that go ominously dead at night," Jane Jacobs would point out.[72] Refracting the sentiment against the black boxes, the director Stanley Kubrick in his film *2001: A Space Odyssey* used a Seagram-like black monolith as the symbol of a future in which men would be controlled by their machines. Already by 1960, Mies was said to be curiously contrite. When asked by Arthur Drexler, then the curator of architecture and design at the Museum of Modern Art, how he spent his day, Mies responded, "We get up in the morning, and we sit on the edge of the bed and we think 'What the hell went wrong?' "[73]

5

ORGANIZATION MEN AND WOMEN

Success in industry and commerce requires a lot
of stamina, yet industrial and commercial activity
is essentially unheroic in the knight's sense—no
flourishing of swords about it, not much physical
prowess, no chance to gallop the armored horse
into the enemy, preferably a heretic or heathen—
and the ideology that glorifies the idea of fighting
for fighting's sake and of victory for victory's sake
understandably withers in the office among all the
columns of figures.

> —JOSEPH SCHUMPETER, *Capitalism, Socialism, and Democracy*[1]

If you wanted to see signs of the paroxysms of affluence that seized the United States after World War II, there were few better places to look than the country's offices. Looking back at the offices of mid-century America, you might think the office worker had reached the pinnacle of comfort and prestige. What had started as a dank cavern, with towers of files crowded everywhere like dark stalagmites, had by the 1950s become clean and blindingly lit from within. Around the serried rows of L-shaped desks in the steno pool were offices partitioned by glass; these were filled with couches, desks made of mahogany and sometimes topped with marble, lounge chairs, and ottomans, all done up by the very best names in American design—Charles and Ray Eames, Florence Knoll, George

Nelson. Inspired by the wilder reaches of Abstract Expressionism and Pop Art (or, maybe, vice versa), bolder colors began to spread around offices, from the sea-green or whiskey-dark glass panels of the curtain wall to the pastel baby blues and salmon pinks of the partition doors. Air-conditioning blasted newly wide offices into an icy temperateness.

The luxury never stopped. Take the elevator up to the executive suites on the top floors, and you would find an extraordinary lavishing of care and detail, snugly insulating the top brass from the ricocheting clacking of the typewriter pools below. The film *Executive Suite* (1954), about the struggle for power facing a furniture manufacturer following the death of its CEO, dramatized this difference precisely: when a visitor to the company stops on the steno floor to let someone step into the elevator, we are overwhelmed by a wave of typewriter noise and a roar of conversation; when he arrives at the top floor, the corresponding silence is surreal. He enters a carpeted space decorated in neo-Gothic arches and columns, as solemn as a monastery. Devotion to business had become a sort of religion.

Executive suites crowning skyscrapers weren't the only symbol of a powerful America; the office didn't just expand vertically. In those years, many companies began to follow thousands of white Americans out of the cities toward the greener pastures of suburbia. At the peak of American industrial strength—by the late 1940s the country's businesses controlled 60 percent of global industrial production—relocating to the suburbs seemed to offer a way for business, and the office workers who made up business, to cope with rapid growth and change, much as the organic motifs in Chicago skyscrapers had mollified the potential coldness of business architecture. Downtowns had also steadily lost their appeal to businesses. Cities had been overrun by cars, and offices by congestion; the size of corporate staff had doubled between 1942 and 1952, but there was no corresponding increase in office space. General Foods, in 1921, leased space in a single Manhattan office building. By 1945, its thirteen hundred staff members occupied multiple floors over three separate buildings, an extremely inefficient arrangement. Three years later, it was scouting for new locations in the suburbs.[2]

Some less sanguine reasons prompted the corporate exodus.

Many white Americans were alarmed by more and more people of color moving into their cities. "New York is becoming an increasingly Negro and Puerto Rican city," *Fortune* reported. "Some companies are reluctant to hire a large proportion of Negro and Puerto Rican help."[3] What corporations wanted instead were white, educated, middle-class women—who, they believed, were increasingly easy to find in suburbs. So, too, did the presence of urban industry, with its contingents of unionized workers, begin to frighten the executives. *Fortune* suggested that corporations were moving to the suburbs "in the hope that this will reduce friction . . . between unionized workers and unorganized office personnel."[4] And there was one more fear peculiar to the climate of the postwar era: the threat of nuclear war. Especially after 1949, when the Soviet Union tested its first atomic bomb and American civil defense spending and research increased accordingly, central business districts were seen as dangerous. Each executive of a corporation seeking an escape from New York to Westchester County privately revealed in a survey "that, among other things, [he] wanted to avoid target areas."[5] The city, increasingly perceived to be dirty and crowded, beset by labor agitation and race riots, had lost its charm. Far from the gray and beige towers of downtown one could find green hills and false lakes—"nature" (as well as an easier-to-enforce ethnic, class, and gender uniformity). The suburbs were signs of health, contemplation, repose—in a word, security. Green, in mid-century America, was good.

Among the earliest examples of the suburban office park—and still, in the memory of many, a model—was AT&T's Bell Labs in Murray Hill, New Jersey. It had been driven out of downtown chiefly because of the nature of its particular research, especially into acoustics, which needed more quiet than New York's downtown could offer. In hunting for new space, AT&T overcame the objections of suburban residents by presenting the civilized credentials of their managers. They cemented a new zoning law that would allow for "laboratories devoted to research, design and/or experimentation"—the first such law in the country and one that opened up the suburbs for more such corporate campuses. Not just a few observers felt that Bell resembled the bucolic pastures of universities like nearby Princeton. "At Bell Labs, Industrial Research Looks like Bright College Years," ran the headline of a 1954 *BusinessWeek* article.[6] And like many American universities, it was isolated and surrounded by gates. The buildings were low and boxy; fenced in by greenery and a heavily secured entrance, its researchers faced no distractions except from the inside.

Unlike on a university campus, however, all the various buildings were connected via long corridors. As a result, everyone was deliberately placed in the way of everyone else. Labs were separated from offices; in order to return to their office, or to get to the cafeteria, physicists ran into chemists who ran into mathematicians who ran into developers.[7] Here was the origin of what later generations of designers would call a "serendipitous encounter"—unexpected collisions between people on otherwise totally different sides of a company, thanks to the soft coercion and subtle manipulations of architecture (a precursor as well to the "nudge" effect prevalent in behavioral economics). Still, the designers of Bell Labs took into account (as many offices today do not) the other side of this coin—space for quiet, self-directed thought. At Bell Labs, pay and job security were divorced from productivity—the goal was to invent, not to meet an arbitrary deadline—and the work space was accordingly apportioned between social and private areas. Even generous common areas enjoyed floor-to-ceiling windows, for views of the artificial landscape; it was space for individual contemplation as well as for socializing and casual discussion.[8] And Bell Labs engaged in a stronger kind of coercion as well, in ensuring rigorous entry requirements for people who worked in the lab: as *BusinessWeek* put it, "All this freedom, this almost relaxed freedom, seems a little at odds in the family of Mother Bell whose business communications empire is the largest nonfinancial company in the world . . . Partly the Freedom is illusory. The lab has firm plans and knows precisely what it wants . . . Over the years men have been meticulously selected and precisely trained. Men chosen to fit the mold will fall into the desired pattern without any pressure from the mold itself."[9] The quiet pastoral research facility, with its "relaxed" and "illusory" freedom, eventually bore fruit: by 1948, scientists in its offices had invented the transistor and the "bit" (the unit of electronic information), two fundamental pieces of technology that merit the otherwise overused term "revolutionary."

Seeking the Bell effect (in 1958, by which point it employed forty-two hundred employees, *Fortune* called Bell Labs, with not too much hyperbole, "the world's greatest industrial laboratory"),[10] other companies began relocating to the suburbs. Even more iconic, architecturally, than Bell Labs was the headquarters for the insurance company Connecticut General designed by Skidmore, Owings and Merrill (SOM), the highly organized and powerful firm that had built Lever House. It was perhaps the most considered and thoroughly planned building since Wright's Larkin Building; there wouldn't be an equivalent in the United States until the era of dot-com campuses. Set in three hundred rolling acres just outside Hartford, Connecticut, it consisted mainly of a long, expansive three-story office surrounded by a moat: a sort of white-collar castle. The floor was wide open, with demountable partitions easily sliding into the modular ceiling (and out of it, when people needed to be shifted around), which was itself illuminated panel by panel, an analogue to the pattern of the curtain wall. As if to point out the sheer American pluck even more strongly, the interior furnishings—from doors to lockers—were bright with red, white, yellow, orange, and blue patterning, suggestive of farmhouses and sunsets and the American flag. Every furniture product was scaled to a module; desks and par-

Connecticut General: the pastoral corporation. *Ezra Stoller, ESTO*

titions, chests and cabinets, were proportioned to line up perfectly and to be separated and recombined flexibly. Though the building imposed itself heavily on the surrounding landscape, reshaping it to its will, inside virtually nothing was permanent.

Behind the conception of the interior lay one of the most formidable architectural minds of the twentieth century, Florence Schust Knoll. Born in Michigan to a Swiss-immigrant father and an American mother, Knoll studied design and architecture with the great architects of the age, Eliel Saarinen and Mies van der Rohe among them. But her innovation—as intelligent as it was obvious—was to push architectural knowledge, otherwise limited to shaping the interior space, into *planning* interior space. In other words, Knoll planned a layout for a company as rigorously and thoroughly as architects responded to a client's general needs for the building as a whole. The idea is elementary now, but before Knoll got into the furniture and planning business, there were hardly any furniture companies, let alone architecture firms, that considered the office as an entire organism. Businessmen often hired their wives' interior decorators to handle their offices; furniture for the open floor came from a catalog and usually followed other precedents. Without conscious planning, conspicuously modern buildings on the outside often contained musty, stuffy, or unintentionally retro environments on the inside. Knoll changed all that. Together with her husband, Hans Knoll, she had become the most successful purveyor of the "Bauhaus approach" to interior design—namely, the idea (following the Bauhaus school of Weimar Germany) that superior design should be manufactured through industrial means for a wider public. She had achieved considerable success mass-producing modernist designs, such as Mies's tilted, leather-backed Barcelona chair, as well as Eero Saarinen's white, sinuous Womb chair with its sunken seat (which became doubly famous when it made it into one of Norman Rockwell's portraits of "traditional" American life for the *Saturday Evening Post*). She had made it normal—even positively American—for companies to use the best in European modernist design in piecing together their offices.

When she was hired to design the interior of the CBS Building in 1952, she formed the Knoll Planning Unit, which analyzed a client's space requirements and took responsibility for handling furniture, mechanical equipment, colors, and fabrics, as well as general art and design for the office.[11] Knoll's signature move was to use the "paste-up" in presentations to clients. Usually a black cardboard sheet to which a designer could affix fabrics and swatches, the paste-up was a common tool in fashion and set design; Knoll translated these "feminine" arts into the male-dominated realm of architecture and design.[12] (She insisted on referring to herself as a designer rather than an interior decorator—at once professionalizing her discipline and rendering its gendered connotations moot.) The paste-up made color and texture more vivid and tactile. The actual results were warm and domestic. Many observers would note that the lounge areas for her projects resembled comfortable modern living rooms. Knoll helped render modern office environments more human; her work was one of the elements that helped transform modernism itself from a European avant-garde tactic into the symbol of the new "concerned parent" style of American corporate capitalism.

The partnership of Knoll and SOM had produced an office environment more bucolic and cozy than nearly any around, but it would take more, the executives of Connecticut General thought, to draw people out from urban settings to the "country." To attract the mostly female staff away from New York, where the original headquarters were located and where most of the staff lived, the campus offered a bevy of amenities: swimming pools, sunbathing facilities, a snack and soda bar, shuffleboard courts, a Ping-Pong table, a card room, a game room, a lounge for noontime meditation, a lending library, services for dry cleaning and shoe repair, as well as flower and grocery delivery, twelve bowling alleys, two softball diamonds, four tennis courts, six horseshoe pits, and a large cafeteria offering cheap, sometimes free food.[13] Like an off-site Katie Gibbs school, it offered classes in languages and singing—as well as (a bit less like a Katie Gibbs school) automobile repair, one of the most popular. A four-hundred-seat auditorium was available for amateur theatricals and musical performances. Buses carried people to and from train stations and even farther afield. Women accustomed to active urban lives began to lead substantially more sedentary ones; they reportedly began to gain weight in their first year. Calorie counts were accordingly posted for the meals.[14] Even the biological lives of its workers had become a subject of keen interest to the corporation.

As a self-professedly "caring" company, Connecticut General was also concerned to make its spaces as democratic as possible. Though this didn't mean abolishing the distinction between private offices and desks out on the open floor, let alone changing the actual relations of power between higher-ups and lower-downs, it did mean not having a special executive wing. This was a desire that brought the management of Connecticut General into conflict with SOM. The architects had wanted a separate executive building for "Class II" offices (along with the executives, this included departments like legal and securities, whose staff levels remained largely static), in order to keep the interior as flexible and open as possible for Class I workers (clerical labor, with more turnover and shifting around of personnel). When these plans were unveiled, they were received with a slight measure of embarrassment; grumblings among the members of the Connecticut General building committee accumulated, with some middle managers publicly deploring the existence of an "ivory tower" for executives. At an informational meeting about the building, a Philadelphia client of the insurance company said, witheringly, "Well, I suppose it makes some sense, but in our part of the country we are more democratic than that and just don't believe in a separate club for officers."[15] Eventually, Frazar B. Wilde, the company CEO, bowed to the logic of the architects and agreed, certainly with great reluctance, to the separate wing.

The zeal that Wilde, his colleagues, and Connecticut General's clients attached to the semblance of a democratic workplace should strike us as curious. Many corporations followed the old mission of industrial betterment and "welfare capitalism" in providing amenities for their employees, but very few shied away from constructing extravagant executive floors, replete with separate bathrooms and elevator entrances. Something else appeared to be at stake in the desire to keep management and staff in close proximity.

It was not that the staff and the executives did comparable work. On the contrary: it might have been the sheer mechanical nature of the work done by the clerical workers, and the lonely decision-making goals of the higher-ups, that motivated the construction of a more harmonious-seeming (and less hierarchical-seeming) workplace. The basic features of insurance work were factory-like. Ensuring an even flow of paperwork was an important concern of SOM and Knoll's design; as a result of their meticulous planning the entire building hummed with the smoothness of an assembly line. Even the fact that escalators rather than elevators conveyed people through the various floors enhanced this impression. Shirley New-man, one of the office workers, testified in the *Saturday Evening Post* to the efficiency of the teams of operations, referring to her own as a "five girl assembly-line":

> The girl at the end . . . is the clerk on our team. She opens and sorts mail. The next girl is our doer. She does whatever the mail calls for—a cancellation, a receipt or whatnot. Then I check the papers she hands me, and add whatever notations are necessary before I pass them along for copying to the first girl on my left, our team's typist. She, in turn, gives the whole batch to the last girl, our assembler, who puts the papers together in proper order and forwards them, maybe to another depart-ment, or to central filing, or possibly back to a policyholder.[16]

Where the women office workers described the mechanical nature of the work, Wilde testified by contrast to the intimate, serendipi-tous effects of the arrangement of corridors. "In vertical buildings, where quick elevators take one from a small work level to the street level, there are few spontaneous meetings, few casual interchanges of work experiences," Newman told the press, apparently attentive to the pressure of marketing the building. "Here in the cafeteria and lounges and on the daily routes of travel through the building we are getting to know each other better."[17] This was not meant to be like Bell Labs; there were no expectations that the clerical workers would run into their managers in a "serendipitous encounter" and produce a new innovation. The idea was rather to create a workplace in which status barriers *seemed* to dissolve, in which participation and friendliness all around made the work environment look less like the white-collar factory it was. And no detail was spared in making

The totally organized interior of Connecticut General. *Ezra Stoller, ESTO*

this impression. "The entire building is *designed*," wrote a critic for *Architectural Forum*, "and there are no cracks showing between the approach to the over-all plan and the corners of the wood paneling. It is pervasively complete; the patterns of rectangles—everything is rectangles—range from the minute to the mammoth, but they are all so subtly related that the architect renders himself almost invisible."[18]

☐

The scary side of the total corporate environment wasn't lost on observers. In fact, during the 1950s, it became an obsession, which millions of readers bought into. *The Lonely Crowd*, *The Hidden Persuaders*, *The Power Elite*, *The Affluent Society*, *The Human Condition*, *The Organization Man*: from the works of social criticism, the doom-laden message of despair was relentless. People were told that society was tending toward a soft totalitarianism, shaped by hidden networks of elites or by tyrannical managers; by sinister human relations experts or callous economists; and, of course, by manipulative admen, who got you to buy things you didn't need. And the overall shape of society was tending away from American individualism to a cage-like conformity. The 1950s are known as a golden age of this sort of sonorous, endlessly throat-clearing criticism, in which "ideal-types" sprang up like mushrooms after a spring rain. Not a small portion of it was inspired, or even written, by the German émigré sociologists who had found refuge in the United States after World War II. They carried with them their Freudian-Marxist obsession with *der neue Mittelstand*. As with the white-collar-girl novels of a generation prior, the protagonists of these books were the target audience as well: office workers who had emerged from a decade of depression and war to be inundated by waves of prosperity.

Perhaps it proved their rightness about conformity that a good number of these books turned out to be crazy best sellers. Since everyone was talking about them, you had to buy in. Terms that the sociologists had introduced as technical became common features of everyday middle-class speech. *The Lonely Crowd*, for example—a spectacularly successful, dense work of sociology—rimmed the martini glasses of not just a few cocktail parties with intellect, contributing terms like "inner-directed" (that is, self-motivated) and "other-directed" (that is, requiring and seeking the approval of others). The inner-directed man had pushed forward the American frontier, had built the railroads, forded the rivers, thrown up the dams that made the country great; he operated by an "inner gyroscope." The other-directed man, a new type in larger metropolitan areas, depended on the approval of others, whether those he associated with or the masklike personalities he encountered in the mass media; lacking an inner compass, he moved through life as if watching it from above, by "radar."

Meanwhile, the title *The Organization Man*, much like *The Man in the Gray Flannel Suit*, came to provide an easy shorthand for designating a conformist corporate stooge. "Are you an ORGANIZATION MAN . . . who's sick of his organization? Are you a STATUS SEEKER . . . who's disgusted with his status? Are you a

CONFORMIST . . . who's sick of conforming? Then this book is for you!" ran the jacket copy of *Mad* magazine's cartoon parody, *The Organization Mad* (1956). The psychoanalytic and sociological tone that was taking over everyday conversation (psychology was the most popular college major of the 1950s) apparently became so insistent that even the practice of talking about conformism became the object of caustic satire—as in Richard Yates's powerfully depressing novel *Revolutionary Road* (1961), where gutless suburban office workers routinely get together for boozy dinner parties in which their conversation invariably revolves around "the elusive but endlessly absorbing subject of Conformity, or The Suburbs, or Madison Avenue, or American Society Today."[19] Titles like *The Man in the Gray Flannel Suit* had also exploited the new market for books about conformity. Its author, Sloan Wilson, was a relative unknown when his book was published; however, his story about a PR man who joins a major broadcasting corporation and resists the pressures to conform was immediately identified by its editors as capturing the spirit of the age—or at least it could be *marketed* that way. An entire apparatus sprang up around the book in order to suggest that it was *the* book about corporate conformity. Movie rights were sold in advance of the book's publication; the silhouette of the suited businessman on the cover was taken from a photograph of Gregory Peck, who would play the character in the (extremely tedious) film.

It was true, of course, that the world of business had tended toward gigantism, dwarfing the individual worker much as the skyscraper loomed over the average pedestrian. "Our home office has 31,259 employees," C. C. Baxter (Jack Lemmon) says at the opening of Billy Wilder's satirical masterpiece *The Apartment* (1960), describing his work at the giant Consolidated Life Insurance company; a bell rings at the end of each workday, staggered by floor, so all the thousands don't try to jam the elevators at once. With companies this size, the old remnants of middle-class entrepreneurship were being extinguished. By the 1950s, small firms existed—millions of them—but they operated in the shadow of larger firms that they depended on; these firms had consolidated monopoly or oligopoly power over entire industries. Already by the 1920s, as the business historian Richard Edwards has written, "consolidation had taken place in industries producing goods such as dairy products, grain mill products, meat, bakery products, refined sugar, tobacco, soaps and toilet articles, chemicals, petroleum, tires and rubber, shoes, shoe machinery, steel, aluminum, copper, fabricated metal, electrical products, household appliances, communications equipment, motor vehicles, railroad equipment, photographic equipment, telephones, and gas and electricity, and services such as life insurance and commercial banking."[20] Firm sizes had grown as well; their financial bases grew accordingly. In 1919, there were five or six firms with over $1 billion in assets; by 1969, there were nearly one hundred.[21] These same firms diversified, with merger after merger leading companies to take on business activities that had hitherto been completely separate from their core business. Larger firms gained access to political power in a way they never had before, affecting regulatory policy as well as securing lucrative government contracts.

Overall, though economic growth had slowed by the end of the 1950s, leading to a substantial increase in private direct investment overseas by American multinationals (at a faster pace, too, than domestic investment), the United States remained largely protected from foreign competition, and, therefore, safe.[22] From the inside of the corporate world, office workers expressed this as a kind of unholy postwar calm—the feeling of having walked away from a train wreck that injured everyone else, not only unscathed, but healthier, happier, and stronger. "There arrives a day when the corporate sanctuary becomes our whole world," wrote Alan Harrington in his memoir of being a PR man in a major corporation, *Life in the Crystal Palace* (1958). "We can't imagine existing outside of it. From our safe place we watch others struggling amid uncertain currents, and thank our stars and the lucky winds that brought us here." From the outside, the brilliant Austrian émigré economist Joseph Schumpeter verified the paradox of safety/sapping of human vim and heroic entrepreneurship. In his masterpiece of political economy, *Capitalism, Socialism, and Democracy* (published in multiple editions from 1942 to 1950), he argued that, with the rise of monopolistic practices in industry and the consequent vanishing of investment opportunity, managerial bureaucracy was starting to replace the entrepreneur, the economy was drifting toward central planning, and bourgeois life was becoming unheroic, tedious. "The bourgeoisie . . . needs a master," he wrote in scorn.[23] They needed entrepreneurs questing like medieval knights after invention; otherwise they would choke themselves in bureaucracy—leading to inevitable socialism. Harrington tacitly agreed. "Every so often I hear my seniors at the corporation inveigh against socialism, and it seems strange," he wrote. "I think that our company resembles nothing so much as a private socialist system. We are taken care of from our children's cradles to our own graves."

What they meant by "bureaucracy" was chiefly the size and hierarchy of administration—what one conservative theorist, James Burnham (in his book *The Managerial Revolution*), interpreted as a budding bureaucratic takeover of the United States. The hugeness of the corporations had derived in no small part from the growth in the number of office workers. Manufacturing and farm employment actually declined relative to the growth of white-collar workers: a consequence of consumers (many of them white-collar workers already) demanding more in the way of services (entertainment, education, travel) than commodities.[24] More services meant more kinds of white-collar employment. Sales teams of independent agents came to be employed by the firms themselves. The incorporated sales teams needed administrative staff. Employees became directly involved in advertising; the popularity of "psychological" approaches to selling products and services required marketing and public relations—the quintessential mid-century jobs (precisely why Wilson made the protagonist of *The Man in the Gray Flannel Suit* a PR man)—which in turn became professionalized. In order to measure white-collar productivity, companies imposed cost accounting, financial reporting, budgeting, and controls for inventory, which in turn required more staff. The ratio of non-production staff to production staff began to become more balanced (or, depending on your perspective, grew completely out of whack); in 1960, white-collar workers were a full third of the total workforce.[25] Being middle-class in America used to mean starting your own business; by 1950, it meant, almost invariably, that you put on a suit and tie and went to work in an office, alongside millions like you.

Sometimes the modular, repetitive surfaces of the glass curtain wall really did symbolize an even deeper sameness within. The technology company International Business Machines, or IBM, was among the biggest of the big corporations (Big Blue, they called it), and it made no bones about the importance it put on loyalty to the organization. In its Eero Saarinen–designed flat glass-box complexes out in Minnesota and upstate New York, it developed a thoroughgoing culture of corporate uniformity that rivaled any college fraternity, with employees asked to learn songs and slogans . . . about IBM. In every room hovered an image of the CEO, Thomas J. Watson Sr., sitting behind a shiny wooden table, arms folded, his gray facial features expressionless; above the built-in bookcase behind him was a sign with the company slogan in capital letters: "THINK."[26] Watson insisted on a uniform dress code of dark gray suits, black ties, and white shirts with extremely stiff, starched collars. The uneasiness of a computer company having slotted its employees into a uniform corporate dress, like so many lines of indistinguishable code, was lost on nobody—including the company. In a publicity booklet from 1955, IBM reminded its customers, "[We] first came into your life when your birth was recorded on a punched card. From then on many such cards have been compiled, giving a lifetime of history of your important decisions and actions. If you went to school, entered a hospital, bought a house, paid income tax, got married or purchased an automobile, the chances are that permanent punched records were made of these and other personal stories."[27] Just as it had no problem fitting its employees into the same uniform and commanding them to think, it had no compunction about telling everyone in the world that all their significant life milestones, including their births, could be reduced to hole punches on a card.

IBM was frightening to people outside their offices as well. Its machines symbolized the ruthless automation of everything, which in turn meant tossing people out of work. Automation in the workplace—blue- or white-collar—became the subject of congressional hearings, as well as a stream of business press writings.[28] Giant computers, such as Remington Rand's UNIVAC (Universal Automatic Computer), began to be deployed in offices to process the increasingly gargantuan amounts of paperwork, such as payroll, cost accounting, and insurance billing. The mainstream press regularly ran stories with headlines like "Office Robots" and "Will Machines Replace the Human Brain?," scaring enough people into imagining an all-robot future.[29]

The response of the computer companies was to conduct an enormous public relations campaign, assuring office workers that their jobs would not be obviated—on the contrary, automation would make their lives brighter and would take the drudgery out of labor. UNIVAC appeared on the news with Walter Cronkite in 1952, successfully predicting the election that brought Eisenhower to the presidency. In 1955, an IBM 701 appeared on the *Today* show to solve a math problem. The star designers Charles and Ray Eames were hired to make an animated film, *The Information Machine: Creative Man and the Data Processor* (1957), which would show the importance of machines for a cleaner, brighter human future. The film depicted the progress of technology from the wheel onward, and it showed the results of that progress: an older, urban, industrial environment filled with smokestacks and crisscrossed with electrical and telephone wires. But hope remained: "Something has now emerged that might make even our most elegant theories workable. The recent acceleration has been fantastic. The electronic calculator has already become a tool upon which much of our daily activities depend."[30] The film segues to an office floor patterned with squares and neatly filled out with gleaming computers. A man in shirt and tie, a creative white-collar worker, labors at his desk (with "THINK" just over it) to make the data that he can feed into the machine. The message is clear enough: Life after computers will be clearer, healthier, and offer more opportunities for better work. Individuals will at last be able to realize themselves.

□

The corporate world described by the mid-century critics—indeed, the world that many office workers felt themselves belonging to—was one characterized by robust affluence as well as pervasive fear, by a sense of individual autonomy that was nonetheless not *too* free. This was the culmination of continuous growth in private bureaucracy, which had resulted, they felt, in a new social type, an inner change in the American character. Self-contradictory or paradoxical phrases proliferated in order to describe this situation. There was the "illusory freedom" that *BusinessWeek* applied to the research environs of Bell Labs; C. Wright Mills, typically more caustic, would call the white-collar class a group of "cheerful robots." David Riesman and his junior research collaborators on *The Lonely Crowd* concluded from their interviews that the typical new middle-class man was an "antagonistic cooperator." Desiring the approval of others, he nonetheless feels himself to be constantly in competition with others. His job entails both the emulation and the manipulation of other people. He begins to work even longer hours and breaks up the time by socializing—itself a kind of work—and on blowing tons of money on his expense account as a kind of "occupational therapy." The office, in turn, becomes a scene of constant "glad-handing":

> The shortening of hours has had much greater effect on the life of the working class than on that of the middle class: the executive and professional continues [*sic*] to put in long hours, employing America's giant productivity less to leave for home early than to extend his lunch hours, coffee breaks, conventions, and other forms of combining business with pleasure. Likewise, much time in the office itself is also spent in sociability: exchanging office gossip ("conferences"), making good-will tours ("inspection"), talking to salesmen and joshing secretaries ("morale").[31]

For Riesman, the newly sociable office—far from the disciplined and heavily watched ideal of the Taylorists—carried the manager and the executive far from domestic life; work took on the psychic pleasures of home, and sociability itself became an essential ingredient in work. The obverse of this was the new internal "radar" that one carried—the constant, wearying attentiveness to the needs and judgments of others. The American novelist Joseph Heller masterfully exploited the paranoid potential of this setup in *Something*

Happened (1974). The novel's manager narrator Bob Slocum is a socially affable but privately high-strung middle manager, popular among the various secretaries in the insurance office where he works, whom he sleeps with on occasion. But he lives in a constant state of low-level tension, mild despair, and fear. "I get the willies when I see closed doors," the novel begins. It's a feeling he associates with a primal scene in childhood, when he stumbles upon his older brother having sex behind a closed door. But it applies equally to the world of the mid-century corporate office, with its casual blend of tedious, bland paperwork and unexploded emotional mines lying between and around people one sees more than one sees one's own family. Rather than the site of great passions and vehement emotions, office sociability offers, at best, a low-level dread:

> In the office in which I work there are five people of whom I am afraid. Each of these five people is afraid of four people (excluding overlaps), for a total of twenty, and each of these twenty people is afraid of six people, making a total of one hundred and twenty people who are feared by at least one person. Each of these one hundred and twenty people is afraid of the other one hundred and nineteen, and all of these one hundred and forty-five people are afraid of the twelve men at the top who helped found and build the company and now own and direct it.[32]

In describing his own private fears, Slocum was also describing the nature of private bureaucracy: its self-protecting, easily wounded nature, the need for higher-ups ceaselessly to be flattered by their lower-downs. For the critics who wanted more "individualism," this was stifling to business itself. The team structure of business, Harrington wrote, "requires that we *not* do our best because it would make the boss look bad. In other words, the inefficient boss's security is more important than getting the job done."[33]

Fear in another sense—the unwillingness to take risks—pervades the signature classic of the era, William H. Whyte's *Organization Man*. Whyte—a reporter for *Fortune* magazine, extraordinarily enough—saw conformity, an "idolatry of the system," produced in every sector of society. An entire system had locked into place to foster the new social demand to *participate*, no matter what the cost; the "inner-directed" ethos that Riesman insisted still lingered in the American consciousness was, for Whyte, all but extinguished. Whyte's primary target was middle management, where two generations of theorists about the office, from Taylor to Mayo, had placed their hopes. Whyte, by contrast, singled the middle managers out for a scathing condemnation. In his view, America had once been the natural home of the "Protestant work ethic," the ethos of individual striving that had fueled the growth of capitalism. But gradually, as more and more workers became employees and filled the ranks of the ever more capacious middle of corporations, the Protestant ethic was turning into a "social ethic." For the middle manager of a corporation, the individual was no longer a hero; society was.

Whyte's argument was crude, far cruder than any tossed-off aperçu of *The Lonely Crowd*, but it was effective. And much of his research was strong. To understand the beginnings of the process of turning free men into organization men, Whyte spent time talking to college seniors. He discovered that universities were now neglecting humanities educations for engineering and business education, under pressure to compete with the science-heavy Soviet Union.[34] Years of financial hardship had made new students—members of what would later be called "the silent generation"—shy away from risk, and they made depressing statements about economic depression. "I don't think AT&T is very exciting," he quoted one senior as saying, "but that's the company I'd like to join. If a depression comes there will always be an AT&T."[35] Big corporations, which to people like Whyte once seemed enormous and impersonal, now offered the womb-like safety and security that colleges provided. On-campus recruiting campaigns, then a novelty, promised prospective employees a world of adventure in the rolling landscape of American business: "A MAN CAN GROW AND KEEP ON GROWING WITH OWEN-ILLINOIS GLASS CO." "VITRO OFFERS YOUR GRADUATES THE ENGINEERS OF TOMORROW!" "THE SKY IS OUR WORLD." "THE SKY IS THE LIMIT!"[36] A smooth pipeline from the dorm room to the desk made organization life irresistible. And though production jobs were available to them, only 12 percent of the seniors he studied went into factory work; the majority preferred to be in an office, on staff.[37] The average college senior, Whyte concluded, "does not want to rebel against the status quo because he really likes it." "Whatever their many differences, in one great respect they are all of a piece: more than any generation in memory, theirs will be a generation of bureaucrats."[38]

Whyte had long been businessmen's favorite critic. They let him into their offices because he worked for a reputable magazine, and he proceeded to excoriate them on their practices. Skilled at invective and sarcasm, and gifted with an unerring bullshit detector, Whyte lambasted the rise of business-speak—for which he coined the term "businessese." He noted two general trends: one was the massive increase in jargon; the other was seemingly counter to it, the penchant for plain talk. The jargon he found is familiar even today: "please be advised," "in reference to yours of . . . ," "we wish to draw attention," "to acknowledge your letter," "in the process of," "at this time," "under consideration," "in the not-too-distant future," "company policy." Stenographers were even taught shorthand for these phrases.

But the other trend, one equally and balefully with us today, was what Whyte called a kind of *"reverse* gobbledygook." Rather than long-winded empty phrases, this "shirtsleeve" English was full of gruff exclamations and terseness. There were never people, only "folks." You never endured anything; you only "took it on the chin." The employees were always your "greatest asset." All businessmen were "forward-looking." And they were all quarterbacks, leading the team. For when there was a football metaphor in sight, it was pretty much a crime for a businessman not to take it. Why say, "Employees and management should work together," when you could say something much more pungent? Here is a real example: "The team can't put the ball across for a first down just by wishing it. The guards and the tackles can't do their job if the quarterback doesn't let them in on the play. And we, the quarterbacks, are muffing the ball."[39]

The amazing thing about shirtsleeve English was that it could be traced to a single source: *The Art of Plain Talk,* by Rudolph Flesch, a linguist who had turned his PhD thesis at Columbia into a best seller. "Do not use rhythm"; "do not use periodic sentences"; "do not use rhetorical questions"; "do not use irony (half the people won't get it)": these were the choice words of advice that Flesch spiraled at his receivers downfield. Even Churchill's blood, sweat, and tears speech was singled out for censure. "The reader gets a vague notion," Flesch writes confidently, "that Churchill used a little word picture of three wet things instead of saying *war*; and that's that." Almost overnight, businessese found a partner in the clenched terseness of tough-sounding, manly business-speak.[40]

American conformity and conformist business-speak didn't come out of nowhere; internal pressure within business wasn't sufficient. As with the rise of public relations, the fastidious attention to language came out of the corporations' profound need to justify themselves to what they saw as a potentially hostile public. Business in the 1940s and 1950s was gripped in the (almost totally unfounded) fear that Americans might be rejecting the capitalist system. The National Association of Manufacturers (NAM), a lobby group that, alongside the Chamber of Commerce, sought to promote the political interests of business, saw free enterprise as imperiled by government planning, on the one hand, and agitating labor unions, on the other. It launched a campaign to win. "Today's challenge, today's dire necessity," NAM's president, Claude A. Putnam, said in 1950, "is to sell—to resell, if you will—to free Americans the philosophy that has kept us and our economy free."[41] The Advertising Council produced eight thousand posters and three million radio spots testifying to the importance of free enterprise. NAM distributed a comic book to hundreds of thousands of workers that showed how the American Revolution had been sparked by "government planners" in London, seeking to take away our freedoms.[42] "It is an unfortunate fact," one Chicago businessman said at a dinner as part of the campaign, "that the majority of the American people are ready to destroy business for state socialism."[43] All of Whyte's reporting suggested that this wasn't quite the case. But business persisted in attempting to refine its communications apparatus, transforming the language itself in the process.

□

Not content to mangle its workers' language, the corporate office set out to mold their personalities as well. This strategy surfaced in the postwar mania for personality testing. Possibly because their leader Taylor had been so maniacal, the scientific managers of a previous generation had been little interested in their workers as human beings: their brute interest lay in testing aptitude, to make sure that organizations were efficient and got things done. Rather, it was the human relations school of Mayo that wanted a warm and friendly workplace, with personalities to match. But if human relations was the spirit presiding over the tests, the source of their actual content was distinctly more sinister. Applied psychologists for years had been working in asylums and prisons, developing tests to understand the roots of madness and abnormality, and "in the course of this work," says Whyte, "they had developed some ingenious pen and pencil tests." It took no leap of the imagination to think of applying these tests to otherwise "normal" individuals. Though they had originally been designed to measure abnormality, it was of course only possible to figure out what was abnormal by having first determined what was normal. Soon these tests became widespread measures for corporations to figure out whether their prospect would be a willing organization man: Was he radical or conservative? Did he have good practical and social judgment? Would he persevere or fold under pressure? Was he stable or unstable? Was he happy or unhappy? Was he a reforming type or a status quo man? Did he have a sense of humor or not? Refusing to answer the questions was itself revealing, for the tests made provisions for understanding what the answers, or lack of them, had suppressed.[44]

In theory, the testing regime might have helped to slot congenial types into proper departments and work groups. In practice, it made corporate culture more uniform across the board. By steadily eradicating abnormalities, the tests enforced loyalty. Besides tending to select participants who were more conservative, cautious, and modestly "other-directed," testing produced its own Hawthorne effect: just the fact of being tested meant that you were more likely to reshape your personality according to some perceived company doctrine. Answering the test questions became a game in guessing what the company wanted. If "Have you enjoyed reading books as much as having company in?" and "Do you sometimes feel self-conscious?" elicited positive answers, that might tell you something about an employee's degree of introversion, which was usually a bad thing. But trying to fake being extroverted might lead to the charge of excessive sociability, a sign of an unreflective and unthinking personality, just as bad as excessive inwardness. But were you supposed to agree with "It is worse for a woman to have extramarital relations than a man"? Answering yes might indicate a strong, manly conservatism and put you in good standing with the executive boys. But too many affirmative answers to things like "Modern art should not be allowed in churches," and you might start to seem like a John Birch Society loon. All in all, people who did best on the questions tended to be middle-of-the-road or good at making themselves seem that way—perfect for the enforced gregariousness of the mid-century corporate office.

The testing regime was so exciting to the new "human relations" corporation that it became a staple of American corporate life after the war. In 1952, one-third of U.S. corporations used testing. In 1954—just two years later—it was over 60 percent, including signature firms such as Sears, General Electric, and Westinghouse.[45] Pseudoscientific research and consultancy firms sprang up by the hundreds, competing with each other to gain coveted testing contracts at corporation personnel departments. These tests were mostly used for screening job applicants. But occasionally tests would be used internally on people already in the company workforce. Sometimes this was deliberately to conduct layoffs, when business was slow. Other times this was to make it easier to get rid of managers who were now over the hill, their wits blunted by age—which a test could easily be designed to confirm. In the eyes of the corporation, office workers were converging with their tests, the tests with their people. Since companies were already using IBM punch cards to tabulate every other important statistic, Whyte suggested, it was only a matter of time before test scores were punched in too, making the card as complete a picture of a life as any man could want.

Testing registered widely in popular culture as one of the more potent symbols of office conformity. In *The Man in the Gray Flannel Suit*, the suburban protagonist Tom Rath gets an unusual test for a PR job at the fictional United Broadcasting Corporation. Walker, the personnel man, asks Rath to take an hour to write up his autobiography. It's a test that he's administered to the twenty or thirty other applicants for the job. The one requirement of the genre is that Rath has to finish by completing the sentence "The most significant fact about me is . . ." "You'd be surprised how revealing the results are," Walker says. Rath sits and agonizes, stifled by the question. The one thing he can't talk about is the one that comes insistently to his mind, a fact as powerful as any. It's "seventeen men": the tally of men he killed in the war. One of them was his best friend, who died walking inadvertently into one of Rath's errant grenades. Rath knows it would be "melodramatic" to say something so baldly on the test, yet every other note he tries to strike, from plainly cynical to cheaply humorous, rings false. Finally, fed up with the whole purpose of the exam, he writes down the bare biographical facts of his life: his birth date; his educational history; his marital status and dependents—indeed, everything that might be contained on a company's IBM punch card. "From the point of view of the United Broadcasting Corporation," he concludes, "the most significant fact about me is that I am applying for a position in its public-relations department, and after an initial period of learning, I probably would do a good job. I will be glad to answer any questions which seem relevant, but after considerable thought, I have decided that I do not wish to attempt an autobiography as part of an application for a job."[46]

If *The Man in the Gray Flannel Suit* were the scathing indictment of a conformist society that it has been held to be since its publication, Rath might not be rewarded for such willful insubordination. But in the world of the novel, he does, in fact, get the job. And every act of nonconformism thereafter only pushes him higher up the ladder. When he is asked to evaluate a speech written by his boss—Hopkins, the chief executive of the United Broadcasting Corporation—Rath considers not saying what he really thinks: that the speech is terrible. Instead, goaded on by his wife, Rath ditches the last shred of his yes-man garb and, gingerly, speaks the truth. Though he is initially stunned by Rath's uncommon forthrightness, Hopkins quickly recognizes its value. He promotes Rath to his personal assistant and tries to mold him after his own image—that of an imperious executive whose entire life is devoted to work. Yet Rath resists again. He sees the danger—to his health, home, and family—of committing himself fully to his job. His boss, jealous and admiring of Rath's sheer lack of ambition, gives him a lower, easier middle-management position that pays pretty well. Fortuitously, Rath's suburban life works out too: he gets permission from the local town council to parcel out his grandmother's enormous estate, which he had inherited at the beginning of the book, so he can sell the additional lots and make more money. The novel concludes with Rath held up as a hero by the society that allows him to pursue all of his small-bore needs, a model corporate citizen.

Rather than criticizing the office world for its repressive conformity, then, Sloan Wilson appears to be admiring its capacity to respond to simple truth telling. *If only the men in the gray flannel suits would occasionally show a little nerve—and stick to the absolute middle of the road!* is its tepid message. Not exactly the sort of stuff to get an office worker's blood boiling. Though *The Organization Man* and Wilson's novel were often mentioned in the same breath, Whyte scorned *The Man in the Gray Flannel Suit*. For him, it was a novel that wanted to "have it both ways,"[47] suggesting that men could retain their moral center and still make it in the go-go marketplace of the 1950s. Rampant materialism and spiritual life could be unified in a "self-ennobling hedonism"—another one of those phrases, like "antagonistic cooperation," that seemed to nail the conflicted world of the mid-century office worker.[48] Lest anyone doubt the novel's conservatism, Wilson opens and concludes his book with fulsome panegyrics to his wife's fastidious attention to all the household details while he was busy writing. In addition to keeping the children away, she "managed all the household finances, repaired the children's bicycles, made excuses about why I didn't have any social engagements," and, proper to the feminine mystique of being seen and not heard, "was cheerful and ornamental."[49]

Still, a current of unease courses through Wilson's otherwise cheerful encomium to the corporate workplace. It comes from Rath's memories of the war, which—in the book and the film as well—are triggered by passing details: a man's bald head, a scar on someone's neck. In these long, discursive accounts of grim battles, and a brief but intense love affair with an Italian maid, Rath—otherwise laconic to the point of straining credulity—exhibits some semblance of an inner life. It is one that his daily existence forces him to repress—much as the interview test was no place to recount the single most important memory he had. All the talk of conformity wasn't necessarily wrong, but its emphasis was misplaced. The monumental conflicts of the early twentieth century, in which so many office workers' lives had been defined, somehow disappeared in the quiet hum of the desperately unheroic office environment. "Each alley between desks quivers with secret romance as ceaselessly as a battle-trench": Sinclair Lewis's satire, written during a previous war, seemed to be echoed in the more melancholy postwar passages describing white-collar experience.

In *Life in the Crystal Palace*, Alan Harrington, a PR man like the fictional Rath, describes a corporate munificence as bounteous as it is stifling, at once coddling and completely inadequate to real, deep, unspeakable human needs. When one of the workers in his office, "tall, blonde . . . one of those nervous, efficient unmarried girls in a man's world," at last takes a three-week vacation in Spain, she returns and tells stories of adventure, some of them implicitly sexual, that startle her office compatriots. "The stories this lonely and excited girl told about her vacation were the kind that evoke a humorous response at the Crystal Palace," he writes. "One of our girls somehow ought not to have such marvelous experiences." Yet, Harrington goes on,

> many of us have been rovers and known the edges of life. Ralph Butler, for instance, was an engineer for five years in Turkey and had a mountain girl for a mistress. Arthur Moore led guerrilla troops in the Burmese jungle. On the bridge of a cruiser at Okinawa, Carleton Bell says, "I roared with terror" when a kamikaze leveled out a few inches above his head. Carl Jensen stunted and wire-walked at air shows in the early days. George O'Brien was a cub reporter dancing with excitement at Le Bourget when Lindbergh landed. And in his senior year Robert Cloud actually won the big game with a sixty-yard run.

"Today," Harrington concludes, ruefully, "you see such formerly robust individuals, now mild of mien, poking along our corridors in groups and committees with administrative papers in their hands. They have lost something . . . verve . . . appetite."[50]

Yet the perquisites of the Crystal Palace are anything but drab, and its denizens are as well treated as any human beings have been in the history of the planet. Their job security is mostly assured; their pension plans generous; their work lives as slow and easy as they want them to be. "We are not worried about our jobs, about the future, about . . . much of anything," Harrington writes. "This is a curious sensation, not to have any real worries." He calls it a "private corporate welfare state," European-style social democracy for office workers, a bastion against the brutalities of the American free-enterprise system that, in Harrington's view, made the country great. Its success permits the members of the newly great American corporations to snooze through days that all seem to blend into one another. In a typical day, the company bus takes them from the commuter rail station to the Palace. Light music—provided by the Muzak corporation—starts up, going off and on every fifteen minutes. "It is said that this music increases office productivity by a sizable percentage," Harrington says, "but I find that if I listen to it at all it puts me in a revery. It makes me feel as if I were in a cocktail lounge." The entire scene conveys unbelievable comfort and a drowsy atmosphere of pleasant boredom, like the episode of the Lotus-Eaters in Homer's *Odyssey*:

> Our employees . . . have a view unequaled by any offered to a group of employees since time began. Rolling hills go on to the horizon; they will burst into flower next week, and when autumn comes they will flare red and gold, and winter will put snow on them like frosting. Our landscaped grounds, too, will flower. We can smell honeysuckle; our lawns are so green that they hurt your eyes. Meadows extend to the hills and beyond like a perpetually green future.[51]

This almost frighteningly blissful portrait of a work environment already suggests all the leitmotifs of all the corporate critiques that proliferated in the 1950s and 1960s. The zoned-out cool of the mid-century corporation, Harrington argued, depended on divesting its workers of any opportunity for initiative or creativity. It was a critique from inside the office world that cohered with the journalistic and sociological accounts from without. But the moral had become too simple: the office had squelched entrepreneurship, and the meritocracy wasn't set up to encourage it; in its place lay bureaucracy. Riesman and his ilk were after something much greater: a critique of the American character itself, and the class politics of the country, as revealed in and outside the workplace. But in the shallow reception of their writings, the parable had turned into one about encouraging more entrepreneurs and cutting down on bureaucracy—an elision that would come to have enormous ramifications.

□

So, the office was destroying the frontier-exploring spirit in man; it was forcing excessive sociability and inane attentiveness to others; it was digging into his very soul, uprooting his native genius, trimming its wildness to fit the willful impulses of the organization. The solution that the situation begged for was as overdetermined as the original premises of the critique had been. For what Whyte and Riesman and the others seemed to imply—or sometimes say more explicitly—was that the old sources of *manhood* were being crushed in the office. When they spoke about individuality, they did so purely in the terms of one sex. Which isn't to say that women were irrelevant to their picture. As Riesman wrote, "Depleting the expense account can serve as an almost limitless occupational therapy for men who, out of a tradition of hard work, a dislike of their wives, a lingering asceticism, and an anxiety about their antagonistic cooperators, still feel that they must put in a good day's work at the office."[52] There's a poisonous mushroom lurking amid the sociological weeds: *dislike of their wives?*

The corporation had usually displayed a certain interest in the family lives of its male employees. When CEOs like Thomas Watson Sr. referred to the "IBM Family," it was meant to suggest, warmly, that IBM hired not only an engineer but his wife and children as well.[53] But the phrase was not so facetious: wives—particularly executive wives—found themselves performing a multitude of tasks for their husbands employed in corporations. And the corporations knew it. They frequently screened the wives of potential employees, either by strongly suggesting that a wife attend an interview with her husband or by arranging an informal breakfast or dinner with the prospect and his wife. According to a study by *Fortune* in 1951, half of all companies screened prospective employees' wives; one company estimated that 20 percent of candidates were turned down because of their wives.[54] Corporate control extended in mid-century America well beyond the office; it reached deep into the family as well. Or—perhaps more precisely—the office worked to incorporate the family, and the family began to bear the imprint of the office. "We control a man's environment in business and we lose it entirely when he crosses the threshold of his home," one executive told Whyte. "Management, therefore, has a challenge and an obligation to deliberately plan and create a favorable, constructive attitude on the part of the wife that will liberate her husband's total energies for the job."[55]

Who was the Mrs. Executive that the companies were looking for? In Whyte's summary of his interview findings, "she is a wife who is: (1) highly adaptable, (2) highly gregarious, (3) realizes her husband belongs to the corporation."[56] But the implication of item number three also meant that the wife inevitably belonged to the corporation as well (she was not supposed to be working). In the management theorist Rosabeth Moss Kanter's study of a major corporation in the 1970s, which she called "Indsco," she found wives who similarly felt that their entire private lives were structured around the corporation:

> Until two years ago, when I thought about going back to school, I was an Indsco wife, married to the company as much as to Fred. No one ever demanded anything of me *per se* except going out to dinner with so-and-so. But in my own being, I was very dependent on Fred's experiences in Indsco. It chose the area we lived in. Our friends, except for a few neighbors,

were Indsco friends, made *because* of the company. I always felt that our goal was to settle down, to set down roots when the kids were in junior high school. Now they are, and the company tells us to move, so we move, pushing that goal further ahead . . . If Fred was doing well, I felt *I* was doing well. I'm the woman behind the man, I could take some pride in his achievements.[57]

On the one hand they had to act as a "stabilizing" influence at home. "A man gets so frustrated at the office," one interviewee reported. "It's such a rat race—he should be able to come home to calmness."[58] On the other hand they had to attend corporate events—dinners, parties, conferences, golf tournaments—and incessantly pluck the grace note that might enhance their husbands' reputations. And because of the various assumptions about proper women's behavior, there were often greater expectations placed on corporate wives than on the men themselves. A charming wife could save an unpopular husband's career. Deciding to have that fourth martini and making mildly off-color comments could just as easily end it.

As a man climbed the corporate ladder, his wife faced tough choices. For the deeper her husband got into the institution, the more entangled she became in her role as institutional helpmate. It wasn't just that social choices were determined by living in or around the company: as a corporate wife, one made friends for strategic reasons, to help one's husband *in* the company. Sentimental choices became corporate choices: office politics pervaded everything. "You have got to leave behind your old friends," the wife of an upwardly mobile plant manager reported. "You have to weigh the people you invite to parties. You have to be careful of who you send Christmas cards to and who you don't. It sounds like snobbery, but it's just something you have to do. You have to be a boss's wife."[59] It was a form of employment that never made it into the statistics.

The powerfully restricted role of women in mid-century almost seemed to be a retrenchment from the "out to work" years that marked their entry into the office. Low-level clerical worker or corporate wife? Neither was an option that spoke of freedom, let alone power. In lieu of a major change in the way the workplace functioned, there was one thing left to do: play pranks. One of the most popular was a game called scuttle. A famous description of it from a former office worker (then working at a radio station) goes like this:

> The Scuttle rules were simple to get the hang of. All announcers and engineers who weren't busy at one particular time would select a secretary or file girl, chase her up and down the halls, through the music library and back to the announcing booths, catch her and take her panties off. Once the panties were off, the girl could put them back on again if she wished. Nothing wicked ever happened. De-pantying was the sole object of the game. While all this was going on, the girl herself usually shrieked, screamed, flailed, blushed, threatened and pretended to faint, but to my knowledge no scuttler was ever reported to the front office. As a matter of fact, the girls wore their prettiest panties to work.[60]

"Nothing wicked ever happened": the line is defensive, knowing that the description of the game can be read by some—perhaps many—as appalling. When the TV show *Mad Men* repeated the game, the show's writers couldn't help but tame it down: Ken Cosgrove chasing down the secretary Allison and merely finding out what color her panties were, without removing them. But the author of the anecdote, Helen Gurley Brown, had made it her business to counter the notion that an office was somehow a minefield for women. The girls wore their prettiest panties: they *wanted* to get scuttled. All the shrieking was a melodramatic act, a secret acknowledgment that everyone was in on it. Not dangerous, and certainly not as soporifically boring as the anti-conformity authors made it out to be, the office was in fact the most sexually exciting place on earth. "Based on my own observations and experiences in nineteen different offices," Brown wrote in her tremendous best seller *Sex and the Office* (1964), "I'm convinced that offices are sexier than Turkish harems, fraternity house weekends, Hollywood swimming parties, Cary Grant's smile or the *Playboy* center-fold, and more action takes place in them than in a nymphet's daydreams."[61] The system was there to be taken advantage of; you just had to *work* it.

Helen Gurley Brown in
the photo department of
Cosmopolitan. *Sophia Smith Collection,
Smith College*

Brown had become the most notorious writer in the country
in 1962, with *Sex and the Single Girl*, an advice book/memoir that
informed the prurient and the horrified alike that sex was pleasur-
able, and women not only could but should take as much of it as they
could get—especially before marriage, if they could help it. Readers rewarded her by buying her book in huge quantities. In three
weeks, it had sold two million copies. But her success wasn't just due
to her subject. Her style, in particular, was charming to many, and
largely inimitable, though it of course spawned thousands of imita-
tors (the creator of the show *Girls*, Lena Dunham, among them): at
once chatty, frank, debauched, and frothy, it seemed to millions to
be the voice of uncompromised female common sense—at last liberated from male strictures on propriety. Unlike *The Feminine Mystique*, which it preceded by a year, *Sex and the Single Girl* spoke to
women already ensconced in the workplace: working-class secretaries rather than middle-class housewives. And unlike Betty Friedan,
Brown didn't call for a repressive order to be overthrown. The existing order only offered opportunities to be conquered and pleasures
to be snatched, through strategies of small subversion. *Sex and the*

Office extended the franchise to speak directly about the workplace, in a way that scandalized conservatives and offended many liberals. Later, when Brown became editor of *Cosmopolitan*, she was seen as totally opposed to second-wave feminism; editors from *Ms.* once occupied her office. But she was as much a part of the movement as anyone—and her obsessive focus on the workplace distinguished her.

Brown's air of unshakable confidence, her assurance to all that the office was a sexual playfield as rich as a college dorm (but cleaner and with better-dressed inhabitants), belied a trying work life. She was born in rural Green Forest, Arkansas, in the Ozarks, the child of a schoolteacher and a housewife. Green Forest was a place she almost never acknowledged in later years, because it lacked the glamour of skyscraper cities like New York and Chicago, where her message pealed most clearly.[62] "I had no money, no college degree, I had wall-to-wall acne, and my family were hillbillies," she recalled in an interview in 1980.[63] She attended a business-secretarial school, working at a radio station after classes—the same radio station where others were scuttled, a favor Brown herself, supposedly, never enjoyed. "Sometimes I would look up hopefully from my type-writer to see three or four scuttlers skulking in the doorway mulling it over, but the decision was always the same—too young, too pale, too flat-chested . . . Clearly I was un-scuttleable."[64] Working in Los Angeles for a film studio, she began to accept the favors of an executive, whom she called M. in her autobiography. Eventually, she became his mistress. M. set her up in her own apartment, gave her money to furnish it, and asked that she simply behave as a classic mistress must: learn to switch naturally from work clothes to lingerie when he was coming over, ensure that he had drinks to accompany their assignations, and give him the latest gossip.[65] It was an arrangement she soon grew to hate: M. was a virulent anti-Semite who hated Brown's Jewish friends, and he insisted Brown stay home most nights on the chance that he could escape his wife.[66] Yet it was also an experience that, stripped of complexity and difficulty, she turned into a source of sassy advice in *Sex and the Office*, in which she advised her readers about how best to conduct an office affair with a married man. After the relationship, she continued to remain proudly and defiantly single for years, even during the doldrums of the 1950s, when marriage rates were high and average marriage ages hovered around the early twenties.[67]

When it came to writing about work-life satisfaction in the office, Brown was her own best example. (Her autobiography was called *Having It All.*) Though she got married in 1959, she had worked in all those offices, could tally quite a number of relationships and casual flings, and was successful *in* the working world—as an ad copywriter and a magazine writer—before she became wildly successful out of it. But Brown's unique solution to the problem of professional success versus marriage and home life was simply to deny the opposition—or perhaps to outline a third path. Women didn't have to get married, and being single in an office wasn't a liability. A thoroughgoing romantic life and climb up the business ladder (at least as far as one could go, as a woman) were complements rather than contradictions. All the hand-wringing of previous generations could simply be tossed out the skyscraper window. (If it *had* a window.) Though Brown strained to detail all the powerful obstacles that women had to navigate in the workplace, she believed she was preaching a philosophy of liberation. And her influence suggests that it was received that way by millions.

The office world that Brown spoke to was one seized by one of its now-habitual upsurges of fear over moral breakdown: women were always emasculating men, and men were constantly debauching women. The film *The Best of Everything* (1959), made from Rona Jaffe's best-selling novel of the same title, was supposed to expose the terrible choices that women faced in the callous, amoral corporate environment. "This is the story of the female jungle," the trailer voice-over intoned ominously, "of the girls who didn't marry at twenty, and of the men who wanted them—*but not as wives.*" Filmed in CinemaScope, *The Best of Everything* took full advantage of the large floor plates of the mid-century office and the wide gridded streets of Manhattan: it opens with shots of Park Avenue at dawn, with women pouring off buses and out of subway stations, wearing white gloves and skirts, filing en masse into mid-century skyscrapers; the enormous steno pool it depicted way up in the Seagram Building seemed to speak of possibility, opportunities. Holding an ad in her hands, Caroline Bender (Hope Lange) arrives at the Seagram plaza, fresh out of Radcliffe, bearing an ad for the Fabian Publishing Company:

> SECRETARIES. You deserve the Best of Everything!
> The Best Job—The Best Surroundings
> The Best Pay—The Best Contacts!!

As the film unfolds, it poses as an open question what the "best of everything" means: whether it's an adoring husband or a successful career. It was one of the few pieces of popular culture to suggest, plausibly, that a woman might be able to have both. It also seemed to imply that a woman might *need* both.

The portrait of office friendships, the casual intimacy between and among the women in the office, is careful and loving: in the early morning hours, a loud, chattering chorus of typists comes in, pulling off the typewriter covers, putting on last-minute makeup, adjusting their girdles. There's an easy solidarity at work. People

Caroline Bender (Hope Lange) and April Morrison (Diane Baker) in the steno pool in *The Best of Everything* (1959). *Photofest*

talk about boyfriends saving checks for a wedding ring. And they exchange tips about work. When Caroline gets her first lunch hour, the head of the typing pool, Mary Agnes (Sue Carson), advises her to take a long lunch. Her boss, Amanda Farrow (Joan Crawford), "doesn't get back till 3:30."

CAROLINE: She doesn't?
MARY AGNES: Of course not, she's an executive.
CAROLINE: How does she get any work done?
MARY AGNES: Executives don't do any work. The higher up you go, the less work you do.

But the friendships only conceal deeper divisions in the office: between generations and between classes of people. The head of Fabian, Fred Shalimar (Brian Aherne), occupies the corner office; he's a lizard from an earlier generation, with irrepressible frisky hands, an alcoholic glaze to his bright blue eyes, and an affected British-sounding accent that thickly coats his constant enunciation of the name of his old friend Eugene O'Neill—an acquaintance he brings up to gull (unsuccessfully) the younger female staff members into "having a little fun." His counterpart is the editor, played by a steely Joan Crawford, her eyebrows darkened and sharply arched into condor wings. She is demanding and inhuman, and her every jagged word bears the scars of an unspoken history of struggling to rise to the position of editor in a hostile environment. Caroline's friend at the company, the heavy-drinking Irish American editor Mike Rice (Stephen Boyd), warns her against her own ambitions: rising to the position of editor will make her "a ruthless, driving, calculating woman," like Farrow.

But Caroline's destiny is different. She has the aura of being one of the elect. Unlike the girls in the steno pool, who went to business college, she went to Radcliffe. Her friends either are seeking jobs elsewhere or come from provincial backgrounds; they don't understand the city or the men who prey on them. Caroline instinctually takes work home with her; when her long-distance boyfriend ends up leaving her for another woman, she commits herself to a career wholeheartedly. She ducks the "organization woman" impulse simply to play along, and she recommends manuscripts that Farrow rejects. Before long, she gets promoted—first to a reader and then to editor. "Why do you want this job?" Farrow asks her. "Because this is what I went to college for," she replies, "this is what I worked for. It means everything to me." Farrow herself attempts to restart her romantic life—to no avail. For her generation, the film implies, it is too late. But by the end of the film, Caroline not only has a successful career but ends up attached to Mike Rice, the man from her office. The powerful intimation is not just that work and romantic life can coexist; it's that they can only coexist when your romantic life is at your office—which is what it means to have the "best of everything."

A bleaker spin on the argument lies in *The Apartment* (1960), a Hollywood film whose depth of feeling and dark portrait of the workplace might make it the best office film of all time. It put paid to all the common nonsense over middle-class respectability in the office while seeming to push further the general idea that offices were full of repressed single women and amoral married men. C. C. Baxter (Jack Lemmon), a bachelor and clerk at desk number 861, sits at the very center of an exaggeratedly large accounting pool in his insurance company. The establishing shot that locates him is a classic of the office film—from the opening scene of *The Crowd*, with its sea of desks, all the way to *Office Space*, with its sea of cubicles. Charming in his lack of confidence and congenitally hapless with women, Baxter serves as a kind of john for his bosses, arranging to have his apartment available for after-work dates between his married superiors and the women in the steno pool and switchboard room. The general conceit turns out to be a joke about the office meritocracy: while Baxter does nothing special in his actual job to move up the ladder, his efforts on behalf of his bosses' sex lives quickly move him up to the highest rungs. People use office language ("You're executive material!") to describe actions that have nothing to do with work. "I put in a good word for you with Sheldrake [the company president]," one of the middle managers and one of the apartment regulars, Al Kirkeby (David Lewis), says to

Baxter. "We're always on the lookout for young executives. You're on the way up, buddy boy!" When Baxter gets his first promotion, the man at the neighboring desk cries, "Say, what's the deal, Baxter, are you getting promoted, or fired? . . . I've been here twice as long as you have!" Seniority means nothing; merit—with all its dubious sources—is everything. Meanwhile, the working-class elevator girl Baxter has a crush on, Fran Kubelik (Shirley MacLaine), moves physically up and down the building all day and is having an affair with the president of the company, Sheldrake, but can't get anywhere, job-wise.

The Apartment imagines the office as oozing with sex, but more like a grotesque fraternity than the harem of *Sex and the Office*, with men ogling the new girls and routinely pinching secretaries as they emerge from the elevators. The office Christmas party, true to legend, turns into an incredibly drunken and powerfully unpleasant make-out party. But sex is entirely attached to office hierarchies. The steno pool and the telephone operators sleep with the bosses with the closed-door offices, but drones out on the floor like Baxter haven't got a chance. As he moves up the ladder, he tries to parlay

C. C. Baxter (Jack Lemmon) gets a promotion in *The Apartment* (1960). *Photofest*

his new authority into sexual charisma—by trying to grant Fran favors. He invites her to the Christmas party and into his office to discuss her job:

> KUBELIK: I'd better get back to my elevator, I'm going to be fired.
> BAXTER: You don't have to worry about that, I have quite a bit of influence in personnel. (*Takes a drink.*) You know Mr. Sheldrake?
> KUBELIK: (*Warily.*) Why?
> BAXTER: He and I are like that. (*Twisting his fingers.*) . . . I thought I could put in a word with Mr. Sheldrake, get you a little promotion. How would you like to be an elevator *starter*?
> KUBELIK: I'm afraid there are too many girls around with seniority over me.
> BAXTER: No-o *problem*! Why don't we discuss it sometime over the holidays?

Fran considers him cute and charming, but it's only when Sheldrake completely humiliates her (by giving her a cash gift for Christmas) that she even considers his innocent proposals. At the end of the film, Fran seems to end up with Baxter, but there's never a question of the office hierarchy being overturned. Only two people, among the thousands in the building, are saved.

Helen Gurley Brown's achievement, such as it was, was to see a way to carve out a realm of freedom for secretaries in what was destined, as far as Brown could see, to be an unequal environment. In the bright assurance of her prose—which, in her typically accurate and annoying way, she called "pippy-poo"—all the anxieties of the old guidebooks just floated away. There was no problem with looking good and being taken seriously as a professional, with being aggressively feminine and making a living: "In an ideal world we might move onward and upward by using only our brains and talent but, since this is an imperfect world, a certain amount of listening, giggling, wriggling, smiling, winking, flirting and fainting is required in our rise from the mailroom."[68] What about getting stuck as a secretary? "Secretarial work isn't a bad thing to be 'stuck' in, anyway. Executive secretaries are close to some of the most glittery men in the world and have great lives."[69] What about flattering your bosses? It was a good idea, she said. "If you can imply that the prettiest girl in the filing room has a secret crush on him, your profit-sharing might really amount to something by Christmas."[70] There was a wry manner to Brown's way of treating office difficulties that thrilled some and irritated others. She tended to satirize her subjects and indulgently excuse them at the same time: for example, teasing male executives for being insecure and needing flattery while nonetheless suggesting that women go ahead and flatter their bosses. Working was great, and sex was great—ergo, Brown concluded, "being great at a terrific job is sexy."[71] Everything could seemingly be resolved in a warm bath of dirty talk and double entendres about work. When it came to office politics, Brown said, "abstinence won't save your job."

In the end, there was an undercurrent of strategy to it. Brown knew that office jobs were hard to come by and easy to lose— something especially true for women, who not only were paid less but had less power. The only way to win that power was to spin everything as positive. This included saying yes to propositions by men at the office. Being able to say yes, affirmatively and ecstatically, was the only way that it would also be meaningful to say no (calmly, without wounding men's pride). While Brown conceded an actual power gap between men and women, she believed that women should still take as much power as they could get—and this meant the ability to be completely in control of their sexuality, if not, in fact, their jobs. In retrospect, much of what Brown argued for seems naive or reckless—affirming so much of what one easily sees as harassment or powerlessness. But it was powerlessness that Brown was determined not to concede. Within, of course, the rules of the game.

6

OPEN PLANS

*The caveman was undoubtedly very pleased to find
a good cave but he also undoubtedly positioned
himself at the entrance looking out. Protect your
back but know what is going on outside is a very
good rule for survival. It is also a good survival rule
for life in offices.*

—ROBERT PROPST, *The Office: A Facility Based on Change*[1]

In the French director Jacques Tati's film *Playtime* (1967), the hero, the Chaplinesque, more or less silent Monsieur Hulot—a stereotypical Gaul, trench-coated and sharp-nosed—finds himself on an unnamed mission in a futuristic Paris of slab skyscrapers and wide streets. Entirely constructed from sets, it is the dream of Le Corbusier realized: a *ville radieuse* of pure rational planning, with every detail mapped out in advance and seemingly nothing that can go wrong. The old Paris, symbolized by the Eiffel Tower, is always spied in the background, reflected in the glassy facades of the curtain walls and the massive transparent doors that open into the wide lobbies of the modern buildings. The film lingers on how long it takes to cross the new, enormous distances inside the buildings, to emphasize the homogeneous, empty time of the zealously bureaucratic future. Though Hulot discovers that it takes forever to move from one end of a building to another, or to rise in the elevator from the ground floor to the top, the message the film sends is of a civilization that has

Jacques Tati's uncannily prescient image of the future in *Playtime* (1967). *Photofest*

moved too fast, has grown too large, for its poor human inhabitants to understand. Hulot is constantly lost or misdirected; the electricity in the gleaming modern restaurants fails routinely; the brand-new architecture turns out to be poorly made and falling apart.

And there is one scene that, for modern viewers, will come as a hallucination: ascending an escalator in a modern office building, he finds himself standing above a wide, open floor, where all the suited clerks are working, isolated in square boxes. Tati lingers on it, to convey its absurdity and mild horror. In the future, he seems to say, there will be no more offices. We will all work inside these cube-like shapes—hidden from each other and from ourselves.

☐

In 1958, the Herman Miller Company hired Robert Propst, a professor of art at the University of Colorado, to head the company's new research wing. The company was aiming to expand beyond its traditional realm, office furniture design, and into realms hitherto untouched by designers—agriculture, hospitals, schools—and Propst seemed an ideal candidate. Though moonlighting as an arts academic, he was in fact an exuberantly, almost maniacally creative freelance intellectual, sculptor, and theoretician. A sandy-haired and brash westerner, he came to Herman Miller with patents in playground equipment, airplane parts, heart valves, timber-harvesting machines, and livestock-tagging machines.[2] Yet he had no formal training in design. This appeared to be a selling point. Untethered from the traditional concerns of designers, he could explore deeper problems and come up with solutions that they could make real. Propst's polymathic mind, the Herman Miller executives thought, might help them take their company in new directions.

Working with Propst was "fascinating," said Bill Stumpf, one of Herman Miller's chief designers. "In one hour, he would reinvent the world. His mind went off like fireworks."[3] Propst's inquisitive soul was coupled with—indeed fed on—a perpetual discontent with his environment. This sometimes translated into discontent with anyone around him who disagreed with him. "Those who were not supportive of his ideas or way of thinking found their personal relation with him changed," said Tom Pratt, another Herman Miller associate. "He believed his way was the right way and usually he was right."[4] Many of the people who worked with him testified to his impatience with things as they were and his irrepressible desire to fix them. In seeking design solutions, he always started from the premise that human beings were mismanaging the world they had built—that in fact they had gone about it all wrong. Only the smallest amount of empirical research, which few bothered to conduct, would naturally confirm his hypothesis. In the lore surrounding Propst, one prominent example is retold endlessly. Early in his career as Herman Miller researcher, Propst slipped a disk and had to spend several weeks in the hospital, bedridden. He immediately began to observe inefficiencies in the delivery of care. A nurse informed an administrator that one of the patients was taking reams and reams of notes. When the administrator spoke to him about his activity, Propst took out his notebook and showed him his exhaustive studies of the wasted energy, the lost time, and the useless motions that he observed. Years later, Propst would turn his insights into a modu-

lar system of cabinets, trays, and medical furniture—Co/Struc—
easily constructed, moved, and dismantled, which came to be
adopted throughout hospitals everywhere.

Despite occasional forays into areas like patient care, Propst
returned obsessively to the one area that Herman Miller was trying
to get away from: the office. Propst "immediately began flooding
us with ideas, concepts, and drawings ranging from agriculture to
medicine," Hugh De Pree, who was Herman Miller's president at
the time, told John Berry, a historian of the design company. "It is
interesting, though, that despite our mutual desire to explore other
fields, the first project that attracted his continuing attention was
the office."[5] Interesting, perhaps, but unsurprising. Propst, in his
move from art and academia to corporate life, simply discovered
what millions have always discovered—that anyone who works in
an office spends an extraordinary amount of time thinking about
the arrangement of offices.

He had set up his research camp in a small building in Ann
Arbor, Michigan. Herman Miller was based on the eastern side of

Robert Propst at work. *Courtesy of Herman Miller*

Lake Michigan, in Zeeland, a hidebound hamlet made up of descendants of Dutch burghers. Propst found the baccalaureate air of Ann Arbor more conducive to his ideas; it also furnished him with a greater variety of postgraduate researchers. Freed from the arbitrary arrangements and furniture demanded by the office industry, Propst had relative autonomy to manage his own work space. Immediately bored with the traditional single, flat desk space, he fabricated over time a number of different "workstations," including a stand-up desk and a display surface for magazines and other reference materials he needed for his work. Noticing that keeping things in files created the problem of "out of sight, out of mind," he developed an open display surface and a color-coded system of visual cues to remind himself of what he should be doing at any given moment. And rather than the sedentary monotony of normal office work, Propst found himself constantly in motion, moving from one working area to another, standing to sitting. All this activity made him feel more productive, alert, vital.

At the same time, he was reading voraciously in journals of sociology and behavioral science. It was the early 1960s, and a new attitude toward man and his relationship to his environment was coming into view. Norbert Wiener was one voice; the influential founder of cybernetics, he argued that technology had the potential to take on human characteristics and become an extension of man. Marshall McLuhan followed with his analogous arguments regarding media. A particular influence was the anthropologist Edward T. Hall. His popular book *The Silent Language* (1959) focused on the varieties of nonverbal understanding among the cultures of the world, including space. "Literally thousands of experiences teach us unconsciously that space communicates," he wrote. "Yet this fact would probably never have been brought to the level of consciousness if it had not been realized that space is organized differently in each culture."[6] He followed this with a book explicitly focused on the unconscious attitudes toward space, *The Hidden Dimension*, which held enormous fascination for architects, designers, and planners of all sorts. A gently meandering discussion of "social and personal space and man's perception of it," *The Hidden Dimension* coined a term for its branch of study: "proxemics." As a field, it grew out of Hall's argument that "*man and his environment participate in molding each other*. Man is now in the position of actually creating the total world in which he lives . . . a frightening thought in view of how very little is known about man."[7] Hall was speaking to Americans experiencing the pummeling of their cities by urban renewal and their heated descent into the crucible of racial integration. But the drama of a civilization that had forgotten its own understanding of its surroundings also took place, Hall showed, in the banal setting of an office—since inattentiveness to one's environment was even more common in spaces people cared the least about, like their workplace. Based on more than one hundred interviews, Hall disclosed that an office contained three "hidden zones," which most designers tended to ignore:

1. The immediate work area of the desktop and chair.
2. A series of points within arm's reach outside the area mentioned above.
3. Spaces marked as the limit reached when one pushes away from the desk to achieve a little distance from the work without actually getting up.[8]

Taylor's disciple W. H. Leffingwell had studied similar minutiae of office life. His reaction, however, was to rationalize inefficiencies in the use of those spaces out of existence. If one followed Hall, however, the "inefficient" use of space began to seem less like a bad habit and more like the expression of a human need—or of a tacit dimension to a worker's knowledge that could be neither replicated nor eradicated.

This was the sort of material that seized a man like Propst. As a restless intellectual without a proper profession, he devoured these items, ranging freely across the worlds of anthropology, sociology, and social psychology, propelled by curiosity; nonetheless, as a designer manqué, he also began to imagine practical applications in the office. The language of the office and the language of social science were, to Propst, coterminous. He set out on research trips, interviewing workers, doctors, psychologists, and scholars of industrial relations. They confirmed the insights that he had developed in his own office: the importance of balanced physical activity; the need for an environment conducive to concentrated work; the practical function of visual stimulus and an open work space. He gradually began to feel the need for a new way of working, one more sensitive to the manifold varieties of how people reacted to their space. It contained prototypes for a stand-up desk with closable top, visible color-coded file folders, a communications workstation, and a low desk with flip-down display. Each interviewee was asked about twenty-five somewhat leading questions regarding their work spaces: "Do you feel deskbound and too sedentary?" "Are you improperly insulated from key information?" and—most important—"Is your office adaptable to change?"

In these early, amateur attempts at defining a better working environment, we see Propst developing the rudiments of what would become known as "ergonomics" (from the Greek, meaning something like "the rules governing tasks"). What has since become a banal discourse about lumbar support began with men like Propst seeking to understand the relationship between human beings and their environment—the very nature of how one labored. And it mattered that Propst was specifically concerned with *office* work, that he considered it an altogether unique kind of activity. Since the Taylorists had ratified the mechanical order that saw office work as largely akin to factory work, nearly no one had bothered to undertake a holistic examination of the office as being fundamentally different. Though office work enjoyed all the status privileges associated with white collars and clean environments, designers had yet to confer on it a system—a layout, a plan—that would actually make its specific work easier and more productive. Propst was among the first designers to argue that office work was mental work and that mental effort was tied to environmental enhancement of one's physical capabilities. To change a desk, then, was to change one's entire way of being in the world. As George Nelson, one of Herman Miller's most illustrious designers, stated loftily, "The Lord never meant a man to be immobilized in one position . . . These are not desks and file cabinets. They are a way of life." Office design was coming into its own.

□

It hardly needs adding that in societies throughout the world, the 1960s more generally saw deep transformations in relationships and culture. But it would be a mistake to see these currents as uniformly hostile to business and to the gray flannel suits of the office world. As Thomas Frank showed in his book *The Conquest of Cool*, business—and particularly the softer arts, like advertising, management theory, and public relations—took warmly to the new spirit of individualism pervading the nascent counterculture. Rather than co-opting the counterculture, business anticipated many of its changes, incorporated them, and in fact propagated several of its currents. The old obsession with conformity and bureaucracy had been internal to business itself. So too would the interest in individuality. Members of Students for a Democratic Society and middle managers alike were avid readers of *The Lonely Crowd*. And of course we recall that *The Organization Man* was written by an editor at *Fortune* magazine. Only incidentally an indictment of a society, it was specifically a goad at business leaders to shape creative workplaces, which could cease churning out Whyte's much-loathed conformist drones and foster individuality instead.[9]

The management guru Douglas McGregor's book *The Human Side of Enterprise*, from 1960, was only the most famous of the new, "spiritual" guides to corporate life. McGregor seemed to be speaking alongside figures like Hall, calling for a new, social scientific approach to the question of human values and needs. "Management's freedom to manage has been progressively curtailed in our society during the past century," he wrote. "One approach to these problems is to see all restrictions on management as unreasonable and to fight blindly against them . . . The other approach is to become more sensitive to human values and to exert self-control through a positive, conscious, ethical code."[10] Like all successful business books since, McGregor had a groundbreaking "theory," which he condensed into a short, easily digestible handle—one that any time-strapped businessman, after quickly browsing the executive summary, could comfortably wrap his mouth around. As many would do, McGregor positioned himself against Frederick Taylor, whom he associated with the "Theory X" version of management. Theory X was hierarchical; it involved coercion, manipulation, supervision. Theory X supposed that men and women had a natural inclination against working; the managerial prerogative, then, was to control, direct, and threaten workers into work. The personality testing that Whyte saw as the sign of a control society, McGregor, too, singled out for censure, as an invasion of privacy: Why should the smallest details of a person's preferences and social attitudes be available to a private company?

"Theory Y" was the alternative. It proceeded from the idea that pleasure in work was "as natural as play or rest,"[11] and so, too, were self-direction and self-control the necessary correlates. A worker's intellectual potential was enormous and only partially realized in contemporary life: management needed to be open to recognizing a junior staffer's individual initiative, subtly encouraging him toward realizing his individual goals rather than terrorizing him with the fear of discipline. McGregor used New Agey phrases out of the psychologist Abraham Maslow to describe Theory Y, like "the satisfaction of higher-level ego" and "self-actualization needs." He spoke of participation, openness, humanism. In an environment already seeded by frank discussions of stifling conformity, McGregor's book was immediately and widely accepted. It was one of the most discussed and influential books of the 1960s—perhaps the management treatise most quoted by managers themselves.[12] Though management books since, such as the former Intel CEO Andy Grove's *Only the Paranoid Survive*, have rediscovered the value of Taylorist coercion and brutality, they still insist on the need for respecting a worker's individuality. Few adopt McGregor's gentle, New Age tone, but they follow in McGregor's footsteps—or, as Frank puts it, "the bloated corpus of recent management literature seems like one long tribute to McGregor's thought, an interminable string of corollaries to 'Theory Y.' "[13] In fact, McGregor was himself the culmination of two decades of human relations theories—people who had dissented from Elton Mayo's pessimistic view of industrial progress but who saw the need for psychological training all the same.[14] And the growth in human relations theories was connected to the implacably growing ratio of office workers to production staff. With the incredible number of office workers, it became impossible for all the employees to be promoted; human relations practices tried to get workers to find satisfaction in their work rather than in the possibility of advancement. It became useful, too, to use one's knowledge of human relations—the ability to slyly manipulate others or to "win friends and influence people," in Dale Carnegie's phrase—to rise up an office bureaucracy.[15]

The growth of the friendly, Theory Y–ish workplace had of course more directly been a response to the industrial unrest brought about by labor unions. A backlash to their success on the shop floor in the 1920s and 1930s arrived in the form of the Taft-Hartley Act of 1947, which placed huge legal barriers against strikes and new organizing. But the level of labor union membership would peak in the postwar years, with 35 percent of private-sector workers belonging to a union and strike activity continuing to grow: the average American worker lost 0.55 of a working day to strikes (compared with 0.13 of a day in Britain and only 0.04 of a day in Germany). Yet the unions were facing a silent problem. Thanks partly to automation, their traditional base—the factory worker—was no longer growing at the pace it had; the other side of the workforce was not only growing faster but statistically growing beyond the blue-collar worker. Finally, in 1956 the Bureau of Labor Statistics recorded the sea change: there were just over twenty million blue-collar workers, while white-collar workers numbered nearly twenty-seven million. This was a momentous shift for an industrial powerhouse like the United States, one that organizers and managers alike struggled to grapple with.

For the unions, it was manifestly a growing crisis, though one that for the time being they failed to register. In a piece for *Harper's* in 1957, one labor official tasked with organizing white-collar workers plainly stated that his job was impossible and that unions trying to win them over, unless they changed tack completely, were doomed. The author—writing anonymously for fear of reprisal from his higher-ups—drew the conclusion that so many had refused to draw before but were now conceding: white-collar workers were different. They had clean jobs that didn't force them to shower when they came home each day. They believed ardently in the American dream of relentless upward mobility. They preferred the insecurity of getting promoted based on merit to the steady advance of seniority. Unions promised one thing above all—dignity—which white-collar workers claimed they already had, thanks to the prestige of their professions, the bleached stiffness of their collars. Many children of blue-collar workers were getting jobs in offices because, tacitly or otherwise, they agreed.

Office workers believed their work had skills that could carry them anywhere. According to the writer, people who worked in steel or coal simply saw their jobs as empty vessels: they were more inclined to talk about the industry they worked in than the specific positions they held. Meanwhile, the average office workers identified themselves by profession—as a "stenographer" or a "file clerk." And if they advanced in their positions, it was because of their talents for their particular jobs. "The white collar worker thinks in terms of her skill, which she can carry with her from employer to employer," he wrote. "She didn't fall into her job haphazardly as the result of lining up before a personnel supervisor. She has some training, perhaps some talent, invested in it. She is likely to be just as concerned about what she contributes to the job as she is about how well the job pays."[16] "The Great American Dream still has a firmer hold on white collar workers than on blue collar workers," he concluded.

There was also the nasty atmosphere that people associated with unions. Publicly, the world of organized labor seemed to be filled with frank talk and aggressive strikes. Such confrontational methods were inimical to the subtle arts of office politics, where insinuation and subterfuge prevailed. Unions argued this was only a sign of the white-collar worker's profound exploitation:

> White collar workers are the most exploited group in our economy. Tied to a fixed non-negotiable salary, victims of every price rise (with no escalator clause to help them), without a political voice raised on their behalf, they are truly "on the short end." But, like Steinbeck's tenant in *The Grapes of Wrath*, whom do they shoot? Mr. Turner, the head of the accounting department, who is so grouchy when he comes to work in the morning? The Steelworkers who always get those big wage raises for their members and thus—according to steel

executives—force prices up all along the line? The politicians who never keep their promises? The company for which they work?

No, instead of shooting the company executives or joining a union, they mouse along and live with their hopes.[17]

The organizer's main concern was whether unions could actually accomplish the task they set for themselves and get white-collar workers to organize. But for us, looking back at this moment—and knowing the less than happy results for organized labor—the question is deeper: How did office workers see themselves? For C. Wright Mills, as we know, there was a hopeless and irremediable *mediocrity* to the new middle class: they were unlikely to develop a distinctive profile or form of political agency, and they would only follow whatever political force seemed to be winning. Subsequent surveys of the attitudes of office workers seemed to confirm this middling-ness. In one such study from 1962, office workers were asked to rate their perceptions of high-level business managers and those of average industrial workers, as well as themselves. In all instances, office workers considered themselves distinct from both, but they tended to rate the business managers with total favorability, compared with themselves; meanwhile, blue-collar workers under those same characteristics—"worthy of trust," "conscientious about work," and "dependable"—rated the lowest in the eyes of the office workers.[18] So they felt themselves to be distinguished from the workers "below," if not quite as distinct as the managers "above."

But to hear that labor organizer tell it, there was a different voice emerging: that of the office worker who saw himself possessed of a particular skill, a certain kind of knowledge, that made him professionally mobile. These were figures who saw themselves not as tied to an organization, as Whyte suggested, but as possessing power, agility, the capacity to shift from one place to another. They weren't likely to respond to the human relations injunction to take solace in the satisfactions inherent to the job. Instead, they wanted organizations that responded to the claims of talent: what they were seeking was *meritocracy.*

The understanding that a small but vocal fraction of office

workers had of themselves didn't correspond to the managerial hierarchies set up by a different age. From left to right—labor organizer to business professor—a new conception of the office worker was coming into view.

☐

The task of describing this new kind of worker—almost invariably called "knowledge worker"—has consumed academic sociologists and management theorists for two generations. Among the managers themselves, the task of propagandizing on the knowledge workers' behalf fell to the century's most renowned theorist of management, the Austrian émigré Peter Drucker, who helped to coin the term. He was part of that great wave of Austrian conservatives—Friedrich Hayek, Joseph Schumpeter, Ludwig von Mises, Sir Karl Popper—who departed their country as the Germans completed the *Anschluss*. The crisis of the 1930s was as formative for him as it was for them.

The charismatic and learned Drucker embedded himself in American corporations as a consultant and in American universities as a lecturer. His conspicuously civilized mien, combined with a luxuriant crop of black hair (in later years, his stark baldness would prove equally imposing), made him at once a forbidding and a seductive presence. He produced a stream of books, with unabashedly portentous titles about change—*The New Society*, *The Age of Discontinuity*—that commanded the attention of CEOs. His prose style was aphoristic almost to a fault, full of vatic pronouncements on the future of man, delivered with a tone of authority that no American management guru could muster. For businessmen who read no philosophy, Drucker was their philosopher. His manifest intelligence added luster to the otherwise monochrome language of management: discussing organizations and corporate structure, he moved with relative nonchalance among an impressive number of disciplines (the social sciences, history, economics) and, like his Austrian compatriots, spoke comfortably of epochs and continents, whereas most Americans languished in the faux-spiritual rhetoric of "self-actualization." In the brutal corporate raider world of the

1980s and 1990s, the aging Drucker leveled criticisms against social inequality; he acquired a saintly reputation among executives who were obviously ignoring him. Today, after his hopes for a moral managerial class have drowned in globalization's merciless tide, Drucker's aperçus fill desk calendars and quotation books. Barack Obama has cited him as a favorite writer.

Like McGregor, Drucker was a figure who inadvertently harmonized the impulses of the nascent counterculture with the outwardly stuffy world of business. Though hardly countercultural himself, Drucker's concepts would prove useful to people in later years who wanted to make the office hospitable to the wilder world outside it. Over the course of the 1960s, Drucker came to expound one of the notions that would make him famous: the idea that a swelling group of workers was becoming central to the economy. They were middle-class employees who would never identify themselves with the "proletariat," nor, in fact, with management. They were technical and professional workers who controlled what Drucker believed was becoming the most important resource of all: knowledge. Calling them "knowledge workers"—a term he coined in 1962 at the same time as, but independently of, another social theorist, Fritz Machlup—Drucker saw them as occupying a historic role in the making of a responsible society.

In Drucker's view, what was changing about work was the increasing need to apply knowledge to work. Knowledge as such, in the intellectual sense, was different. The mathematical formulas and theorems that existed in books were a form of knowledge useful to intellectual history, but mathematics as applied to, say, a space program was "knowledge work." So, too, did advertising and marketing and various other new professions require the mental labor of workers, applying what they knew from various disciplines to the techniques of mass persuasion. It was one thing to be an expert in Freud or Newton in a university; another to use the insights of Freud to sell a toothbrush or to use Newton to build a ballistic missile capable of striking the Soviet Union.

Knowledge work itself came from a historic shift, one that Drucker, like so many, traced to Frederick Taylor. But his version of the history was marked by a curious and useful elision. In Drucker's account, Taylor came upon a working world characterized by rote, nearly mindless, activity. It wasn't planned so much as willed: the workers simply worked *harder* rather than "smarter." Until Taylor, that is: "Taylor, for the first time in history, looked at work itself as deserving the attention of an educated man."[19] Drucker's subsequent description of the insensate labor of unskilled men in factories draws almost entirely from Taylor's portrait of them—and accordingly condescends to their abilities to plan and organize work. In actual fact, it wasn't so. Before Taylor, work was already organized by teams of factory workers, who in large part had control over how they worked. The knowledge they applied to work was largely "tacit" in nature, agreed upon among the workers themselves and developed through a silent or coded language, rather than "explicit" (to borrow a famous definition from the sociologist Michael Polanyi). What Taylor sought in particular—indeed, what constituted his signal obsession—was to extract this tacit knowledge from the workers and install it in another set of people, the "industrial engineers." Drucker called them "the prototype of all modern 'knowledge workers' "—a plausible assumption but one that excised the tremendous amount of knowledge that already existed in the work process.[20] (Taylor lamented that after being taught "the one best way," workers had a stubborn tendency to return to their own ways of working.)[21] It was a useful fiction, and a common one, that helped to uphold a new class of technicians and professionals as the masters of an ever more progressive society, dependent on the application of knowledge to work. For the knowledge worker, Drucker held, was not simply a freelance professional but rather "the successor to the employee of yesterday, the manual worker, skilled or unskilled."

Social theorists all over appeared to agree that the labor market in the United States was changing dramatically, becoming less focused on manufacturing and more on goods and services—the age would get its first monumental treatment in sociologist Daniel Bell's *The Coming of Post-Industrial Society* in 1973—but Drucker was the first to give the new age a hero, some years after his compatriot Schumpeter, seeing bureaucracy all around, had demanded one. Drucker's explanation for the rise of the knowledge worker in the

1950s and 1960s remains striking. Rather than work itself changing, he believed the increasing life span of workers was changing the
labor supply, and therefore changing the kinds of jobs available. An
individual could imagine him- or herself working longer—in which
case, it no longer made sense to drop out of high school, or avoid
college, in order to enter the labor force. One didn't *need* a high
school education to land a desk in the steno pool; neither precal-
culus nor the history of the War of 1812 would serve you in your
work. A kind of educational inflation, however, soon made a high
school degree a requirement, as, in our time, a college degree has
become, for working virtually any kind of office job. The jobs had
not gotten more complex; the individuals working in them had. In
other words, "knowledge worker" was the name for an overeducated office worker—someone whose capabilities far exceeded his
or her position. "They expect to be 'intellectuals,' " Drucker writes.
"And they find that they are just 'staff.' "[22] Drucker's explanation, in
other words, was supply side rather than demand side: a larger educated population was prepared to do, and indeed desired, different
kinds of work from before. It remained for the workplace, Drucker
concluded, to adjust accordingly. This meant managing knowledge
workers in order to elicit better performance: they would answer to
the demands of knowledge, not to the demands of arbitrary authority, like a boss. *Excellence*, not output, would be the measure of productivity. This in turn suggested that the workplace had to become
more performance based, less hierarchical, and more open to the
ideas of its employees. It had to change shape, too: Drucker lauded
the "campus" atmospheres of places like Bell Labs and Connecticut
General as conducive to knowledge work.[23]

Nonetheless, Drucker's conception of "knowledge work" was
almost inevitably vague, based on an argument more propagandistic
than analytical. It seemed to answer to a felt need, a spirit of anxiety
in the workforce itself, rather than a change in the kinds of work
being done. Just as William H. Whyte and office workers like Alan
Harrington had named the disease—bureaucracy—Peter Drucker
named the still-to-be-hoped-for cure. The actual boundaries of
knowledge work remained difficult for even more empirically motivated writers to define, its characteristics resistant to cataloging;

still, the term spread among management theorists like an epidemic, suggesting that knowledge work was like pornography: you knew it when you saw it. Fritz Machlup, whose book *The Production and Distribution of Knowledge in the United States* had appeared alongside Drucker's early forays into social theory, attempted to measure the actual worth of knowledge. Machlup—like Drucker, an Austrian émigré who had studied under Hayek and von Mises—argued that "a succession of occupations . . . first clerical, then administrative and managerial, and now professional and technical personnel" were leading "a continuing movement from manual to mental, and from less to more highly trained labor."[24] Yet in his measurements, Machlup was nothing if not inclusive: knowledge workers for him were "all the people whose work consists of conferring, negotiating, planning, directing, reading, note-taking, writing, drawing, blueprinting, calculating, dictating, telephoning, card-punching, typing, multigraphing, recording, checking, and many others."[25] In other words: office work. Naturally, when he estimated its worth, he considered it the fastest-growing sector of the economy.

Machlup was more generous than Drucker: for him, even the most mechanical white-collar tasks were part of knowledge work. Drucker and others would see it as a specific fraction of the workforce, the entrepreneurial elect within the bureaucratic machine of the office, the people who analyzed and judged rather than followed orders. Yet because all sorts of work within the office could qualify as "mental" (as Machlup correctly intuited), it became a futile labor to identify what precisely knowledge work was—and a far easier task to propagate it as a buzzword.

In this respect, it's probably better to think of knowledge work as the name of a desire, or a hope, rather than an actual feature of the workplace. The wispy outlines of the knowledge worker would be filled in, again and again, by designers and management gurus following in Drucker's confident (if evanescent) footsteps. Each new thinker took the idea to mean something different, adding to its multifarious and slippery meanings. Despite this vagueness, and perhaps a little because of it, the idea of knowledge work would drive the central changes in office design up to the present day. Knowledge workers would be the heroes of a coming new society, an "information society," in which they were the chief "symbolic analysts," all the while rehabbing the urban core as a "creative class." The tone of all values being revalued—somberly accounted for in Drucker—would become ever more strident and unhinged. Meanwhile, office designers worked patiently at realizing the material conditions for the utopia, when it arrived, so that it might feel at home. Perhaps creating the right space for knowledge work, the story went, would finally make it a real thing.

☐

Robert Propst, who never saw a new idea that he didn't like, ate up the "knowledge worker" concept and began deploying it in his writings and memos to Herman Miller. With the imaginary knowledge worker filling his dream office design, space planning had more than mere ergonomics at stake. It provided a rationale, a spur, for his work.

And then, as if providentially, a design emerged from Europe that would give his work on furniture an entirely new setting, as well as a vote of tremendous confidence.

By and large, except in inspiring the glass office building envelope, Europe hadn't provided design ideas for work spaces in generations. American offices had been the dominant form of design, with European offices at best furnishing smaller versions of the gargantuan American bull pens and skyscrapers. Indeed, the bull-pen office itself became known in Europe as the "American plan," one that Europeans used sparingly, if at all. Without the enormous building plates characteristic of American offices, corridors and closed-door offices were the norm throughout western Europe. Two devastating continental wars had only sealed the lid on European cautiousness.

But the postwar reconstruction led famously to unbelievable rates of growth, particularly in Germany, the most ravaged nation of all. The lightning-fast emergence of German manufacturing out of its cratered and ashen cities gradually broke the congealed tentativeness of managerial thinking and design. Architects had new license to think of bigger buildings. German émigrés who had spent the war in American exile returned to West Germany. Trailing them

were clouds of American business thinking, from scientific management to human relations, that flooded Germany with an incredible rush. The terrible cost of the war had been a kind of "creative
destruction." With its desperate need to bury and move on from its
recent murderous past, Germany was cleared for new thinking. Out
of the ferment of ideas came a new approach to designing offices.[26]

In 1958, the brothers Wolfgang and Eberhard Schnelle, languish-
ing as assistants in their father's furniture company, decided to light
out on their own. They founded the Quickborner consulting group,
a space-planning firm outside Hamburg. Space planning had hitherto been a negligible function of architectural practice—as long
as the outside was shiny and glassy, and the inside was pleasantly
furnished and Muzak filled, the architect felt he was done (Florence Knoll constituting a lonely exception). The Schnelle brothers, however, spied an opportunity lying dormant in the well-trod
alleys between office desks. Though these regimented rows had
once reflected the deepest impulses of Taylor's acolytes, the gesture
of apportioning a space between desks had over time become rote
and uninspired, much as the corridor offices had been. The Schnelle
brothers wanted to get beyond the conventional ways of dividing up
an office, which claimed to rely vaguely on charts of organizational
hierarchy but in actuality often derived from awards of status and
prestige. Sure, on the level of individual psychology it made sense
to give some managers closed-door offices and higher-ups corner
offices with carpeting. But how did that at all help the work flow
of the entire office? In their view, the office was an organic whole,
made up of finely interlinking parts and an enormously complex
network of paper flow. Yet most offices, whether consisting entirely
of closed-door offices or open bull pens, hardly reflected this work
flow. A new conception of the office was needed—one that was
organic, natural, on a human scale.

Through measurements of communication within offices, the
type of space and level of privacy that each employee needed, and
the amount of time that each employee needed to spend on the telephone versus interacting with other employees, the Schnelle brothers arrived at a solution. They called it *Bürolandschaft*, which
translates literally as "office landscape." As many at the time and

since have noted, the translation is somewhat misleading, because "landscape" in the German phrase doesn't carry any of the connotations of the natural world that it does in English. And yet there is, in fact, an affinity with certain planned "landscapes" of the natural world—namely, the classic Italian Baroque garden. In the sample plans the Schnelle brothers devised, the arrangement of desks seems utterly chaotic, totally unplanned—a mess, like a forest of refrigerator magnets. But, as with the seemingly "wild" overgrowth of a "natural" garden, the office landscape is more thoroughly planned than any symmetrical and orderly arrangement of desks. Imaginary lines wend their way around every cluster, delineating common pools of activity; between and through the undergrowth of clusters are invisible, sinuous paths of work flow. Rather than the coffee carts of the Crystal Palace trundling along at appointed hours, the *Bürolandschaft* insisted on the more flexible "break room," where employees could retreat for conversation and coffee at their leisure. And, most startling of all, there are no closed doors in sight, no one boxed in, no executives enjoying commanding views in snug corners. At most, a few mobile partitions and plants shielded certain sections and workers from others.

The uniformity of previous office design was so rigidly accepted by everyone that the free-form concept seemed at once promising and totally insane. Only the publishing company Bertelsmann was willing to commission the Quickborner Team to spend two years instantiating its ideas. A group of architects, engineers, and interior designers met with Quickborner's systems consultants to work with Bertelsmann employees and devise an appropriate setup. The result was received as a kind of liberation. Signature European firms were soon falling over themselves to transform their stuffy, bottled-up environments into the breathing, lyrical, and above all flexible spaces of *Bürolandschaft*. Within a few years, office landscapes were blooming in Sweden (*kontorslandskap*!), and word began to make its way across the English Channel and the Atlantic.[27] Articles in small architectural presses began reporting on the German phenomenon, snagging readers with their smoothly scattershot arrays of little rectangular desks.

Francis Duffy, a British architect and office historian, was a

A typical office landscape plan.

student when he first came across *Bürolandschaft* in an article by the renowned architectural historian (and fellow Englishman) Reyner Banham in 1964. Many years later he recalled the excitement it caused. "The building's form was excitingly non-orthogonal," he writes. "The interiors were rich in informal break areas, elegant planters and *carpet*! Workplaces were not arranged in regimented rows, like contemporary American offices, but in an organic and free flowing pattern, following, as Banham's text explained, systematic studies of flows of information and patterns of interaction."[28] And above all, it was only an *approach*, not a one-model-fits-all design. "Once seen," he wrote, "*Bürolandschaft* could never be forgotten."[29] The universal office solution had arrived. Duffy had been expected by his professors to follow slavishly the "glamorous" precedents set by the Lever House and its ilk, but he quickly became one of the most articulate advocates of office landscaping outside its home country. Robert Propst, who grew aware of the phenomenon around the same time,[30] became a strong proponent in America. Quickborner established teams in both the U.K. and the United States, and in 1967 the first American office landscape was set up for DuPont. Soon New York's Port Authority would ask Quickborner to propose landscapes for the hundreds of office floors rising at the tip of Manhattan in the two towers of the World Trade Center.

Since each office had different needs and did different kinds of work, the way each office landscape looked should have been as wildly unpredictable as the "American plan" was stolidly always the same. And yet "flexibility" meant that even if the specific arrangements were different, all landscapes in fact had recognizably similar features. Reports from office landscapes by workers all roughly provided the same view. As one enters the office landscape, spartan dinner-table-like desks (reducing the number of vertical planes reduces noise) appear set entirely at random, with acoustic screens shielding noise and plants providing "organic" breaks in the floor's wide, expansive stretch. Over time, however, a certain kind of order emerges. Secretaries are still pooled together, but at odd angles. Large tables enclosed by curved sound partitions make for the sole conference "rooms." The chief executives are out on the floor but get apportioned conspicuously more space. Nearly every aspect of the design is mobile. In a way, the Quickborner Team had only carried out another revolution of the Taylorist wheel; freed from the model of the factory, it had added flexibility to Taylor's sacred quest for efficiency.[31]

And "flexibility"—not by accident still one of the key words of the office environment—was the appeal to executives who otherwise had no interest in giving up their generous corner offices for a desk out in the open. For a flexible office was above all a cheap office. No need for expensive wooden private office partitions, let alone any other amenities that might speak of permanence. The office landscape could be rearranged at will, at virtually no expense at all; shrinking the company would make no dent in the planning budget, since you just had to move the desks around. And with the mass flirtation with a cheaper office came the first hint of danger. Very small status symbols began to reappear in office landscapes: upper-level managers were given more space and better partitioning than junior people; a supervisor might have the benefit of two potted plants shrouding his desk, whereas secretaries had none at all. And then there was the noise. The Quickborner people had foreseen the problem of noise in an open plan—it was after all a constant threat in "American plan" offices as well—and for that reason insisted on carpeting and sound screens. But this failed to counter the problem. In the DuPont offices, people speaking in low tones managed to sound muffled enough, but higher-pitched noises, such as ringing telephones or the unending whir of typewriter strokes, carried unimpeded throughout the office. In the end, noise would always be a problem, when quiet was not placed at a premium. Interaction and communication were conceived of as norms in the landscaped office; introspection and concentration were sidelined. In the rush to open-plan the world, some crucial values for the performance of work were lost.

□

In 1964, a year after the assassination of John F. Kennedy and a year before the escalation of the American ground invasion of Vietnam, the American economy was growing at a nearly inhuman speed, and Herman Miller unveiled the practical results of Robert Propst's research. Called Action Office, it was unlike anything anyone had ever seen. Rather than a furniture item or a collection of them, it was a proposition for an altogether new kind of space.

Most office designs were about keeping people in place; Action Office was about movement. For in keeping with the ergonomic thinking that Propst had been doing for years, the motion of the body assisted—corresponded to—the ceaselessly inventive motion of the white-collar mind. Advertisements for the system show workers in constant motion; indeed, the human figures in the images often appear blurred, as if the photographer were unable to capture their lightning speed. The subjects are rarely sitting; when they are, they seem just on the verge of rising again. The display surfaces show copies of the latest popular science journals; a prickly model of a molecule lies dormant on one of the desks: the knowledge worker is home in the office at last. And the space is porous enough for the "fortuitous encounter" that Propst believed normal offices militated against; two empty espresso cups on a mobile, neutral table—better

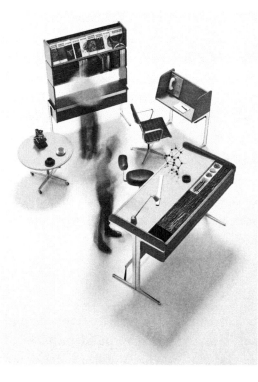

Action Office I (1964).
Courtesy of Vitra Design Museum

for a meeting, Propst believed, than the battlefield of a personal desk—bear witness to an intense conversation with another human performer.

There were many idiosyncratic touches. Because Propst had convinced himself that work out of sight was work out of mind, there were no large desk drawers. Instead, there was a movable display surface, from which items could be retrieved and replaced at ease. A standing rolltop desk—a retro touch, one of the first rolltop desks since the early days of the countinghouses—not only kept workers on their feet but also allowed them to leave work out overnight, securely closed. (Though it only allowed a pile three inches high; anything higher, Propst thought, led to inaction.) This was another one of Propst's hobbyhorses: the fact that managers insisted knowledge workers clear their desks at night, when "few thinking projects are completed in a day, and some are mulled over for weeks."[32] The office as it had previously been constituted was against thinking, against creativity, against knowledge. But what was an office for, if not for cultivating the mind? "An office is a place for transacting abstractions," Propst insisted. "Its function is to be a mind-oriented living space."[33]

Action Office was the happy result of an unusual collaboration. Propst had been thrown together with one of his near opposites— George Nelson, who grew to prominence by converting the ideas of modernism into effortlessly cool pieces of furniture. Propst was laconic, prophetic, intransigent, exuding the tight-lipped silence of the American West's wide expanses; Nelson was a scotch-swilling bon vivant and raconteur. Propst had never left the country; Nelson had spent his youth touring Europe, becoming fluent in Italian, French, and German, and he would later pick up a little Japanese and Portuguese.[34] But both were committed, almost instinctively, to remaking the world around them. Just as Propst seemed to belong outside conventional design tradition, Nelson was perhaps the least self-conscious of any of the modernists; with a slew of products, from multicolored Pop Art swag-leg desks to futuristic shell-shaped chairs, he channeled the idea of modern and new without even seeming to think about it. Looking back on his long career, he stated his belief that "everything that is worth anything is always modern because it can't be anything else, and therefore there are no flags to wave, no manifestoes, you just do the only thing you can honestly do *now*."[35] The items Nelson had designed for Action Office were beautiful, at once homey and utterly modern, nostalgic and forward thinking. His desk surfaces rested on cantilevered die-cast aluminum legs; for the standing desk, a chrome brace doubled as a footrest. A "communications center" with a telephone was acoustically insulated. Above all—and what is impossible to convey with black-and-white photographs—it was colorful: green, bright blue, navy blue, black, and yellow. Like bright magazine advertisements, or the Pop Art of Warhol and Lichtenstein that executives were putting in their offices, Action Office proclaimed its allegiance to the new spirit of the age: rich, advanced, potentially liberating.

In this sense, the Action Office that Propst had conceived and Nelson designed might have been the first truly modern idea to enter the office—that is, the first in which the aesthetics of design and progressive ideas about human needs were truly united. For years, the glass skin of buildings had suggested progress, but inside everything looked much the same as it had for years—only buffed with slightly fancier furniture and cleaner-looking lines and partitions. The worker, these designs implied, was interchangeable and malleable, a cog in a machine. The worker imagined by Action Office was also pictured as a machine of sorts—but less like a robot and more like the Italian futurist images of machine-like soccer players, seething with dynamism and physical intelligence. With *Bürolandschaft*, and now Action Office, it appeared as if the office world were on the verge of a breakthrough, at last able to achieve the work utopia that it had always promised. Voices like Drucker's were clamoring that a new age was coming, one beyond planned socialism and industrial capitalism—a *knowledge* economy. Had this new age at last gotten the furniture it deserved?

When Action Office was unveiled before the press, the answer appeared to be resoundingly affirmative. "Seeing these designs," wrote *Industrial Design*, "one wonders why office workers have put up with their incompatible, unproductive, uncomfortable environment for so long." Meanwhile, the more popular *Saturday Evening Post* cried, "Office workers of America, beware! The Action Office is coming! We are in real danger of being enabled to work at 100 percent efficiency."[36]

Despite the rapturous reviews, Action Office didn't sell. Office managers complained that the entire system was too expensive, because the furniture was made of such quality material. And the space that Action Office created was too vaguely defined, its borders too porous. The "office landscape," for which Action Office was perfectly suited, had yet to catch on in the United States; it was unlikely that managers would quickly leap from their orthogonal bull pens to the terrifying freedom Propst envisioned; despite the Aquarian currents already beginning to waft through the office, they were a conservative bunch. The product won a few awards within the industry but otherwise saw little actual adoption in the workplace.

Propst had run up against a classic problem of design, rooted in his approach from the outset. Office planners and architects tend to imagine that the setup of their own offices should be the way that everyone should work. They pretend that their own subjective methods are objective empirical results. For this reason the most advanced offices usually end up looking like the offices of architects and planners. In the same way, Frederick Taylor had claimed as "scientific" what had in fact been rooted in a personal obsession: the need to make workers stop soldiering and submit to supposed experts like himself. To his credit, Propst had at least attempted to verify his own thoughts by speaking to a handful of other experts. But he had only sought out sympathetic voices; his surveys, likewise, were planned, unconsciously or not, to confirm his own thoughts on the matter. It may be, of course, that office workers themselves would have appreciated the malleability of Action Office—it was certainly better than the imaginatively null kinds of workplaces they were accustomed to. But on this matter, as on most others, their voices are unrecorded, and regardless, there were never enough Action Office installations to test their reactions.

The failure of the first Action Office on the market might finally have been due to another factor: the cynicism of executives. They had the final say on how their offices looked, since they controlled the bottom line, and the last thing they were going to drop a ton of money on was a set of fancy chairs and desks for their junior and middle managers, let alone the steno pool. The news about the junior staff being "knowledge workers" hadn't yet reached the top. And office space was growing at too fast a volume for anyone to be concerned about niceties. Something faster was needed, something more easily reproducible.

Nonetheless, Propst took the design community's enthusiasm over Action Office as a vote of confidence. He went back to his team and pushed forward. He was determined to return with what he believed the office needed, his vision uncompromised.

□

Rather than merely acceding to the market demands, Propst doubled down on his own theoretical work. He became more confident in the essential rightness of his thinking, incorporating more and more of the spirit of the 1960s—individualism, autonomy—into his notes and writing. He became relatively well-known in the world of architecture, with his writings on design solicited by major journals. When the left-wing thinker and artist Ben Shahn presented his paper "In Defense of Chaos" at the International Design Conference in Aspen in 1967, arguing that space needed to be more anarchist, Propst responded with his own paper essentially agreeing, saying that individuals needed more freedom in managing their spaces. (The fact that Shahn's essay was later published in *Ramparts* magazine, one of the antiwar New Left's house organs, begins to suggest the depth of interrelations between the practitioners of design, art, and management theory in the 1960s.)

The concept that Propst came to reiterate again and again was that office design needed to be "forgiving." That is, overly designed and stylized spaces were "unforgiving," barriers against change, and change was coming into the office one way or another. Computers were automating more and more processes, allowing office workers to reduce routine tasks to focus more on "tasks of judgment." What an office design had to do was anticipate these changes as best as it could, through modularity and flexibility. It had to be adaptable, movable. This meant that "design" itself had to be tossed out: anything that made his concept more expensive and less "forgiving" to user needs was against the concept. This meant that Nelson, whose relationship with Propst had never been close, had to go. Though he had been integral to the conception of the Action Office, Nelson was too partial to humanizing and stylish touches in his products. The predilection for beauty of the object was an obstacle in Propst's eyes; it detracted from the beauty of the office worker's motion in space.

By the end of 1967, Propst had made significant improvements. The space was smaller; the interlocking walls were mobile, lighter, and made of disposable materials; storage space was raised off the ground. Action Office II was Propst's attempt to give form to the office worker's desire. A "workstation" for the "human performer," it consisted of three walls, obtusely angled and movable, which an office worker could arrange to create whatever work space he or she wanted. The usual desk was accompanied by shelves of varied heights and variable placement, which required constant vertical movement on the part of the worker—because "man," as Propst observed, is a "vertically oriented machine."[37] Tackboards and pushpin walls allowed for individuation. Intentionally depersonalized, the new Action Office would be a template for any individual to create his or her own ideal work space.

Action Office II (1968). *Courtesy of Herman Miller*

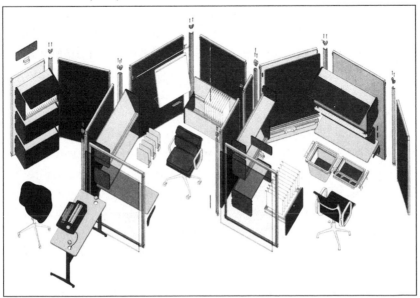

Early brochures for Action Office II play this up—we see modular walls expanded to create broad, half-hexagonal spaces; tackboards are used to great effect, and the walls are adorned by hangings, maps, or chalkboards. Workers are in motion or constant conversation, some even standing to make dramatic pointing gestures to other workers sitting on high swivel chairs (which force them constantly to move between sitting and standing positions).

So it was that in 1968, Propst unveiled Action Office II and published a seventy-one-page pamphlet that trumpeted the theoretical bases of his new design. Called *The Office: A Facility Based on Change*, it was a kind of Port Huron Statement for the white-collar worker. Contained in a single pamphlet was a meditation on work and its changing status in 1960s America. Propst's narrative of the office teems with high historical drama, centered on one key event in the history of labor: the gradual replacement of America's manufacturing base with white-collar work. "We are a nation of office dwellers," Propst asserted. The face of capitalism had changed; the office had become a "thinking place"; "the real office consumer [was] the mind." Repetitive work, of the kind performed in factories and typing pools, was disappearing, to be replaced by "knowledge work"— and the new office was going to have to keep up. Propst noted that in the spring of 1968—that fabled spring of Prague and Paris— the New York Stock Exchange, which he called "the office-of-all-offices," suffered a "hiccup" when the manual machine processing required to run share transactions was suddenly and dramatically outpaced by the volume of trading, forcing the exchange to limit its hours.

Despite the dated references, Propst's thinking is uncannily prescient, foreseeing many of the same obsessions that people in the office are busying about today. Many of the problems he saw as contemporary remain contemporary; many of his solutions are those later proposed by others. He describes the constant state of technological and economic changes that motivate endless innovation in business. He laments the overload of information inundating office workers. He outlines the multitude of positions for conversations that office workers need. Like so many today, he stresses the danger, to one's mental and physical vitality, of sitting too long at one's desk.

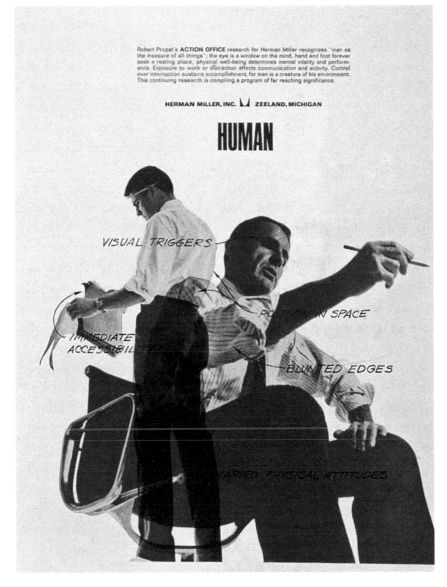

Advertisement for Action Office II. *Courtesy of Herman Miller*

He argues that the ideal office should make room for "meaningful traffic" between knowledge workers and lights upon the constant battle between privacy and openness in the office.[38] And behind it all one can see Propst reflecting on the chaos and ferment of the 1960s: "Our culture shows all the signs of digesting ideas and producing new values at a dismayingly rapid rate. New music forms are innovated, adopted and rejected in a few months. Social evolution is bursting by all the old progress norms."[39] Much of Propst's understanding of ergonomics and the importance of interaction in the office will sound familiar to many today, and even intuitive. At the time, however, the panoramic vision he had of the office—taking in history and psychology, ergonomics and theories of business—was virtually unprecedented.

Yet reading through Propst's book is like peering into a mind concerned only with brains and legs, abstractions and motions. It is unencumbered by personalities and bad behavior. His vision is so complete, so penetrating, that it refines human needs out of existence. He sees only bodily needs, and in his models people are only bundles of mental stimuli. Were they not also bundles of emotions and deeper needs, one day greedy and heartless and competitive, the next warm and collegial? Despite and perhaps a little because of his clear understanding of the poor thinking that had led to the terrible offices he was trying to undo, he had a very clear understanding of where history was going: in his direction. As doctrinaire as any orthodox Marxist, Propst implied that implacable social forces would make human beings recognize the inevitability of his designs. He was unable to imagine a world in which they might be perverted to unfathomable ends. His optimism would be his undoing.

□

Like its predecessor, Action Office II was received as a liberation. In a *New York Post* column titled "Revolution Hits the Office," Sylvia Porter, a reporter rather than a design expert, wrote that in the light of Action Office II the old office was now officially doomed: "You know . . . the completely enclosed 'boxes' in which the bosses isolate themselves behind monster mahogany status symbols;

the inhuman row upon rigid row of steel desks with their clumsy drawers at which you sit all day; the huge file cabinets in which we hide paper until it is obsolete, irrelevant and overwhelming." With Action Office there were changes afoot at last. "As a person who has spent a working lifetime in the open spaces of a newspaper city room," she wrote, "I find the concept entirely appealing. I particularly like the idea of sitdown or standup work stations." And she was enchanted by Robert Propst's language as well: "Incidentally, Propst won't even use the word 'desk.' In the modern office, you, the 'human performer,' will work at 'free standing units' in your 'work station,' choosing either to 'sit down' or 'stand up.' Like it?" For her, "the success of the concept seems assured."[40]

Action Office II received immediate praise from the office furniture industry as well. Herman Miller launched a nationwide marketing campaign to educate designers on the use of the system, simultaneously inaugurating an accompanying lecture series on the future of creative office work (for which Action Office would be the ideal work space). An Action Office II model kit was provided to interested facilities managers. An architecture firm, JFN, installed the first Action Office II system in its workplace. Initially, sales were

Action Office II in action. *Courtesy of Herman Miller*

slow, but after the competitor Haworth produced a rival modular office system, Propst's concept was validated, and sales began to take off. Steelcase's 9000 series and Knoll's Zapf System soon followed.

The federal government helped these along as well. In order to stimulate business spending, the Treasury in the 1960s made a slight but powerfully significant change in the tax code, making it easier for companies to write off depreciating assets. A shorter shelf life was established for furniture and equipment, while more permanent features of buildings had a longer range. In other words, it became cheaper to have an Action Office than an actual office.[41] The Action Office eventually became Herman Miller's most important product and an inescapable feature of office design.

There were concerns early. The jilted Nelson somewhat predictably foresaw problems in Action Office II's design—or the lack thereof. Yet his insights into its flaws, however motivated by hurt, were genuine. In a prescient letter to Herman Miller's vice president for corporate design and communication, Nelson lamented Action Office II's "dehumanizing effect as a working environment":

> This characteristic is not an accident, but the inevitable expression of a concept which views people as links in a corporate system for handling paper, or as input-output organisms whose "efficiency" has been a matter of nervous concern for the past half century.
>
> People do indeed function in such roles, but this is not what people *are*, merely a description of what they *do* during certain hours . . .
>
> One does not have to be an especially perceptive critic to realize that A[ction] O[ffice] II is definitely not a system which produces an environment gratifying for people in general. But it is admirable for planners looking for ways of cramming in a maximum number of bodies, for "employees" (as against individuals), for "personnel," corporate zombies, the walking dead, the silent majority. A large market.[42]

Meanwhile, the copycat Action Offices were starting to have strange, unforeseen effects on other workplaces. Rather than making them more flexible, they in fact appeared to be making them more regimented. Douglas Ball, a designer for the rival furniture company Haworth, came up with one of the many knockoff designs for the Canadian company Sunar. Initially excited, he emerged from the completed space utterly depressed. "I went to see the first installation of the Sunar system, a huge government project. The panels were all seventy inches tall, so unless you were six-foot-three you couldn't look over the top. It was awful—one of the worst installations I'd ever seen," Ball said. "We thought it was extremely flexible in the plan view, but we had never considered the vertical elevation."[43] And it was too late to fix the problem. He had trapped people in giant fabric-wrapped walls, when he had meant, like Propst, to free them. The open-office plan that had descended like a thunderbolt from Germany in the 1960s was becoming crowded with screens and partitions. The use of Action Office, one designer wrote in the late 1970s, "will almost certainly modify planning in a way that leads away from the original *Bürolandschaft* concept."[44] This would turn out to be a great understatement.

What is happening? was the sentiment of designers at the time. In the wake of two massive changes in the thinking about offices— *Bürolandschaft* and Action Office—the sense of ultimate progress, of "human performers" (as Propst called them) growing more and more powerful, seems to reverse. The space is taking them over. The designers feel history slipping away from them, perverting everything they hoped for into everything they had fought against—their creation suddenly alive and powerful and monstrous in ways they could not predict. For it turned out that companies had no interest in creating autonomous environments for their "human performers." Instead, they wanted to stuff as many people in as small a space for as cheaply as possible as quickly as possible. By 1978, Propst was composing memos on repositioning his design, panicked over the obsession with "easily defined and accountable cost savings." "Meanwhile, other matters of more profound influence on the real productivity of organizations have slipped into the background," he worried. "Action Office, which was conceived as a tool for managers, now has lost much of its initial broad dialogue with management."[45] Action Office had been meant for flexibility; instead, a new

Action Office II (1978)—the denouement. *Courtesy of Herman Miller*

rigidity set in—though it was wrapped disingenuously in humanistic fabric. Propst's memos seemed to have no effect. Soon the designs for Action Office in the Herman Miller brochures began to seem more box-like. They were selling what the companies wanted.

□

Whether due to the dystopian visions of *Playtime* or more concrete reasons, European office workers saw the writing on the wall. Offices were going in a bad direction, and nobody but they seemed to notice it. In a powerful shift, inspired by the industrial revolts taking place in France and Italy and Germany in the 1960s and 1970s, white-collar workers began to form "councils," demanding an end to *Bürolandschaft* and all the supposedly progressive ideas of the designers. They had had enough of being imposed upon. They would decide their workplaces for themselves. In one country after the other—Italy (1975), Germany (1976), Sweden (1977), and the

Netherlands (1979)—laws were passed mandating that employee representatives be allowed to sit on the supervisory boards of companies.[46] Through their new organs of dissent, employees voiced their collective hatred of *Bürolandschaft*. Surveys suggested that the offices had "unpleasant temperature variations, drafts, low humidity, unacceptable noise levels, poor natural lighting, lack of visual contact with the outside, and lack of natural ventilation."[47] But there was another factor as well: the open-office plan also ran up against a strong cultural propensity for privacy that had built up in northern European offices and was difficult to contravene.

From that point on, the European office diverged sharply from American office design. The Action Office made no inroads into the tightly wound, narrow floor plates of European office buildings. But rather than getting less innovative as a result, European offices became more daring. Stricter regulations led to better and more humane forms of experimentation. The landmark Centraal Beheer office building in the Netherlands, designed by Herman Hertzberger and unveiled in 1972, was one such example. Hertzberger insisted that the building's employees "have the feeling of being part of a working community without being lost in the crowd."[48] In other words, Hertzberger wanted to keep the offices relatively open but without compromising the ability of individuals to have their own space and to organize their spaces in whatever way they chose. His solution was to make the office into something like a raised village or community tree house: Open-office areas for around ten people were connected by walkways and common spaces. Workers were encouraged to bring in plants and other decorations so that their spaces could become their own.[49] It was, in fact, like Action Office II—except these spaces were made of concrete and had the aura of permanence about them. The workers in them were both protected and invited to stay. A similar focus on worker comfort would characterize the major offices of the 1980s, such as the Scandinavian Airlines building (1988) in Stockholm. In what would prove a hugely influential move, the building was designed as a small "city," with a central "street" running directly through the plan, branching off into "neighborhoods" of private offices. Workers could choose to interact in the street if they liked, or they could retreat to their offices to do concentrated work. In the years to come, as the cube-shaped monster invading American offices became ever more frightening, designers would look to the European exception as inspiration—or as a means of escape.

☐

In 1998, a journalist was sent to interview Robert Propst—then seventy-seven years old—for *Metropolis* magazine. Propst noted that his design proved irrepressibly popular: forty million employees in America alone worked in—by his own count—forty-two different versions of the Action Office. But he failed to note that by that point they were all known by the same name: the cubicle.

He defended the features that had made his design so popular: its austerity, its flexibility. But he conceded what he hadn't been willing to understand then. "The dark side of this is that not all organizations are intelligent and progressive," Propst says. "Lots are run by crass people who can take the same kind of equipment and create hellholes. They make little bitty cubicles and stuff people in them. Barren, rat-hole places. . . . I never had any illusions that this is a perfect world," he concluded.[50] Two years later he was dead.

"I saw it happen . . . there was a moment when the orthogonal came in. Someone figured out that you didn't need the 120-degree [angle], and it went click. That was a bad day," Francis Duffy told me in an interview. "It took only five seconds for Action Office to turn into a box. Such a nice guy, Robert Propst. Couldn't have happened to a nicer guy."[51]

7

SPACE INVADERS

The aspiring executive woman is engaged
in a perpetual battle with hangovers of past
discrimination as well as the renegade troops
of continuing discrimination. She must take
extraordinary measures to insure that her player
status signals are registering on the same wavelength
as those of comparable or superior men, and that
message is, "Yes, I'm ready to play."
——BETTY LEHAN HARRAGAN, *Games Mother Never Taught You*[1]

In the 1970s—that beige, dishonest decade—drinking at lunchtime was still a necessity, but the de rigueur two-martini habit was slowly giving way to a few glasses of wine.[2] Afterward there was always the postprandial haze, the opiate fatigue that even a stiff coffee chaser couldn't forestall. "In the early afternoon it was always quiet, the whole place tossing slowly in tropical repose," wrote Don DeLillo in *Americana*, "as if the building itself swung on a miraculous hammock . . . [T]here was something wonderful about that time, the hour or so before we remembered. It was the time to sit on your sofa instead of behind the desk, and to call your secretary into the office and talk in soft voices about nothing in particular—films, books, water sports, travel, nothing at all."[3]

When there weren't fun lunches, there were business lunches (also boozy). There were the dinners for trainees. Superiors flew in, and they had to be entertained. One manager at a major corporation of the time thought he would spend about nine days of the first quarter of the year simply entertaining.[4] The rest of the time, there was the work, an endless amount of responding to communications and an endless amount of meetings—the latter making for nearly one-third to one-half of their day. Meanwhile, for the contemporary office worker who complains about the overload of e-mail, the pileup of mail and telegrams in the older, pre-digital office was nearly as onerous. In one list of a manager's duties from the time:

> Paper work and mail; sales calls and negotiating contracts; reviewing telegrams at the office and at home; receiving and making phone calls (including unsuccessful repeat calls); talking to subordinates; interviewing recruits; reviewing with secretaries; teaching trainees; contracts, monthly summaries, weekly summaries, forecasts, sales plans, and quarterly reviews; reviewing subordinates' expense accounts, career reviews (preparation and feedback); performance appraisals; meetings with others in the function, including technological, professional and associated functions; entertainment such as golf and skiing, travel; training programs; handling specific crises . . . ; active recruiting on campus; discussions with others about competitors' activities; organizing meetings; reviewing business plans continuously; watching video tape cassettes sent from headquarters; travel, and time waiting for planes or appointments; solving problems of interface with people in other functions; and special task force meetings.[5]

When it wasn't about commuting, lunching, and drinking, office life had become chiefly about meetings, training, and paperwork. For people down a level, there was still the routinization: the typing pool, the adding machines, the new automation of the computers.

Yet the human element persisted: where systems of bureaucratic control, or simply a nasty boss, threatened to empty out the mild pleasures of work, there always arose a tendency for office workers to find ways of coping. The need for personalizing the workplace accounted partly for the persistence of the secretary—a stubborn remainder of an old workplace paternalism. Having a secretary to type or take dictation wasn't necessary so long as you had a steno pool; computer automation was already making certain functions obsolete or ensuring that they were better done when not attached to a boss. But for managers, having a secretary (or two) was a status symbol that had accrued to their forebears, and one that they were not inclined to give up. For secretaries, too, the work required personality traits—affability, charisma, aplomb—that more mechanized kinds of office work ruled out, or at least didn't consider valuable. Each day could prove unpredictable, based on the whims of a boss, who might need you to entertain and care for visiting clients or—it wasn't in the job description—want you to return his wife's shoes or stay at his home and dog-sit while he went on vacation. In Rosabeth Moss Kanter's study of a large 1970s corporation, she found that the two most important traits in performance ratings meted out to secretaries were "initiative and enthusiasm" and "personal service orientation" (which one manager glossed as the "ability to anticipate and take care of personal needs"). And in her study the secretaries liked it that way. The work was organized in such a way as to make it entirely personalized—the skills that they got praised for were entirely personality based, and most of them felt that they had no other particular abilities. Much of their prestige was derivative, coming from the high status of the people they worked for. Limited opportunities for advancement, too, had curtailed the worldviews of the staff. Some went out of their way to verify the old stereotypes of "the office wife." As one executive secretary put it:

> I think if I've been at all successful with men, it's because I'm a good listener and interested in their world. I enjoy it, I don't become bored with it. They tell me about their personal life too. Family problems, financial, and the problems of raising children. Most of the ones I'm referring to are divorced. In looking through the years they were married, I can see this is what probably happened. I know if I were the wife, I would be interested in their work. I feel the wife of an executive would be a better wife had she been a secretary first. As a secretary, you

learn to adjust to the boss's moods. Many marriages would be happier if the wife would do that.[6]

This was the unchanging, staid world the office cubicle entered: it was simply another piece of furniture, whose appearance hardly seemed to register in the consciousness of office workers. From the stoned placidity of *Life in the Crystal Palace* to the 1970s, it would seem as if nothing had fundamentally changed. Of course, there was a new permissiveness in the fashions. "For years I've been taking the same train to New York that an advertising executive takes," one Connecticut commuter quoted in *Newsweek* said. "He gets on at Darien, and used to be strictly a gray-flannel, button-down, crew-cut type. But now he wears flowered jackets, broad ties and side-burns down to here. I guess that's what's happening on Madison Avenue."[7] But things were changing in the office in a more profound way, with a kind of silent stirring that was difficult to sense; the office was becoming at once more hopeful and more confused, happier for some who had never been in it, less happy for those who were used to the way things were. Social changes outside the curtain walls were beginning to make their presence felt within, in ways that management theory had not fully anticipated.

After 1964, when the passage of the Civil Rights Act led to the establishment of the Equal Employment Opportunity Commission (EEOC), pressure began to build on corporations to hire African Americans. But transformations in the color of the workplace became more significant in the following years of militancy; in studies at the time, managers reported that the urban rebellions by blacks in cities across the country compelled them more seriously. "The riots affected everyone's attitude," one lower-level white bank manager attested. "They prompted a realization of the problem. It was an unfortunate way to do it, but it helped. And it's not an unusual way for this country—it's always been violent."[8] In 1972, Congress passed H.R. 1746, which gave the EEOC the power to sue noncompliant firms directly. Affirmative action programs sprang up at many companies, and the hiring and promotion of blacks increased dramatically.

Discomfort and resistance soon followed. Sociological studies confirmed outright racism from white managers. "I keep hearing the old clichés like, 'We don't see why you niggers want so much' and 'You blacks are getting all the breaks,'" one black manager at a large manufacturing firm said. Another at the same firm mentioned a company-wide memo from a manager which said that "he didn't want any more blacks in his department because they were lazy and didn't work."[9] But more often it seemed that office workers expressed a low-level coded or euphemistic fear of environmental change—one that stemmed directly from the old pressure toward social cohesion and conformity for which the office environment was renowned. Black workers, and many people of color more generally, often found themselves coming up against vague currents of prejudice; as a result, they would experience even more acute feelings of paranoia and dread than office life already tended to encourage. When working lunches or casual get-togethers took place, they would routinely not be asked to join. One black woman reported that her peers "never invite me to informal discussions, meetings, and luncheons, and many times they discuss issues related to my job."[10] "I saw younger whites come into the organization and other whites take them aside and tell them things, share information," one black manager said, recalling his first days in an organization. "I saw the new whites interacting with other people I didn't even know. That wasn't done with me or for me. Now I'm feeling really strange." But because of his isolation, he wasn't immediately ready to see these actions for what they were: "At first—not for a long time, really—I didn't attribute my weird feelings to racism. I thought it was me! I thought I was doing something wrong."[11] Only when that same manager began to mention his concerns to other black workers at the company did he get confirmation of the same kinds of biases: "Glory! Man, I felt . . . *good*! I was relieved. It wasn't just me!"[12]

It wasn't just me: though the specific feeling of being a black manager in a white corporation led to a very particular kind of isolation, the feeling of being alone and responsible for one's fate was more likely in the office environment in general. The willingness to blame oneself for failures or mistakes was a powerful temptation. Partly this stemmed from the hopeful prognostications about knowledge work and the increasing importance of education.

Boosters throughout the 1960s and 1970s, such as Drucker and the economist Gary Becker (coiner of the term "human capital"), held that education naturally led to employment and that a more deeply educated populace would lead to better and more thoughtful jobs.

But with office work, this proved not only untrue but spectacularly so. Not only had white-collar work changed little, but much of it had arguably gotten less demanding and more rationalized. Yet to get a job in an office increasingly required higher levels of education than were strictly necessary for the job. In fact, the growth in white-collar employment by 1970 had been on the lower rungs of the ladder rather than the "knowledge work" prophesied by so many. And in various measurements of white-collar work—such as one study of 125 branch offices of a New York bank—the level of education and the level of performance of these workers were *inversely* related.[13]

Offices were filling up with overeducated workers whose expectations were gradually running up against their actual possibilities for advancement. And the "human relations" paradigm was losing its ability to soothe them. Education had the use of creating a certain aura around work in an office that the office usually failed to fulfill. Yet rather than forming a frustrated "white-collar proletariat" and demanding changes, they tended to blame themselves in the same breath that they (borrowing some language from the student movement) blamed "the system." In one interview, a manager in a multinational, called Howard Carver, decried the "aridity, the petty politicking and the scary power scramble" of his world. "The fact is, the company, the bureaucracy, can only use a small part of a man's capabilities and yet it demands so much in time, in loyalty, in petty politics, in stupidities . . . the ratio of morons, time-wasters, time-servers, petty politicians and scared rabbits is so high here that it's discouraging, and I'm beginning to feel only little bully boys and smart operators can claw their way through middle management." Yet the same man blamed the failure of his career, its dead-ending in the very middle of middle management, on a small social mistake, when he wondered aloud, in the presence of a vice president, when the CEO of his company would finally retire. It turned out the vice president was secretly the right-hand man of the CEO, his eyes and ears for the rest of the company. "That's how I blew it," he said. "It's been ten years since that day and while I've gotten on the escalator and gone up routinely, all the good posts have eluded me." It was a minor moment of office politics, and because he knew the game, he believed he had failed. Yet his final description of the corporate world is bleak—as grim as any of the factory worker tales that littered Studs Terkel's *Working* and far from the stirring tales of corporate power at mid-century:

> I've looked around . . . and I can see, not malevolence, not conspiracy, not a sinister force operating in the world for its own hidden purposes or trying to bend the public to its will nor, on the bright side, as so many would have you believe, a hard-working fulfilling existence, a set of challenges and excitements that can command the best of truly good men, but a trivialization of human effort and aspiration in a chaotic and mindless drudgery, a sidetracking of valuable human resources, and, for most truly intelligent men who have so much to offer, as I once did, in the end a career in a wasteland.[14]

□

On the outside, the offices were changing as well, in a way that refracted the ill will inside them in a peculiar way. Until the 1970s, some brand of architectural "modernism"—usually meaning the International Style—had prevailed without question, almost monolithically consistent across the country. Developers, planners, and politicians supported modernism, at once inflexible as a form and adaptable for multipurpose use, amenable to both government and corporations, an all-purpose glassy, boxy style—or occasionally a "brutalist" concrete—for any kind of building. The building as glass envelope had gone essentially unquestioned: despite the rise in space planning, few architects devoted any kind of mind toward the interiors of these buildings.

At the same time, despite two oil shocks, stagflation, and, in 1982, a spike in real interest rates, knocking the jobless rate up to 10 percent and precipitating what was then the worst economic crisis since the Great Depression, the blast radius of the speculative boom in office development, detonated in the 1960s, expanded implacably through the 1970s and 1980s. Nothing could stop the office space binge. Fifty-four million square feet of office space were added in New York in the 1970s, forty-six million in the 1980s. The two main towers of the World Trade Center, the tallest buildings on the planet, steadily grew to cast a long shadow on a city that, in the mid-1970s, was on the verge of bankruptcy. Designed by Minoru Yamasaki, one of the premier architects of modernism, their unbroken upward sweep of tiny windows and neo-Gothic tracery was then perceived by many critics as a bizarre and anonymous—not to say hubristic—testament to New York's new emphasis on the banking and finance sectors of its economy. Lewis Mumford described their enormousness as "purposeless gigantism and technological exhibitionism." Meanwhile, the critic Charles Jencks saw specters of fascism:

> The effect of extreme repetition may be monotony or a hypnotic trance: positively it can elicit feelings of the sublime and the inevitable because it so incessantly returns to the same theme. A musical figure, repeated at length, such as that in *Bolero*, acts not just as a form of mental torture but as a pacifier. Repetitive architecture can put you to sleep. Both Mussolini and Hitler used it as a form of thought control knowing that before people can be coerced they first have to be hypnotized and bored.[15]

When they opened in 1973, their ten million square feet of space wasn't filled and wouldn't be for several years. In 1977, the city suffered a catastrophic blackout; the towers loomed over the city, lightless, a symbol more forbidding than anything dreamed up by Kubrick in *2001*.

Downtown business districts all over the country added tower after tower in a desperate attempt to refill empty city coffers with a new corporate tax base. San Francisco, which had been a dense but low-rise city for decades, began to capitalize on the growing computer industry to its south and its connection with the Pacific Rim economies to its west, led by Japan. It added an exorbitant amount of office space in just a few years, prompting a movement by many residents against what they saw as a catastrophic "Manhattanization." By 1981, the city had nearly quadrupled its annual increase in office space, to 2,156,500 square feet a year from an average of 573,000 in 1964. Only Boston had a higher proportion of office space to population. Boston itself crowned its skyline with I. M. Pei's glassier-than-thou John Hancock Tower in 1976. Soon after it was built, it became uncomfortably clear that it was structurally unsound, unprepared for the city's chill blast of high-speed winter winds. Like something out of a disaster movie, large panes from the building's curtain wall began to loosen, dislodge, and careen to the ground, littering the downtown pavement with shards of glass. In any case, the slow return of corporate headquarters to metropolitan cores hadn't stopped the flight of back-office operations out to the suburbs (possibly fleeing all the falling glass in the cities). A pastoralia of office parks was springing up in commuter corridors with delirious abandon: the Raleigh–Durham–Chapel Hill Triangle; the Boston Tech Corridor; Silicon Valley; and the D.C.-centered swath of the Northern Virginia suburbs.

Even if the amount of office space grew, the way it was housed was starting to signal a change in the way people were thinking about architecture—with implications about how people should work as well. All precepts of modernism that had attempted to legislate how people should live, move, and labor were coming under attack. In 1961, Jane Jacobs had delivered the monumental treatise *The Death and Life of Great American Cities*, a devastating attack on the effect of architectural modernism on the American city. Ostensibly a brief against the planning mistakes and social costs of urban "renewal" programs, *Death and Life* also lodged an aesthetic critique of the way modernism had insisted on spacing superblocks—housing and office towers—against the natural, spontaneous, and time-honored order of street life. Where people like her political opponent Robert Moses had set up cities to be amenable to cars, the city of Jacobs's imagination was rooted in tightly knit communities that depended on pedestrian life. It was a version of cities heavily tilted in favor of face-to-face interaction, small public spaces, and low-rise density over high-rise grandiosity. One could hear echoes of the critique in Robert Propst's own thinking about "fortuitous encounters" in the office and his emphasis on flexible, "forgivable" design—design that catered to human needs, that didn't destroy already existing cultures.

Without quite intending it, Jacobs's critique might have become one of the first foundation stones in the giddy edifice housing all the artistic movements gathered up under the term "postmodernism." It had its first strong proponents in the field of architecture. In the hands of architects and critics like Charles Jencks and Robert Venturi, modernism—especially in the figure of Le Corbusier—came under attack for its blind utopianism, its willingness to ignore context and scale and landscape in favor of large-scale projects of social reengineering. Jencks cited the infamous failure of a public housing project, the Pruitt-Igoe homes in St. Louis, as the death knell of modernism. "Modern Architecture died in St. Louis on July 15, 1972, at 3:32 p.m. (or thereabouts)," he wrote in *The Language of Post-modern Architecture*, "when the infamous Pruitt-Igoe scheme, or rather several of its slab blocks, were given the final *coup de grâce* by dynamite."[16] Jencks noted that Pruitt-Igoe had been sanctified by the Le Corbusier acolyte organization, the International Congress of Modern Architecture, and had won an award from the American Institute of Architects when the buildings were inaugurated in 1951. Consisting of fourteen-story blocks spaced apart by swaths of greenery, it was perfect Corbusianism. But though hospitable to rational ideals, it was seen by many as hostile to human needs. Over time the buildings began to fall apart, and crime within them began to rise. Though the reasons for this were complex—largely deriving from the disappearance of St. Louis's manufacturing jobs—the legend swiftly arose that it was the building's *design* that had destroyed the building from within.

Critics drew the necessary conclusion: that modernism was antihuman. And it was the commercial architecture that revealed this best. For Jencks, modernism had ignored context to such an extent that it had essentially modeled every building as an office building. He claimed that no architect stopped to ask himself, "Are I-beams and plate glass appropriate to housing?" Nor, when they subsequently and deliberately confused the language of architecture for working and living, did they realize that "the net result would be to diminish and compromise both functions by equating them: working and living would become interchangeable on the most banal, literal level, and unarticulated on a higher, metaphorical plane. The psychic overtones to these two different activities would remain unexplored, accidental, truncated."[17]

Yet the answer that the postmodernists proposed wasn't to separate work and life more, to pursue a deeper purism, but rather to confuse everything more vigorously and in a playful spirit. One of the founding documents of the movement, Venturi's *Learning from Las Vegas* (co-authored with the architects Steven Izenour and Denise Scott Brown), said it all with its title. Rather than proclaiming the tragic purity of contemporary architecture, as the modernists did, architects would borrow from the historical landscape with a kind of studious abandon, combining in a single building styles from neoclassical predecessors and neo-Gothic motifs (it was often the "revived" style, rather than the original, that attracted them). Venturi, Scott Brown, and Izenour also paid special attention to the vernacular or pop cultural landscape—kitsch hotels, classic American diners, even gas stations and hot dog stands—that had been constructed by developers or second-rate builders instead of star architects. The gaiety of this mélange was what attracted Venturi in particular, who had redescribed it, in an uncharacteristically haughty phrase, as "complexity and contradiction in architecture." Although it attempted to look wild and populist, the effect of superficiality was a kind of *diligens negligentia*, a cultivated negligence: the postmodernists' thinking was in fact being processed with deep self-consciousness through a new brand of hypertheorization of the nature of building (often taking place in the heady pages of the journal *Oppositions*). Men trained as modernists (and they were virtually all men) began to make their names as postmodernists: Frank Gehry, Charles Moore, Robert A. M. Stern, Michael Graves, Peter Eisenman. Their houses and projects were deliberately eclectic, scaled down, making more than halfhearted genuflections to the context of their surrounding landscape. Their position of openness to bizarre forces moving in from the fringes paralleled the movement in office design toward letting the users articulate their own spaces, such as Robert Propst's hope that the Action Officers would decorate their walls to express their individuality.

But while postmodernism was deployed in a smattering of houses, museums, and university buildings, it would take an office building—a symbol of corporate power—to cement its arrival as a cultural force. One figure emerged from the shadows to set the tone for postmodernist office buildings. It was Philip Johnson, erstwhile partner of Mies van der Rohe—the man who had brought the International Style to the United States. Now in his seventies, bald, ever more impish, donning thick round glasses in the style of Le Corbusier, he had outlived the modernists he had supported, confronting a future of which he would be proclaimed the living master. Whatever fervors had led him to linger in the wilds of fascism or subsequently embrace the fastidious cool of modernism, he had shed. In his grand old age, he cultivated a charmingly weak attention span. "My direction is clear: traditionalism," he said, seemingly soppy-stern in the old modernist, aphoristic way, before coyly and folksily describing his lax habit of combining various styles in his buildings: "I try to pick up what I like throughout history . . . I pick up anything, any old point in time or place."[18] Following his conviction that the truth was not found but made by personality, he had developed a conspicuous persona, one that could be easily talked about by carefully selected friends and reproduced in a fawning media. "Architecture in the main is something that is more apt to be run by popes, kings and generals than by public vote," Johnson once said, explaining his way of working, "and so I got interested in getting things done in a grand way."[19] Johnson held court at the Four Seasons Restaurant in the Seagram Building that he had designed. Its theatrical lighting was perfect for highlighting the most powerful power lunch in the world of architecture. Commissions came to him there, though he also dispensed largesse among the younger architects who crowded around him. In a manner hitherto unknown, the figure of the revolutionary architect had become a celebrity.

When the American Telephone and Telegraph Company—AT&T, popularly known as Ma Bell—asked him to design its new headquarters in New York, it had found the perfect choice. Johnson's playful, witty approach to architecture's past made him at once a paragon of the postmodernist revolt and a natural medium for corporations wanting to express their renewed power. Whatever corporate, futuristic ethos modernism had once expressed was now gone, dissipated amid a profusion of black boxes and gray civic centers that everyone now hated. Glass and concrete were the media of bureaucracy, of the creaking old American welfare state that, in the 1980s, a bold president would be given a tremendous mandate to dismantle.

The design that Johnson (through the aegis of his firm, Johnson/Burgee) provided would be the most admired and reviled building of the new decade, a consummate symbol of a new corporate culture. Following the past masters of the skyscraper form, like Burnham and Sullivan, the building was divided like a column, with base, shaft, and capital. AT&T's original headquarters from 1922 was also a classic skyscraper in this way, lavishly outfitted in marble, bronze, and alabaster and peppered with a profusion of ornamental columns.[20] Johnson therefore gestured back to the 1920s, when he chose to cover his steel frame not, as per usual, with a glass curtain wall but rather with acres of rosy-pink granite. Consisting of stacked panels running up to ten inches thick, the facade shone richly through the long summer months of Manhattan sunshine—and required six thousand more tons of steel than usual to support.[21] Other aspects of the building were exaggerated as well. He elongated the base of the building vertically, making it into a large, yawning loggia; the lobby was perhaps the most lavish entrance to any office building in the city. This was a thirty-eight-story building that rose sixty stories.[22] Rather than creating an open public space as he and Mies had earlier done with the Seagram Building, Johnson opened up a corridor framed with columns. Johnson would later explain that this space "was basically tailored to AT&T—it is an imperial space. AT&T didn't want lingerie stores in the lobby. They said 'Make it the front door into our empire. Let's make it so you'll be impressed when you go by.'"[23] And, most controversially and impishly, Johnson split the usual flat pediment with an angled inverted arch, scooped out of the air, nicknamed Chippendale after the eighteenth-century English furniture maker who used that gesture as his signature. It instantly made the building the most recognizable and infamous new addition to the crowded Manhattan skyline and earned it the nickname Chippendale Building. An aging George Nelson commented favorably, arguing that it was "high time things got dinguses on top."[24] Acerbic *Village Voice* critic Michael Sorkin had more choice words. "Not to put too fine a point on it, the building sucks," he wrote in his review. "The so-called 'post-modern' styling in which AT&T has been tarted up is simply a graceless attempt to disguise what is really just the same old building by cloaking it in this week's drag and by trying to hide behind the reputations of the blameless dead."[25]

The design and opening of the AT&T Building were a media event, the likes of which the public hadn't seen since the opening of the GM research facilities in the 1950s. *Time* magazine put Johnson on its cover: unsmiling, a gray wool coat draped over his shoulders and trailing like a cape, he clasped a miniature AT&T Building–shaped slab, like Moses bearing the tablets of the law: Johnson leading his children on an exodus from the tyranny of modernism into the promised land of plentiful building commissions. Michael Graves, one of the regulars at the Four Seasons table, got a commission to design the Portland Municipal Services Building for Portland, Oregon, in 1982, thanks chiefly to Johnson's intervention. In the same city where Pietro Belluschi's Equitable Building, the first aluminum-and-glass-skinned building of the International Style, had appeared, Graves's Municipal Services Building was a garish fever dream of terra-cotta and navy blue, an even more daring version of postmodernism than Johnson's corporate tower. Making the building squat and boxy where AT&T was thin and soaring, Graves pushed the absurdity of the design to its limits. He studded his facade with deliberately undersized windows, some as small as four feet square, crowded around a central glass curtain wall framed by two seven-story beams, which had the inadvertent appearance of a liturgical cross. Seven-story fake maroon columns culminated on two faces in keystone figures, on two others in blue-and-gold ribbons that were styled to look like prizes granted at a county fair. Belluschi himself, then eighty years old, called it "an enlarged jukebox" and "oversized beribboned Christmas package" that would have been

Philip Johnson, bearing the
AT&T Building. *Time & Life
Pictures*

better on the Las Vegas strip than in sober Portland.[26] It was the
kind of attack the postmodernists loved.

How did office workers deal with the architects' pretensions?
In Graves's building, not so well. The deliberate wackiness that led
him to produce such small windows meant that the dwellers of the
central open-plan, cubicle-ridden offices enjoyed little in the way of
natural light. In the AT&T Building, however, Johnson was aware
that he had to attract employees who largely commuted from the
New York suburbs, and so he had successfully imitated all the benefits of the suburban corporate campus. Besides having its own medical office, gym, and multiple dining rooms, the office building had
an impressive two-story-tall "sky lobby," an entrance five stories
above the ground floor, where workers got off one set of elevators
to enter another set, surrounded by walls of gleaming white marble.
The cubicled work floors, surrounded by corridors of private offices,
were ten feet high, two and a half feet more than the standard, and

the core of the building was only thirty feet away from the windowed periphery, meaning that workers got a significant amount of natural light. In a nice touch, they were also given adjustable task lighting in addition to the usual fluorescent ceiling panels. Of course, given the imperial leanings of AT&T, the company had a grand staircase leading to a three-story executive floor, filled with faux-Georgian panels and moldings.[27]

Soon after it appeared, the AT&T Building began to symbolize a changing American workplace in a very different way than its owners and designers had imagined. An antitrust case launched against the company in 1974 came to a conclusion in 1982. AT&T, which had held a monopoly on U.S. telecommunications for generations, had lost. Its new building opened in 1984, just as it was tasked with carrying out its divestiture order. AT&T sold off two-thirds of its assets; in the first two years of divestiture, it laid off 56,000 people. Between 1984 and 1992, 107,291 unionized employees were discharged—one of the biggest business discharges ever, in a decade that would see many more such mass layoffs.[28] Johnson had made AT&T's office spaces flexible, with ceiling grooves designed for easy slotting and removing of office walls. Now the kind of reorganization AT&T was engaged in meant getting rid of offices—and the people in them—altogether. "Flexibility," that sacred word in business, came to have a sinister meaning. By the end of the decade, when the country was sliding into yet another recession, AT&T was questioning the need of having a fifteen-hundred-person corporate headquarters at all. In 1992, it paid New York City the $14.5 million tax abatement that it no longer qualified for. Many of the employees were shifted to an old building; still more were told that they should "work from home"—an unusual phrase that most office workers had not heard before. A number of unassigned cubicles were available to anyone who needed to come in. Otherwise they sat empty.

□

"Stress is high in my life right now," an AT&T manager wrote in his diary in 1983. "Principally because of the job. The problem is that I see myself standing alone . . . It's damn near impossible to keep from going crazy . . . Sometimes I feel that this stress is self-induced, because of my conscientiousness . . . In this era of ambiguity, uncertainty and inordinate turf battles, the manager who *really* cares may well kill himself with anxiety and worry and what those emotions generate—stress."[29] This was a former organization man who now confronted the total collapse of his world. Just ten years prior, office workers still believed that they were essential to their companies—so essential that many of them stayed where they started until they retired, having moved steadily up the ladder. But a new breed of executives, threatened by waves of global competition from Germany and Japan and seeking more and more profits to deliver to shareholders, sliced through their ranks. All the old certainties seemed to have dissolved in an instant.

In the early 1980s, things were looking so desperate that people of all stripes, especially managers and managers-to-be, began to buy business books. Hitherto these were objects so shameful that people might, or should, have covered them in brown paper, but in 1982, the worst year of the U.S. recession, people bought Tom Peters and Robert H. Waterman's study of high-performing companies, *In Search of Excellence*, in such massive quantities that they kept it on the best-seller list for the entire year. This was despite the fact that in writing the book, as Peters himself later admitted, they "had no idea what [they] were doing."[30] A year before, readers had similarly devoured William Ouchi's *Theory Z*—a sequel, of course, to Douglas McGregor's Theories X and Y that had so influenced Propst—a glimpse into the world of Japanese management, whose secrets appeared to be the reason the United States was getting its ass kicked, economically speaking. These books and ideas were so pervasive in the 1980s that they were all encapsulated in the Mike Nichols film *Working Girl* (1988). Melanie Griffith's Staten Island secretary, Tess McGill, arrives at her new job at the opening of the film and unloads her books at her desk, among which is *In Search of Excellence*, a sign of her entrepreneurial spirit and appetite for creative destruction. Later in the film she surprises a potential investor by confronting him at his daughter's wedding, and tries to seduce him into doing a deal by flattering his foresight in breathy tones of excitement, enumerating the high points of 1980s business thought:

"You're the man who . . . applied Japanese management principles while the others were still kowtowing to the unions, the man who saw the Ma Bell breakup coming from miles away."

And yet the theories were often antithetical to the message that American corporations appeared to take from them. For example, Japanese management theory, as Ouchi had it, was not antiunion. Indeed, Ouchi argued that any attempt by management to drive out a union would give employees "further proof of the duplicity of management."[31] He pointed out (however duplicitously himself) that Japanese companies had developed a cooperative rather than adversarial relationship with labor. Moreover, Ouchi spoke passionately of the lifetime employment policies of the Japanese corporation. (These in fact had been influenced by American thinking developed by the business theorist W. Edwards Deming, who had taught management to the Japanese during their period of postwar reconstruction.)[32] Overarching trust and symbolic gestures toward egalitarianism were the keys to Japanese management. "Theory Z" was a model for making corporations more clannish and the hierarchy less authoritarian. Ouchi even advocated an open-plan layout, over private offices and partitions, to capture more fully the trust that higher-ups were supposed to place in their subordinates. For Peters and Waterman, too, the problem was definitely not in the fact that Americans had to deal with unions or tough regulations; they noted that the Germans had tougher unions, and both the Germans and the Japanese had stricter regulations.[33] They agreed with Ouchi, and most office design theorists, that looseness and openness in office design were the keys to superior management. All of these made for the success of the books; they were also conspicuously ignored.

There was one message that Americans obviously took from the business books: the need to cut staff, to achieve—in the argot of *In Search of Excellence*—"lean form." Ouchi had noted that the Japanese were light on managerial ranks, and so did Peters and Waterman. Somehow, the Americans had to get there. And the only way to get there was to cut. "The numbers in many companies—both levels and employees—are staggering," Peters and Waterman wrote, in one of the book's few somber moments. "Ford over the last twenty-four months, in an effort to become more competitive with the Japanese, has cut more than 26 percent of its middle management staff; President Donald Petersen believes this is only the beginning. Reductions in the neighborhood of 50 percent, or even 75 percent, in levels and bodies are not uncommon targets when businessmen discuss what they could honestly do without."[34]

The targets proved about right. The 1980s became known as one of the meanest decades for corporate America in many generations; the 1990s, which were perhaps even meaner (statistically at least), somehow avoided the designation—perhaps because by then people had gotten inured to the practice. In those two decades, the generous benefits and stable wage increases that had defined a generation would vanish. Largely through brutal mass layoffs, American manufacturing workers would decline from a peak of 19.4 million in 1979 to 14.3 million in 2005. Of the country's five hundred largest manufacturers in 1980, one in three would disappear by 1990.[35] A spree of mergers and acquisitions and corporate raids, fueled by soon-to-be-infamous junk bonds, became regular headlines. The union movement had its spine split by newly emboldened corporations; it declined from a peak of about 35 percent of the labor force in the 1950s to 12.7 percent of the workforce today, hovering around 6 percent of the private-sector labor force. The aggressiveness of the new era was signaled by one government action, unrivaled in spectacle: Ronald Reagan's decision in 1981 to fire 11,345 striking air-traffic controllers, whose union had endorsed him for president.

Many job losses were in blue-collar sectors, due to deregulation of industry, plant closings, and offshoring. As for the office itself, insecurity had crept in by at least the mid-1980s; for instance, in 1985 BusinessWeek reported that at least one million white-collar or "non-production" jobs had been lost since 1979, because of the even heavier losses in what it called "smokestack America." (In a particularly grim irony that year, the New York Times reported that companies were purging their ranks of in-house business economists. That same year, the World Design Congress declared Propst's Action Office to be the most influential design of the previous quarter century.) But the fact remained that the office side of America was still safer than the factory side of it. Office workers were certainly told—constantly—that it was. The economy—as Propst, Drucker, and so many others had promised and continued to promise—would become perpetually more "postindustrial" and knowledge oriented. Machines and machine-made goods could be produced anywhere. Knowledge, however, unique to the character of the ever more individualized white-collar worker, was best produced at home. Perhaps the office worker labored in a cubicle, not a cozy corner office, but he might ascend to the corner office someday, and in the meantime his semipermanent walls were better than the laborer's open shop floor, which seemed more and more like a dangerous no-man's-land.

By the end of the decade, whatever remained of that fantasy would at last be punctured. On or around October 19, 1987, everything changed. The Dow shed 23 percent of its value in a day, and in the recessions that followed, white-collar workers—particularly managers and mid-level executives—began to recognize themselves as the targets of mass downsizing. Between 1990 and 1992, 1.1 million office workers would be laid off, exceeding blue-collar layoffs for the first time. In the ten days following the 1992 election of Bill Clinton, the pace of white-collar layoffs quickened (General Motors, 11,000 jobs; BellSouth, 8,000; Travelers, 1,500; Chevron, 1,500; DuPont, 1,243). The rate of layoffs in the early 1990s ended up being much higher than that of the mean years of the 1980s.

The chief victims of the cuts were middle management—the organization men (by the 1980s, about a third of them were organization women as well) who had defined American business in the preceding decades. Despite the critiques of organization man ideology, their ranks had swelled in the 1970s, growing at twice the rate of the lower rungs (clerks, typists, secretaries) of the white-collar workforce. Managers had in fact grown at twice the rate of the rest of the workforce: 43.1 percent. Meanwhile, thanks in large part to automation, which ended up creating more jobs for technical workers than production workers, manufacturing employees fell considerably. As a result, the ratio between workers in management and those in production had flipped. After World War II, around three-quarters of corporate employees did production work, while only a quarter did administration. By 1980, these numbers had changed places.[36] Executives looking around at Germany and Japan, which appeared to be outcompeting the United States in the early 1980s, saw much lower rates of managers to manufacturing. American companies seemed fat—and so the phrase "trimming the fat" became one of the millions of gross euphemisms ("downsizing," "restructuring," even "dehiring") executives used for mass layoffs.

But the cost of shedding middle management would prove high, for middle managers had been the basis of the American middle class itself. The promise of stability, clean work, and relatively high pay, all tied to company loyalty, had provided stability to American politics and work for two generations. The fact that Tom Rath—of *Gray Flannel Suit* fame—could turn down an executive position so that he could work less and spend time with his family (but still earn enough money to maintain a large home in suburban Connecticut) was part of the dream of middle classness that the United States had genuinely extended to thousands of men and, increasingly in later years, women. In the 1980s and 1990s, the U.S. corporate world broke that silent contract. Of course, when contracts are unspoken, they're so much easier to break. The cushy, boring world of the office described so well in *Life in the Crystal Palace* became a more frightening place, ruled by a deep-seated psychological fear of being fired. By the 1990s, fear was not only the casual effect of workplace reorganization; it was the goal. The Intel CEO Andy Grove, in his classic book of management theory *Only the Paranoid Survive*, put it succinctly, slyly contrasting his philosophy with that of the original practitioner of Japanese management:

> The quality guru W. Edwards Deming advocated stamping out fear in corporations. I have trouble with the simple-mindedness of this dictum. The most important role of managers is to create an environment in which people are passionately dedicated to winning in the marketplace. Fear plays a major role in creating and maintaining such passion. Fear of competition, fear of bankruptcy, fear of being wrong, and fear of losing can all be powerful motivators. How do we cultivate fear of losing in our employees? We can only do that if we feel it ourselves.[37]

What had been a supposedly unintended by-product of corporate restructuring gradually became a business principle. Succumbing to one of their many fits of italics, Peters and Waterman had written that, as workers, *"we simultaneously seek self-determination and security."*[38] As it happened, the new office would provide neither. And nothing symbolized this transfigured world better than its furniture.

☐

The surest sign of trouble for a worker was when he lost his office. "I came back to the home office," one Kodak employee recalled, in the midst of the mass layoffs of the 1980s, "and I knew that the company had really changed. My office in Texas was as big as a living room, and I had a secretary in a private office outside. When I went back to Rochester, I had a cubicle. I could hear the two people alongside me, and could hear the secretary who sat nearby."[39] Peters and Waterman, and Ouchi as well, might have argued for a loose, open-plan arrangement for the newly competitive American economy. Instead, corporations responded by giving a privileged elite the few remaining offices while cramming everyone else into partitioned spaces.

The fierce and unyielding new corporate ethos had changed the image of the cubicle. As we remember from Propst, those three walls had once been meant to liberate office workers, to guarantee them autonomy and freedom. But they had finally taken on the image that they have today: the flimsy, fabric-wrapped, half-exposed stall where the white-collar worker waited out his days until, at long last, he was laid off. The media caught on. In news stories the word "cubicle" rarely appeared in dignified solitude; instead, it was prefaced with some inevitable epithet: "windowless" or "dreary," "cubicle warrens," "bull pens," or "infernos." People labored in "cube farms" and were stuck next to each other in six-by-six standard sets known as six-packs. Douglas Coupland's epoch-defining book, *Generation X*, coined the phrase "veal-fattening pen" and provided a mock-serious "dictionary" definition: "Small, cramped office workstations built of fabric-covered disassemblable wall partitions and inhabited by junior staff members. Named after the small pre-slaughter cubicles used by the cattle industry."

To add insult to injury, they shrank. According to a *Business-Week* editorial from 1997, between the mid-1980s and the mid-1990s the average size of a cubicle decreased between 25 and 50 percent. Ironically, the editorial was spurred by *BusinessWeek*'s editorial staff being "informed that most of us will lose our private offices in a year or two. This prompted a closer look at cubicles," they wrote, "which are occupied by some 35 million of the 45 million white-collar workers in this country."[40] *BW* forecast only half humorously that at those rates the average cubicle in 2097 would be eight square feet. By 2006, when the average cubicle was seventy-five square feet, half of Americans would report that they believed their bathroom was larger than their cubicle; one wonders to what extent the extravagant growth of the American bathroom, and of the suburban home in general, is partly a reaction against the shrinking of cubicles, where the owners of those bathrooms spend so much of their time.[41] Still others, more melodramatically, compared cubicles to prisons. Rushing to help this analogy was the fact that certain prison systems, such as that in Texas, responded to overcrowding by redesigning their jails along the lines of an open-plan office, replete with cubicle partitions.[42] Prison inmates employed by the company with the classic 1990s name Unicor (combined words were always the sign of a merger) were set to work manufacturing cubicle walls and occasionally the chairs that people sat in in those cubicles.[43] At night, while others left their cubicles to go back home, some prisoners by contrast left the manufacturing plant to go back to their cubicles.

Complaints about the office environment began to mushroom. Cubicles restricted air circulation and made workers sick (this was called sick building syndrome).[44] Bosses were enriching their own offices with wood-trim furnishings and credenzas while foisting more cubicles on their employees.[45] Apple's workers stayed home because they couldn't work in their cubicles; as a result, Apple eliminated cubicles.[46] In one company seeking to get rid of cubicles, the workers were afraid of losing their minimal bit of privacy.[47] Employees of IBM found themselves crammed into ever smaller cubicles;

they believed that the company was making its cubicles so small and miserable that people would never come to work and it wouldn't have to spend money on office space.[48]

It was in the midst of the great cubing of America that its poet arrived, with the unassuming, appropriately bland name Scott Adams. In the mid-1990s, his comic, *Dilbert*, provided a kind of solace to millions of white-collar workers by converting day after day of fungible dullness into concise, portable satire. It satirized the office world with necessary self-deprecation—for to be its protagonist, Dilbert, as everyone was and is Dilbert, was to be hastily sketched, basically featureless, and frankly doomed. "I worked in a cubicle for seventeen years," Adams wrote in *The Dilbert Principle*, his monster best-seller book of cartoons and fake business advice. "Most business books are written by consultants and professors who haven't spent much time in a cubicle. That's like writing a first-hand account of the experience of the Donner party based on the fact that you've eaten beef jerky. Me, I've gnawed an ankle or two."[49] Just as important as its being true to life was the fact that *Dilbert* came in a form—the daily comic—that could match the pounding regularity of office routine. It arrived early every morning, just like the white-collar worker, and gave that worker something to look forward to. Even the three panels of the newspaper strip were turned to a purpose, mimicking as they did the contours—even the three-wall shape—of cubicle life: cramped, square, colorless, and infinitely replicable. Soon *Dilbert* was accommodating itself to the office it satirized in all kinds of ways. It turned out that Propst's tackboards, which were meant to create individuality, were best used as spaces for clipped *Dilbert* cartoons. It soon became a cliché fixture of the office environment, with ubiquitous desk calendars, coffee mugs, mouse pads, and plush toys (all available in the online store's Cubeware section of the Web site). At the end of his life, Propst was being prodded for being responsible for *Dilbert*. "I don't even feel faintly guilty about Dilbert," Propst said. "The things expressed in that comic are the very things we were trying to relieve and move beyond. It was a Dilbert world even back then. Everything we worked toward tries to express something more interesting."[50]

□

Imagine what it was like to work in a typical office during the first years of the personal computer. Many people don't have to imagine: they were there; or perhaps some workplaces have changed so little that their current setups closely approximate those early days. The blinding glare of fluorescence doesn't compensate for the lack of natural light; the recycled atmosphere is stuffy, even poisonous. Thanks to the energy crisis of the 1970s, buildings have been shut up and sealed against too much sun or fresh air; chemicals from carpeting and construction materials, like asbestos and formaldehyde, circulate with impunity, along with airborne illness.[51] The chatty atmosphere of the open plan might once have made it hard to concentrate; now the conspicuous silence hovering over the partitions, interrupted only by the tapping of keys, comes from the enforcement of surveillance. Machines ensure that data-entry clerks type their minimum of keystrokes per second; talking, let alone getting up to take a walk, results in error. Even the green characters of the visual display terminal of the new personal computer suggest some kind of menace; reports in the news appear daily about their potential radiation hazards and about women who have had miscarriages thanks to them.

Computers and automation had brought the blues to the white-collar workplace. Office worker apathy had been growing for some time, especially among the clerical ranks. An extraordinarily candid report from 1972 commissioned by the Nixon administration, *Work in America*, offered a bleak confirmation of worker discontent, whether at the assembly line or in front of a typewriter. (For this reason, Nixon attempted to suppress the contents of the report.) "Secretaries, clerks, and bureaucrats were once grateful for having been spared the dehumanization of the factory," wrote the authors of the report. But, they said, "the office today, where work is segmented and authoritarian, is often a factory. For a growing number of jobs, there is little to distinguish them but the color of the worker's collar: computer keypunch operations and typing pools share much in common with the automobile assembly-line."[52] Clerical worker pay had dipped below that of average blue-collar production workers. Turnover rates were high; union membership was growing. Managers were well aware of the apathy. A survey indicated that they believed office workers were producing at only 55 percent of their potential. One of the reasons they cited was "boredom with repetitive jobs."[53]

The effect of the personal computer was equivocal: the sort of deeply transformative item that also seemed to leave everything pretty much the same. One of its achievements was to break the "office monogamy" (as the journalist Barbara Garson has called it) between secretaries and their bosses—the old "office wife" relationship that had held steady since the earliest days of women's entry into the workforce. Companies like IBM began to promote the concept of an "administrative support center," where "word originators" (managers) could send their requests to be filled by "specialists" (typists on word processors). Of course typing pools had always existed, and even the noise wasn't diminished by word processors. "The printing out is so steady . . . it gets to you more than a whole room of old-fashioned typewriters," one word-processing specialist said.[54] But the level of control offered by clusters of word processors was greater. Keystrokes could be monitored and an employee's progress and speed measured. Whatever personal control the old secretarial relationship seemed to offer was stripped from the job. In one sense, this was a kind of liberation from old strictures; in another, it led to not more control by the staff but less.

One would think it was only a matter of time before the soullessness of the new workplace would have prompted revolts by the disgruntled: workers parking their cars in executive spots, smashing their VDTs, and tearing down their cubicle walls and using them to erect barricades. And in a few cases, there *were* office shootings, prompting the brief media buzz phrase "cubicle rage." More often, however—in typical office worker, or perhaps American, fashion—resistance to routine and work degradation usually took the form of apathy and foot-dragging, stealing time and control over one's work rather than demanding it. Clerks in Citibank bank-card-processing centers, forced to deal with customer calls in under two minutes, would often hang up on their customers in order to beat the clock. Or insurance claims processors could type fake data into their computers to meet their quota for the day. People in offices everywhere are still familiar with this kind of everyday resistance to routine.[55]

Resistance of that kind naturally remained limited, infrequent, and disorganized. The office that emerged from the 1980s, however lean and mean it was, did offer a new sense of "entrepreneurial" possibility to a handful of people, and for many this seemed to be enough. The newsmagazine trend-spotting figure of the age, "the yuppie," corresponded to a real social type. Looser banking regulations, crushed unions, and granite skyscrapers combined to give corporate life a peculiar feel of exhilaration for the people whose voices were the loudest in sanctioning the transfigured, deindustrializing American economy. The correlate to pervasive insecurity among the mass of workers was euphoria among a handful of executives. With middle management in decline, organizations *seemed* to be more open to merit. The hope that you might rise out of the crowd, through the skillful manipulation of office politics, and into the executive suite became stronger for those not already overwhelmed by apathy. This prevailing belief held offices together in a way vastly more powerful than any mechanical surveillance installed in the new computer systems.

The yuppies, or what sociologists have called the "professional-managerial class," tended not to complain about cubicles; or they knew that they would eventually make it out of one of them into an office. Investment banking—until the 1980s, a relatively staid and dull profession—became the signature industry of the time. As Karen Ho has shown in her granular, sensitive anthropology of bankers, *Liquidated,* the frenzied culture of banking has been part of its mystique since the shareholder value revolution: insane work hours on trading floors that crammed people together, most of them men, sometimes in six-by-six modules with low partitions, made the atmosphere of banking offices legendarily heated and fratty. The investment bank that Ho observed was typical: a "bull pen" like the American plans of yore, with a plastic gate affixed to the entrance of the hallway as a kind of joke. "Inside the gate, cramped desks, shelves, and floors overflowed with pitch books, PowerPoint presentations, and old binders of previous deal books, not to mention soda cans, footballs, gym bags, weights, change of clothes, deodorant, and an extra suit hanging just in case."[56] Bankers were increasingly recruited from top universities, which took the place of the "old boys' networks" that had hitherto populated the ranks of finance, and they brought into the workplace a cult of "smartness": one part recognizable intelligence mixed with several parts attitude and "master of the universe" confidence. Smartness had surmounted bureaucracy.

The importance of intelligence in the new "knowledge" workplace was a theme of *Working Girl,* which opens in a messy, male-dominated banking office not unlike the one Ho described in *Liquidated.* But Tess McGill leaves the workplace and ends up working for a woman. Initially her boss, Katharine Parker (Sigourney Weaver), appears to be interested in her thoughts. "I welcome your ideas and I want to see hard work rewarded. It's a two-way street on my team," she says. It's one of the film's many pungent evocations of canned business-speak, and it's because it's canned that we the audience (if not Tess herself) can immediately scent the pure bull; it's not too long before we see Katharine stealing all of Tess's good ideas. Tess's real breakthrough only comes when Katharine gets injured in a skiing accident abroad, and Tess gets to pretend that she *is* her boss. She lives in Katharine's apartment, dresses in Katharine's clothes, shows up to parties that Katharine is invited to, and even sneaks into a wedding that neither she nor Katharine is invited to, all to talk to big shots who otherwise wouldn't bother to learn her name. At the end of the film, her game exposed, a high-placed investor offers her a manager's job because of her "gumption." Office politics, the film seems to say, can be such a skillful game that playing it well is often counted as a kind of merit.

There was another factor that the office could count on its side: isolation. Whatever the terrors of assembly-line work, it had the unintended effect of forcing people together on the same shop floor. Workers often entered and left at the same time, and they spent day after day together. Few had any illusions of getting "promoted" to the head of their factory. This was a situation where people might get organized, or could at least speak to each other on a regular basis. Office work tended to siphon people off from each other. The individualism inherent in the office—something managers have counted on since the union upsurge in the 1930s, as we've already seen—also found its expression in work and design. Being tied to a computer could mean, as boosters often argued, that one was connected to an invisible network much larger and more powerful than any series of merely personal relationships. But in daily practice, and certainly before the spread of the Internet and the laptop computer, one was more often stuck at a VDT the way one would be chained to an assembly line. And the range of activities that most people could do on a computer was highly limited—as limited, in its way, as a ledger was to the bookkeeping staff of a Taylorist office in the 1920s. The cubicle had the effect of putting people close enough to each other to create serious social annoyances, but dividing them so that they didn't actually feel that they were working together. It had all the hazards of privacy and sociability but the benefits of neither. It got so bad that nobody wanted them taken away; even those three walls offered some kind of psychological home, a place one could call one's own. All of these factors could deepen the frenzied solitude of an office worker.

□

And yet, despite everything, discontent *did* brim over into protest, and it began in the place where the work was dullest and most routine and therefore, paradoxically perhaps, togetherness was strongest: the secretarial typing pool. For generations herded together in vast caverns and condemned to positions above which they could never rise, secretaries had the strongest claim to being the office proletariat. There was the deep and enduring crime, too, of their sex preventing them from enjoying anything resembling equal opportunity in the workplace. The few male secretaries would receive higher pay for the same work and get to skip the degrading kinds of harassment that were de rigueur for their female counterparts—the kind that, just a few years before, Helen Gurley Brown had told them to turn to their advantage.

The signs of discontent were few and scattered, but thanks to tremendous media coverage they began to seem like a groundswell. In the infamous 1968 protest against the Miss America Pageant, more than a hundred women tossed their symbols of subjection into the trash—and among the thickly padded bras, fake eyelashes, gushing women's magazines, lay many steno pads and typing manuals.[57] The symbolic protests grew. Soon others began shirking the one duty expected of every secretary: getting coffee for their bosses. In 1973, Leonor Pendleton was fired for—in the words of her bosses—"incompetence, insubordination, and failure to comply with job instructions." In the words of her attorney, it was her refusal "to follow a sexist practice based on the erroneous stereotype that only females, even in their employment situation, should perform household chores."[58] It turned out that Pendleton, one of the secretaries in the all-female secretarial staff of her office, had refused to make coffee and wash the dishes. A secretary in a naval air station was fired in the same year for failing to make coffee. In 1975 another was stopped in the hallway by a man she didn't know asking her to get "four regulars," which she refused. The man turned out to be her vice president; she was terminated twenty minutes later.[59]

What was it about making coffee—or the failure to do it—that made workers and their bosses so upset? For secretaries, it was one of the features of their job that virtually no secretarial manual spoke of; it was simply assumed that as "office wives" they would know to do it. It was just an expectation, one that went hand in hand with the expectation of harassment. "My boss expected me to get his coffee and lunch and run his personal errands during my lunch hour," a secretary at CBS said. "He constantly cracked jokes about my (and every other secretary's) legs, hips, and breasts, and so did the other men."[60] Another secretary pointed out that it seemed to be the way things were always done:

> In this firm the men wear the suits and ties and sit in the offices, and the women get their coffee, get their sandwiches, fix their bouillon. A lot of women say they don't mind doing it, but at the same time they *hate* doing it. It's tradition. They're afraid to go in and say, "I'm sorry, I don't want to do it anymore." Men will even get up, walk to the women standing at

Secretaries love this file.
It's the strong, silent type.

File drawers opening and closing all day make a lot of noise. Enough to drive a girl to aspirin.

So we designed our file with drawers that just won't slam or screech.

Another nice thing about our file drawers. They pull out all the way. The "zebra" folder is as easy to remove as the one on "aardvark".

There's nothing tinny or weak about our file, either. It's built to take on big loads without getting out of alignment. You know what happens when files lose their alignment. They get stuck.

Our "500" file has a clean, beautiful face. Easy on the eyes. No drawer pulls that stick out like sore thumbs. And you don't need a magnifying glass to read the labels.

In two, three, four and five drawer units. Letter and legal size. In gray, black and beige finishes.

Art Metal furniture looks beautiful and works beautifully—a solid investment for management. We'll be happy to send you a brochure on the "500" files, and tell you where they can be seen. Write today. You'll hear from us, posthaste.

ART METAL INC
JAMESTOWN NEW YORK

© 1967 ART METAL INC., JAMESTOWN, N.Y.

From a *BusinessWeek* ad from 1967: the sort of images that fueled office feminism.

the coffee wagon, dump a dime in their hand, and say, "Can I have a regular?" I mean they're *right there*! We're told to "Xerox this for me" or "would you get me a pack of cigarettes downstairs."[61]

So it was the simple assumption on the part of the bosses that women would not only be expected to do their actual work, which was dreary enough, but also cheerfully perform "home" tasks in the office that made the coffee duty, and things like it, so irksome. It was the insult that pointed most clearly to the deeper injury.

Finally, an organization took hold. In 1970, a group of secretaries working for a downtown accounting firm in Boston, sick of the way their work was apportioned and organized, had banded together to come up with a solution. They circulated a memo redrawing the lines of hierarchy and expanding the responsibilities—hitherto menial—of the office secretaries. One of the secretaries responsible for the memo was fired. A few years later, she became one of the founding members of the organization 9to5, a Boston-wide organization of women clerical workers.[62] One of the many "locals" springing up in cities all over the country, 9to5, headed by the charismatic Karen Nussbaum, a New Left antiwar activist who had been a clerk and typist at Harvard, quickly became the most famous. Media savvy, 9to5 invited the press to all of its events, ensuring that even the smallest actions would get coverage. It began circulating a newsletter, *9to5 News*, which quickly garnered six thousand subscribers.[63] And it began to initiate an impressive number of direct-action activities to further its goals of achieving rights for women office workers.

One of the typical moves of the 9to5-ers was to subvert office hierarchies as they were expressed in layout and design. After all, no one knows better how an office can express status and privilege than a secretary chained to a metal desk in a noisy typing pool. In one action, a university group managed to secure a meeting with the vice president of personnel (after eight months of attempts). The members of the group arrived before he did. Naturally, the desk was set up executive-style, back against the far wall, with enormous windows on either side, so that the sun beamed into the eyes of anyone sitting in the chair across from the vice president. It was meant, of course, to convey the vice president's immense authority. The leader of the group said, "I don't like to have the sun shining in my eyes, do you?" The group accordingly lined up behind the desk, so when the vice president walked in, he was unnervingly confronted with a line of women occupying the position he would normally take. He took the only seat available to him—an ordinary chair. In a similar example in Chicago in 1975, a group of legal secretaries protested against a new plan to square more secretaries into less space in cubicles. They circulated a petition, which actually forced the attorneys to come up with a redesign. "I really believe this is the first time the Administrative Committee actually sat down and discussed secretaries as people," one of the secretaries said. "And the fact that they actually called the architects and told them to go back to the drawing boards is a very important thing."[64]

The secretarial revolt hit the mainstream in 1980, when the Jane Fonda–produced feminist classic 9 to 5 appeared in movie theaters. A satire-farce about sex discrimination in the office, it concerned three clerical workers (Lily Tomlin, Dolly Parton, and Fonda) who suffered from the undeserved abuse, or unwanted attentions, offered up by a man they call only "the boss" (Dabney Coleman). One evening, debilitatingly high after sharing a joint, they each conjure up stoned fantasies of treating their boss to his comeuppance, including hog-tying him, shooting him with a hunting rifle, and—of course—pouring rat poison in his coffee. A series of more or less implausible plot twists result in their sequestering him in his own home in an impressively S&M-like bondage getup, while they take over the workplace and institute then-novel reforms: flexible hours, job sharing, day care at work. In a blatant argument for how design is tied up with work, they even reshape the office. By the end of the film, it has changed from a gray open-bull-pen typing pool, with the usual rows of serried desks, to a swirling mélange of variegated partitions, flourishing plants, and desks arranged into unorthodox angles. The vision 9 to 5 offered of the liberated workplace was in fact a *Bürolandschaft*, an office landscape.

The amazing thing is that all of these details—save tying up the boss—were taken from workers' own experiences. Fonda had gone to Nussbaum to ask her about what office workers thought of their jobs. She visited the Cleveland chapter of Nussbaum's organization, Women Working, and she and a scriptwriter spent a night speaking with forty office workers, from which emerged the story that they told. Nussbaum joined Fonda on a speaking tour promoting the movie. "It was the best example I've ever seen of popular culture helping to lift organization and movement," Nussbaum would later say. "You had to fight hard on this issue about whether there was discrimination or not," continued Nussbaum, "and then Jane Fonda makes a movie that mocks discrimination in the workplace and the argument is over, because women have been poised on the edge of their chairs, ready to understand it this way and then this capped it and made it, the behavior of the bosses and the discrimination, the object of ridicule."[65]

Yet, in hindsight, 9 to 5 also might have made a casualty of the movement that it sought to promote. As a film, it makes sex discrimination the central issue of the workplace and suggests that by ending it, the workplace can become a utopia. The chief message that seemed to emerge from the movie was that flextime and an end to harassment were all that stopped women from being free as workers. But 9to5 and organizations like it were about something bigger. They seemed to promise that organizing women office workers would in fact result in more humane workplaces altogether. Sex and class went hand in hand, since sex discrimination had created a gendered "working class" within the office. Collections of interviews with office workers in the movement suggested that racism was also a problem that they wanted to address, and of course they were concerned that office work itself, regardless of the gender of the person doing it, was a nightmare. In a survey of women office workers conducted in 1981, respondents indicated that "lack of promotions or raises" was the chief complaint (52 percent). This was followed by "low pay," "monotonous, repetitive work," "no input into decision-making," and "heavy workload/overtime."[66]

Thanks to sex discrimination, women were indeed disproportionately slotted into jobs that were degrading and soulless. But the jobs themselves would not disappear if women were taken out of those positions. Working Girl, in many respects a more conservative film than 9 *to* 5, acknowledged this. Though Melanie Griffith's Tess suffers sex discrimination early in the film, she suffers even more because of her class—indicated above all by her viscously thick Staten Island accent—which slots her into a secretarial role that no one takes seriously. It's thanks to the secretarial revolt—or to feminism more generally—that women are able to be bosses at all, but sisterhood didn't (yet) have enough to say about the divide between the middle and the working classes. Pointing the moral even further, the film indicates that it's Tess's working-woman smarts that end up providing her with her business knowledge: unlike the middle-class Katharine, Tess reads the tabloid newspapers, which tell her more about the scandalous private lives of businesspeople—which in turn gives her special insight into where a CEO or investor might take his or her company next. At the end of the film, Tess ends up with a secretary of her own, whom, the film implies, she promises to treat better than Sigourney Weaver treated her, thanks to her own working-class experience.

This is of course a fantasy as strong as anything offered by 9 *to* 5. And interviews with office workers in the 1970s suggested that at least a few women clerical workers were not inclined to believe it. "Even girls who have been pretty good kids as clerks—once they become supervisors, they change," one worker was quoted as saying. Her co-worker concurred: "I think they get into positions that they have someone to answer to, and I think they forget to be human beings; they become part of the establishment. Perhaps they're told, 'The workers are the workers and you are the boss, and you keep the workers in their place and you stay in your place.' And I think that after a while they feel as though they are the king. They begin to believe it."[67]

An interviewer asked the workers what they would do if they could change their office in any way they wanted. "Get rid of management!" one responded. "We'll run the business for a while!" the other said. "I think when you sit there as a clerk," the first worker went on, "you see a lot of things that they do backwards. You would maybe use a more logical approach. I think I'd like to see more flexibility. And I think I'd do away with job levels and just make everybody more equal."[68]

8

THE OFFICE OF THE FUTURE

*From some distant cubicle comes a tinny electronic
melody Maxine recognizes as "Korobushka," the
anthem of nineties workplace fecklessness, playing
faster and faster and accompanied by screams of
anxiety . . . Has she entered some supernatural
timewarp where the shades of office layabouts
continue to waste uncountable person-hours playing
Tetris? Between that and Solitaire for Windows, no
wonder the tech sector tanked.*

—THOMAS PYNCHON, *Bleeding Edge*[1]

Office worker discontent didn't only inspire organizing; union-ization, as well as groups like 9to5, remained rare. But there was another branch of discontent: one that led straight into reshaping the physical world of the office. As with the countercultural ideas that made their way into management textbooks of the 1960s, a handful of disgruntled white collars translated their unhappiness into design. Looking back at the 1970s unexpectedly discloses a fertile moment for the future of the office. Many of the things said then could be said now—or, perhaps, were realized in the future that is *our* present.

Seeing that they were on the cusp of some hitherto invisible computer revolution, a number of researchers began predicting vast changes in the nature of office work. These were accompanied by a significant number of writers who, unlike the researchers, had done virtually no research. Though they had little intellectual capital to offer, they became well-remunerated professional futurologists, whose job was to get people excited about the brave new world of work that was coming into being. Thanks to the cunning of history, many of their predictions would in fact come to pass.

In 1975, *BusinessWeek* coined a phrase with its series of articles on "the office of the future." Reporting on the as-yet-unseen future of the computerized office, experts predicted the end of everything that the office was known for: the end of typewriters; the end of secretaries; and the end, above all, of paper. George E. Pake, head of Xerox's research division, accurately predicted the emergence of an electronic form of correspondence. He described a "TV-display terminal with keyboard." "I'll be able to call up documents from my files on the screen, or by pressing a button," he said. "I can get my mail or any messages. I don't know how much hard copy [that is, printed paper] I'll want in this world."[2] Though confidently imagining a paperless office, experts were quick to say that changes were not around the corner. "It will be a long time—it always takes longer than we expect to change the way people customarily do their business," said the president of Redactron Corporation, a manufacturer of text-editing typewriters (that is, typewriters that could also correct documents).[3] And yet just a few years later, the National Science Foundation (NSF) encouraged a group of its workers to try out having all their work "on-line." Excluding any kind of paper use except what was necessary to communicate with people outside their group, a manager, four professionals, and a secretary stored all of their work using digital means. Amazingly, despite the rudimentary quality of computer storage at the time, the NSF recorded productivity gains.[4] The world of *The Jetsons* might not be that far off after all.

Only a few years earlier, and little noticed, a group of product engineers at IBM had tried something that was, in their words, "radically new." They moved into a new office space that was not only without walls but without permanent workstations. Calling it a "non-territorial office," they tried to set up a space that would accommodate motion between different kinds of work setups, based on the particular task at hand. In addition to common tables and work benches, scattered throughout the work area, engineers had access to quiet areas where they could escape for concentrated work if necessary. The goal overall was to "improve and increase the sharing of problems and experience" within the group. Freeing people from their workstations would naturally result in greater interaction between other isolated people, the story went. The workers approached the project with trepidation; they said, in the words of the researchers who reported on the experiment, that "the opportunity to decorate a personal space has become one of the few remaining avenues for expression of individuality in large organizations."[5] But afterward, they couldn't have been more enthusiastic. "Don't fence me in again," one engineer said. "I was skeptical before, but I'd hate to go back to closed office now," said another. Data suggested that internal communication had indeed improved. The non-territorial office was, in this instance, a success.[6]

Visions of paperless and non-territorial offices were contemporary with another kind of visionary idea: that there wouldn't really need to be offices at all. Alvin Toffler predicted in the early 1980s that telecommunications technologies would revolutionize the workplace. People would no longer work in offices; instead, they would be housed in "electronic cottages" in the countryside, linked to a worldwide network that made office buildings obsolescent. In a suitably apocalyptic (but not too exaggerated) image, he imagined downtowns "stand[ing] empty, reduced to use as ghostly warehouses or converted into living space."[7] Though "working from home" was a concept decidedly in its infancy, Toffler's idea had precedents. Stuck in a traffic jam on his way to his L.A. office one day in the 1970s, the American researcher Jack Nilles (who was, quite literally, a rocket scientist) began to imagine ways that people might be able to avoid costly and frustrating commutes altogether. Long commutes were polluting, encouraged wasteful sprawl, and above all were inefficient. With a grant from the National Science Foundation, he began a feasibility study for an L.A. insurance firm of something he called "telecommuting." Because the firm was located in an old crumbling building in a neighborhood with an aging population, it had to attract younger workers from far away, who were loath to brave the arduous travel time to work in a crummy office, no matter how attractive the company was. (And the company was attractive: it provided a higher salary than most comparable places, free hot lunches, and a reduced workweek of 37.5 hours.) Nilles enthusiastically concluded that telecommuting was a viable option. He mentioned hesitations: supervisors would no longer be able to control their employees; and workers themselves might miss out on the social atmosphere of office life. But the company went forward with it. As soon as it began to be effective, the project was canned. It turned out managers felt threatened by telecommuting: they weren't able to control their employees in the same way as before and had to change their methods.[8]

Things in 1980s offices often seemed grim, but in the late 1990s a utopia seemed to emerge on the horizon. It was way out, beyond the highest ranks of the corporate world in New York or Boston or even Tokyo. In this new land, the story went, the workplaces were full of the smartest people on earth, knowledge workers in the truest sense, starting companies left and right, some of them crashing to earth, others lighting up the sky like streaking comets. In the 1990s, the office world suddenly seemed—once again—full of promise, and the whisper in everyone's ears was the old one: *Go west . . .*

□

Drive on U.S. 280 down from San Francisco in the springtime, and you find yourself emerging from the thick, fogbound hills of South San Francisco and Daly City, San Bruno, and Millbrae into a sinuous, verdant landscape, poppy-ridden, glinting here and there with teal reservoirs. Take the exit onto Sand Hill Road, backed by hills filled with California oaks, and you'll find yourself in the bucolic regions of what is often taken to be the future. Soon you crest a hill and see below you a classic oasis of sprawl, striated by highways and dotted with low-rise corporate campuses. On your right is the endless sandstone campus of Stanford University (Stanford, where it always seems to be late afternoon, like a de Chirico painting). On your left, row after row of squat brick-and-glass boxes, one partnership after another: venture capital firms, whose partners can walk across the street to meet the students they plan to make rich. Here was where the office of the future at last met the people who were determined to make it real.

At least since the 1980s, Silicon Valley was the source of no end of utopian prognostications about the workplace. Not only were its soft- and hardware innovations supposed to be lightening the burden on everyone else's work by making it less laborious and more streamlined, but the workplaces of the Valley were also seen as idylls of enlightened capitalism. Even after muckraking journalists began sneaking into its light-manufacturing chip factories and exposing toxic working conditions there, the offices were still held up as models for the rest of the country. The Valley was the world's truest merit system, it was said; the only aristocracy there was the aristocracy of talent. Job turnover—what business writers called "churn"—was terribly high, but not, the Valley people said, because of constant layoffs. Rather, turnover was a reflection of job mobility and the relentless pace of technological change. Companies grasped eagerly at excellence, prompting people to move constantly; it was also the case that those same companies often went under and were replaced by new ones. Some individuals were serial entrepreneurs themselves: they no sooner founded a company and loaded it up with venture capital than they moved on to their next gig. Nobody needed job protection, because they had freedom instead. And they worked constantly.

The late Steve Jobs, Apple's co-founder, whose black-turtlenecked ghost looms powerfully over every budding Valley entrepreneur, set the tone at the first Stanford Conference on Entrepreneurship in the early 1980s. "There is something going on here on a scale which has never been seen on the face of the earth," he said, with characteristic portentousness, describing what he called the area's "critical mass of entrepreneurial risk culture." "A lot of people ask if Silicon Valley is ever going to be unionized," Jobs went on. "I say everybody's unionized . . . There's much greater union here than I've seen anywhere. What we're starting to see is the redefinition of the corporation in America."[9] It was a sign of the times that Jobs could pretend not to know the meaning of the word "union." Yet he was right in describing the workplaces of the Valley as being knotted together by powerfully, almost desperately strong forms of corporate culture. The hierarchies were flatter, the amenities were better, and the stock options were plentiful, making for offices that often evinced, at least on the surface, high degrees of teamwork. It helped, paradoxically, that at any minute one team member might pick up and leave, to start a new, competing team somewhere else.

Appropriate to its churning, libertarian ethos, Silicon Valley was born in an office revolt. In the lore they are known as the Traitorous Eight—the young engineers who in 1967 walked out of Shockley Semiconductor Labs to found their own company, Fairchild Semiconductor Corporation, the first company to manufacture chips exclusively in silicon. In 1968, two of those eight, Robert Noyce and Gordon Moore, resigned; they each put up $250,000 to found Intel Corporation,[10] one of the first companies with a nonhierarchical, open-plan office, replete with secondhand metal desks.[11] Three years later, they had produced the world's first microprocessor. The rest of the iconic Valley companies have similar stories, which have spread far beyond its traffic-choked two-freeway peninsula into postindustrial folklore: Dave Packard and William Hewlett working out of their garage (now a landmark); Jobs and his co-conspirator Steve Wozniak, who had left Atari and Hewlett-Packard, respectively, presenting the Apple 1 at the Homebrew Computer Club in Palo Alto; and of course the thousands of students for whom late-night hacking binges in dorms and rec rooms on college campuses like Stanford formed their early idea of what a "workplace" should be like. This pervasive culture, or cult, of informality, coupled with an intense devotion to all-hours work, would have an enormous influence on the work environments of the Valley.

Another key factor in the rise of the Valley was the counterculture. The first generation of Valley pioneers was unimpressed with the goings-on at nearby Berkeley and San Francisco State. "We are really the revolutionaries in the world today—not the kids with the long hair and beards who were wrecking the schools a few years ago," Gordon Moore told *Fortune* in 1973. People like Packard, one of the prosecutors of the Vietnam War, were often objects of student protest. Valley computer geeks often had little compunction about supporting the American war machine. But the second generation—Jobs and Wozniak's generation—was different. They enjoyed a well-chronicled relationship to recreational drug use and, less often, political activity. *Pirates of Silicon Valley*, a 1990s film chronicling the dual rise of Jobs and Microsoft's co-founder Bill Gates, makes this point explicitly, having Jobs and Wozniak weaving in and out of a pot-smoke-ringed antiwar protest, carrying computer parts back to their home. Jobs and Gates were famously dropouts, and so were countless others—a common feature of the Valley career that would be exacerbated in the 1990s by the promise of gargantuan venture capital payouts based on slivers of wisps of ideas. The disaffection with figures of authority meant that most Silicon Valley types couldn't tolerate university learning for long, even though, ironically, they would go out of their way to make their offices resemble college campuses.

At first the signature Valley office was filled with cubicles. That sounds of course like yet another callous business environment. In the Valley, however, cubicles were adopted as a deliberate affront to the traditional office arrangements still on offer in the rest of the corporate world. Like the *Bürolandschaft* that made it possible, the all-cubicle office was a symbolic gesture toward equality. Whatever its aesthetic value, forcing all employees, whether bosses or staff, to wade into a sea of flimsy partitions was more egalitarian than having most out in the snake pit with others snug in closed-door offices, let alone executive suites. And though the office layouts themselves were uninspiring, the surrounding amenities were enormously better than at most places. Besides the fabled Foosball tables and basketball hoops that soon became the boilerplate references in the media, many, if not most, Silicon Valley companies offered rec centers and swimming pools; they usually didn't insist on suits and ties; work hours followed flextime, while job rotations and autonomous work teams were normal; and to foster corporate bonding, they hosted picnics, barbecues, and end-of-the-week "beer busts," where workers got together, drank beers—and inevitably did more work. It was the college lifestyle extended into the early days of a startup and then institutionalized as the startup got bigger. Not uncommon in Silicon Valley, this fun office lifestyle became the subject of legend. In 1984, the *New York*

Times reporter Robert Reinhold wrote that workers at the Rolm Corporation, a Silicon Valley telecom company, "eat subsidized meals in the restaurant-like cafeteria, choose their own hours, and enjoy a company recreation center that offers two pools, volleyball, racquetball and courses ranging from skiing to pregnancy care." In those anxious, global-competition-fearing times, he compared it to Japanese techniques of worker involvement. "The methods vary widely," Reinhold wrote, "but [all the Valley companies] have one thing in common: a belief that the traditional hierarchical structure of older Eastern-based companies has hobbled American industry in an age when technological change is so rapid that a few weeks lost can mean the difference between failure and success."[12]

But for the workers, over time these companies ceased to be the vanguard organizations of a future utopia and became instead just like big businesses of old. Embodied above all in lumbering behemoths like IBM (and later replaced by the idea-stealing giant Microsoft and its nasal-voiced overlord, Bill Gates), they were the companies to beat—the ones stifling, rather than fostering, innovation. And workers felt it immediately in the design of the offices. In a typical Silicon Valley reminiscence from the 1980s, one worker held the workplace utopia up to critical scrutiny:

> Management took great pride in being an exponent of the "Office of the Future" concept, which was touted as effecting a radical transformation of conventional office relations and designs. Since it is said that change begins at home, I looked around the office. It consisted of a series of cubicles with tall dividers; in order to speak to anybody, I had to stand up and peer over the partition. Each cubicle was unbelievably cramped; there were no windows; the ceilings were claustrophobically low; and fans spread the stale air around equitably and democratically. The supervisor's fan was at floor level, a detail I discovered after almost shredding my pants leg in the blades. Most workers didn't even have a phone at their desks—no doubt, such a "privilege" would have been "abused" to the detriment of the productivity level . . .
>
> The message? Office of the Future = More of the Same.[13]

When the largest tech corporations expanded in the mid-1990s, each needed to consider the benefits of closed offices versus an open-plan office with cubicles. Microsoft added more closed offices. So did Apple, which by the late 1980s was dealing with chronic absenteeism from its employees; its workers had found the noisy cubicle environment so detrimental to concentration that they often stayed home. Its redesign adopted the "cave and commons" approach pioneered by Marvin Minsky at MIT, where a common meeting space determined the shape of windowed offices in the periphery.[14] Most tech companies, however, despite employee complaints, followed the lead of Intel. Intel did not pretend that the cubicle was a great place to be; instead, it pretended that it could foster an egalitarian work environment by insisting that even the staff of upper management work in cubicles, that there should be no "mahogany row" at Intel. Intel used only two sizes and styles of office furniture; as in a kind of state socialism for design, everyone would be starved of beauty equally.[15] Introducing Grove at the Los Angeles Times Annual Investment Strategies conference, reporter James Flanagan described visiting Intel's workplace in 1996: "Here were cubicle dividers, and behind the cubicle dividers was a desk, a computer, and a man, Andrew Grove. And you looked at that and you thought, well, wait a minute: What kind of business is this?"[16] Another employee, introducing Grove at an Intel International Science and Engineering Fair, said, "Andy has nurtured an egalitarian culture at Intel . . . We all work in a company where Andy Grove's cubicle—which I think is about eight by nine—is just like everybody else's."[17]

Yet Grove's was a gesture of pure irony. The cubicle had come to *represent* the exploitation and unhappiness of white-collar workers, but the idea that those modular walls, those tackboards, actually determined anything was patently false. You could hardly be said to occupy a cubicle if you could leave whenever you pleased, probably spent most of your working hours flying around the country in the company jet, and earned $100 million a year. This was not, incidentally, a nuance lost on Grove's employees: his "egalitarian culture" led to the employee-constructed Web site FACE Intel (Former and Current Employees of Intel), an enormous blog-like register of complaints about overwork and employee abuse. A quotation from Elie Wiesel headlined the home page ("There may be times when we are powerless to prevent injustice, but there must never be a time when we fail to protest"), and the Web site's creators were well aware that Grove himself, a Hungarian Jew, had spent the war hiding out in a cellar.

It was this experience, repeated at tech companies everywhere, that prompted much of the hatred of traditional offices that was specific to the Valley in the 1990s. *Dilbert* had made the cubicle the perfect symbol of business callousness in general, revealing how its antihierarchical symbolism only concealed real hierarchies. But many of the Microsoft engineers, all of whom enjoyed private offices, didn't necessarily feel that having four walls was conducive to good thinking and innovation. Partitioned or not, the design at the big Valley companies was felt to be unexciting; it didn't seem to correspond to the brave new workplace that was perpetually being promised and was forever out of reach. Something more informal, and yet more thoroughly human, was necessary. In Douglas Coupland's 1995 novel, *Microserfs*, a group of programmers at Microsoft (former art-school students like the author) find themselves disgusted with their evil company and their endless work lives: "the first generation of Microsoft employees faced with reduced stock options and, for that matter, plateauing stock prices." "I guess," the narrator concludes, "that makes them mere employees, just like at any other company."[18] They accordingly leave to found their own company in Silicon Valley. Where their previous Redmond, Washington, company was a corridor-private-office setup (and modeled after the real Microsoft), their new Palo Alto, California, office resembles something more "dorm-like." And they suddenly find themselves enjoying their work, sliding effortlessly in and out of it, as if it were merely one with their biological cycles. The endless search for venture capital is finally denounced as beside the point by one of the programmers, for whom the work was everything. "I would have come here for *nothing*. I never *had* to get paid," he insists. "It's not the money. It's *never* been the money. It rarely ever *is*."[19]

Anxiety over the dreams of what many were increasingly calling a "New Economy" and its reality built up an impressive amount of repressed energy in the Valley offices. The result, as journalist-scholars of the changing workplace like Andrew Ross have noted, was a kind of religious atmosphere, more akin to a Pentecostal revival meeting than the corporate world, where proclamations of the coming insurrection of knowledge workers were issued in thunder. Manifestos began to appear, especially in new institutions like *Wired* magazine, that heralded the coming techno-utopian future. Tom Peters, on the success of yet more dubious books, quit his role at McKinsey and restyled himself as a wild-man business guru, a Timothy Leary of the management world, hailing the new loving and feeling and hearing that was on the verge of coming into rapturous being. If only we would taste what he was tasting, we would know! His titles became increasingly unhinged: from *Thriving on Chaos*, a paean to the junk-bond 1980s that he had helped foster, he arrived at last with *Liberation Management*, a nearly nine-hundred-page tome on the glorious disorder of the "nanosecond nineties." "If you don't feel crazy," he cried, "you're not in touch with the times! The point is vital. These are nutty times. Nutty organizations, nutty people, capable of dealing with the fast, fleeting, fickle, are a requisite for survival."[20] It was a new region, Peters said, that had given him religion. "When I worked on *In Search of Excellence*, from 1978 to 1982, my eyes still mostly turned eastward (Detroit, etc.), toward yesterday's big manufacturers," he confessed. But Silicon Valley had changed everything, he argued, in increasingly "radical" prose. "I've had all of my assumptions about 'organization' ripped asunder as I've watched the Valley thrive," he cried. "It has elbowed its way into the planet's consciousness, largely courtesy of failure after failure after failure (and, along the way, many more than its fair share of successes—mostly by-products of the most exciting failures). It's instructive to think about how Silicon Valley pulled off its coup: It provides many people with a heavy dose of liberation, and, God knows, it's disorganized. By living in its midst, I've been forced to acknowledge that it's time to shed—make that shred—the old images."[21] He went on to praise "non-territorial" offices as part of the liberation—the kind that IBM had tried in the 1970s but that more and more Valley companies were just beginning to experiment with. In the informal office, Peters suggested, lay salvation.

Finally, the heavens opened up, just as Peters had predicted. In the year of Bill Clinton's reelection, economic growth rates unexpectedly surged, and investors were ecstatic. For years, the fabled promises of the computer age had appeared "everywhere except in the productivity statistics," as the Nobel laureate economist Robert Solow famously put it. But in the years after 1995, the output-per-hour rate rose 2.8 percent—the delayed result, economists claimed, of investment in IT infrastructure. Soon, venture capital began washing through the industry in great, titanic waves; at its peak in 1999, $20 million a day was being thrown at companies in and around San Francisco. The money was pouring into Silicon Valley with such Niagara-like force that no one was able to retain the kind of earnestness purveyed in *Microserfs*. Nor, too, did the counterculture put up any resistance. Hackers who had hailed the utopian promise of the Internet now spoke of the utopian promise of their companies. Indeed, the counterculture became the willing accomplice of the New Economy—the marker that made it hip and attracted a whole host of slackers, hitherto unwilling to join, into the willing arms of the dot-com companies. They would make their workplaces into palaces of informality to house the knowledge workers whose time, at last, had come.

Working in the typical dot-com office was an admixture of frenetic pace and a relaxed overall atmosphere, exemplifying that chilled-out anxiety which was the general mood of the 1990s. New Economy offices tended to have a cultivated negligence to them: picnic-table desks spread out at odd angles, piles of paper and crisscrossing wires everywhere, scruffy workers crouched in front of their screens in their pajamas, sporting carefully sculpted bed-head haircuts, while classic rock—the new era's Muzak—blared overhead. Compared with earlier generations of offices, this one arguably looked worse: more chaotic, less manageable. And the truth was that everything was moving too fast for anyone to design in the thorough way once imagined by Skidmore, Owings and Merrill, with those tilted Mies van der Rohe chairs and wood-paneled partitions siphoning off luxurious offices.

This was not because the programmers didn't care about design. On the contrary: the dot-commers, the moment they got a little money in their pockets (and in the 1990s, as many will remember, it didn't take long), tried to scale up their offices as quickly and as painlessly as possible. They needed to plan for an office that could accommodate fifteen people one week and sixty the next. Teams would have to assemble for a quick deadline and then drop everything on a dime to move on to a new project. What they needed was an office that was much like the one Robert Propst imagined thirty years before: an office design that could be changed at a moment's notice; a design that didn't look like design; a design that was "forgiving."

But it had to be forgiving not just to work but also to something more vague and intangible, though inescapable in those years: company culture. The concept was a descendant of the old human relations school of thinking about work. The employees of Razorfish (covered in detail in Andrew Ross's book *No-Collar*) embodied this sort of concern. Razorfish was one of the iconic dot-com Web design firms, having grown from a startup in an East Village apartment in 1995 to, in 2000, a multinational consulting firm, with offices in Boston, San Francisco, San Jose, Los Angeles, London, Amsterdam, Helsinki, Milan, Stockholm, Oslo, Hamburg, Frankfurt, and Tokyo. Proud of their workplace atmosphere, employees there told Andrew Ross that "culture" had to be fostered through permissiveness. One worker called it "the permission to give permission, to yourself and to others" (a formulation she confessed was "hopelessly abstract"). Another more plainly said, "There was the official party line on culture, which was enforced fun, and then there was what we created for ourselves."[22] No one could point out examples of this culture, but they knew what it was not: buying a video game system for the office or having Nerf wars. Nor was it one of the amenity-rich big corporations that the Valley was full of, many of which were Razorfish's clients. They had been there and seen those, with the usual cube farms, empty work relationships, and, worst of all, enforced fun. Office design was important. But rather than legislate a culture, it had to allow one to come into being.

This was not something that designers were necessarily prepared to do. Design is normally the enemy of culture (in the Silicon Valley sense): if something needs to be designed, that means putting some kind of limit on space and personal or even group expression. Architects and designers were more interested in thoroughly conceived spaces, of putting their marks on the world through a project. Designers like Nelson and Eames, and architects like Mies and Johnson, wanted to convey an entire worldview through their work. But this was too much for the Valley people to handle. They were too arrogant to countenance anyone else's imagination impinging in the slightest way on their own. "When we began working with an outside interior designer," Razorfish's chairman, Craig Kanarick, said in an interview, "the issue was to get stuff done super fast and relatively inexpensively and with some specific functions in mind. That person had her own ideas about what she wanted to express as an artist. I think it's what makes her great as a designer. But it also made it difficult to work with her."[23] And above all, they needed it faster; the speed of design was too slow. "A dot-com client always wants a facility that's faster, cheaper, and better," one design firm principal told *Interiors* magazine. "He's the client from hell." The designer added, wryly, "That's not necessarily a bad thing."[24] In fact, the dot-com era, in its brief period of efflorescence, might have changed design irrevocably—and, many designers were saying, for the better.

Designers stepped up to meet the dot-com model, often by establishing their own departments specifically geared for dot-com clients. These departments developed new ways of working—usually meaning that they worked insane hours—to meet the always-on schedules of the dot-commers. "Image is everything for dotcom companies," a project manager from the design studio Swerve said at the time. "Most of them don't acknowledge old systems of doing business."[25] As a result, designers had to come up with "hip" spaces and furniture, indicating the dot-commers' rebellion against the status quo, while doing it quickly. Places like Swerve came up with designs from scratch: colorful, enamel-covered workstations with boomerang-shaped desks for Evolve, which they managed to produce in eight weeks. They made conference tables that could split in quarters; sidecar tables that could "dock" onto desks when one worker needed an instant powwow with another. For the company Blue Hypermedia, Specht Harpman Architects came up with desks, dividers, storage units, and lighting that could be shuffled into team spaces or separated into private work spaces at will. A series of custom-made, slip-fit metal clamps assisted the assembly and disassembly. All of it had to coexist in a space that was open, the view unfettered by partitions. In an era when Peter Gibbons tearing down his cubicle wall in *Office Space* had become the most resonant image of workplace rebellion, the open plan was the image of the coming revolution.

There was another rationale to the open plan, which went as far back as the original open plan, the *Bürolandschaft*: the idea of the "spontaneous encounter." Propst had floated the idea during his development of the Action Office, though it never took hold then. In the dot-com boom, however, the idea that two workers from different departments or on different rungs of the ladder might run into each other by chance and, through the sheer friction of their sudden meeting, combust into a flaming innovation became sanctified as the key to company culture. In traditional offices, according to the dot-com ethos, CEOs were insulated from people lower down through spatial constraints: they were literally cushioned in an executive floor, in an executive suite, and, because they had an executive bathroom, didn't even run into people in the urinal or the stall. But in the dot-com office, the story went, a chairman might be lightly bonked on the head by a Nerf arrow flying freely through open-plan space, loosed from an engineer's bow as he careened around on his kick scooter—and, as in the fable of Newton bonked by an apple, thereby discover the secret of the universe. It was yet another spin on the human relations school of management, whereby "culture" could solve any potential conflict in the workplace and produce benefits in productivity.

The emphasis on spontaneity, fraternally connected to the overwhelming emphasis on fun, was eliminating an old—and, many Valley people thought, outdated—distinction between work and leisure. The New Economy offices were infamously some of the most intense workplaces in the United States, but not because people were working constantly. In fact, the work rhythms were largely unscheduled—and that was the danger. With the Internet providing inexhaustible modes of distraction, alongside its growing bounty of pornography, work tended to stretch out over hours. The dot-commers would work for twenty minutes, take a coffee break, go back and work for an hour, run to the gym, sprawl out in the company lounge and look at Webzines for an hour or so, head back to their computer for more work, order dinner, play video games, and so on, until some sixteen hours had passed, much of it spent sitting in front of a computer.

It was for precisely this posture that Herman Miller produced the Aeron chair in 1994, the most powerful symbol of the dot-com bubble. Designed by Bill Stumpf—hitherto famous for designing the Ergon chair, the first ergonomic chair for the office—and Don Chadwick, the first version of the Aeron, the Sarah, was originally intended for the elderly in nursing homes who had otherwise been content with the traditional La-Z-Boy. But the Sarah was too futuristic and expensive for anyone to consider using in a nursing home. Getting rid of the foam cushions that they had used in the Sarah, they stripped down their new chair into a basic woven-plastic-and-fabric mesh. What had originally been designed to prevent bedsores would now protect the sore asses of engineers. It was practically the first ergonomic chair without cushioning—and it sold for $750. It was a phenomenon. Companies bought it by the boatload; an entire episode of the show *Will & Grace* was devoted to Will's attempt to get an Aeron chair. But its success was a sign not of the endless mobility and freedom of the dot-com office but of its simultaneously lackadaisical and profoundly intense pace, which kept people essentially confined to one place for hours on end.[26]

Workers were motivated not only by the money, though, but also by the famous company culture, the widespread practice of making dot-com workers feel as if they were artists, autonomous and free. As long as workers believed they were creating something new, and that they were doing a new kind of work, not for others, but for themselves, it was easier to work long hours. Though Silicon Valley in the dot-com years embodied this ethos in its purest form, it was something that well exceeded its geographic and corporate cultural boundaries. Arlie Russell Hochschild's study *The Time Bind* (1997) had shown how the changing dynamics of corporate culture at a Fortune 500 company—"autonomous" work teams and the rest—encouraged workers to seek the satisfactions of family life increasingly at their companies. They posted longer hours at the office than they did at home. Though Whyte had warned against the tendency of office life to incorporate family life, he had not anticipated the unraveling of the nuclear family. Stepping up to take its place was the office.

Business books had advocated a more familial office environment since the 1980s; Peters and Waterman had connected it to upholding the autonomy of lower-level workers and had encouraged collaborative teamwork. Typically, they had given it an unintentionally Orwellian spin, by calling it the "illusion of control." "If people think they have even modest personal control over their destinies," they wrote in *In Search of Excellence*, "they will persist at tasks. They will do better at them. They will become more committed to them . . . [T]hat we think we have a bit more discretion leads to *much* greater commitment."

□

The idea for the most audacious office experiment in the dot-com era arose, the story goes, at Telluride. Jay Chiat, then sixty-two, was mid-slope, careening skillfully through fresh powder, when he came to his realization. Technology had made the old office obsolete; it was time to use that technology to create the office of the future. By the time he reached the bottom, he had come to a decision. His office would have to go through a fundamental change in the way it did business.

Perhaps it was the speed he was going at—gravity pulling at his skis like fate—or the sheer hubris he had accumulated over a lifetime of accolades. Perhaps it was both. With his blinding white hair, implacable gaze, and fidgety manner, Chiat was an immediate presence in any room. And he had the characteristic impatience and restlessness of a man who constantly felt that he was surrounded by stupid people. Like the classic admen—Dowd, Ogilvy, Bell, Bernbach—he tried his hardest to be effortlessly quotable; his lines had the added benefit of sounding imperious and authoritarian. "Taking risks gives me energy." "Don't be afraid of failure unless you're working for me." "Money hasn't changed me. I've always been an asshole." The staff of his agency, Chiat/Day, liked to compile gems like these into an in-house book: *Quotations from Chairman Jay.* When entering a presentation, he immediately launched into critiques. "This doesn't hang together," he would say. "You don't have one single idea." "He would terrorize people," a former vice-chairman was quoted as saying. "When things were going well, he would walk around the agency complaining, moaning and abusing everyone." Chiat clearly had a touch of Steve Jobs ("the quickest study I've ever met," Chiat said of Jobs, though, in a classic case of the pot calling the kettle black, he also called Jobs "moody and erratic").[27] Both had the habit of counting on vast teams of people whom they were relentless in pushing as hard as they could. And Chiat reportedly forced ads down his clients' throats, gagging them until they cried uncle. Some of those clients became ex-clients.

No matter what you thought of him personally, he had been successful. Chiat/Day, Chiat/Night, his employees called it—because they worked at all hours to make what became the most iconic ads of the 1980s. His company had created the Energizer Bunny (*it keeps going and going and going . . .*); it had done the famous "1984" Super Bowl spot for the first Apple Macintosh, in which a female American athlete hurled a sledgehammer at a gigantic screen on which Big Brother was delivering his latest motivational lecture. His ads glittered with a veneer of erudition and intelligence, of being in the know. According to one associate, the "roiling stew" of his ads might consist of "a dash of Moby, a sprinkling of Sontag, and bits of Lenin and Lennon, served on a dish designed by Walter and Margaret Keane"—thus, the associate went on, had Chiat moved advertising "into the postmodern era."[28] In 1990, the industry trade magazine *Advertising Age* had crowned Chiat/Day "the agency of the decade." Chiat had been fast in other respects too—adopting the cubicle in his L.A. offices earlier than most. Despite the growing bad feelings about the cubicle, it hadn't hurt Chiat/Day's business: on the contrary. Jay Chiat and his company had done everything right. Why change it all now?

It turned out things weren't right after all. The downturn of the early 1990s had been hard on Chiat/Day. It lost two big clients,

Shearson Lehman and American Express. It closed its San Francisco office. It hired a big adman, Tom McElligott, and lost him nine months later. To recoup losses, it sold an Australian ad agency it had acquired in 1989. Its creative powers were apparently suffering too. *Advertising Age* had been scathing about some commercials for Benetton: "so very mundane, very Fox TV, very Sherman Oaks," it said; the ads reeked of "adolescent sniveling."[29] By 1993, snowbound in Telluride, Chiat knew it was time for a shake-up. And Chiat was sure his office was the problem.

Offices, Chiat thought, are ruined by politics. People become obsessed with each other rather than the work. They defend their privileges over the needs of other people; their status over genuine space requirements. Higher-ups hide in offices when they should be out on the floor; lower-downs get stuck in noisy open floors when they sometimes need a room to concentrate. The office, Chiat argued, had become the site of a turf war, not a place to do work. Changing the office "means focusing on doing great work instead of focusing on agency politics," he argued. "You come to work because the office is a resource."[30]

Chiat had already revolutionized his offices once before. In 1986, he had hired the architect Frank Gehry, then floundering after an early critical succès de scandale with his Santa Monica home, to design his agency offices in Venice, California. Working with the inescapable, and inescapably arch, Pop artist Claes Oldenburg, Gehry produced one of Southern California's iconic buildings, whose focal point was a giant pair of binoculars. (Each "eyeglass" housed a conference room.) The layout was unusual, with pizza parlor booths for informal meetings, trash-can lids directing the light from ceiling lights, and all around Jay Chiat's sterling collection of contemporary art. Opening in 1991, it was "the Oz of offices," *New York* later said, turning Frank Gehry's career around and becoming one of the grandest of work spaces—appropriate to an agency that had ruled the decade before it. And yet Chiat still continued to carp and whine, complain and moan. It wasn't enough. And the agency was no longer doing well.

In November 1993, at an *Advertising Age* conference in New York, Jay Chiat announced his new plan: the walls, desks, and cubicles were going. So were the desktop computers and the phones. Anything that anyone might have once called "theirs" was gone. He called it a "team workroom," but everyone else called it a "virtual office." The work had been "deterritorialized." Everyone would be given a cellular phone and a laptop computer when they came in. And they would work wherever they wanted. According to Adelaide Horton, the chief operating officer of Chiat/Day, people would naturally work in teams, and the teams would work in conference rooms—or, as Chiat/Day preferred to call them, "strategic business units" (which sounded suspiciously like the "strategic hamlets" of the Vietnam War). If anyone was carrying personal effects—like pictures of his dog or family, or plants—he would be kindly requested to place them in a locker of his choosing. It sounded to some like high school. For Chiat, he saw it as more like higher, rather than secondary, education, and it was all to avoid the childish atmosphere of primary school. "We're trying to structure things more like a university, rather than an elementary school. Most businesses are run like elementary schools—you go to work and you only leave your office when you have to go to the bathroom. That sort of thing breeds insularity and fear, and it's nonproductive. The important thing is to focus on what kind of work you do."[31]

Chiat's office plans became the talk of not just the industry but the entire world of business. Coming from a bold agency, and a bolder chairman, it seemed like the most exciting move that an office could possibly make. It was the root, the zero degree of offices: this far, and no further, could the radical office go. "Thoroughly armed with the modern weaponry of the road warrior," *Time* magazine wrote breathlessly, "the telecommuters of Chiat/Day . . . are among the forerunners of employment in the information age."[32] Soon everyone was talking about the possibilities of making their offices virtual. Ernst & Young established a "hoteling" service in its Chicago office, where traveling workers, who were out most of the time anyway, found a desk if and when they came in. Cisco Systems and Sprint also began experimenting with the "virtual office." No attempt, though, was more thoroughgoing than Chiat's, and he didn't hesitate to trumpet its eventual success as the future of the office. He also convinced, or perhaps bullied, everyone at the firm into accepting the idea, despite their objections to the lack of private space. It would have been a mistake to see the changes as cost cutting, which some had accused Chiat of doing, because none of it came cheap: buying all the new computers and phones and furniture took much more money than Chiat/Day could really afford. But the vision of a new workplace was more powerful than any anxious glance at a balance sheet, let alone a finance officer's querulous whining.

The furniture came first. As promised, the office walls came down, along with the lighter cubicle walls. In their place were couches and tables in common areas, like in a rec room. Lockers were color coded red, green, black, and blue (Chiat's designer, Gaetano Pesce, had a penchant for garish colors). Most famously, Chiat had Tilt-A-Whirl domed cars installed, which had been taken from a defunct amusement park ride, for two people to have private conferences. They became the only place where people could take private phone calls.

Within a year, the experiment was going awry. As *Wired* reported during the fallout, the office politics that Chiat thought his experiment would expel came back in a new and even more aggressive form. Anything that could have gone wrong went wrong. People arrived and had no idea where to go, so they left. If they stayed, they found there was nowhere to sit; there were too many people. Not allowed to leave anything out on the collective tables—especially not paper (Chiat insisted that the office had to be "paperless"), they stuffed unfinished work in their lockers. The lockers turned out to be too small. People used their car trunks instead. (One employee used a toy wagon to cart her stuff around.) It turned out Chiat and his designers had miscalculated how many computers or phones they would need (and the agency couldn't afford more). People who lived nearby would arrive early, stash their computers and phones in a locker, and catch a couple hours of sleep before starting work. Sometimes they'd sequester them overnight to be sure to have work in the morning. People began playing hooky. Managers couldn't find their staff. No work was getting done. It was a disaster. In 1998, the experiment was declared over—a more traditional, or at least less chaotic, design would be commissioned.

In an interview with *Wired*, Chiat conceded few mistakes. There should have been more computers, he agreed. But he was right about privacy, he argued, right that the virtual experiment was the future. It was, he said, "the only thing I ever did in business that I was satisfied with." The moral of the Chiat/Day story was so simple that Chiat himself was unable to draw it. In almost comic accordance with his personality, Chiat had been prescient and willful, egalitarian and autocratic, all at once. His experience in advertising had led him to believe that people should be pushed to achieve nothing short of excellence and that no one was better qualified than himself to judge whether they got there. In the name of upending hierarchies, he hierarchically instituted an egalitarian system whose fundamental truth only he was positioned to recognize. In a classic case study in unintended consequences, the experiment failed, and the subjects of the experiment came to be blamed. You can't have egalitarian offices, it was said, because people aren't set up for them. Some are fit to rule, and others to be ruled: hierarchy alone is natural. "Deep down, we're all still cave dwellers," one survivor of the experiment said. And Chiat blamed the desire for a corner office as the culprit: "We all have been taught the corner office is a badge of success. It's difficult to change that." Despite the revolutionary air at the end of the millennium, it was impossible to ask whether the office workers themselves should be consulted, whether they had ideas about how a workplace should be run. Under this rubric, the last people who knew anything about anything were the knowledge workers.

Chiat/Day cleared out of its offices in September 1998 and moved into a different space. Two years later, the Nasdaq crashed, and the dot-commers began vanishing one after the other. There was little money left to be spent on fancy offices, and it seemed that the heady experiment of the 1990s was over and the office of the future was dead.

9

THE OFFICE AND ITS ENDS

*The office could be any office. Cove fluorescents on
a dimmer, modular shelving, the desk practically an
abstraction. The whisper of sourceless ventilation.
You are a trained observer and there is nothing to
observe.*

—David Foster Wallace, *The Pale King*[1]

After the stock market crash, which emptied out the lofts and
warehouses of San Francisco, eroding in an instant the frictionless,
cloud-kicking fantasies of the dot-commers, another white-collar
recession slung into place, and the office seemed to resume its role as
the workplace everyone loved to hate.

Few cultural objects expressed this miasma of ill will better than
the film *Office Space*, which appeared in 1999 at the very peak of
the boom. Its theatrical run was a modest failure, but in retrospect
it's no surprise that a film so relentlessly dark and nasty would be
overpowered by the delirium that gripped the end of the millennium. (From a reporter visiting a Microsoft annual meeting in 1997:
" 'Why are we at Microsoft?' bellowed billionaire Steve Ballmer,
then the company's executive vice president, to a crowd of nine
thousand employees packed into the Kingdome, Seattle's indoor sta-
dium. 'For the money!' he screamed. 'Show me the money!' The
crowd responded with a roar: 'Show me the money!' ")[2] Running
gags about staplers, misplaced memos, "Hawaiian Shirt Day," and

the specter of working lives wasted in dead-end, purposeless jobs for a gray tech company: no one appeared ready for that sort of humor in an era of raging exuberance—and anyway, the cubicle was dead, right? Then the bubble burst; people woke up the following morning with their stock options erased; the beanbag chairs were gone, and they were in a cubicle again or unemployed and desperately searching for a cubicle. *Office Space* found new life on the small screen, a medium that suited the office worker existence depicted in the film: long days huddled in front of a computer, followed by short nights exhausted on the couch, staring at a television. In 1999 it barely recovered its $10 million budget in box office receipts; by 2003, it had become a cult classic, with more than two and a half million copies sold on video. (It screens on Comedy Central with the sort of mindless regularity that suggests a bored television office staff behind it all. "What do we fill the 2:00 to 5:00 p.m. slot with?" "Fuck it, let's just put on *Office Space* again.")

Everyone knows very happy white-collar people who can quote *Office Space* with as much fervor and accuracy as a pastor does the Gospels, and it's a plausible and routine assumption that repeated watchings of the film might offer a kind of therapy for stressed office workers: a vent for an inarticulate rage that helps keep them humming away at bad jobs. But anecdotally, at least, it's led to people quitting their jobs, and one Portland, Oregon, Webmaster started a site, Bullshit Job, that doubled as both a tribute to the film and a page where workers could post all the insulting memos and e-mails their bosses sent out.[3] In other words, *Office Space*, and subsequent works in the general fraternity of office satire, helped office workers recognize themselves as belonging to a particular kind of group—a recognition that the office always seemed to deny, since no matter where you were in the office, you were always presumed to be on your way up. (Think of that line from the Stanwyck film: "Baby Face is *moving out of your class*.") And part of the brilliance of the film was its insistence that the jobs weren't bad simply because the office workers were oppressed: they were intrinsically bad jobs, in a bad environment.

The setup for *Office Space* represents a larger shift in the understanding of office life. The paradigmatic narrative had been the entry of the rural woman into urban white-collar life, with its attendant sexual terrors; by mid-century, it was the travails of the middle manager attempting to avoid the conformist spirit of organizational life. But the plot of *Office Space*—reflecting the larger changes in the American economy—is about people being forced to leave an environment they hate, through layoffs; the same is true of the British show *The Office* (called, in an even more insulting euphemism, "redundancies") and of the recent American novels of office life *Then We Came to the End* and *Personal Days*. The prospect of losing one's job forces the personal crisis: you come to know who your friends are, what your loyalties are worth, and what your job really is. In *Office Space*, consultants come to examine the company's structure to give it a leaner form; though their method is unjust, they really do find people working useless jobs:

> BOB SLYDELL (JOHN C. McGINLEY): What you do at Initech is you take the specifications from the customers, and you bring them down to the software engineers.
> TOM SMYKOWSKI (RICHARD RIEHLE): Yes, yes, that's right.
> BOB PORTER (PAUL WILLSON): Well, then, I have to ask—why couldn't the customers just take them directly to the software people?
> TOM: I'll tell you why. Because engineers are not good at dealing with customers.
> SLYDELL: So you physically take the specs from the customer?
> TOM: Well . . . no, my secretary does that. Or the fax.
> PORTER: So then you must physically bring them to the software people?
> TOM: Well, no. I mean, sometimes.
> SLYDELL: What would you say you do here?
> TOM: Well, look, I already told you. I deal with the goddamn customers so the engineers don't have to. (*Screaming.*) I have *people skills*! I am good at dealing with people! Can't you understand that? What the hell is wrong with you people?

Tom Smykowski is defensive about his job, even though he can't explain what it is he does. Peter Gibbons (Ron Livingston), the main protagonist, knows that his job—updating software for the Y2K switch—sucks, and he knows that it's meaningless; from the vantage point of the new millennium, it seems especially useless. Struggling to explain it to a waitress, Joanna (Jennifer Aniston), he says, "I sit in a cubicle, and I update bank software for the 2000 switch. Well, see they wrote all this bank software, and to save space they used two digits instead of four, so like 98 instead of 1998, uh, so I go through these thousands of lines of code and uh . . . It doesn't really matter. I don't like my job." Later Peter confesses to the consultants that his average workday consists of coming in fifteen minutes late and "just sort of spac[ing] out for about an hour . . . I do that for about another hour after lunch too. I'd say in a given week, I only do about fifteen minutes of real, actual work."

The twist is that this honesty is exactly what the consultants prize—a kind of ironized version of the "truth-telling" organization man of *The Man in the Gray Flannel Suit*. Though Peter stops showing up to work and wrecks his work space by dismantling his cubicle walls, the consultants offer him a promotion. "[He's] just a straight shooter with upper management written all over him," one consultant says to Peter's boss. In return, however, they fire two engineers with actual experience, who happen to be Peter's friends. This sets in motion the increasingly madcap (and implausible) third act, when Peter and his laid-off friends try to program a virus that would scam the company they despise out of thousands of dollars. At the end of the film, one of the company's disgruntled employees, the sublime mutterer Milton Waddams (Stephen Root), sets the building on fire. Peter's engineer friends have moved from Initech to its competitor Initrode; Peter himself takes a blue-collar job in construction—preferring the outdoor life to his stationary warren of cubicles.

Office Space occupies such a tremendous place in the American office worker's imaginary about his workplace it's a shame that its effect—or the effect of the larger discourse it's a part of—has tended to be shallow and focused on the cubicle and dumb bosses. The "space" in *Office Space* was largely a symbol—of an uncaring, even ruthless organization. Its real targets were the unholy expectations of the modern workplace, which asked for dedication and commitment, offering none in return. It doubled the force of its condemnation by extending it to other kinds of workplaces. The waitress Joanna works in a chain diner called Chotchkie's, whose absurd expectations closely resemble those of the office. Part of her job involves donning wacky buttons with slogans and symbols on them, called "flair." At one point, her boss takes her aside to chastise her about her flair.

> STAN (MIKE JUDGE): Joanna! . . . We need to talk about your flair.
> JOANNA: Really? I have fifteen pieces on (*demonstrating*).
> STAN: Fifteen is the minimum, mmkay. It's up to you whether you want to just do the bare minimum. Brian for example has *thirty-seven* pieces of flair—and a *terrific* smile.
> JOANNA: Okay, so you want me to wear more?
> STAN: (*Sighing.*) Look, Joanna, people can get a cheeseburger anywhere, they come to Chotchkie's for the atmosphere and the attitude. That's what the flair's about. It's about fun.
> JOANNA: So . . . more, then.
> STAN: Look, we want you to express yourself. Mmkay? Now, if you feel the bare minimum is enough, well, okay, but some people choose to wear more, and we encourage that. You do want to express yourself, don't you?

Joanna's boss occupies the same place as the office consultants: looking for intangible, personality-based outward expressions as signs of being a "straight shooter"—rather than establishing obvious benchmarks that one meets simply to garner a paycheck. Her suspenders laden with flair suggest nothing so much as cubicle walls, decked out to show one's "individuality." The human attachments in *Office Space* were so strange and obsessive—Milton and his now infamous need to keep his red Swingline stapler—that it was hard to believe there was anything still left to express. Those still immune to the satire of flair, however, are encouraged to check out the catalogs of the office supplier Baudville, which offers, among other choice items, rhinestone-encrusted lanyards as well as T-shirts for appreciation weeks with slogans like "Smells like Team Spirit" and "I Put the 'Zing' in Amazing."

After such knowledge as *Office Space* offered, what forgiveness? How could one acknowledge the essential failure of the office to deliver on its promised utopia—and go on as if nothing had happened? For many, the question was merely rhetorical: they were out of work and stringing together temporary gigs as best they could. But for others, the dream of a better office lived on in different ways: some saw technology as still offering a way of moving office work out of the office, into a broader sphere of public life; others saw that the office needed to be made vastly more humane and responsive to its increasingly apathetic denizens. These two paths were united by a single goal: the desire to make work enjoyable, to return it to an innocence that generations of workplace mistakes had rendered corrupt. In an arresting and bleak phrase, the sociologist Max Weber had described the progress of rationality and scientific demystification as leading to a gradual "disenchantment of the world." Something like that had happened to office work: the rosy image of the office as a distinct, and distinctly middle-class, alternative to the travails of factory work and other manual labor had suffered too many jolts to survive. The office would have to be re-enchanted.

□

You enter the new headquarters of TBWA\Chiat\Day through a yellow staircase that rises up from a parking lot into an undistinguished-looking warehouse. The entrance leads past a circular reception desk into a fifty-foot sloping tunnel, which deposits you into what is easily one of the most whimsical offices anyone has ever had the wherewithal to build. Rather than the usual rows of desks or packs of cubicles—that same endless view, repeated in films from *The Crowd* to *The Apartment* to *Playtime* to *Office Space*, of anonymity and dreariness—you gaze into the middle distance of a block-length street, running past an indoor park and a full-sized basketball court. A three-story cliff-like tower with a handful of warmly lit offices nestled inside provides the only immediate sense that one is indeed in an office, but it feels like an outdoor scene, a glimpse you might catch of late-night work from the pavement as you walk by. And covering it all is a penumbra of buzzing conversation, the sound of workers excitedly greeting each other in the morning as they suck down coffee underneath the black ficus trees in the park.

TBWA\Chiat\Day hired the architect Clive Wilkinson to redesign its offices in 1997, once the Chiat virtual office experiment had conclusively failed. The design he came up with seemed to have the opposite goal in mind from Chiat's original vision: rather than condemning workers to the terrifying freedom of a nomadic existence, Wilkinson came up with an office as thoroughly *designed* as any workplace has ever been since Connecticut General. It was filled with enclosed spaces for meetings, informal and otherwise. One conference room had a table made up of stacked surfboards. Scattered throughout were large white spandex tents hung from the high ceiling; extraordinary to look at, they turn out to tear easily and are expensive to replace. In a nose thumbing at the virtual office, workers still had their own desks, crowded together in broadly segmented, low-partitioned stations; in the cavernous space, they felt as if they were outdoors. (I was told that the crowding was a result of enormous company growth.) A cafeteria serving out six hundred meals a day doubled as a work space: people congregated in the buzzing booths with paninis steaming beside the glow of their laptops. On the wall were creative posters advertising sandwiches that each worker got to create every month—another "culture"-building exercise, a work activity that seemed like leisure. In fact, because there were endless spaces for lounging and goofing off—pool tables, espresso bars, and the basketball court, of course—you had to keep reminding yourself that you were in an office and playtime was only the supplement, or necessary spur, to work time.

And it turned out that TBWA\Chiat\Day employees had quite a lot of work time. Carol Madonna, a director of office services who had worked there for many years, having even survived the bloodshed of the virtual office days, told me that weekends and nights were pretty common, even when they were punctuated by sweaty five-on-five basketball games, where people got to blow off steam.

"Advertising is a team sport," she kept repeating to me, where people "thrive on chaos" (a line I recognized as a Tom Peters title). This meant that people needed to be in the office together; ideas needed to "cross-pollinate," something TBWA\Chiat\Day's mix of private and communal spaces was designed to foster. When I asked about how different this office was from the original radical version that Jay Chiat had wanted, Madonna told me that in the end "Jay had it right." "He didn't want you to shut yourself in and hide," she said.[4] And indeed, as I looked around, a good number of the staff seemed to be out, walking from place to place or milling around together. It was shocking how pleasantly noisy the space was, considering its enormous size; I didn't think I had ever been in an office so filled with conversation that also felt so quiet.

In its totalizing design, the office was in a sense faithful to the authoritarian spirit of the late Chiat, who had died in 2002. The old virtual office forced workers out of their comfort zone in one way; the Wilkinson design did so even more flagrantly. "Both Utopian

The new interior of TBWA\Chiat\Day's offices. *Photograph by Benny Chan, Fotoworks*

commune and Orwellian nightmare," wrote the architecture critic Nicolai Ouroussoff in his review when it opened, "whose inhabitants are carefully sealed off from the outside world with their common goal—the subtle manipulation of public desire."[5] From what I could tell, it was neither utopian nor Orwellian; instead, the pervasive whimsy reminded me of nothing so much as Disneyland—which turned out to be, in fact, a deliberate, postmodernist reference by the architect. (The street was called Main Street, after the theme park's Main Street, U.S.A., section.) Later, Malcolm Gladwell, impressed by the indoor street, would compare the office to the supersubtle network of Greenwich Village that Jane Jacobs described in *The Death and Life of Great American Cities*. This was a beautifully apt description of what the offices were trying to do, and yet it concealed a fundamental difference. Jacobs's point about Greenwich Village was that it was partly organic, growing out of the common work of the city inhabitants. The paradise of TBWA\Chiat\Day was a pleasant but definitely artificial one; if we were thinking in city terms, we might imagine something more like a cul-de-sac in Celebration, Florida, than the corner of Bleecker and MacDougal.

In its bravura, encircled, thorough design, TBWA\Chiat\Day was at once breathtaking and scary. As a space, it soared, and to walk around as a visitor made you long, briefly, to work there—or at least get in a game of basketball. If this was a city, it was one that curiously made no reference to the massive city outside. In some respects, the city inside was *better*. Few streets in Los Angeles were as walkable as the one inside the TBWA\Chiat\Day warehouse. Strolling around the place, cresting pedestrian bridges and lingering underneath the deep red hoops, reluctantly recalling my car and the freeway and the flight out I had to catch, I thought, why would you ever leave?

Something similar occurred to me when I visited the offices of Google in Northern California. Campus offices like Google's totally incorporate everything we do into one area. At Google you not only get free food all day and the gym anytime you want but also have day care, on-campus health and dental service, a resistance pool, and the ability to get your oil changed. If a preference for urban life causes you to move away from the main campus in Mountain View, you can take the Google bus from several points in San Francisco and begin your workday on the bus. (In fact, steep rent and housing increases have occurred in neighborhoods with proximity to Google bus pickup points, suggesting that the effect of offices carries well beyond their immediate glass-and-concrete bounds.)

Visiting Google's Mountain View offices is initially an underwhelming experience. The large campus is superficially indistinguishable from many office parks: low-slung, glassy buildings, encircled by trim lawns, all ringed by heavily trafficked streets and highways. To be sure, the beach volleyball court and "community" garden add a certain California-progressive air to the general tech company aesthetic—not to mention the strategically placed, goofy-looking small bicycles, slathered with the eye-popping Google quadricolor of yellow, blue, green, and red, that you're supposed to be unembarrassed riding from building to building. It's when you enter the buildings that you begin to sense a slight shift in the atmosphere. What looks from the outside like just another sunny chain of cubicle warrens turns out to be something that takes the word "campus" rather seriously.

Like TBWA\Chiat\Day, Google's headquarters—the Googleplex —is meant to be a self-contained universe. You shouldn't ever have to leave the campus to do the work you want; in fact, with endless amounts of free snack food and treadmill desks, you pretty much never have to leave, even to sustain your own biological existence. But the point of reference for this all-encompassing universe isn't, as with TBWA\Chiat\Day, the city; it's the university. This isn't a European-style university, plopped down in the middle of the city. The model is clearly Stanford University, which the Founders (as they are called), Sergey Brin and Larry Page, attended for a time, before dropping out to found their more lucrative corporate university—many of whose employees come, of course, from Stanford.

The idea behind Google has been to make the normally wrenching transition from university life to corporate life as seamless as possible. Google had inherited the campus in 2004 from defunct Silicon Graphics, which had established the now hackneyed urban idea: a "Main Street" running through the building, spoking off into "neighborhoods," encouraging people to use stairways rather than elevators for random encounters. The architect Clive Wilkinson (also the designer for TBWA\Chiat\Day) was hired to push the idea of circulation even further, adding links between buildings, while emphasizing the campus life of the company. Outdoor sports, lots of food, various common rooms, a park—these were the first signifiers of campus life. Zones within the building were designated as "hot" and "cold": the hot areas were meeting rooms and lounges, collaboration spaces for teamwork; the cold areas more like libraries and study rooms, for seclusion and private work. Finally, for the engineers who needed to code, "tents" were provided to house two to three people. This, according to the Founders, was the right size for coding.

Google's Mountain View office, which I visited in the spring of 2012, was an extraordinary conglomeration of spaces and furniture, not all of which, pleasantly enough, pushed the envelope of innovation. Aside from the treadmill desks (which I didn't see anyone use), some of the spaces had cubicles. Many of the workstations were tightly packed together. And yet Google seems to care immensely about its workers' preferences. New lighting, chairs, and desks were being tried out constantly. In one of the buildings, the Google rep Christopher Coleman told me, the company was trying out "ten different lighting systems, four different mechanical systems, and five different furniture manufacturers," all to see which worked best for the Googlers.[6] In that respect, Google seemed to hark back to older kinds of campus and familial work environments—Connecticut General, or even the Larkin Building. Google liked to mix traditional arrangements, such as cubicles, and "wackier" concepts, such as egg-shaped private nests (which it uses in its Zurich office), where people can have private conversations or even settle down and take a nap.

Like TBWA\Chiat\Day, Google seemed to want its employees to stick around, something its spokespeople confirmed. When I asked Coleman whether Google permitted workers to telecommute, he replied, "No—and we discourage it." Google wanted its employees to be productive on campus, he argued, and coordinating with workers not at the office wasn't helpful in that regard. But an employee I spoke to, who asked to remain anonymous, suggested that the policies weren't so strict. She had worked at Google for several years, before moving to a dot-com start-up, only to move back to Google. "They're the most flexible company I've ever worked for," she said. "If people commute a lot, they'll often work from home on a Friday. It is fairly lax, I would say, in terms of being at work and getting things done. They just assume you're doing good things for the good of the company, and they trust you."[7]

Coleman took me into a large amphitheater with a two-story screen, where, he mentioned, the Founders would speak every Friday to the Googlers about what was going on in the company. Meant to be charmingly paternalistic, it struck me as scary: I had a slightly melodramatic vision of the giant poster of Citizen Kane, leering down at a mass of people in thrall. But soon afterward, Coleman showed me into what he indicated was one of the Googlers' favorite places in the building. "They just love this place," he said, as we walked into a small café space, buzzing with talk and the whir of a blender. It was a juice bar. Coleman pointed to the juices written on the chalkboard. *This* was their favorite place? He asked me why I thought people liked it so much. The juices? I replied. He pointed to the floor-to-ceiling windows, letting in a glimpse of green, and the late afternoon California springtime sun. "It's the proximity to nature," he said.

The simplicity and cheerful haphazardness of Google tended to contradict the rather elaborate image it had constructed for itself. The same employee I spoke to above seemed to confirm this. She mentioned that the cafeterias have "these strange designs: you return your tray in a place where people are lining up for food. There's this very inconvenient crossroads." The Founders had set it up to encourage—of course—random encounters and encourage fraternizing among engineers. But when I asked her whether she thought Google's long corridors did anything, she said, "You'll run into people to get to know them and form relationships—it inspires innovation, I *guess*," before confessing, "I don't know *why* they did that." What was more important in her view turned out to be the least prepossessing aspect of the office's design: the company's permissive dog policy. It was running into people with dogs that would prompt more human interactions: with dogs, she said, "for whatever reason, people are much more social." In other words, long corridors where people might run into each other are fine, and their effect is equivocal, but what might work even better are policies that allow you to bring your pet to work.

□

The Google and TBWA\Chiat\Day models of workplaces have a kind of unquestioned authority to them, as well as outward popularity. Many on the outside are trying to get in: Google receives about seventy-five thousand job applications a week, in no small part because it's reputed to be a good work environment. It's also, as a result, a very exclusive environment, and there *is* a kind of self-selecting quality that contributes to the informality of Google's atmosphere: it's an open secret, as an employee told me, that Google tends to seek out Ivy Leaguers for its office, ensuring that everyone has the same cultivated attitude of intelligence.

Yet the model of an office that caters to all your needs (and mostly keeps you there) came under severe public strain when a Google alumna, Marissa Mayer, tried to apply its lessons to the company where she had recently become CEO, the struggling Silicon Valley search engine company Yahoo! Roughly contemporary with Google, Yahoo! had fallen conspicuously behind, becoming widely seen as a Valley has-been. Hiring Mayer in 2012 away from Google—where she was employee number twenty, and therefore something of a multimillionaire—was seen as both a last-ditch effort and a brilliantly bold move. Much of this boldness apparently had to do with the fact that Mayer, at the time of her hiring, was pregnant. How would she manage a company while also being a mother? people asked. Some of the testimony about Mayer's insomniac prowess and even-the-early-Protestants-weren't-like-this work ethic suggested the path forward. "She used to put in 130 hour weeks at Google," explained *Business Insider*, and "she managed that schedule by sleeping under her desk and being 'strategic' about her showers."[8] As for her efforts to be a working mother, there was the unspoken and obvious idea that Mayer would be able to afford some in-home help. Still, there was hope among many that she would institute model work-life policies as a mother. Such hope suffered tremors of dismay when she announced that she would be taking only a paltry two-week maternity leave.

And when an internal memo from Yahoo! leaked in late February 2012, indicating that the company's policy on telecommuters would be abrogated, and all work-at-home employees asked to start putting their days in at the office, the fiercest outrage came from working parents, who took it out on Mayer. "Rather than championing a blending of life and work," Lisa Belkin wrote at the *Huffington Post*, "she is calling for an enforced and antiquated division. She is telling workers—many of whom were hired with the assurance that they could work remotely—that they'd best get their bottoms into their office chairs, or else." "Did Marissa Mayer actually have a baby or was that like a ploy for press or something?" one blogger at the site *Scary Mommy* wrote. In an industry—and a region—that had pioneered techniques of flexible working, many said, the fiat decision to end a progressive practice was nothing but a reactionary move. These sentiments were widely echoed.[9]

The move itself had an obvious and plausible, if nonetheless cruel, rationale: that, faced with a beleaguered company, the CEO had made a "tough decision" to weed out the workers who were using their remote status to collect paychecks while remaining unproductive. A source close to Mayer suggested that at Yahoo! "a lot of people hid. There were all these employees [working remotely] and nobody knew they were still at Yahoo!" Many of them no doubt would not be able to come to the office as requested and would be forced to leave. It was a way, the same source attested, of "carefully getting to problems created by Yahoo!'s huge, bloated infrastructure." The supposition that her Google training had led to the decision was also probably specious, since flexible work remains a practical reality there, if not something the company advertises. What's more, a few months after the controversy over her decision—and despite and perhaps a little because of it—Mayer announced an extended maternity and paternity leave policy of eight paid weeks: this was nothing compared with, say, Sweden's national policy of sixteen months' leave at 80 percent pay, but in the United States, where paid maternity leave isn't even required, it was a step in the right direction.

Although this was not the intention, the decision at Yahoo! had set off a wide-ranging discussion about the nature of the workplace, one it appeared that office workers were increasingly desperate to have. At the heart of it was the issue of control. There was the old suspicion that workers shouldn't be too far from management, who needed to keep a close eye on people to ensure that they worked, which many affirmed. Some insisted that despite all the trendy discussions of mobile work, people still worked better together, in an office. Others—following a long if sinuous line of management theorists—suggested that workers were better educated than ever before and had correspondingly high expectations and need for autonomy: they didn't have to be corralled or watched in order to work and in fact worked better when not under surveillance.

Whatever the truth of these arguments, there's no question that in the last decade workplace "control" in the old sense has been subject to a certain kind of unraveling; in its stead have come workplaces characterized, at least on the surface, by more informality and autonomy on the part of workers themselves. Most people suggest that the increased mobility of technology is the prime mover in this. And there's of course a great deal of truth to that: as everyone knows, contemporary technology enables us to work in ways that permit—as well as demand—work outside the bounds of the workplace. Of course, not all of the workplaces that produce mobile technologies encourage such work within their own offices. As the Dutch architectural historian Juriaan van Meel pointed out to me, "The small irony of these new ways of working is that the people who produce the tools that allow us to work in the cloud, to work anywhere we want to—this software is being produced by people sitting in offices . . . It's highly personalized—at Google at least—people in cubicles, people working in groups. It's not being done on an iPad from a café . . . roaming and working wherever you want to."

The hold of the office over its workers began to dissipate well before the "cloud." The rise of temporary, freelance, and contract work in particular coincided with the gradual breaking of lifetime employment policies in American corporations in the "lean and mean" 1980s. As the cycle of mergers and layoffs became at once more intense and more routine, a larger proportion of workers were being hired on a contract basis, among them thousands of former employees forced out of the permanent workforce. Some of them, of course, sought out semipermanent work. Well before people felt comfortable about working from home, the change in the labor force began to prize apart the idea of "work" from any particular "place." In her superb book, *The Temp Economy*, the historian Erin Hatton traced the rise of the temp industry from the early 1950s to the present. The early temp offices, like the "Kelly Girls" agency, explicitly linked work and gender: most temps were (and are) women, who performed work outside the home for needed cash—though the assumption was always that their *real* work was inside the home. It was only by the 1980s, when companies became less committed to having permanent workers, that temping became a fundamental, even paradigmatic, part of the American economy: temps were hired to replace striking workers, and the figure of the "permatemp"—the de facto permanent employee who conveniently received no benefits—became a common feature of the tech company landscape.[10] When we see nomadic and non-territorial offices, with official policies about flexibility, it's just as much the influence of this history of work as it is technology that's the source.

□

During the same years that Jay Chiat was trying to force his virtual office onto unexpectedly recalcitrant employees, a self-styled visionary consultant named Erik Veldhoen was doing something similar at a Dutch insurance company called Interpolis. Like Chiat/Day, Interpolis was doing badly in the early 1990s. It hired the ubiquitous consulting firm McKinsey to come in to do some consulting work, which naturally led to the ham-fisted solution of layoffs. But layoffs didn't solve the problem. In desperation, Interpolis turned to Veldhoen. In 1995 he had become somewhat notorious for having published a book called *The Demise of the Office*, which argued, as many others were suggesting at the time, that telecommunications would soon put an end to the office as we knew it. Veldhoen and his company came up with a simple plan. They assigned teams to floors and created a variety of work settings on each floor—private offices, semi-open spaces, and totally open spaces. Private desks were abolished. Workers now had lockers, a home zone where they worked each day, and an internal mobile telephone. And workers were now permitted to work from home as much as they needed—which typically meant one to two days a week. The people Interpolis had trouble convincing were not the workers themselves, as might be expected, but the managers. Managers were too used to being in positions where they could constantly watch their workers. The idea that workers might work anywhere in the building, let alone anywhere outside it, was frightening. "They think that if I see somebody he works," Louis Lhoest, a consultant at Veldhoen + Company, told me. "It is not true. Most managers are quite lousy managers. If you're really in contact with your people, you don't have to see them every day, or every hour."[11]

The fear on the part of management that workers would disappear turned out to be unfounded. According to one study from the Center for Buildings and Places, a Dutch workplace research institute, workers appeared to seek each other out more, and internal communication increased.[12] Environmental psychology studies, which suggested that requirements of status, privacy, and personalization were large barriers to flexible working, turned out to be disproven. After some initial resistance, workers adapted quickly to their new arrangements—though they did tend to seek out the same spot to work, despite the idea that the "activity-based" arrangement within the office was supposed to get people working in different spots.

When I visited Interpolis, I spoke to Lhoest over lunch at the company's Tivoli Plaza, a communal space added in the second stage of making the company more flexible. What might have otherwise been an empty atrium (something like what they have at the Pixar office), connecting the various buildings that make up the Interpolis complex, had been subdivided and given over to various artists and architects to design. Each of the seven "clubhouse" areas was connected by "streets" (the old urban metaphor again), and each was created by someone different. In one section, Aeron chairs surrounded a large yellow conference table in the shape of a palette, near a bar lined with stools; it was all overhung with lamps in the vague shape of bowling pins and carpeted with a light-yellow-and-green pattern reminiscent of a medieval tapestry. Elsewhere in the vicinity were giant huts and chairs in the shape of artist models. Lhoest showed me to an "ear chair," a high-backed couch with wings extending outward to guard the sitter's head. Superficially, it seems to have the texture and color of concrete but turns out to be quite plush and comfortable—and amazingly, it blocks out most sound. You can face two "ear chairs" together and have something resembling a private conversation. All the clubhouses had varieties of spaces like this, designed for meetings, conferences, or private work. It was pleasingly extravagant for a workforce that was only at the office three to four days a week.

Interpolis was ingenious, but something troubled me about the imposition of the concept. Lhoest kept insisting to me that instituting "activity-based working" meant getting a commitment from the top management levels. Executives had to agree, and to believe, before anything could be done. But what about the bottom? Didn't they have to agree too? It never came up, even though "trust," Lhoest told me, was the central idea behind activity-based working—trust, that is, between employees and managers, since constant supervision was out of the question. What Lhoest called "trust" I suspect might be better termed, from the staff perspective, "consent"—a willingness to go along with changes made by the executives. In other companies, the consent had frayed. While studies of Interpolis suggest that satisfaction with the space and work had increased since the change to flexible work, other workplaces in the Netherlands that had adopted similar environments had suffered enormous drops in satisfaction. At the Dynamischkantoor in Haarlem, a building housing parts of the Dutch Ministry for Housing, Spatial Planning, and the Environment, the proportion of workers who believed the activity-based environment contributed to productivity dropped from 60 percent to 25 percent after the new arrangements were introduced. The complaints were legion: lack of proper space for concentration and privacy; constant noise and interruptions; and too much time wasted planning for work.[13] This was despite

The Tivoli Plaza at Interpolis (1998). *Photograph by Kim Zwart, courtesy of Veldhoen + Company*

the fact that all the necessary components were in place: cellular offices for concentrated work; informal spaces for collaboration; and closed-door conference rooms for formal meetings.

It turns out that imposition of a concept by fiat can easily result in a workplace that looks "creative" but works terribly. Drawing on a utopian concept, rather than the actual experience of actual workers, the plans fail not for lack of trying but for lack of listening. For example, following the MIT professor Thomas Allen, who famously discovered that interactions decrease exponentially the farther people work from each other, designers have tended to cram people together—something that not so incidentally decreases costs exponentially—while making nominal gestures toward private space. The result is noise and distraction. Or, following the "cave and commons" approach, a designer might place a central space in the midst of an area between private offices, thinking that this would be a great spot for those sacred serendipitous encounters. The result might be no interactions at all, or at least not meaningful ones. In one study, a shared space at a media agency was passed through constantly, but there was no combustion of innovation flames, as the collaboration ideologists always hope. There was too much traffic in general, and the agency's director was often in the space having coffee, which made more junior workers fearful of being overheard.[14]

Erik Veldhoen, who eventually sold the company he started (for obscure reasons, he appears to have left when there were differences between partners over the design of Microsoft's Amsterdam headquarters), is someone who insists grandly on the autonomy of workers to decide their environments. One of the more famous and oddly charismatic personages in the dense, creative world of Dutch design, he has become a freelance consultant, working on books and expounding his theories at conferences. I met him at his usual table in Dauphine in Amsterdam—the sort of buzzy, Parisian-style café that proponents of his method often cite as one of the new working environments for modern-day "knowledge workers." When I asked him about autonomy, he got right to the point. "Hierarchy models," he told me, "are based on control . . . People are owners of their own activities." He began to hold forth on the future of the digital revolution, something he believes (and many others believe along with him) is as enormous a change as the Industrial Revolution—something that is already changing the way people experience time and place. Explaining his understanding of the Industrial Revolution as two hundred years of error, which cruelly required people to work every day at a specific place, he suggested that the new era would return us to a *pre*industrial time. "We are at the end of labor," he said. "We [will] go back to craftsmanship." Information technology had made work more time and place independent. People could organize time as they liked. "When you see people working, for example, 40 hours a week—a week is 168 hours. Let's say that from the 40 hours, 20 hours are labeled 'time with others.' Cooperation. And 20 hours are just for you to do your work alone . . . to organize . . . in the time frame you want. That's a possibility. It has a lot of influence on how you organize your life and your life-work balance. That will change dramatically."[15]

I asked him what would happen to the system of hierarchy as a result. "In the future we don't need managers anymore," he said. He took off his glasses and self-consciously widened his large blue eyes. He knew he had made a grandiose statement, and he took care to emphasize it. "The labor contract will change dramatically. It's not 'You work for me, I'm the boss, and you do what I say.' It's 'We have a target in our company, and what can you deliver to reach that target?' And then we make a deal, but you have to deliver that. You're organizing your own way to get that result, you're responsible for that, not the company." I was confused momentarily, since it seemed to me that he was eliminating managers from his system but not executives or the old forms of ownership that had made the Industrial Revolution possible—before it turned out he had another semi-scandalous statement in store. "You know Karl Marx?" he asked, eyes again expanding. "He has to live now. Because his dream comes now. Power to labor, to the people."

□

Veldhoen's supposedly Marxist claims for the increasing autonomy of workers, and the return to a preindustrial world of labor organization, mirrored the sorts of arguments I heard from another writer on contemporary work arrangements, Richard Greenwald. I met him in a café in Williamsburg, Brooklyn, which was full of the laptop-affixed workers he's spent the last several years studying: namely, freelancers. A professor of labor history and sociology at St. Joseph's College in Brooklyn, where he is also the dean, Greenwald did his early work on more traditional subjects, like the rise of the garment workers' union. But in his work as a labor activist and journalist, he began to realize that the world he saw around him made little reference to the unionized precincts of the urban industrial workforce he had studied; indeed, it was far different from the corporate world of flush benefits and high pay that had characterized corporate life for generations. Nor did it seem to consist of knowledge workers "controlling the means of production" in a "post-capitalist society," as the late Peter Drucker had come to prophesy in the last decades of his life. Rather, he saw people moving from gig to gig, in an ever more jagged and precarious path of nearly permanent underemployment.

"Freelancing is the fastest-growing sector of our economy," he told me. It's difficult to come up with an accurate count of how many freelancers there actually are—filing a self-employment tax form doesn't mean you don't also have a permanent job, and the Bureau of Labor Statistics hasn't done an estimate since 2005—but reasonable estimates put the number anywhere between 25 and 30 percent of the American workforce; their numbers are growing in European countries as well, leading some writers to speak of a precarious office proletariat, or "precariat." Some of these precarious workers choose to leave the permanent workforce; most others are pushed out. Most don't have health insurance; many are in constant and "desperate need of money." And they suffer from "the illusion that not many of them are being exploited."[16] These are the same people who, according to Veldhoen, were harbingers of the end of capitalism.

Of course, as Greenwald went on to explain, the picture is complicated. Drawing on his many conversations with freelancers and people who hire them, he discovered that contract work does offer a kind of freedom. He found in their attitudes "a sense of pride and identity with work" that—if we're to believe *Office Space* anyway—has gone missing from the larger economy. The people in the creative industries, like graphic design, spoke of the satisfaction they took in their work. Freelancers who do well have substantial control over their hours and the work that they produce; like anyone else, they sell their labor for a price, but the best can set the terms of what they offer.

At the same time, along with the satisfaction, comes "a lot of worry." When the freelancers *are* exploited—when they have to do a lot of work for not much money, and there's nothing else coming their way, and bills are due—they feel "helpless to prevent that exploitation." Much of the pleasure of being a freelancer also seems to entail many of the problems. Freelancers usually work alone and many refer to themselves as "entrepreneurs," which often means that they see themselves as unique. It also means that when they fail, they put the failure entirely on themselves rather than ascribe it to some kind of system. Greenwald, in a rather uncompromising phrase, called it "a persistence of the white-collar delusion." He blamed a whole host of freelance self-help books for promoting a boosterish attitude toward contract work—one that rarely informs a freelancer of the difficulties he or she is likely to face.

What did the rise of contract work mean for the future of work more generally? Here Greenwald too saw the return of older styles of independent entrepreneurs pursuing their craft. With, of course, a key difference: the large, transnational companies weren't disappearing but in fact were growing, taking on larger shares of the workforce. The change was that the workforce was increasingly taking on a precarious aspect. Greenwald thought the only way to make freelancing work was to increase a frayed safety net—to allow for flexibility while making sure failure didn't mean catastrophe. He suggested that something along the lines of the old nineteenth-century guilds could operate as greater protection against the headwinds of economic change or crisis. In a cheerier vein, Veldhoen had voiced the same idea: but neither the optimistic nor the pessimistic view seemed to reflect the coming of a socialist utopia.

If the increasing contingency of work could be said to have one bright side, it would be the emergence of a workplace characterized less by hierarchy and management control, and the potential of greater control by workers themselves over the labor process. Management theorists have been prophesying the coming of this world for decades, of course; Tom Peters and similar figures have long urged executives to upend hierarchies; and in his last book Peter Drucker suggested, in another inversion of Marxism, that knowledge workers would at last come to control the "means of production"—knowledge—and bring about a new, "post-capitalist" society. Other theorists, such as labor scholar Charles Heckscher, have seen a "post-bureaucratic" world emerging, again characterized more by trust than by control. The problem has been that such conjectures rarely describe actual workplaces; rather than in the sector of so-called knowledge workers, job growth is projected mostly to take place in low-wage clerical sectors, while the expansion of heavily monitored call centers puts the lie to the idea that Taylorism is coming to an end.[17] One professor of business has suggested, influentially, that employees in the new era need to develop a "mindset flexibility," or a "self-employed mindset," in which they treat their employers as "customers" of their services, and ensure that they are satisfied, in order to retain their customers' "business."[18]

Among a rash of new companies, however, chiefly in the tech sector, one does see significant gestures toward loosening forms of work. These have become known as "bossless" offices—among the most famous are Menlo Innovations and the video game company Valve—in which hierarchies are supposed to be flatter than usual, work is done on a group basis, and leadership emerges and subsides on a project basis, rather than being functionally apportioned by a bureaucratic rationale. GitHub, a San Francisco–based software company that came up with a fantastically popular means of sharing and editing open-source software, is one such workplace. I visited them in September 2013, just after they had moved into a giant new warehouse office, which expressed a newfound sense of security and power after several years of profitability. Spread out over three floors, it resembled some of the dot-com offices of an earlier boom in its many touches of expensive wackiness. The vast reception area had been designed as a replica of the Oval Office; one secret wall opened into a mahogany-paneled library with musty leather furniture, while another led to the internal office "speakeasy." Breaking up the wide loft floors into mini conference rooms were dismantled shipping containers: a reference to the company's jargon for "shipping" code. Some workers had assigned desks; many, perhaps most, were mobile or nomadic; private rooms were available for concentrated work. The bottom floor was open for events. It reflected the most intelligent contemporary ideas in office design. Over 70 percent of the workforce worked offsite, or would end up in one of GitHub's new offices opening around the world; all of the important work-related conversations tended to take place online, or in forums that were otherwise available to people after the fact. Yet Scott Chacon, one of the company's founders and COO, kept referring to the importance of employees being able to "serendipitously encounter" each other throughout their workday (in a slightly unserendipitous phrasing). When I asked how people were supposed to have these encounters, given the fact that most of the staff wasn't actually required to come into the office, he mentioned, sensibly, that he wanted these encounters to be rare, once a month, or once every two months, and to be "deeper interactions." He suggested that people could run into each other at a company event as well as at the office, and actually have longer, more profound conversations. "That's way more valuable to me than 'I saw this person when I was going to the bathroom,' or 'I had to wait in line behind them when I was waiting for food' . . . that's not a valuable interaction."[19] It was a rebuke to the lazier ideas of fortuitous encounters that proliferated in office design–speak around the world.

The permissive attitude toward coming into work had its correlate in the lightly articulated management structure of the company. GitHub has gotten a substantial amount of press for not having managers. Tim Clem—who was described to me by Liz Clinkenbeard, a GitHub press representative, as being on "our, I guess . . . *management* team, if you would?"—suggested it was "a little bit of a falsehood that we have no management. The reality is we expect most individuals to perform most of those managerial functions." The idea was that management wouldn't be the structure above the coding and more entry-level work that one ascended to after years of service; it was something that was supposed to emerge. Chacon described this as coming out of the open-source model: "A lot of the ways that we worked [when we were starting the company] was the same way we would work on an open-source project . . . You have all these projects that you can work on, and people choose the crossover of what they're good at . . . leadership can be ephemeral." Though others were hesitant to recommend the practice as a model, Clinkenbeard mentioned that the way it tended to cut through traditional aspects of the division of labor could be salutary for other companies. For example, rather than a project commencing with a small group of engineers, and enlisting publicity only at the very end, the fluidity of the structure made it possible, even likely, for people from various departments to comment and participate in work from the beginning. "It can be frustrating to get things done," Chacon commented. "You have to convince people . . . It's taken a lot of experimentation, and frustration, but a lot of great stuff has come out of it."[20]

GitHub has begun subtly to affect the practice of governments as well, with municipalities and states releasing data to the public to manipulate through GitHub's software. What effect this could have on general attitudes toward bureaucracy, and whether places like GitHub represent an emerging "post-bureaucratic" workplace, remain open questions. For now it's clear that, like other widely admired work environments, the company remains an exception; even internally, its loose management practices leave GitHub's ownership structure unclear. Still, its approach reflects a wider sense of unease with the systems of managerial control that developed during a century in office environments—something the debate over Marissa Mayer and Yahoo! signified as well. Organizations that insist on hierarchy are becoming harder to defend; the "mindset flexibility" demanded of workers has the potential to transform itself from contingency and precariousness into something that might very well look like autonomy.

□

When I asked Francis Duffy whether he believed that Dutch offices like Interpolis and its ilk were the future of the office, he replied that they seemed to be "chinks of light in the situation" but that they weren't radical enough. To go further, we had to change not just offices but cities themselves. Office design was advanced; it was the supply of offices that was regressive.

For over a century, the dominant model of office development—in the United States and the U.K. particularly, but now also in emerging economies, like China and India—has been speculative. Offices get built not for specific purposes but to satisfy imagined future demand. This has resulted in the spectacular skylines that people admire, from Vancouver to New York and from Kuala Lumpur to Shanghai, at a terrible cost: human, environmental, and otherwise. Development schemes, whether grand or minimal, rarely survive financial crashes, and the 2008 crisis has left a lot of office carcasses lying around. Drive around office park corridors near Princeton,

New Jersey, and in Northern Virginia, and you'll see dozens, maybe hundreds of boxy office buildings with "For Lease" signs out front, advertising their many thousands of square feet of rentable space. Across China, you can find ghost cities of empty business districts, with towers crowding empty downtowns, rising over unused streets into skies viscous with smog. In Caracas, the capital of Venezuela, an unfinished office tower, Torre David, has infamously been taken over by squatters, who have developed their own informal skyscraper community.

But even offices that are used are wasteful. Most of the time they're empty (though the lights are often still on), and even during working days some estimates suggest that people are at their desks only about a third of the time. Businesses can use that sort of statistic to cut down desk sizes and crush people into less space, but the lesson is much larger than a real estate one. In Bengaluru, India, where my family is from, the sprawling campus of the software company Infosys is out in a special economic zone called Electronic City. It has a water and electric supply separate from, and better than, the city of Bengaluru itself. The campus is extraordinarily well landscaped, filled with careful floral arrangements haunted by rare butterflies. Bengaluru was once known as the "garden city," and I still recall it as a sleepy, relatively small South Indian town in the 1980s. A decade later, the country's economy had liberalized, and Bengaluru became the center of the country's burgeoning information technology sector, and the fastest-growing city in India. But its infrastructure was never maintained at a level to sustain such growth; most of the city's best companies moved out to special zones like Whitefield and Electronic City—to garden cities of their own.

Infosys's campus consists of many "modern"-looking glass buildings, originally designed to project a "global" image to visitors; among the most striking, or bizarre, on the Electronic City campus is a solid-glass reflective block with a transparent sphere scooped out of the center, known affectionately to Infosys employees as "the washing machine building." A representative of the company insisted to me that such buildings are part of Infosys's past and are gradually being greened.[21] Green or not, outside a city with a level of poverty hovering around 30 percent, the benefits being apportioned among the offices seem to be particularly unequal, not to mention unsustainable. What's more, the design inside is hardly progressive. Infosys's buildings were packed tightly with cubicles; and another campus I visited, General Electric's research facility out in Whitefield, was the same. When I asked a representative of GE why they had chosen to use cubicles, he replied, "How else do you design offices?"[22]

In his book *Work and the City* (2008), Duffy suggests that the supply chain needs to be completely reordered so that use becomes the primary criterion for creating offices, not speculation. The suggestion isn't purely a fanciful one. The phenomenon of "co-working," something that has exploded in the last decade, is evidence of a new attitude toward building use. Co-working can take several forms, but the most basic is the provision (for a fee) of a shared office facility (desks, conference rooms, coffee) for freelancers who want to get out of their apartments and be sociable in an office setting. These office settings are almost universally classic millennial "creative" offices: open plan, vintage furniture, bicycle racks, whiteboards. One of the co-working spaces I visited, Indy Hall in Philadelphia, consisted of cheap IKEA furniture that was easy to put together and just as easy to dismantle and throw out. Most members had "flex" memberships, which meant that they came in rarely; most didn't use it as their primary office. Alex Hillman, one of the co-founders of the space, told me that Indy Hall was competing not with other offices but with its members' homes. The space was outfitted with well-indented couches and slightly rickety bookshelves, a full kitchen with freshly washed dishes drying next to the sink, and a fridge full of homemade beer. On the shelves I saw the usual business classics with some slightly more hacker-ish additions: a biography of Steve Jobs, Lawrence Lessig's works on free culture, and *The Essential Drucker*.

The hidden promise of co-working is of course serendipitous encounters with like-minded entrepreneurs. The amount of business-speak expounded on the virtues of co-working—and the conditions it creates for "creative collisions" and "radical collaboration"—has been voluminous. (Said Tim Freundlich, one of the founders of HUB, a co-working space for social entrepreneurs: "The tectonic shift in how people, especially millennials, want to physically go to work and the understandings emerging around the utility of rapid prototyping, collaboration and 'creative collision,' married to the surge in having sustainability and one's values incorporated into our work all make this type of model successful."[23] Got that?)

And yet co-working has more potential than a one-company office to make encounters a genuine proposition: It seems more likely that you would meet someone useful outside your delimited field of work than you would in it. If you're working on, say, a toy design, but you know nothing about social media, it's possible that you might strike up a conversation with someone who understands marketing and would be willing to help (also for a fee). Despite the impressive strangeness of actually paying to go to an office (when freelancing was supposedly going to keep you out of one), co-working has proved immensely popular. As of 2012, there were eighteen hundred co-working spaces in the United States—a figure that has doubled every year since 2005—and there were at least ninety thousand people who were dues-paying members of a facility, half of whom were in the United States.[24] Some companies have predictably seen co-working as an opportunity to decrease costs. In 2011, the California electronics company Plantronics told about 175 members of its staff that they no longer had desks. They had the option of working from home; commuting to the office (where presumably they'd have to share space); or taking a desk at NextSpace, a co-working building, in San Jose. About a dozen took Plantronics up on the offer—though it wasn't one that they could exactly refuse.

But co-working also offers the model in which a company shares a space or small building with other companies, such as GRid70 in Grand Rapids, Michigan, where the furniture company Steelcase, the marketing company Amway, the grocery chain Meijer, and the shoe company Wolverine Worldwide all overlap, and all share ideas, meetings, and, occasionally, food. Zappos in Las Vegas and Google in London have opened up their office spaces to strangers—hoping for yet more "creative collisions" to take place.[25] When I visited GRid70 in May 2013, I was impressed by the genuine openness and informality of the work spaces. Presentation spaces were shared across the companies, and I saw people from different organizations popping in to watch how other businesses did work.

For the flexible workplace, a new crop of flexible furniture styles are coming up. In their book, *Make Space: How to Set the Stage for Creative Collaboration*, the Stanford Design School professors Scott Doorley and Scott Witthoft take examples from their work with students to come up with designs for office environments. Moving screens for impromptu partitions, foam blocks for informal seats, whiteboard sliders to segment rooms and start meetings, large tables for projects, and flip-top tables for storing unfinished projects: it's the old Robert Propst model of creating space, one that is flexible and "forgiving." Though Doorley and Witthoft make allowances that people will occasionally need to find space and room to think, the emphasis falls firmly and irrevocably on collaboration. Even their offices, which I visited in the spring of 2012, were designed along an open plan.

In a world of upheaval, the old furniture companies that dominated the office market—particularly Steelcase and Herman Miller—are struggling and shifting back to basics: to detailed

Indy Hall, a co-working space in Philadelphia. *CJ Dawson Photography*

behavioral studies of office workers and their needs. The prospect of a single supplier catering to an entire office building—as Steelcase did in the 1970s with the Sears Tower—no longer animates the industry. Paul Siebert, director of research and strategy at Steelcase, told me that he saw tremendous difficulties facing office designers in the years ahead. "I think in terms of work-space design, in some ways, there needs to be or there's likely to be a new kind of emergent discipline that's integrative. In other words, interior designers are struggling, hard, to be relevant and so are architects. And so are space planners and so are product designers."[26] Both Steelcase and Herman Miller have intensified their use of anthropological techniques—participant observer, video ethnography, object testing—to understand office workers' behavior and to design around behavior rather than attempt to influence or change it. Herman Miller's most recent furniture solution, Living Office, represents a stripped-down approach to the office along the lines of old Robert Propst. Short, waist-high partition walls were constructed out of big foam blocks that could be easily shifted around. Tall blue cushioned three-seat couches with wings could be massed together to form impromptu conference rooms. Everything was flexible. Reaching back for an old metaphor, the company called each potential arrangement a "Living Office landscape." "In a Living Office," it advised, "people should immediately grasp what they can do, where they can go, what things are for, and why they are the way they are." The same company that had given birth to the most reviled feature of the American workplace was now looking back to its very human-scaled origins.

When I visited the Herman Miller offices in Zeeland, Michigan, it was chiefly to plumb the Propst archives, to see the genesis and apotheosis of the Action Office. But in the company's own new work space, it had shifted to a largely open-plan space: you entered confronted by an espresso bar and saw executives out alongside the junior staff. Though there were tons of private meeting rooms and colorful offices with George Nelson swag-leg desks, there was not an Action Office in sight. Eventually, I was taken to the local manufacturing plants. As I walked along the steel pedestrian bridge above the assembly-line floor, I was overwhelmed with the sweet smell of

GRid70, a co-working space for multiple companies, in Grand Rapids, Michigan.
Courtesy of Steelcase

Herman Miller's retort to its own Action Office—the Living Office (2012).
Courtesy of Herman Miller

plywood. There, beneath me, workers in goggles were wrapping giant sheets of plywood in fabric: the still-booming business of the cubicle.

□

For the moment, despite the adoption of co-working-style spaces by larger companies, the phenomenon appeals to only a small segment of the workforce. But that segment is expected to grow. Projections by software company Intuit suggest that by 2020 freelancers, temps, day laborers, and independent contractors will constitute 40 percent of the workforce; according to Greenwald's calculations, it might even be 50 percent. Even this might underestimate the amount of casualized labor the country should expect. Not all of these, of course, will be office workers. But it seems likely that a substantial number of office workers will go freelance, or at least spend some significant portion of their lives freelancing.

Here is where the question of "autonomy" returns. From the perspective of those employed in the permanent workforce, freelancers and temps might seem to enjoy more autonomy: they determine either the kind of work they do (freelancers) or the length of the contract they want to serve out (temps). But contingent labor is also the sort that doesn't easily get to make demands beyond that. Freelance contracts are notoriously difficult to enforce; the looser the labor market, the tighter the control companies have over their workforces. According to Freelancers Union, which helps independent contractors get health benefits and other protections, over 77 percent of freelancers have had trouble collecting payment at some point in their lives. The number of freelancers and other forms of informal employment may itself be underestimated. In this respect, the United States is returning to the preindustrial era in a different way from what Erik Veldhoen implied. Back in the mid-nineteenth century, the labor market was vast and unregulated, and workers weren't counted in any systematic way. With an increase in precarious employment, or the precariousness of permanent employment, work appears to be moving not forward but back: back to an earlier era of insecurity. It's not a coincidence that the office itself may also be disappearing, at least in the form that it arose at the beginning of the twentieth century.

Flexibility doesn't have to be one more trick in the managerial guidebook for keeping workers docile and consenting. Flexibility, like technology, is a tool, an opportunity: it lies there, inert, until someone uses it. The willingness of workers to discard status privileges like desks and offices is not just a sign of giving in to executive demands for cost control; it also suggests that the career path that defined the white-collar worker for generations—from the cubicle to the corner office, or even from the steno pool to the walk down the aisle—is coming to a close, and that a new sort of work, as yet unformed, is taking its place. It remains for office workers to make this freedom meaningful: to make the "autonomy" promised by the fraying of the labor contract a real one, to make workplaces truly their own. "Whatever history they have had is a history without events; whatever common interests they have had do not lead to unity; whatever future they have will not be of their own making," wrote C. Wright Mills in the middle of the last century. The coming years will test the truth of that prophecy.

Acknowledgments

This book is chiefly a work of synthesis; without the incredible and ongoing labor of scholars whose work I cite in my notes, it would not be possible. I am also grateful to the libraries of the following institutions, and to their librarians, staff, and security officers: the New-York Historical Society; Columbia University; Stanford University; University of Utah; and University of Pennsylvania.

For editorial and research assistance: Donald Albrecht, Bette Alexander, Karina Bishop, Carla Blumenkranz, Benjamin Buckley, Kim Buckley, Judy Candell at the Department of English at Stanford, Amanda Claybaugh, Liz Clinkenbeard at GitHub, Georgia Collins at DEGW, Nicholas Dames, Marije den Hollander at Rijksgebouwendienst, Stephen Distinti, Francis Duffy, the staff of Joseph Fox Bookshop, Edward Morgan Day Frank, Brian Gallagher, Joe Gallagher, Richard Greenwald, Mark Greif, Katie Hasse at Steelcase, Lara Heimert, Coralie Hunter, Gloria Jacobs and Linda Baron at the Herman Miller Archives, Sadaf Khan at Infosys, Kate Kingen, Benjamin Kunkel, Mark Lamster, Alexandra Lange, Louis Lhoest at Veldhoen + Company, Allison Lorentzen, Chidambaram Maltesh at General Electric, Mark McGurl, Jeremy Medina, James Melia, Franco Moretti, Joan Ockman, Bruce Robbins, Marco Roth, Jim Rutman, Mark Schurman at Herman Miller, Jacob Shell, Katherine Solomonson, Nathaniel Sufrin, Dayna Tortorici, Juriaan van Meel, Astrid Van Raalte at Microsoft Schiphol, Erik Veldhoen, Jon Vimr, Kanye West, Alex Woloch, Hannah Wood.

For their mentorship and support: the Garrisons, everyone at *n+1*, Keith Gessen, Chad Harbach, Edward Orloff, Gerald Howard.

For everything: my parents, and my brother.

This book and its author are dedicated to Shannon.

Notes

INTRODUCTION

1. In neglecting the wider world of work, I less justifiably focus on films and novels to the exclusion of television, more powerful a cultural force now than in Mills's time. *Cubed* is in that sense a partisan work, not seeking to tell the entire cultural history of the office, but seeking out those moments in culture where narratives of office life responded to or even helped shape its social world.

2. C. Wright Mills, *White Collar: The American Middle Classes* (1951; New York: Oxford University Press, 2002), 353.

I: THE CLERKING CLASS

1. Benjamin Browne Foster, *Down East Diary*, ed. Charles H. Foster (Orono: University of Maine Press, 1975), quoted in Michael Zakim, "Business Clerk as Social Revolutionary; or, A Labor History of the Nonproducing Classes," *Journal of the Early Republic* 26, no. 4 (Winter 2006): 580.

2. Herman Melville, "Bartleby, the Scrivener" (1853), in *Billy Budd and Other Stories* (New York: Penguin, 1986), 8.

3. Herman Melville, *Moby-Dick; or, The Whale* (1851; New York: Penguin, 2001), 4.

4. Melville, "Bartleby," 4.

5. Ibid.

6. Ibid., 8.

7. Ibid., 11.

8. Ibid., 12.

9. Ibid.

10. "Marginalized: Notes in Manuscripts and Colophons Made by Medieval Scribes and Copyists," *Lapham's Quarterly* 5, no. 2 (2012): 155.

11. Evelyn Nakano Glenn and Roslyn L. Feldberg, "Degraded and Deskilled: The Proletarianization of Clerical Work," in *Women and Work,* ed. Rachel Kahn-Hut, Arlene Kaplan Daniels, and Richard Cloward (New York: Oxford University Press, 1982): 204.

12. Brian Luskey, *On the Make: Clerks and the Quest for Capital in Nineteenth*

Century America (New York: New York University Press, 2010), 6. Luskey notes, however, that the census did not disaggregate private-sector workers from those in municipal government, nor those in law offices from clerks in countinghouses.

13. *American Whig Review*, April 1853, 75; *American Phrenological Journal* 17 (1853); *Vanity Fair*, February 18, March 17, 1860, quoted in Zakim, "Business Clerk as Social Revolutionary," 570.

14. Quoted in Michael Zakim, *Ready-Made Democracy: A History of Men's Dress in the Early Republic, 1760–1860* (Chicago: University of Chicago Press, 2003), 109–10.

15. Edgar Allan Poe, "The Man of the Crowd" (1840), in *Poems, Tales, and Selected Essays* (New York: Library of America, 1996), 389–90.

16. Walt Whitman, *New York Dissected* (New York: Rufus Rockwell Wilson, 1936), 120.

17. Quoted in Michael Zakim, "Producing Capitalism," in *Capitalism Takes Command: The Social Transformation of Nineteenth-Century America*, ed. Michael Zakim and Gary J. Kornblith (Chicago: University of Chicago Press, 2012), 226.

18. Stuart Blumin, *The Emergence of the Middle Class: Social Experience in the American City, 1760–1900* (Cambridge, U.K.: Cambridge University Press, 1989), 73–74.

19. Willis Larimer King, "Recollections and Conclusions from a Long Business Life," *Western Pennsylvania Historical Magazine* 23 (1940): 226, quoted in Ileen A. DeVault, *Sons and Daughters of Labor: Class and Clerical Work in Turn-of-the-Century Pittsburgh* (Ithaca, N.Y.: Cornell University Press, 1990), 9.

20. Quoted in Robert G. Albion, *The Rise of New York Port*, 264, quoted in Alfred Chandler, *The Visible Hand: The Managerial Revolution in American Business* (Cambridge, Mass.: Belknap Press, 1977), 37.

21. Michael Zakim, "Producing Capitalism," 229–30.

22. Chandler, *Visible Hand*, 15.

23. Blumin, *Emergence of the Middle Class*, 83.

24. Ibid., 95.

25. Ibid., 116.

26. Edward N. Tailer, Diary, January 1, 1850, New-York Historical Society.

27. Harry Braverman, *Labor and Monopoly Capital: The Degradation of Work in the Twentieth Century* (1974; New York: *Monthly Review Press*, 1998), 204.

28. Quoted in Blumin, *Emergence of the Middle Class*, 78.

29. Ralph Waldo Emerson, "Self-Reliance," in *The Essays of Ralph Waldo Emerson* (Cambridge, Mass.: Harvard University Press, 1987), 43.

30. Quoted by Tailer, Diary, December 2, 1848.

31. Tailer, Diary, December 15, 1849.

32. Ibid.

33. Tailer, Diary, January 17, 1850.

34. Luskey, *On the Make*, 129–31.

35. Tailer, Diary, November 12, 1852, quoted in ibid., 186.

36. Luskey, 191–93.

37. Quoted in ibid., 137.

38. *New York Daily Tribune*, August 16, 1841, 2.

39. *New York Daily Tribune*, September 2, 1841.

40. Quoted in Luskey, 138.

41. "Familiar Scenes in the Life of a Clerk," *Hunt's Merchants' Magazine* 5 (1841): 56, quoted in Margery Davies, *Woman's Place Is at the Typewriter: Office Work and Office Workers, 1870–1930* (Philadelphia: Temple University Press, 1982), 21.

42. See Martin J. Burke, *The Conundrum of Class: Public Discourse on the Social Order in America* (Chicago: University of Chicago Press, 1995), 108.

2: THE BIRTH OF THE OFFICE

1. Henry Adams, *The Education of Henry Adams* (New York: Houghton Mifflin, 1918 [1907]), 445.

2. William C. Gannett, "Blessed Be Drudgery," in *Blessed Be Drudgery, and Other Papers* (Glasgow: David Bryce and Sons, 1890), 2.

3. Ibid., 7.

4. Horatio Alger Jr., *Rough and Ready; or, Life Among the New York Newsboys* (Philadelphia: John C. Winston, 1897), 262.

5. Eric Sundstrom, *Work Places: The Psychology of the Physical Environment in Offices and Factories* (Cambridge, U.K.: Cambridge University Press, 1986), 33.

6. Susan Henshaw Jones, preface to *On the Job: Design and the American Office*, ed. Donald Albrecht and Chrysanthe B. Broikos (New York: Princeton Architectural Press, 2001), 18.

7. Jerome P. Bjelopera, *City of Clerks: Office and Sales Workers in Philadelphia, 1870–1920* (Chicago: University of Illinois Press, 2005), 26.

8. As scholars have argued since, Chandler greatly exaggerates the efficiency of the "managerial revolution." So, too, did he neglect the broader economic changes, such as the depression of the 1890s, which fueled consolidation and price competition in industry. See William G. Roy, *Socializing Capital: The Rise of the Industrial Corporation in America* (Princeton, N.J.: Princeton University Press, 1997), 21–40, and Naomi Lamoreaux, *The Great Merger Movement in American Business, 1895–1904* (Cambridge, U.K.: Cambridge University Press, 1985), 153–55.

9. Olivier Zunz, *Making America Corporate, 1870–1920* (Chicago: University of Chicago Press, 1990), 47.

10. See Lamoreaux, *The Great Merger Movement in American Business*, 85–87.

11. Ibid., 33.

12. Marshall McLuhan, *Understanding Media: The Extensions of Man* (New York: McGraw-Hill, 1966), 262.

13. Sinclair Lewis, *The Job* (New York: Grosset & Dunlap, 1917), 234.

14. JoAnne Yates, *Control Through Communication: The Rise of System in American Management* (Baltimore: Johns Hopkins University Press, 1989), 34.

15. Mills, *White Collar*, 189.

16. Aldous Huxley, *Brave New World, and Brave New World Revisited* (1932; New York: Harper Perennial, 2005), 20.

17. Quoted in Yates, *Control Through Communication*, 9.

18. Sharon Hartman Strom, *Beyond the Typewriter: Gender, Class, and the Origins of Modern American Office Work* (Urbana: University of Illinois Press, 1992), 20–22.

19. Quoted in Sundstrom, *Work Places*, 31.

20. James S. Russell, "Form Follows Fad," in Albrecht and Broikos, *On the Job*, 53.

21. Quoted in Sudhir Kakar, *Frederick Taylor: A Study in Personality and Innovation* (Cambridge, Mass.: MIT Press, 1974), 168.

22. Daniel T. Nelson, *Frederick Taylor and the Rise of Scientific Management* (Madison: University of Wisconsin Press, 1980), 29.

23. *The Taylor and Other Systems of Shop Management: Hearings Before Special Committee of the House of Representatives to Investigate Taylor and Other Systems of Shop Management, Under Authority of H. Res. 90*, Vol. 3, 1912: 1414.

24. Quoted in Daniel Rodgers, *The Work Ethic in Industrial America, 1850–1920* (Chicago: University of Chicago Press, 1974), 53.

25. Frederick W. Taylor, *The Principles of Scientific Management* (New York: Harper & Brothers, 1913), 69.

26. Ibid., 7.

27. Ibid., 83.

28. Robert Kanigel, *The One Best Way: Frederick Winslow Taylor and the Enigma of Efficiency* (New York: Penguin, 1997), 433–34.

29. Strom, *Beyond the Typewriter*, 34–35.

30. Quoted in Kakar, *Frederick Taylor*, 2.

31. *Providence Labor Advocate*, November 30, 1913, 1, quoted in David Montgomery, *The Fall of the House of Labor: The Workplace, the State, and American Labor Activism* (New Haven, Conn.: Yale University Press, 1987), 221.

32. Montgomery, *Fall of the House of Labor*, 221.

33. John Dos Passos, *The Big Money* (New York: Houghton Mifflin, 2000 [1933]), 15, 19.

34. *System*, January 1904, 484–85.

35. Robert Thurston Kent, "Introduction," in Frank Gilbreth, *Motion Study* (New York: D. Van Nostrand Company, 1921), xiv.

36. William H. Leffingwell, *Scientific Office Management: A Report on the Results of the Applications of the Taylor System of Scientific Management to Offices, Supplemented with a Discussion of How to Obtain the Most Important of These Results* (Chicago: A. W. Shaw, 1917), 214.

37. Ibid., 16.

38. Ibid., 35.

39. Ibid., 33.

40. Ibid., 19.

41. Ibid., 7.

42. Ibid., 11.

43. Lee Galloway, *Office Management: Its Principles and Practice* (New York: Ronald Press, 1919), ix.

44. Angel Kwolek-Folland, *Engendering Business: Men and Women in the Corporate Office, 1870–1930* (Baltimore: Johns Hopkins University Press, 1998), 110.

45. Kwolek-Folland notes the similarities between the arts and management in ibid., 108.

46. Upton Sinclair, *The Brass Check* (Pasadena, Calif., 1920), 78.

47. "When Wall Street Calls Out the Reserves," *BusinessWeek*, December 11, 1929, 36, quoted in Daniel Abramson, *Skyscraper Rivals: The AIG Building and the Architecture of Wall Street* (Princeton, N.J.: Princeton Architectural Press, 2001), 160.

48. Russell, "Form Follows Fad," 50; Jack Quinan, *Frank Lloyd Wright's Larkin Building: Myth and Fact* (Chicago: University of Chicago Press, 2006), 44.

49. Quinan, *Frank Lloyd Wright's Larkin Building*, 15.

50. Ibid., 18.

51. Darwin Martin, app. C, in ibid., 133.

52. Quoted in ibid., app. G, 144.

53. *Frank Lloyd Wright, An Autobiography* (New York: Duell, Sloan and Pearce, 1943), 143.

54. Quinan, *Frank Lloyd Wright's Larkin Building*, 62.

55. Quoted in ibid., 156.

56. Ibid., 44.

57. Quoted in ibid., 153.

58. Quoted in ibid., 143–44.

59. Ibid., 180.

60. Rodgers, *Work Ethic*, 88.

3: THE WHITE-BLOUSE REVOLUTION

1. Quoted in Kwolek-Folland, *Engendering Business*, 94.

2. Lewis, *The Job*, 5.

3. Christopher Morley, *Plum Pudding: Of Divers Ingredients, Discreetly Blended and Seasoned* (Garden City, N.Y.: Doubleday, 1922), 232.

4. Lewis, *The Job*, 42.

5. Strom, *Beyond the Typewriter*, 177.

6. Davies, *Woman's Place Is at the Typewriter*, 51.

7. Bjelopera, *City of Clerks*, 13.

8. Lisa M. Fine, *The Souls of the Skyscraper* (Philadelphia: Temple University Press, 1992), 31.

9. Quoted in Wilfred A. Beeching, *Century of the Typewriter* (Bournemouth, U.K.: British Typewriter Museum Publishing, 1990), 35.

10. Quoted in Davies, *Woman's Place Is at the Typewriter*, 54.

11. William H. Leffingwell, *Office Management: Principles and Practice* (New York: A. W. Shaw, 1925), 620–21.

12. Strom, *Beyond the Typewriter*, 189.

13. National Industrial Conference Board, *Clerical Salaries in the United States* (New York: National Industrial Conference Board, 1926), 11–21, 29.

14. Kwolek-Folland, *Engendering Business*, 27.

15. Kim Chernin, *In My Mother's House* (New York: Harper & Row, 1984), 47–48, quoted in Strom, *Beyond the Typewriter*, 274.

16. Strom, *Beyond the Typewriter*, 276.

17. Bureau of Vocational Information Survey of Secretaries and Stenographers 915 (444), California, Schlesinger Library, Radcliffe College, quoted in Strom, *Beyond the Typewriter,* 323.

18. Fine, *Souls of the Skyscraper*, 53–54; Fessenden Chase, *Women Stenographers* (Portland, Maine: Southworth, 1910), quoted in Fine, *Souls of the Skyscraper*, 59.

19. Egmont quoted in Fine, *Souls of the Skyscraper*, 58.

20. Ibid., 59.

21. Julie Berebitsky, *Sex and the Office: A History of Gender, Power, and Desire* (New Haven, Conn.: Yale University Press, 2012), 43–44. My account of the trial draws heavily on Berebitsky's work.

22. Quoted in ibid., 103.

23. Ibid., 108.

24. Ibid., 87.

25. Ibid., 88.

26. Zunz, *Making America Corporate*, 119–20.

27. Faith Baldwin, *The Office Wife* (Philadelphia: Triangle Books, 1929), 91.

28. Lynn Peril, *Swimming in the Steno Pool: A Retro Guide to Making It in the Office* (New York: W. W. Norton, 2011), 42.

29. " 'Katie' Gibbs Grads Are Secretarial Elite," *BusinessWeek*, September 2, 1961, 44.

30. Ibid., 46.

31. Rosabeth Moss Kanter, *Men and Women of the Corporation* (New York: Basic Books, 1977), 27.

32. Ibid.

33. Peril, *Swimming in the Steno Pool*, 42.

34. Judith Krantz, *Scruples* (New York: Crown, 1978), 122.

35. Ibid., 122–23.

36. Ibid., 126.

37. Quoted in Peril, *Swimming in the Steno Pool*, 42.

4: UP THE SKYSCRAPER

1. Le Corbusier, *When the Cathedrals Were White*, trans. Francis Hyslop (New York: Reynal & Hitchcock, 1947), 68.

2. Juriaan van Meel, *The European Office: Office Design and National Context* (Rotterdam: OIO, 2000), 31.

3. Hugh Morrison, *Louis Sullivan: Prophet of Modern Architecture* (New York: W. W. Norton, 2001), 111.

4. Max Weber, *The Protestant Ethic and the Spirit of Capitalism, and Other Writings*, trans. Peter Baehr and Gordon Wells (New York: Penguin, 2002), 121. Pedants, watch out! The phrase has been influentially mistranslated as "iron cage" (by Talcott Parsons), but the original is *stahlhartes Gehäuse*.

5. Quoted in Robert Twombly and Narciso G. Menocal, *Louis Sullivan: The Poetry of Architecture* (New York: W. W. Norton, 2000), 34.

6. Daniel Bluestone, *Constructing Chicago* (New Haven, Conn.: Yale University Press, 1991), 105.

7. Ogden to George S. Boutwell, January 27, 1982, Public Building Service Records, RG 121, entry 26, box 8, National Archives, Washington, D.C., quoted in ibid., 112.

8. Joanna Merwood-Salisbury, *Chicago 1890: The Skyscraper and the Modern City* (Chicago: University of Chicago Press, 2009), 29–30. My account of the anarchist influence on skyscraper architecture is indebted to Merwood-Salisbury's work.

9. Lucy Parsons, "Our Civilization: Is It Worth Saving?," *Alarm: A Socialist Weekly*, August 8, 1885, 3, quoted in ibid., 32.

10. Henry B. Fuller, *The Cliff-Dwellers*, ed. Joseph A. Dimuro (Toronto: Broadview, 2010), 75.

11. Editorial, *Building Budget*, August 1886, 90, quoted in Merwood-Salisbury, *Chicago 1890*, 37.

12. *Chicago Tribune*, February 16, 1890, quoted in Donald Hoffman, *The Archi-*

tecture of John Wellborn Root (Baltimore: Johns Hopkins University Press, 1973), 112.

13. Bluestone, *Constructing Chicago*, 140.

14. Henry James, *The American Scene, Together with Three Essays from "Portraits of Places"* (New York: C. Scribner's Sons, 1946), 78.

15. John J. Flinn, *The Standard Guide to Chicago* (Chicago: Standard Guide Company, 1893), 47, quoted in Bluestone, *Constructing Chicago*, 119.

16. Faith Baldwin, *Skyscraper* (1931; New York: Feminist Press, 2003), 13–14.

17. Ibid., 15.

18. Edith Johnson, *To Women of the Business World* (Philadelphia: J. B. Lippincott, 1923), 40–41, quoted in Strom, *Beyond the Typewriter*, 318.

19. Bluestone, *Constructing Chicago*, 141.

20. "The New Pullman Office and Apartment Building," *Western Manufacturer*, March 31, 1884, 41, quoted in Bluestone, *Constructing Chicago*, 141.

21. "The Pullman Palace-Car Company," *National Car-Builder*, February 1873, 38, quoted in Bluestone, *Constructing Chicago*, 141.

22. Hardy Green, *The Company Town: The Industrial Edens and Satanic Mills That Shaped the American Economy* (New York: Basic Books, 2010), 37–41.

23. Quoted in Bluestone, *Constructing Chicago*, 115.

24. William Dean Howells, *Impressions and Experiences* (New York: Harper & Brothers, 1896), 3:265.

25. Ibid.

26. For a discussion of the "hive" metaphor in architecture, see Katherine Solomonson, *The Chicago Tribune Tower Competition: Skyscraper Design and Cultural Change in the 1920s* (Chicago: University of Chicago Press, 2003), 208–11.

27. The standard line, though Sullivan's actual phrasing was "form ever follows function."

28. Jürgen Kocka, *White Collar Workers in America, 1890–1940*, trans. Maura Kealey (London: Sage, 1980), 156.

29. Ibid., 174.

30. Ibid., 164.

31. Lynn Dumenil, *The Modern Temper: American Culture and Society in the 1920s* (New York: Hill and Wang, 1995), 87.

32. Margaret Mather, "White Collar Workers and Students Swing into Action," *New Masses*, June 5, 1934, 17.

33. "What Can the Office Worker Learn from the Factory Worker?," *American Federationist*, August 1929, 917–18.

34. Quoted in Mills, *White Collar*, 301.

35. Emil Lederer, *Problem of the Salaried Employee: Its Theoretical and Statistical Basis*, trans. Works Progress Administration (New York: Department of Social Welfare, 1937), 121–22.

36. Siegfried Kracauer, *The Salaried Masses*, trans. Quintin Hoare (New York: Verso, 1998), 32.

37. Ibid., 88.

38. Ibid., 39.

39. Ibid., 48.

40. Ibid., 46.

41. Ibid., 82.

42. Val Burris, "The Discovery of the New Middle Class," *Theory and Society* 15, no. 3, May 1986, 331.

43. Charles Yale Harrison, "White Collar Slaves," *New Masses*, May 1930.

44. Stanley Burnshaw, "White Collar Slaves," *New Masses*, March 1928, 8.

45. Michael Gold, "Hemingway—White Collar Poet," *New Masses*, March 1928, 21.

46. Lewis Corey, *The Crisis of the Middle Class* (New York: Covici Friede Publishers, 1935), 259.

47. Malcolm Cowley, letter to Edmund Wilson, February 2, 1940, in *The Long Voyage: Selected Letters of Malcolm Cowley, 1915–1987*, edited by Hans Bak (Cambridge: Harvard University Press, 2013), 163.

48. See Michael Denning, *The Cultural Front: The Laboring of American Culture in the Twentieth Century* (New York: Verso, 1996).

49. Whiting Williams, "What's on the Office Worker's Mind?," *Proceedings of the Annual Conference of the National Office Management Association* (1935): 98–99.

50. Harold C. Pennicke, "Important Aspects of the Personnel Problem: Selection and Training," *Proceedings of the Annual Conference of the National Office Management Association* (1936): 40.

51. See, for example, the comment by Coleman L. Maze in response to W. M. Beers, "Centralization of Office Operations—Why and to What Extent?," *Proceedings of the Annual Conference of the National Office Management Association* (1935): 66.

52. Williams, "What's on the Office Worker's Mind?," 99.

53. Elton Mayo, *The Human Problems of an Industrial Civilization* (New York: Macmillan, 1933), 175–76.

54. Le Corbusier, *Towards a New Architecture*, trans. Frederick Etchells (1927; New York: Dover, 1986), 270.

55. Ibid., 288.

56. Ibid., 289.

57. Le Corbusier, *When the Cathedrals Were White*, 51–53.

58. Ibid., 52.

59. Ibid., 54–55.

60. Ibid., 53.

61. Reyner Banham, *The Architecture of the Well-Tempered Environment* (Chicago: University of Chicago Press, 1969), 157–58.

62. Ibid., 172–74.

63. Carol Willis, *Form Follows Finance* (New York: Princeton Architectural Press, 1995), 136.

64. Ibid., 137.

65. Mumford, "The Lesson of the Master," *The New Yorker,* September 13 (1958): 141.

66. Lewis Mumford, "A Disoriented Symbol," in *From the Ground Up: Observations on Contemporary Architecture, Housing, Highway Building, and Civic Design* (New York: Harcourt, Brace, 1956), 49–50.

67. Quoted in Carol Herselle Krinsky, *Gordon Bunshaft of Skidmore, Owings and Merrill* (Cambridge, Mass.: MIT Press, 1988), 18.

68. Mumford, "House of Glass," in *From the Ground Up*, 161.

69. Manfredo Tafuri and Francesco Dal Co, *Architettura contemporanea* (Milan: Mondadori, 1976), 381.

70. Quoted in Franz Schulze, *Philip Johnson: Life and Work* (Chicago: University of Chicago Press, 1994), 139.

71. See Phyllis Lambert, *Building Seagram* (New Haven, Conn.: Yale University Press, 2013), 170–71.

72. Jane Jacobs, *The Death and Life of Great American Cities* (New York: Random House, 1961), 168.

73. Arthur Drexler, "Transformations in Modern Architecture," lecture delivered at the Museum of Modern Art, April 10, 1979, on the occasion of exhibition #1250, Transformations in Modern Architecture, on view February 21–April 24, 1979. Sound Recordings of Museum-Related Events, 79:29, Museum of Modern Art Archives, quoted in Felicity D. Scott, "An Army of Shadows or a Meadow: The Seagram Building and the 'Art of Modern Architecture,' " *Journal of the Society of Architectural Historians* 70, no. 3 (September 2011), 331.

5: ORGANIZATION MEN AND WOMEN

1. Joseph Schumpeter, *Capitalism, Socialism and Democracy* (New York: HarperCollins, 2008 [1947]), 128.

2. Louise A. Mozingo, *Pastoral Capitalism: A History of Suburban Corporate Landscapes* (Cambridge, Mass.: MIT Press, 2011), 23.

3. Philip Herrera, "That Manhattan Exodus," *Fortune*, June 1967, 144, quoted in ibid., 24.

4. "Should Management Move to the Country?," *Fortune*, December 1952, 143, quoted in Mozingo, *Pastoral Capitalism*, 24.

5. "Should Management Move to the Country?," 168, quoted in Mozingo, *Pastoral Capitalism*, 26.

6. Mozingo, *Pastoral Capitalism*, 62.

7. Jon Gertner, *The Idea Factory: Bell Labs and the American Age of Innovation* (New York: Penguin, 2012), 77.

8. Mozingo, *Pastoral Capitalism*, 63.

9. "At Bell Labs, Industrial Research Looks like Bright College Years," *BusinessWeek*, February 6, 1954, 74–75, quoted in Mozingo, *Pastoral Capitalism*, 62.

10. Francis Bello, "The World's Greatest Industrial Laboratory," *Fortune*, November 1958, 148, quoted in Mozingo, *Pastoral Capitalism*, 63.

11. Phillip G. Hofstra, "Florence Knoll, Design, and the Modern American Office Workplace" (PhD diss., University of Kansas, 2008), 65.

12. See Bobbye Tigerman, " 'I Am Not a Decorator': Florence Knoll, the Knoll Planning Unit, and the Making of the Modern Office," *Journal of Design History* 20, no. 1 (2007): 65.

13. "A Dramatic New Office Building," *Fortune*, September 1957, 230.

14. Alexandra Lange, "Tower Typewriter and Trademark: Architects, Designers, and the Corporate Utopia" (PhD diss., New York University, 2005), 46.

15. "Dramatic New Office Building," 169.

16. Joe Alex Morris, "It's Nice to Work in the Country," *Saturday Evening Post*, July 5, 1958, 70, quoted in Lange, "Tower Typewriter and Trademark," 44.

17. Quoted in Lange, "Tower Typewriter and Trademark," 45.

18. "Insurance Sets a Pattern," *Architectural Forum*, September 1957, 127, quoted in Lange, "Tower Typewriter and Trademark," 21.

19. Richard Yates, *Revolutionary Road* (1961; New York: Vintage, 2000), 59.

20. Richard Edwards, *Contested Terrain: The Transformation of the Workplace in the Twentieth Century* (New York: Basic Books, 1979), 74.

21. Ibid., 77.

22. See Robert Brenner, *The Economics of Global Turbulence: The Advanced Capitalist Economies from Long Boom to Long Downturn, 1945–2005* (New York: Verso, 2008), 58–59.

23. Schumpeter, *Capitalism, Socialism, and Democracy,* 138.

24. See Everett M. Kassalow, "White Collar Trade Unions in the United States," in *White Collar Trade Unions: Contemporary Developments in Industrialized Societies,* ed. Adolf Sturmthal (Chicago: University of Illinois Press, 1966), 308.

25. Ibid., 85.

26. Reinhold Martin, *The Organizational Complex: Architecture, Media, and Corporate Space* (Cambridge, Mass.: MIT Press, 2003), 166.

27. Quoted in ibid., 159.

28. Merrill Schleier, *Skyscraper Cinema: Architecture and Gender in American Film* (Minneapolis: University of Minnesota Press, 2009), 256.

29. Ibid., 233.

30. Quoted in ibid., 240.

31. David Riesman, *The Lonely Crowd: A Study of the Changing American Character,* with Nathan Glazer and Reuel Denney (1961; New Haven, Conn.: Yale University Press, 2001), 136.

32. Joseph Heller, *Something Happened* (New York: Alfred A. Knopf, 1974), 14.

33. Harrington, *Life in the Crystal Palace,* 148.

34. William H. Whyte Jr., *The Organization Man* (New York: Simon & Schuster, 1956), 82.

35. Ibid., 71.

36. Ibid., 72–73.

37. Ibid., 74.

38. Ibid., 64.

39. William H. Whyte Jr., *Is Anybody Listening? How and Why U.S. Business Fumbles When It Talks with Human Beings* (New York: Simon & Schuster, 1952), 57.

40. Ibid., 65, 72.

41. Ibid., 4.

42. Quoted in Robert B. Reich, *The Work of Nations: Preparing Ourselves for 21st-Century Capitalism* (New York: Alfred A. Knopf, 1991), 43.

43. Quoted in Whyte, *Is Anybody Listening?,* 15.

44. See Whyte, *Organization Man,* 171–201.

45. Ibid., 173.

46. Sloan Wilson, *The Man in the Gray Flannel Suit* (New York: Simon & Schuster, 1955), 15–17.

47. Whyte, *Organization Man,* 251.

48. Ibid., 132.

49. Wilson, *Man in the Gray Flannel Suit,* 304.

50. Alan Harrington, *Life in the Crystal Palace* (New York: Alfred A. Knopf, 1959), 32–33.

51. Ibid., 112.

52. Riesman, *Lonely Crowd*, 163.

53. Schleier, *Skyscraper Cinema*, 226.

54. Whyte, *Is Anybody Listening?*, 180.

55. Ibid., 146.

56. Ibid.

57. Kanter, *Men and Women of the Corporation*, 105.

58. Quoted in Whyte, *Is Anybody Listening?*, 151.

59. Quoted in Ibid., 162.

60. Helen Gurley Brown, *Sex and the Office* (New York: B. Geis & Associates, 1964), 285.

61. Ibid., 183.

62. Jennifer Scanlon, *Bad Girls Go Everywhere: The Life of Helen Gurley Brown* (New York: Oxford University Press, 2009), 1.

63. Ibid., 15.

64. Brown, *Sex and the Office*, 286.

65. Scanlon, *Bad Girls Go Everywhere*, 24.

66. Ibid.

67. Ibid., 28.

68. Brown, *Sex and the Office*, 3.

69. Ibid., 9.

70. Ibid., 12.

71. Ibid., 59.

6: OPEN PLANS

1. Robert Propst, *The Office: A Facility Based on Change* (Elmhurst, Ill.: Business Press, 1968), 25.

2. Stanley Abercrombie, *George Nelson: The Design of Modern Design* (Cambridge, Mass.: MIT Press, 1995), 210.

3. *Salesmarts* magazine, Herman Miller Archives.

4. Tom Pratt, "A View of Robert Propst," March 8, 1985, Herman Miller Archives.

5. John R. Berry and Herman Miller: *The Purpose of Design* (New York: Rizzoli, 2009), 117.

6. Edward T. Hall, *The Silent Language* (Garden City, N.Y.: Doubleday, 1959), 169.

7. Edward T. Hall, *The Hidden Dimension* (1966; New York: Doubleday, 1982), 4.

8. Ibid., 54.

9. Thomas Frank, *The Conquest of Cool: Business Culture, Counterculture, and the Rise of Hip Consumerism* (Chicago: University of Chicago Press, 1997), 21–22.

10. Douglas McGregor, *The Human Side of Enterprise* (New York: McGraw-Hill, 1960), 12.

11. Ibid.

12. According to Paul Leinberger and Bruce Tucker, *The New Individualists: The Generation After "The Organization Man"* (New York: HarperCollins, 1991), 189.

13. Frank, *Conquest of Cool*, 22.

14. See Mauro F. Guillén, *Models of Management: Work, Authority, and Orga-*

nization in Comparative Perspective (Chicago: University of Chicago Press, 1994), 58–65.

15. Ibid., 67.

16. Anonymous, "Why White Collar Workers Can't Be Organized," *Harper's*, August 1957, 48.

17. Ibid.

18. Harry R. Dick, "The Office Worker: Attitudes Toward Self, Labor, and Management," *Sociological Quarterly* 3, no. 1 (1962): 50.

19. Peter Drucker, *The Age of Discontinuity: Guidelines to Our Changing Society* (New York: Harper & Row, 1969), 269.

20. Ibid., 270.

21. See Taylor, *Principles of Scientific Management*, 61.

22. Drucker, *Age of Discontinuity*, 277.

23. Peter Drucker, *The New Society: Anatomy of Industrial Order* (New York: Harper & Row), 357.

24. Fritz Machlup, *The Production and Distribution of Knowledge in the United States* (Princeton, N.J.: Princeton University Press, 1962), 396–97.

25. Ibid., 41.

26. Francis Duffy, "The Case for Bürolandschaft," in *The Changing Workplace*, ed. Patrick Hannay (London: Phaidon Press, 1992), 10.

27. "Landscaping: An Environmental System," in *Office Landscaping* (Elmhurst, Ill.: Business Press, 1969), 13.

28. Francis Duffy, "Commerce: The Office," unpublished, 1.

29. Francis Duffy, "The Princeton Dissertation," in Hannay, *Changing Workplace*, 79.

30. Propst mentions it in his article "The Action Office," *Journal of the Human Factors Society* 8, no. 4 (1966): 303: "This work was given considerable additional impetus by information coming from Germany concerning a system of office planning called *Bürolandschaft*, which literally means 'office landscape' and which emphasis [*sic*] open offices with free furniture grouping. The resulting irregular arrangements eliminate the possibility of using traditional rectangular office areas, and this outcome is claimed to increase flexibility in the consideration and use of space, result in a more intensive use of space, reduce office noise by eliminating sound-reflective partitions, and provide window views for more workers."

31. This picture is a composite of Henry Panzarelli, "A Testimonial to Life in a Landscape," in *Office Landscaping*, 55–59; and Duffy, "Case for Bürolandschaft," 11–23.

32. Propst, quoted in Howard Sutton, Background Information, Action Office, January 25, 1965, Herman Miller Archives.

33. Ibid.

34. Abercrombie, *George Nelson*, 9.

35. George Nelson, "Peak Experiences and the Creative Act," *Mobilia* 265/266, 12.

36. Mina Hamilton, "Herman Miller in Action," *Industrial Design*, January 1965, quoted in Abercrombie, *George Nelson*, 213; William K. Zinsser, "But Where Will I Keep My Movie Magazines," *Saturday Evening Post*, January 16, 1965, quoted in Abercrombie, *George Nelson*, 213.

37. Propst, *The Office: A Facility Based on Change*, 49.

38. Ibid., 25.

39. Ibid., 29.

40. Sylvia Porter, "Revolution Hits the Office," *New York Post,* June 3, 1969.

41. Julie Schlosser, "Cubicles: The Great Mistake," *Fortune*, March 2006, http://money.cnn.com/2006/03/09/magazines/fortune/cubicle_howiwork_fortune/.

42. Quoted in Abercrombie, *George Nelson*, 219.

43. Peter Hall, "Doug Ball Digs Out of the Cube," *Metropolis*, July 2006, http://www.metropolismag.com/story/20060619/doug-ball-digs-out-of-the-cube.

44. John Pile, *Open Office Planning* (New York: Whitney Library of Design, 1978), 14.

45. Propst, "Notes on Proposal for Repositioning Action Office," January 23, 1978, Herman Miller Archives.

46. Van Meel, *European Office*, 38.

47. Quoted in ibid., 37.

48. Quoted in ibid., 39.

49. Ibid.

50. Yvonne Abraham, "The Man Behind the Cubicle," *Metropolis*, November 1998.

51. Francis Duffy, interview with author, July 14, 2012.

7: SPACE INVADERS

1. Betty Lehan Harragan, *Games Mother Never Taught You: Corporate Gamesmanship for Women* (New York: Warner Books, 1977), 286–87.

2. See Kanter, *Men and Women of the Corporation*, 34.

3. Don DeLillo, *Americana* (New York: Penguin, 1971), 20.

4. Kanter, *Men and Women of the Corporation*, 57.

5. Ibid., 56.

6. Studs Terkel, *Working: People Talk About What They Do All Day and How They Feel About What They Do* (New York: Pantheon Books, 1972), 56.

7. "Advertising's Creative Explosion," *Newsweek*, August 18, 1969, quoted in Barbara Ehrenreich, *Fear of Falling: The Inner Life of the Middle Classes* (New York: Pantheon Books, 1989), 176.

8. Quoted in John P. Fernandez, *Black Managers in White Corporations* (New York: John Wiley & Sons, 1975), 39.

9. Quoted in ibid., 95.

10. John P. Fernandez, *Racism and Sexism in Corporate Life* (New York: D. C. Heath, 1981), 53.

11. Floyd Dickens Jr. and Jacqueline B. Dickens, *The Black Manager: Making It in the Corporate World* (New York: AMACOM, 1982), 56.

12. Ibid., 57.

13. See Ivan Berg, *Education and Jobs* (New York: Praeger, 1970), 93.

14. George de Mare, *Corporate Lives: A Journey into the Corporate World*, with Joanne Summerfield (New York: Van Nostrand Reinhold, 1976), 57.

15. Quoted in Eric Darton, *Divided We Stand: A Biography of New York's World Trade Center* (New York: Basic Books, 2011), 141.

16. Charles Jencks, *The Language of Post-modern Architecture* (New York: Rizzoli, 1978), 9.

17. Ibid., 15.

18. Philip Johnson, "Whither Away: Non-Miesian Directions," in *Philip Johnson: Writings* (New York: Oxford University Press, 1979), 227, 230.

19. Quoted in Emmanuel Petit, introduction to *Philip Johnson: The Constancy of Change* (New Haven, Conn.: Yale University Press, 2009), 2.

20. Marisa Bartolucci, "550 Madison Avenue," *Metropolis*, October 1993, 28.

21. Kazys Varnelis, "Philip Johnson's Empire: Network Power and the AT&T Building," in *Philip Johnson: The Constancy of Change*, 128.

22. Mark Lamster, "Highboy Hullabaloo," *Design Observer*, September 11, 2010, http://observatory.designobserver.com/entry.html?entry=20608.

23. Maurice Carroll, "AT&T to Build New Headquarters Tower at Madison and 55th Street," *New York Times*, March 31, 1978, quoted in ibid., 129.

24. "His Office Designs Fulfill Human Needs," *Milwaukee Sentinel*, July 21, 1978, 12.

25. Michael Sorkin, *Exquisite Corpse: Writing on Buildings* (New York: Verso, 1991), 12.

26. Quoted in John Pastier, " 'First Monument of a Loosely Defined Style': Michael Graves' Portland Building," in *American Architecture of the 1980s* (Washington, D.C.: American Institute of Architects Press, 1990), xxi.

27. Bartolucci, "550 Madison Avenue," 33. See also Lamster, "Highboy Hullabaloo."

28. Jeffrey H. Keefe and Rosemary Batt, "United States," in *Telecommunications: Restructuring Work and Employment Relationships Worldwide* (Ithaca, N.Y.: International Labor Relations Press, 1997), 54.

29. Quoted in Jill Andresky Fraser, *White-Collar Sweatshop: The Deterioration of Work and Its Rewards in Corporate America* (New York: W. W. Norton, 2001), 129.

30. Tom Peters, "Tom Peters' True Confessions," *Fast Company*, December 2001, http://www.fastcompany.com/44077/tom-peterss-true-confessions.

31. William S. Ouchi, *Theory Z: How American Business Can Meet the Japanese Challenge* (Reading, Mass.: Addison-Wesley, 1981).

32. Ibid., 17.

33. Thomas J. Peters and Robert H. Waterman Jr., *In Search of Excellence: Lessons from America's Best-Run Companies* (New York: Harper & Row, 1982).

34. Ibid., 15.

35. Quoted in Fraser, *White-Collar Sweatshop*, 117.

36. Amanda Bennett, *The Death of the Organization Man* (New York: Simon & Schuster, 1991), 98.

37. Andrew S. Grove, *Only the Paranoid Survive: How to Exploit the Crisis Points That Challenge Every Company and Career* (New York: Currency/Doubleday, 1996), quoted in Fraser, *White-Collar Sweatshop*, 155.

38. Peters and Waterman, *In Search of Excellence*, 80.

39. Quoted in Bennett, *Death of the Organization Man*, 141.

40. "Commentary: Help! I'm a Prisoner in a Shrinking Cubicle!," *BusinessWeek*, August 3, 1997.

41. "Nearly Half of Americans Indicate Their Bathroom Is Larger Than Their Office Cubicle," Fellowes press release, July 17, 2007.

42. "Texas Reduces Prison Overcrowding with Breakaway Construction Program," PR Newswire, June 29, 1994.

43. Catherine Strong, "Prison Labor Has Monopoly Contracts but Delivers Late," *Associated Press*, August 11, 1998.

44. "Air Makes Workers Ill," *Reuters*, June 6, 1991.

45. Scott Haggert, "Making the Office Fit to Work," *Financial Post* (Canada), November 25, 1991.

46. John Markoff, "Where the Cubicle Is Dead," *New York Times*, April 25, 1993.

47. Sheila McGovern, "Working in Comfort," *Gazette* (Montreal), January 17, 1994.

48. Kirk Johnson, "In New Jersey, I.B.M. Cuts Space, Frills, and Private Desks," *New York Times*, March 14, 1994.

49. Scott Adams, *The Dilbert Principle: A Cubicle-Eye View of Bosses, Meetings, Management Fads & Other Workplace Afflictions* (New York: HarperBusiness, 1996), 4.

50. Yvonne Abraham, "The Man Behind the Cubicle," *Metropolis,* November 1998.

51. See Stewart Brand, *How Buildings Learn* (New York: Viking Penguin, 1994), 170.

52. *Work in America: Report of a Special Task Force to the Secretary of Health, Education, and Welfare* (Cambridge, Mass.: MIT Press, 1973), 38.

53. Ibid., 40.

54. Quoted in Barbara Garson, *The Electronic Sweatshop: How Computers Are Transforming the Office of the Future into the Factory of the Past* (New York: Simon & Schuster, 1988), 172.

55. Robert Howard, *Brave New Workplace: America's Corporate Utopias—How They Create Inequalities and Social Conflict in Our Working Lives* (New York: Penguin, 1985), 102.

56. Karen Ho, *Liquidated: An Ethnography of Wall Street* (Minneapolis: University of Minnesota Press, 2009), 52.

57. Peril, *Swimming in the Steno Pool*, 194.

58. Ibid., 203.

59. Ibid.

60. Ethel Strainchamps, ed., *Rooms with No View: A Woman's Guide to the Man's World of the Media* (New York: Harper & Row, 1974), 12.

61. Anonymous worker quoted in Jean Tepperman, *Not Servants, Not Machines: Office Workers Speak Out!* (Boston: Beacon Press, 1976), 33.

62. Ibid., 63–64.

63. John Hoerr, *We Can't Eat Prestige: The Women Who Organized Harvard* (Philadelphia: Temple University Press, 1997), 47.

64. Tepperman, *Not Servants, Not Machines*, 64.

65. Quoted in Jefferson Cowie, *Stayin' Alive: The 1970s and the Last Days of the Working Class* (New York: New Press, 2010), 351–52.

66. Answers by 915 respondents to a survey conducted in Boston and Cleveland by Working Women Education Fund in the fall of 1980, quoted in Joel Makower, *Office Hazards: How Your Job Can Make You Sick* (Washington, D.C.: Tilden Press, 1981), 128.

67. Tepperman, *Not Servants, Not Machines*, 21.

68. Ibid.

8: THE OFFICE OF THE FUTURE

1. Thomas Pynchon, *Bleeding Edge* (New York: Penguin Press, 2013), 43.
2. "The Office of the Future," *BusinessWeek*, June 30, 1975, 40.
3. Ibid.
4. Juriaan van Meel, "The Origins of New Ways of Working: Office Concepts in the 1970s," *Facilities* 29, no. 9/10 (2011): 361.
5. Ibid., 359.
6. Ibid.
7. Quoted in Juriaan van Meel and Paul Vos, "Funky Offices," *Journal of Corporate Real Estate* 3, no. 4 (2011): 323.
8. Jack M. Nilles, *Making Telecommuting Happen* (New York: Van Nostrand Reinhold, 1994), xiii.
9. Howard, *Brave New Workplace*, 4.
10. "What Matters Is How Smart You Are," *BusinessWeek*, August 25, 1997, 69.
11. David Manners and Tsugio Makimoto, *Living with the Chip: How the Chip Affects Your Business, Your Family, Your Home, and Your Future* (London: Chapman & Hall, 1995), 41.
12. Robert Reinhold, "Mixing Business and Pleasure for Profit in Silicon Valley," *New York Times*, February 12, 1984.
13. Christopher Winks, "Manuscript Found in a Typewriter," in *Bad Attitude: The "Processed World" Anthology*, ed. Chris Carlsson with Mark Leger (New York: Verso, 1990), 20.
14. John Markoff, "Where the Cubicle Is Dead," *New York Times*, April 25, 1993.
15. William Scott, "Intel Corp. Serves as Role Model for Aerospace Companies in Transition," *Aviation Week and Space Technology*, August 24, 1992, 60.
16. Intel Keynote Transcript: "Los Angeles Times 3rd Annual Investment Strategies Conference," May 22, 1999, http://www.intel.com/pressroom/archive/speeches/cn052499.htm.
17. Intel Keynote Transcript: "Intel International Science and Engineering Fair," May 9, 2001, http://www.intel.com/pressroom/archive/speeches/grove20010509.htm.
18. Douglas Coupland, *Microserfs* (New York: Regan Books, 1995), 16.
19. Ibid., 319.
20. Thomas J. Peters, *Liberation Management: Necessary Disorganization for the Nanosecond Nineties* (New York: Alfred A. Knopf, 1992), 18.
21. Ibid., xxxiii–xxxiv.
22. Andrew Ross, *No-Collar: The Humane Workplace and Its Hidden Costs* (New York: Basic Books, 2003), 98–99.
23. Marisa Bowe and Darcy Cosper, "The Sharper Image: A Conversation with Craig Kanarick," *Interiors*, October 2000, 105.
24. Roger Yee, "Connecting the Dots," *Interiors*, October 2000, 61.
25. Quoted in Raul Barreneche, "Industry Non-standard," *Interiors*, October 2000, 83.
26. Cliff Kuang, "The Secret History of the Aeron Chair," *Slate*, November 5, 2012, http://www.slate.com/articles/life/design/2012/11/aeron_chair_history_herman_miller_s_office_staple_was_originally_designed.html.
27. "Virtual Chiat," *Wired*, July 1994.

28. Randall Rothenberg, "A Eulogy for a Whiner: My Experience with Jay Chiat," *Advertising Age,* April 29, 2002, http://adage.com/article/randall-rothenberg/eulogy-a-whiner/34339/.

29. Quoted in Thomas R. King, "Creating Chaos," *Wall Street Journal,* April 17, 1995.

30. "Virtual Chiat."

31. Ibid.

32. Leon Jaroff and Saneel Ratan, "The Age of the Road Warrior," *Time,* March 1, 1995, 38.

9: THE OFFICE AND ITS ENDS

1. David Foster Wallace, *The Pale King* (2011; New York: Back Bay Books, 2012), 539.

2. Leslie Helm, "Microsoft Testing Limits on Temp Worker Use," *Los Angeles Times,* December 7, 1997, quoted in Fraser, *White-Collar Sweatshop,* 147.

3. "The Fax of Life," *Entertainment Weekly,* May 23, 2003, http://www.ew.com/ew/article/0,,452194,00.html.

4. Carol Madonna, interview with author, April 23, 2012.

5. Nicolai Ouroussoff, "A Workplace Through the Looking Glass," *Los Angeles Times,* January 31, 1999.

6. Chris Coleman, interview with author, April 26, 2012.

7. Anonymous, interview with author, August 15, 2013.

8. Carolyn Cutrone and Max Nisen, "19 Successful People Who Barely Sleep," *Business Insider,* September 18, 2012.

9. Lisa Belkin, "Marissa Mayer's Work-from-Home Ban Is the Exact Opposite of What CEOs Should Be Doing," *Huffington Post,* February 23, 2013, http://www.huffingtonpost.com/lisa-belkin/marissa-mayer-work-from-home-yahoo-rule_b_2750256.html; Kelly Steele, "New Moms at Work," *Scary Mommy,* http://www.scarymommy.com/new-moms-at-work/.

10. Erin Hatton, *The Temp Economy: From Kelly Girls to Permatemps in Postwar America* (Philadelphia: Temple University Press, 2011).

11. Louis Lhoest, interview with author, July 12, 2012.

12. Paul Vos and T. van der Voordt, "Tomorrow's Offices Through Today's Eyes: Effects of Innovation in the Working Environment," *Journal of Corporate Real Estate* 4 (2001): 53.

13. T. van der Voordt, "Productivity and Employee Satisfaction in Flexible Workplaces," *Journal of Corporate Real Estate* 6, no. 2 (2004): 137.

14. Anne Laure-Fayard and John Weeks, "Who Moved My Cube?," *Harvard Business Review,* July 2011, 104.

15. Erik Veldhoen, interview with author, July 13, 2012.

16. Richard Greenwald, interview with author, August 9, 2013.

17. "Employment Projections, 2010–2020," Bureau of Labor Statistics, February 1, 2012. See also Ursula Huws, "The Making of a Cybertariat? Virtual Work in a Real World," *Socialist Register,* 2001, 12–13.

18. Clive Morton, Andrew Newall, and John Sparkes, *Leading HR: Delivering Competitive Advantage* (London: CIPD Publishing, 2001), 22–23. The authors refer to Amin Rajan's work in Amin Rajan and P. van Eupen, *Tomorrow's People* (Kent, U.K.: CREATE, 1998).

19. Scott Chacon, interview with author, September 24, 2013.

20. Scott Chacon, Tim Clem, and Liz Clinkenbeard, interview with author, September 24, 2013.

21. Sadaf Khan, interview with author, June 5, 2012.

22. K. Santhosh, interview with author, June 5, 2012.

23. Paul Shankman, "Tim Freundlich: HUB, a New Kind of Workspace," *Lincoln Now*, February 28, 2013.

24. Greg Lindsay, "Coworking Spaces from Grind to GRid70 Help Employees Work Beyond the Cube," *Fast Company*, March 2013, http://www.fastcompany.com/3004915/coworking-nextspace.

25. Ibid.

26. Paul Siebert, interview with author, May 5, 2013.

Index

Page numbers in *italics* refer to illustrations.

Abstract Expressionism, 144

accountants, 79, 112

Action Office, Action Office I, Action Office II, 5, 6, 206–10, *206,* 211–18, *211, 213, 215, 218,* 219, 220, 232, 239, 270, 308, *310*

Adams, Henry, 33

Adams, Scott, 244

Addams, Jane, 81

Adding Machine, The (Rice), 114

Adler, Dankmar, 100, 102

advertising, 272

Advertising Age, 273, 274

Advertising Council, 163

Advocate, The, 112

Aeron chair, 271, 294

Affluent Society, The (Galbraith), 152

African Americans, corporate employment of, 224–25

Age of Discontinuity, The (Drucker), 195

Aherne, Brian, 178

air-conditioning, 66, 132, 133, 144

air-traffic controllers, 239

Alarm, 103

Alger, Horatio, Jr., 34–35

Alice Adams (Tarkington), 91

Allen, Thomas, 296

Amazon.com, 64

Americana (DeLillo), 221

American Federationist, 114

American Federation of Labor (AFL), 114

American Institute of Architects, 230

American Phrenological Journal, 14

American Railway Union, 107

American Whig Review, 14

Amway, 306

Apartment, The, 154, 179–81, *180*

Apple, 243, 261, 264, 273

Architectural Forum, 152

architecture:

   black box, *139,* 142

   Chicago school, 100

   early-twentieth-century, 5, 20, 36, 100, 110, 127–28

   "form follows function" principle in, 110, 321

   Greek Revival, 20

   International Style, 131, 132, 140, 234

architecture (continued):
  modernist, 127–28, 131, 132, 134,
    135–42, 227, 228, 229, 230–31,
    233
  pop culture in, 231
  postmodernist, 227–36, 286
  in post–World War II Germany,
    200
  as social engineering, 230
  space planning in, 201
  technological advances in, 36, 100,
    128, 132–33
  see also office buildings; office
    design; skyscrapers
Art of Plain Talk, The (Flesch),
  162–63
AT&T, 145, 236
AT&T Building, 232–36, 235
Atlanta Constitution, 83
Auditorium (Chicago), 102

Baby Face, 85–88, 86
Baker, Diane, 177
Baldwin, Faith, 89, 106, 123
Ball, Douglas, 217
Ballmer, Steve, 278
Balzac, Honoré de, 4
Banham, Reyner, 204
banking, 12, 228, 247–48
Barcelona chair, 148
Barcelona Pavilion, 131
"Bartleby, the Scrivener" (Melville),
  9–11, 13, 31
Bass, Saul, 138
Baudville, 282–83
Becker, Gary, 226
beehives, 109
behavioral sciences, 125, 126, 127,
  187
Belkin, Lisa, 291
Bell, Daniel, 197
Bell Labs, 145–47, 159, 198

BellSouth, 240
Belluschi, Pietro, 234
Beman, Solon S., 107
Bengaluru, India, 304–5
Berlin, Germany:
  office buildings in, 97
  Weimar-era office workers in, 117
Berry, John, 186
Bertelsmann, 202
Best of Everything, The, 140,
  176–79, 177
Bethlehem Iron Company, 45, 48
Bleeding Edge (Pynchon), 256
Blessed Be Drudgery (Gannett), 34
blue-collar workers:
  wages of, 21, 84, 112, 246
  see also factory workers; labor
    movement
Blue Hypermedia, 269
Bluestone, Daniel, 104–5
bookkeepers, 16, 17, 18, 22, 33–34,
  79, 112
Boston, Mass.:
  nineteenth-century office workers
    in, 17
  office buildings in, 229
Boyd, Stephen, 178
Brandeis, Louis, 50–51
Braque, Georges, 61
Brass Check, The (Sinclair), 62
Brave New World (Huxley), 41
Braverman, Harry, 22, 62
Brin, Sergey, 287
"Broadway" (Whitman), 16
Broadway Boogie-Woogie
  (Mondrian), 129
Brooks Brothers, 15
Broughton, Len G., 83
Brown, Denise Scott, 231
Brown, Helen Gurley, 173–76, 174,
  181–82
Building Budget, 104
Bullshit Job, 279

Bureau of Labor Statistics, 192, 299, 310

Burnham, Daniel, 100, 102, 104

Burnham, James, 156

Bürolandschaft, 5, 6, 201–5, *203,* 208, 217, 218, 219, 253, 262, 270

business:

  consolidation in, 154–55

  education in, 21–22, 79, 93–95, 113, 161

  individualist trend in, 190–92, 198, 208, 210, 211, 232, 240, 249

  innovation in, 212, 263

  1960s changes in, 190, 196, 212, 224

  1980s changes in, 233, 236, 237–38, 239, 263

  nineteenth-century changes in, 16–17, 20, 33–34, 38

  office buildings as paeans to, 68, 96, 97, 101, 103, 104–5, 109, 131, 135, 141, 142, 144, 232, 233

  political action by, 163

  post-Depression changes in, 125–26

  railroads' effect on, 38–39

  Silicon Valley's effect on, 260, 265–66, 267

  tax write-offs for, 216

  white-collar labor movement's impact on, 124–25

  see also corporations; management science

business attire, nineteenth-century, 14–15

Business Insider, 290

Business Man's Magazine, 68

business-speak, 162–63, 248, 305–6

BusinessWeek, 56, 62, 93, 146, 159, 239, 243, *251, 257*

California, Gilded Age corruption in, 43–44

call centers, 301

camera, motion-capture, 52

Capitalism, Socialism, and Democracy (Schumpeter), 143, 155–56

Caracas, Venezuela, 304

Carnegie, Dale, 192

Carrier, Willis, 132

Carson, Sue, 178

Carver, Howard, 226

CBS Building, 148

ceilings, suspended, 132–33

Center for Buildings and Places, 294

Centraal Beheer, 219

Chacon, Scott, 301

Chadwick, Don, 271

Chamber of Commerce, 163

Chandler, Alfred, 38, 317

Chase, Fessenden, 81

Cheaper by the Dozen, 56

Chernin, Rose, 78

Chevron, 240

Chiat, Jay, 272–77, 285

Chiat/Day, 273–77

Chicago, Burlington & Quincy Railroad, 103

Chicago, Ill.:

  fire in, 102

  labor movement in, 102–4, 107–8

  office buildings in, 66, 96–97, 100, 101–8, *108*

Chicago Tribune, 109, 111

China, skyscrapers in, 97, 303, 304

Churchill, Winston, 163

Cicero, 12, 13

Cisco Systems, 275

Cité de Refuge, 132

Citibank, 246–47

cities:

  business education in, 22

  corporate flight from, 144, 145

  downtown areas in, 20, 109, 144, 228, 229

cities *(continued)*:
  offices' growth in, 13–14, 16–17,
    20, 97–98, 303
  postmodernist view of, 229–30
  white-collar "islands" in, 130
  see also urban renewal
Civil Rights Act (1964), 224
Civil War, U.S., 32
Clem, Tim, 302
clerks, 9–32, 316
  changing social position of, 13–14,
    17, 21, 22, 23, 25, 26–29, 30–31,
    32, 62
  education of, 21–22, 28, 79
  famous, 12
  Gilded Age transformation of, 33,
    39, 43
  masculinity concerns of, 14, 16,
    22–23, 24, 28, 29
  see also office workers
Cliff-Dwellers (Fuller), 104
Clinkenbeard, Liz, 302
Clinton, Bill, 240, 267
coffee, 250, 252
Cold War, 96, 145
Coleman, Christopher, 288, 289
Coleman, Dabney, 253
Colgate-Palmolive Building, 138
*Coming of Post-Industrial Society,
  The* (Bell), 197
Communist Manifesto, The (Marx),
  115
Communist Party, German, 116
Communist Party of America, 123
computer industry, 228, 301–3
  see also office(s), dot-com era;
    Silicon Valley
computers:
  introduction of, 157–58, 210
  office design ramifications of,
    256–57, 272
  workplace effects of, 245–47, 249,
    256–57, 258
  see also telecommuting

Connecticut General, 147–52, *147,
  152,* 198
Conquest of Cool, The (Frank), 190
Corey, Lewis, 122
corporate campuses, 145, 147–52,
  198, 229, 235, 259, 262, 286–90
corporate ladder, *see* upward mobility
corporations:
  African Americans in, 224–25
  all-enveloping environments in, 64,
    67, 68, 152, 159, 161, 168, 169,
    170–72, 261, 268, 270–72, 284,
    286, 287, 288
  co-working in, 306–7
  growth of, 36
  late-twentieth-century, 238, 239,
    241, 247–48, 292–93
  layoffs by, 236–37, 238–42,
    292–93
  mergers of, 40, 43, 239, 293
  mid-twentieth-century hegemony
    of, 154–56, 158–59
  mid-twentieth-century
    management of, 149, 150, 156,
    159, 160, 161, 165, 168, 169, 170
  mid-twentieth-century public
    relations efforts of, 163
  organization of, 38–39, 42, 43,
    62–63
  skyscraper design for, 111, 138
  social criticism of, 152–54, 158–62,
    169–70, 198, 227
  student recruiting by, 161
  suburban relocations of, 144–49,
    147, 229
Cosmopolitan, 174, 175
Co/Struc, 186
Coué, Émile, 113
countinghouses, 4, 17–20, 22–27, 33,
  36, 39, 42
Coupland, Douglas, 242, 265
Cowley, Malcolm, 123
co-working, 305–7, 310
Crawford, Joan, 178

Crisis of the Middle Class, The (Corey), 122
Crittenden, S. W., 22
Crowd, The, 99, *99,* 113–14, 179
cubicle(s), *ii*
  late-twentieth-century proliferation of, 242–44, 249, 273
  in 1970s offices, 224
  in 1980s offices, 235
  origins of, 6, 217–18, 220
  in Silicon Valley, 262, 264, 265
  Tati's vision of, 184
  twenty-first-century resurgence of, 279, 305, 310
cubicle rage, 1–2, 246
cybernetics, 187

Davies Building, 138
Death and Life of Great American Cities, The (Jacobs), 134, 229, 286
Debs, Eugene V., 108
DeLillo, Don, 221
Deming, W. Edwards, 238
Demise of the Office, The (Veldhoen), 293
Denning, Michael, 123
De officiis (Cicero), 12–13
De Pree, Hugh, 186
desks, 42, 137, 207, 208, 212, 269
 see also workstations
Dictaphones, 40
digital revolution, 297
 see also computers; telecommuting
Dilbert, 3, 244, 265
Disneyland, 286
Doorley, Scott, 307
Dos Passos, John, 54, 120
Down East Diary (Foster), 9
Dreiser, Theodore, 91, 120
Drexler, Arthur, 142
Drucker, Peter, 54, 195–200, 208, 226, 299, 300

drugs, in Silicon Valley, 262
Duffy, Francis, 202, 204, 220, 303, 305
Dunham, Lena, 174
DuPont, 204, 205, 240
Durant, William C., 43
Durkheim, Émile, 127
Dynamischkantoor, 295

Eames, Charles and Ray, 143, 158
Edison, Thomas, 132
education:
  of clerks, 21–22, 28, 79
  in Cold War era, 161
  of female office workers, 78–79, 93–95
  management, 113
  of Silicon Valley workers, 262
  vocational, 79
  white-collar levels of, 198, 225–26, 248
Education of Henry Adams, The (Adams), 33
Edwards, Richard, 155
efficiency:
  early-twentieth-century obsession with, 55–56, 57
  Leffingwell's studies of, 57–59
  Taylor's theories of, 45–46, 47, 48, 51, 52
Egmont, Janette, 82
Eisenman, Peter, 231
Elementary Treatise on Book-Keeping (Crittenden), 22
elevators, 36, 100, 105
Ellison, Ralph, 120
Emerson, Harrington, 51
Emerson, Ralph Waldo, 23
Empire State Building, 97
Equal Employment Opportunity Commission (EEOC), 224
Equitable Building, 234
Ergon chair, 271

ergonomics, 189, 206, 214
Ernst & Young, 275
Essential Drucker, The (Drucker), 305
Europe:
  freelancers in, 299
  modernist design in, 148
  office buildings in, 97
  office design in, 200–204, 218–20
  post–World War I political change in, 115
  privacy tradition in, 219
Evolve, 269
Exception, The (Jungersen), 3
executives, *see* managers
Executive Suite, 144

FACE Intel, 264–65
factories:
  automation in, 192, 240
  college students' disinterest in, 162
  communal nature of, 248
  labor strife in, 43
  lighting experiments in, 126
  management of, 47–48, 197
  offices' modeling on, 6, 33, 44, 59, 118, 151
  offices' separation from, 20, 102, 104, 108, 145
  "piece-rate" system in, 49
  work process in, 47–49, 197
  see also manufacturing
factory workers:
  office workers' perceived superiority to, 5, 26, 30, 62, 63, 104, 106, 115, 118
  Taylorism's effect on, 49–50, 52, 54, 55, 63
  Taylor's opinion of, 47, 54
  see also blue-collar workers; labor movement
Fairchild Semiconductor Corporation, 261

farming, decline of, 16, 36, 76–77, 156
fascism, 119–20
Feminine Mystique, The (Friedan), 174
feminism, 91, 92, 175, 250, *251,* 252–53, 255
Ferris, Joshua, 2
file cabinets, 41
financial crisis of 2008, 303
Flanagan, James, 264
Flesch, Rudolph, 162–63
Fonda, Jane, 253–54
football, 162
Form Follows Finance (Willis), 111
Fortune, 145, 147, 171, 190, 261
Foster, Benjamin Browne, 9
Fountainhead, The (Rand), 134
Fourier, Charles, 32
Four Seasons restaurant, 141, 232
France, white-collar movement in, 218
Frank, Thomas, 190, 191
Franklin, Benjamin, 12
freelancers, 6, 292–93, 298, 299–300, 305, 306, 310–11
Freelancers Union, 109, 311
Freud, Sigmund, 125, 126, 127
Freundlich, Tim, 305–6
Friedan, Betty, 174
Fuller, Henry Blake, 104
furniture:
  modernist, 207
  tax write-offs of, 216
  twenty-first-century, 307–10
  see also office design
futurologists, 257

Galloway, Lee, 60
Games Mother Never Taught You (Harragan), 221
Gannett, William, 34

Garson, Barbara, 246

Gates, Bill, 262, 263

Gehry, Frank, 231, 274

Geiger, Theodor, 119

General Electric, 165, 305

General Foods, 144

General Motors, 43, 240

Generation X (Coupland), 242–43

George, Henry, 32

Germany:

  blue-collar immigrants from, 103

  1980s competitiveness of, 237, 238, 241

  post–World War II economic growth in, 200–201

  white-collar class studies in, 115–19, 153

  white-collar movement in, 218

Gibbs, Katharine, 92–93, 95

Gibbs schools, 93–95

Gilbreth, Frank, 56, 57

Gilbreth, Lillian, 56

Gilded Age, 5, 40, 43–45

Ginsberg, Allen, 98

GitHub, 301–3

Gizmodo, 2

Gladwell, Malcolm, 286

Glass House, 131

globalization, 97, 196

Gold, Michael, 121

"gold diggers," 85

Gompers, Samuel, 114–15

Goodell, R. H., 61

Google, 67, 286–90, 291, 306

Graves, Michael, 231, 234

Great Depression, 85, 87, 98, 122, 125–26

Greeley, Horace, 30

Greenwald, Richard, 298–300, 310

Greenwich Village, 286

GRid70, 306–7, *309*

Griffith, Melanie, 237, 255

Gropius, Walter, 131

Grove, Andy, 191, 241, 264, 265

Guggenheim Museum, 67

gyms, nineteenth-century, 24

Hall, Edward T., 187–88

Hamilton, Alexander, 12

Hammett, Dashiell, 123

Harper's, 192

Harragan, Betty Lehan, 221

Harrington, Alan, 155, 156, 160, 168–70, 198

Harris, Theresa, 86, 87

Harvard Business School, 113

Hatton, Erin, 293

Having It All (Brown), 176

Haworth, 216, 217

Hayek, Friedrich, 195, 199

Haymarket Square bombing, 104

Haywood, "Big Bill," 54

health insurance, 299

Heath, William, 66

Heckscher, Charles, 300

Heller, Joseph, 159

Hemingway, Ernest, 121

Herman Miller Company, 184, 185, 186, 189, 200, 206, 215, 216, 218, 271, 307, 308, *310*

Hertzberger, Herman, 219

Hewlett, William, 261

Hidden Dimension, The (Hall), 187

Hidden Persuaders, The (Packard), 152

Hillman, Alex, 305

Hitchcock, Alfred, 138

Hitchcock, Henry-Russell, 131

Ho, Karen, 247

Hochschild, Arlie Russell, 271

Home Insurance Building, 100

Hood, Raymond, 111, 130

Horton, Adelaide, 275

hospitals, modular units in, 186

Howells, William Dean, 109

Howl (Ginsberg), 98

HUB, 305

Huffington Post, 291
Human Condition, The (Arendt),
    152
*Human Problems of an Industrial
    Civilization, The* (Mayo),
    126–27
human relations movement, 126–27,
    164, 165, 191–92, 226, 270
human resources, 57
Human Side of Enterprise, The
    (McGregor), 190–91
Hunt's Merchants' Magazine, 16,
    21, 22
Huxley, Aldous, 41

IBM, 157, 158, 243–44, 246, 257, 263
immigrants:
    in labor unions, 102–3
    nineteenth-century employment
        restrictions on, 28
"In Defense of Chaos" (Shahn), 210
India, office development in, 303,
    304–5
industrial betterment, 70, 81
Industrial Design, 208
industrialization, 13, 16–17, 297
    Chicago labor movement's
        response to, 102
    Le Corbusier's thoughts on, 128
Industrial Workers of the World
    (IWW), 113
Indy Hall, 305, *307*
*Information Machine, The: Creative
    Man and the Data Processor,* 158
information technology, 304
Infosys, 304–5
In Search of Excellence (Peters and
    Waterman), 237, 238, 272
insurance industry, 247
Intel, 261, 264–65
Interiors, 269
International Congress of Modern
    Architecture, 230

Internet, 270–71
Interpolis, Tivoli Plaza, 293–95, *296*
Italy, white-collar movement in, 218
It Can't Happen Here (Lewis), 120
Izenour, Steven, 231

Jacobs, Jane, 134, 142, 229–30, 286
Jaffe, Rona, 176
jails, cubicles in, 243
James, Henry, 105
Japan:
    management theory in, 237, 238,
        263
    1980s competitiveness of, 237, 241
    Taylor's influence in, 52
jazz, 129
Jeanneret, Charles-Édouard, *see* Le
    Corbusier
Jencks, Charles, 228, 230–31
JFN, 215
Job, The (Lewis), 40–41, 72–73, 78,
    91–92, 119
Jobs, Steve, 260, 261, 262, 273, 305
John Hancock Tower, 229
Johnson, Philip, 131, 140–42,
    232–36, *235*
Johnson/Burgee, 233
Jones and Laughlin Steel
    Company, 18
Judge, Mike, 282
Jungersen, Christian, 3

Kakar, Sudhir, 46
Kanarick, Craig, 269
Kanter, Rosabeth Moss, 80, 171, 223
"Kelly Girls" agency, 293
Kent, Robert Thurston, 57
Kitty Foyle (Morley), 91
Knoll, Florence Schust, 143, 148–49,
    151, 201
Knoll, Hans, 148
Knoll Planning Unit, 148–49, 216

knowledge workers:
  ideal of, 5, 200, 208, 225, 240, 259,
    267, 300
  1960s definition of, 195, 196, 197,
    198–99, 212
  1960s management view of, 210
  1970s reality of, 226
  1980s concept of, 248
  Propst's designs for, 189, 200, 206,
    207, 212, 214
  Silicon Valley, 259–71
  twenty-first-century, 300
Kocka, Jürgen, 115
Kodak, 242
Kracauer, Siegfried, 8, 117–18
Krantz, Judith, 93, 95
Kropotkin, Peter, 127
Kubrick, Stanley, 142

labor movement:
  anarchist factions of, 102–4
  beginnings of, 21, 23, 26, 43, 45,
    54, 55
  in Chicago, 102–4, 107–8
  early-twentieth-century gains of,
    112
  Japanese attitude toward, 238
  mid-twentieth-century, 192–94, 246
  1920s decline of, 113
  1980s difficulties of, 236, 239
  office workers' nonparticipation in,
    84, 114–15, 192, 194
  post–World War II, 145
  Taylorism criticized by, 63
  Taylor's hatred of, 49
  white-collar, 112–13, 118, 121,
    122–23, 124–25
  see also Left
Lacey, Edward, 56
Lambert, Phyllis, 140
Lange, Hope, 140, 177, 177
Language of Post-modern
  Architecture, The (Jencks), 230

Larkin, John, 65
Larkin Administration Building,
  64–71, 69
Learning from Las Vegas (Venturi,
  Scott Brown, and Izenour), 231
Le Corbusier, 96, 127–31, 130, 132,
  133, 230
Lederer, Emil, 116–17
Leffingwell, W. H., 57–59, 76, 124,
  188
Left:
  1960s cultural dominance of, 210
  office workers' scapegoating by,
    113, 119–22
  white-collar class consciousness of,
    122, 123
  see also labor movement
Lemmon, Jack, 154, 179, 180
Lenin, Vladimir, 51–52
Lessig, Lawrence, 305
Lever House, 5, 135–38, 136, 137
Lewis, David, 179
Lewis, John L., 124
Lewis, Sinclair, 40, 72, 73, 91,
  119–20, 168
Lhoest, Louis, 294, 295
Liberation Management (Peters),
  266
Life, 53, 135
Life in the Crystal Palace
  (Harrington), 155, 168–70, 224,
  241
lightbulbs, fluorescent, 132, 133
Lincoln, Abraham, 107
Lippold, Richard, 141
Liquidated (Ho), 247
Liverpool, England, 16
Living Office, 308, 310
Livingston, Ron, 280
London, Jack, 91
London, office buildings in, 97
London Building Act (1894), 97
Lonely Crowd, The (Riesman), 152,
  153, 159, 161, 190

Loos, Adolf, 111
Loring, Charles, 72

Macaulay Company, 122
McElligott, Tom, 274
McGinley, John C., 280
McGregor, Douglas, 190–91
Machlup, Fritz, 196, 199
McIntyre, Shirley, 84–85
McKim, Mead & White, 140
McKinsey, 293
MacLaine, Shirley, 180
McLuhan, Marshall, 40, 187
Mad, 154
Mad Men, 135, 173
Madonna, Carol, 284–85
Make Space: How to Set the Stage
    for Creative Collaboration
    (Doorley and Witthoft), 307
management theory:
  development of, 5, 45–63, 70
  education in, 113
  female workforce's importance
    to, 77
  Japanese, 237, 238, 263
  late-twentieth-century, 237–38,
    241–42, 272, 300
  in 1960s, 190–92, 195–200, 210,
    224
  personality-testing trend in,
    164–66, 191
  post-Depression approach to,
    125–27
  in post–World War II Germany,
    201
  Silicon Valley's influence on, 266,
    270
  twenty-first-century, 302–3
  see also business-speak; human
    relations movement; Taylorism
Managerial Revolution, The
    (Burnham), 156

managers:
  early-twentieth-century increase in,
    33, 38, 39, 42, 43, 45, 55, 59, 317
  factory, 47–48, 63
  1970s duties of, 222
  in 1980s, 237
  worker observation by, 42, 57, 61,
    62, 68, 126–27, 245, 246, 259,
    292, 294, 301
  workers' separation from, 42, 60,
    62–63, 63, 144, 150, 205, 209–10,
    242, 243, 270, 274
  see also middle managers
Man in the Gray Flannel Suit, The
    (Wilson), 154, 156, 165–68, 241,
    281
"Man of the Crowd, The" (Poe), 15
manufacturing:
  late-twentieth-century layoffs in,
    239, 240
  mid-twentieth-century decline of,
    156, 192, 212, 240–41
  nineteenth-century growth of, 20,
    40, 77
  Taylor's ideas about, 45
  see also factories
marketing, 156
Marshall Field Wholesale Store, 102
Martin, Darwin D., 64, 65, 66
Marx, Karl, 32, 115, 116
Maslow, Abraham, 191
Masonic Temple, 108
maternity leave, 291–92
Mayer, Marissa, 290–91, 303
Mayer, Walter, 84–85
Mayo, Elton, 126, 127, 164, 191
media:
  architecture in, 234
  cubicle's image in, 242–43
  feminist protests in, 250, 252
  nineteenth-century clerks'
    portrayal in, 14, 17, 28, 30
Medici family, 12

Meijer, 306
Melville, Herman, 9–10, 31
Menlo Innovations, 301
mercantile business:
  nineteenth-century transformation
    of, 20
  railroads' effect on, 39–40
Mercantile Library Association, 28
meritocracy, 194, 198, 247, 260
Merrill, James, 98
Metropolis, 220
Metropolitan Life Insurance
  Building, 88, *89,* 101
Metropolitan Life Insurance
  Company, 88–89
Microserfs (Coupland), 265, 267
Microsoft, 263, 264, 265, 278, 297
middle class:
  female office workers from, 78,
    79–80, 90
  German studies of, 115–19, 153
  office workers' membership in, 4,
    23, 27, 36, 62, 77, 84, 106, 112,
    115–19, 122, 156, 194, 241
Middle East, skyscrapers in, 97
middle managers, *141,* 190
  discontent among, 6, 150, 226–27
  late-twentieth-century layoffs of,
    238–39, 240, 241, 247
  Whyte's condemnation of, 161
Midvale Steel Works, 47
Mies van der Rohe, Ludwig, 131,
  138, 140, 141, 142, 148, 232
Milam Building, 132
Mills, C. Wright, 4, 7, 8, 41, 115,
  159, 194, 311
Minsky, Marvin, 264
Miss America Pageant protest, 250
Moby-Dick (Melville), 10
Modern Efficiency Desk, 42
modernism, 127, 148, 149, 207
  see also architecture, modernist
Monadnock Building, 109

Mondrian, Piet, 129, 131
Moneyball, 49
Moore, Charles, 231
Moore, Gordon, 261
Morley, Christopher, 73, 91
Morrison, Hugh, 100
Moses, Robert, 229
motion:
  Leffingwell's studies of, 57, 58, 59
  Propst's focus on, 187, 188–89, 206,
    211
  Taylor's studies of, 46, 48
motion pictures, 61
Motion Study (Gilbreth), 57
Ms., 175
Mumford, Lewis, 99, 133–35, 137,
  138, 228
Museum of Modern Art, 131
Muybridge, Eadweard, 52, 61
Muzak, 169, 201

Nation, 75
National Association of
  Manufacturers (NAM), 163
National Labor Relations Act
  (1935), 124
National Office Management
  Association, 124, 125
National Science Foundation (NSF),
  257, 258
Nazi Party, 116, 119
Nelson, George, 144, 189, 207–8,
  211, 216, 234, 308
Netherlands:
  twenty-first-century office design
    in, 293–98
  white-collar movement in, 218
New Deal, 123, 124
Newman, Shirley, 151
New Masses, 120–22
New Republic, 123
New Society, The (Drucker), 195

Newsweek, 224

New York, 274

New York, N.Y.:
  Le Corbusier's travelogue of, 129
  nineteenth-century office workers
    in, 14, 16, 25, 29
  office buildings in, 88, 96, 97, 98,
    100, 101, 108–9, 129, 130, 133,
    134–42, 228, 232, 236
  post–World War II corporate flight
    from, 145, 149

New-York Enquirer, 23

New York Post, 214

New York Stock Exchange, 212

New York Times, 51, 239, 263

New-York Tribune, 29, 30, 51

New York Tribune Building, 100

NextSpace, 306

Nichols, Mike, 237

Nilles, Jack, 258, 259

9 to 5, 253–54

9to5 (organization), 252–53, 254

Nixon, Richard, 245

No Collar (Ross), 268

North by Northwest, 138

Noyce, Robert, 261

Nussbaum, Karen, 252, 254

Obama, Barack, 196

O'Brien, Thomas, *24*

Odyssey (Homer), 169

office(s):
  amenities in, 59, 64, 67, 70, 106,
    107, 130, 135, 138, 149, 202, 235,
    261, 262, 268, 284, 286, 288
  automation in, 157–58, 210, 223,
    245–47, 256–58
  bull-pen, 200
  cleanliness in, 125, 143
  color in, 144, 208
  cultural dominance of, 8, 73
  "democratic" spaces in, 150–51,
    262, 264, 270, 275, 276, 277, 285

dot-com era, 5, 6, 147, 256–77
in early skyscrapers, 105–6,
  109–10, 111, 130, 133
early technological advances in, 5,
  40–41
early-twentieth-century, 33–34,
  42–43, 54–63, 105–6, 109–10,
  111, 112, 118, 125, 129–30
empty labor in, 6, 8, 10, 14, 279
environmental problems in, 243,
  245
equipment in, 34, 36, 216
etymological root of, 12–13
"flexibility" in, 204, 205, 210, 217,
  236, 268, 294, 295, 307, 308,
  311
Gilded Age, 44, 45
individual isolation in, 8, 225, 236,
  248–49, 258
late-twentieth-century, 240–55
mid-twentieth-century, 133,
  134–35, 137–38, *141,* 143–44,
  146, 147–52, *152,* 157–58, 159,
  160, 161, 162, 165–70
modular, 5, 6, 147–48, 185–86,
  212, 216–17; *see also* cubicle(s)
1920s murder case involving, 84–85
in 1970s, 221–27
1970s fashion in, 224
in 1980s, 235–42
nineteenth-century, *see*
  countinghouses
noise in, 205, 264
nonterritorial, 257–58, 266, 275
open-plan, 202–5, *203,* 209, 217,
  235, 238, 242, 261, 264, 270, 308;
  see also Bürolandschaft
origins of, 4, 5, 12–17, 33–71
pets in, 289–90
popular perception of, 4, 11, 12, 13,
  14, 17, 34, 35, 60, 73, 98, 99, 144,
  152–54, 159–62, 165–70, 173,
  175–81, 183–84, *184,* 242–44,
  248, 253–55, 265, 270, 278–83

sexual politics in, 73–74, 77, 80–92, 82, 94–95, 173–82, 252–5; *see also* sexual harassment
Silicon Valley, 262–71, 286–92
social requirements in, 8, 68, 88–89, 159, 161, 165, 172, 221–22, 259, 268
space planning in, 148–49, 188–89, 201, 210, 274, 307; *see also* office design
Taylorism's application in, 54–63, 88, 105, 125, 201, 205, 301
twenty-first-century, 278–311
utopian ideas about, 5, 31–32, 60, 104–5, 108, 130, 200, 208, 254, 255, 259, 260, 263, 266, 267, 272, 275, 276, 277, 283, 285–86, 296, 300; *see also* upward mobility
"virtual," 275–76, 277, 284
waste in, 304
women's roles in, 6, 74–76, 77, 79, 80
worker interactions in, 18–19, 135, 146, 206, 212, 214, 258, 270, 285, 289, 290, 296, 297, 301–2, 305, 306
work flow in, 57–59, 67, 151, 201, 202
see also business; office design; office workers; telecommuting
Office, The, 3, 280
Office, The: A Facility Based on Change (Propst), 183, 212
Office Boy (board game), 35, *37,* 109
office boys, 76
office buildings:
early-twentieth-century, 35–36, 63–71, 88, 112
light in, 65–66, 106, 131, 133, 134, *137,* 141, 143, 235, 236, 245
nineteenth-century, 20
shared use of, 305–7
speculative development of, 303–5
see also architecture; skyscrapers

office design, 6, 183–220
Bauhaus approach to, 148
"cave and commons" approach to, 264, 296–97
college-style, 262, 265, 275, 287–88
in computer age, 5, 6, 147, 256–57
European, 200–204, 218–20
Frank Lloyd Wright's approach to, 65, 66–67
impersonal, 214, 216, 217, 275, 276, 277, 283
Le Corbusier's approach to, 129–30, *130*
management structure's influence on, 42–43, 201
mid-twentieth-century, 137–38, 143–44, 146, 147–52, *152,* 200–204
modular, 147–48, 185–86, 212, 216–17
1960s innovations in, 5, 190, 199–200, 206–14, 217, 232
1970s ideas about, 256–58
Propst's contributions to, 184–89, 206–14, 215, 217, 218, 220, 232, 239, 242, 244, 268, 270, 307, 308, 326
Silicon Valley's effect on, 261, 262–71
subjectivity problem in, 209, 214, 277, 296
Taylorist approaches to, 56, 59, 61, 88, 125, 201, 205
twenty-first-century, 283–90, 293–98, 301, 307–10
urban metaphor in, 283, 286, 287–88, 294
white-collar labor movement's effect on, 125
office landscapes, *see Bürolandschaft*
Office Management (Galloway), 60
Office Management (Leffingwell), 57

office politics, 3, 8, 193, 226–27, 247,
  248, 274, 276
  nineteenth-century, 26
  see also office(s), sexual politics in;
    office(s), social requirements in
Office Space, 2, 3, 3, 179, 270,
  278–83, 299
"office wife," 89, 223, 246
Office Wife, The (Baldwin), 89–90
office workers:
  computers' effects on, 245–47, 249
  conformity of, 3, 93–95, 99, 99,
    113–14, 118, 146, 153, 154, 157,
    158–70, 190, 191, 225
  contemporary problems of, 212
  discontent among, 2, 6, 23, 25, 44,
    71, 221–55, 256, 264–65, 276,
    279–80, 281–82, 283, 291, 292,
    295
  early, see clerks
  early-twentieth-century, 33–34,
    42–43, 60–61, 62–63, 106, 112,
    118
  educational requirements for, 198,
    225–26, 248
  female, 6, 36, 72–95, 125, 240
  hours of, 6, 29–30, 159, 247, 271,
    272, 284
  late-twentieth-century, 240–55
  management observation of, 42, 57,
    61, 62, 68, 126–27, 245, 246, 259,
    292, 294, 301
  mid-twentieth-century, 133,
    134–35, 137–38, 143–82
  1960s conception of, 194–200
  in 1970s, 221–27
  in 1980s, 235–42
  passive resistance by, 246–47
  personality testing of, 164–66,
    191
  popular culture portrayals of, 2–3,
    14, 15–16, 17, 24, 28, 29, 30,
    62, 72–73, 81, 82, 83, 85–88,
    89–92, 93–94, 98, 99, 99, 113–15,

  119–22, 121, 123–24, 152–54,
    159–62, 165–70, 173, 175–81,
    184, 237–38, 248, 253–55,
    278–83
  population of, 2, 4, 13–14, 17, 36,
    74, 133, 144, 156, 191, 192, 226,
    240
  protests by, 249–55, 251
  reactionary stereotype of, 114, 119,
    120–22
  skills' importance to, 193, 194, 198
  Taylorism's effect on, 60–61,
    62–63
  twenty-first-century, 278–83,
    284–92, 294, 295, 297–98,
    300–303, 305–7, 308, 310–11
  twenty-first-century layoffs of, 280
  University of Sydney 2013 study, 2
  see also knowledge workers;
    office(s); white-collar workers
Office Workers Union, 122
Ogden, Mahlon D., 102
Oldenburg, Claes, 274
Only the Paranoid Survive (Grove),
  191, 241
open-source model, 302
Oppositions, 231
Organization Man, The (Whyte),
  152, 153–54, 160–62, 167, 190
Ouchi, William, 237, 238
Ouroussoff, Nicolai, 286
Owen, Robert, 32

Packard, Dave, 261
Page, Larry, 287
Pake, George E., 257
Pale King, The (Wallace), 278
paperwork:
  computer processing of, 158
  early-twentieth-century growth in,
    40, 45, 60
  industrialization's creation of, 13,
    16

office design's effect on, 67, 151
office's connection to, 12
predicted end of, 257, 276
storage of, 41
Paris, France:
  1920s housing shortage in, 128–29
  1930s offices in, 129–30
Park, Ed, 2
Parker Brothers, 35, *36*
Parsons, Lucy, 103
Parton, Dolly, 253
paste-ups, 149
Patri, Giacomo, 123–24, *123*
Peck, Gregory, 154
Pei, I. M., 229
Pendleton, Leonor, 250
Pennsylvania Railroad, *55*
Pepys, Samuel, 12
Peril, Lynn, 94
Personal Days (Park), 2, 280
personnel management, 56–57
Pesce, Gaetano, 276
Peters, Tom, 237, 238, 242, 266, 272,
  285, 300
Philadelphia, Pa., nineteenth-century
  office workers in, 17
Philadelphia Savings Fund Society,
  132
Phillips, Thomas, 56
Picasso, Pablo, 61
Pirates of Silicon Valley, 262
Pixar, 294
Plantronics, 306
Playtime, 183–84, *184*, 218
pneumatic tubes, 40
Poe, Edgar Allan, 15
Polanyi, Michael, 197
Pop Art, 144, 208
Popper, Karl, 195
Porter, Sylvia, 214–15
"porterhouses," 29
porters, 25
Portland Municipal Services
  Building, 234

postmodernism, 227–36, 286
Power Elite, The (Mills), 152
Poyfair, Will, Jr., 52
Pratt, Tom, 185
Pravda, 51
*Principles of Scientific Management,
  The* (Taylor), 52
*Production and Distribution of
  Knowledge in the United States,
  The* (Machlup), 199
Propst, Robert, 5, 183, 184–89, *186*,
  200, 204, 206, 209, 210–14, 215,
  217, 218, 220, 230, 232, 239, 242,
  244, 268, 270, 307, 308, 326
*Protestant Ethic and the Spirit of
  Capitalism, The* (Weber), 100
proxemics, 187–88
Pruitt-Igoe homes, 230
psychology, 125, 126, 154, 156, 164
public relations, 156, 163
publishing industry, labor organizing
  in, 122–23
Pullman, George, 107–8
Pullman Building, 107, 108, *108*
Putnam, Claude A., 163
Pynchon, Thomas, 256

Quickborner, 201, 202, 204, 205

racism, 25, 28, 83, 87, 114, 145, 225,
  254
railroads, 38, 39, 50–51
  labor organizing on, 107–8, 112
Ramparts, 210
Rand, Ayn, 134
Raymond Loewy Associates, 135
Razorfish, 268, 269
Reagan, Ronald, 239
Redactron Corporation, 257
Reinhold, Robert, 263
Remington Rand, 157
Remington typewriter, 36, 75–76

Retail Clerks International
Protective Association (RCIPA),
112
Revolutionary Road (Yates), 154
Rice, Elmer L., 114
Richardson, Henry Hobson, 102
Riehle, Richard, 280
Riesman, David, 159, 170
Ripley, E. P., 39
Rockefeller Center, 111, 130
Rockwell, Norman, 148
Rodgers, Daniel, 70
Rolm Corporation, 263
Rookery Building, 102
Root, John Wellborn, 100, 102, 104
Root, Stephen, 281
Ross, Andrew, 266, 268
*Rough and Ready; or, Life Among
the New York Newsboys*
(Alger), 35
Rousseau, Jean-Jacques, 4

Saarinen, Eero, 111, 148, 157
Saarinen, Eliel, 111, 148
San Francisco, Calif.:
nineteenth-century office workers
in, 17
skyscraper development in,
228–29
Saturday Evening Post, 148, 151,
208–9
Scandinavian Airlines Building, 219
Scary Mommy, 291
Schnelle, Wolfgang and Eberhard,
201, 202
Schumpeter, Joseph, 143, 155–56,
195, 197
Scientific Office Management
(Leffingwell), 57
scribes, medieval, 12
Scruples (Krantz), 93–94
scuttle (game), 173

Seagram Building, 5, 138–41, *139,
141,* 232
Sears, 165
Sears Tower, 308
secretaries, 76, 80, 84, 89–90, 106,
134, 181–82, 222–24, 246,
249–55
"Self-Reliance" (Emerson), 23
Sex and the Office (Brown), 173,
174–75
Sex and the Single Girl (Brown),
174
sexual harassment, 6, 83–84, 86,
249, 250, 252
sexual revolution, 93
Shahn, Ben, 210
Shanghai, China, 97
Sherman, Cindy, 140
Shockley Semiconductor Labs, 261
Sholes, Christopher, 75
sick building syndrome, 243
Siebert, Paul, 308
Silent Language, The (Hall), 187
Silicon Graphics, 287
Silicon Valley, 259–71, 286–92
Simmons College, 92
Sinclair, Upton, 62, 77
Skidmore, Owings and Merrill
(SOM), 135, 147, 150, 151
Skyscraper (Baldwin), 106, 123
skyscrapers, 96–142
American-ness of, 97, 101, 103, 131
antimodern appearance of early,
100–101, 105
critics of, 105, 109, 133–35, 142,
228, 230–31, 234
European restrictions on, 97
file cabinets' resemblance to, 41
glass, 111, 127, 130–32, 133, 134,
135, *136,* 138, 304
labor actions against, 102, 103, 104
Le Corbusier's thoughts on, 129,
130

light courts in, 66
offices in, 105–6, 109–10, 111, 208
ornate entrances to, 105, 233
postmodern, 233
post-1920s design trends in,
  110–12, 127
real estate speculation on, 111, 142,
  228–29
standardized nature of, 110, 111,
  138, 141, 142
wind's effect on, 133
see also architecture; office
  buildings
Smith, Adam, 49
socialism, 32
Social Security Act (1935), 124
Society to Promote the Science of
  Management, 50
sociology, 153, 187
soldiering, 43, 47
Solow, Robert, 267
Something Happened (Heller),
  159–60
Sorkin, Michael, 234
Soviet Union, 126, 145, 161
space:
  cultural understanding of, 187
  see also office(s), space planning in
Specht Harpman Architects, 269–70
Spinner, Francis Elias, 74
Sprint, 275
Standard Oil, 43
Stanford Conference on
  Entrepreneurship, 260
Stanford University, 259, 287
Stanwyck, Barbara, 85, 86, 87
steel, 36, 100, 132, 233
Steelcase Corporation, 2, 42, 216,
  306, 307, 308
stenographers, 74–75, 79, 80, 81–83,
  112, 162
Stern, Robert A. M., 231
Sticks and Stones (Mumford), 99

stopwatch, 48, 52, 54
Stratton Commercial School, *19*
Students for a Democratic Society,
  190
Stumpf, Bill, 185, 271
Sullivan, Louis, 5, 100, 101, 102,
  109–10
Sunar, 217
Sweden:
  maternity leave in, 291
  white-collar movement in, 218
Swerve, 269
System, 56, 57

Taft-Hartley Act (1947), 192
Tafuri, Manfredo, 140
Tailer, Edward, 21, 23–27, 28, 29, 62
"Tall Office Building Artistically
  Considered, The" (Sullivan),
  101, 109–10
Tange, Kenzo, 130
Tarkington, Booth, 91
Tati, Jacques, 183, 184, *184*
Taylor, Frederick, 45–50, *48,* 51, 54,
  55, 190, 196–97
Taylorism, 49–50, 51–54, *63,* 189
  behavioral sciences' overtaking of,
    125, 126
  global spread of, 97
  Le Corbusier's support of, 128
  modern resurgence of, 191
  offices' application of, 54–63, 88,
    105, 125, 201, 205, 301
TBWA\Chiat\Day, 283–86, *285,*
  290
telecommunications, 258
telecommuting, 5–6, 258–59, 283,
  288–89, 291, 292, 293, 301
  see also freelancers
telegraph, 36, 38, 40
telephone, 36, 40
Temp Economy, The (Hatton), 293

Terkel, Studs, 227

Then We Came to the End (Ferris), 2, 280

Theory Z (Ouchi), 237, 238

Thoreau, Henry David, 22

Thriving on Chaos (Peters), 266

Tilt-A-Whirl, 276

Time, 234, 275

Time Bind, The (Hochschild), 271–72

Today show, 158

Toffler, Alvin, 258

Tokyo, Japan, Tange's design plan for, 130

Tomlin, Lily, 253

Towards a New Architecture (Le Corbusier), 127–28

"Traitorous Eight," 261

Travelers, 240

Twitmyer, George, 68

2001: A Space Odyssey, 142

typewriters, 36, 75–76

Uffizi gallery, 12

Understanding Media (McLuhan), 40

Unicor, 243

United Nations Secretariat Building, 133, 134–35, 138

United Office and Professional Workers of America, 123

United States:
  class politics in, 170, 255
  corporate mentality in, 68, 96, 97, 101, 103, 104–5, 131
  female government employees in, 74
  freelancers in, 299, 306, 310–11
  Gilded Age corruption in, 43–44, 45
  landscape of, 36, 38
  maternity leave policies in, 291–92

mid-twentieth-century workforce of, 192, 197–98, 212
  "New Economy" in, 265–66, 267, 270
  1960s economic growth in, 205–6
  1960s social changes in, 190, 224, 261–62
  1960s tax code changes in, 216
  1970s energy crisis in, 245
  1980s economic difficulties in, 227–28, 236, 237, 240, 263
  1980s ethos in, 233, 247
  nineteenth-century depressions in, 40
  open-plan offices in, 204, 209, 217
  post–World War II affluence in, 143–44, 155
  suburban homes in, 243
  tallest buildings in, 97, 108
  temp workers in, 293
  twenty-first-century economic uncertainty in, 278, 280, 299, 311

Unity Building, 105

UNIVAC, 157, 158

Untitled Film Still #14 (Sherman), 140

upward mobility, 4–5
  clerks' focus on, 23, 26–29, 30–31, 32
  in corporate organizations, 39
  mythology of, 34–35, 36, 63, 88, 106, 113, 124–25, 192–93, 226, 240, 241
  1960s view of, 191–93, 194
  post–World War I view of, 112
  in Silicon Valley, 260, 261
  women's exclusion from, 77, 80
  yuppie view of, 247–48
  see also white-collar workers, status concerns of

"Urban Convalescence, An" (Merrill), 98

urban renewal, 98, 134, 229, 230
U.S.A. (Dos Passos), 54

Valve, 301
Vanity Fair, 14
Veldhoen, Erik, 293–94, 297–98, 300
Venturi, Robert, 230, 231
Vidor, King, 99, *99*
Vietnam War, 261
von Mises, Ludwig, 195, 199

Wainwright Building, 100
Walden (Thoreau), 22, 34
Wallace, David Foster, 278
Warren, Clinton J., 105
Waterman, Robert H., 237, 238, 242, 272
Watertown Arsenal, 54, 55
Watson, Thomas J., Sr., 157, 170
Wealth of Nations, The (Smith), 49
Weaver, Sigourney, 248
Weber, Max, 100, 283
Wells, Samuel, 14–15
Westchester County, N.Y., 145
Western Electric, 126
Westinghouse, 165
When the Cathedrals Were White (Le Corbusier), 96, 129
White Collar (Mills), 4, 7, 8, 115
White Collar (Patri), 123–24, *123*
white collars, 15
"White Collar Slaves," 120
white-collar workers:
  in Chicago's "Loop," 101, 104, 108
  emergence of, 7
  European, 218–20
  labor organizing of, 112–13, 118, *121,* 122–23, 124–25, 192, 194
  late-twentieth-century layoffs of, 239–40, 241, 242
  masculinity issue for, 84, 85, 121, *121,* 163, 170
  mid-twentieth-century prestige of, 5, 7, 193
  racial restrictions on, 25, 28, 87, 145, 224–25, 254
  status concerns of, 7–8, 15, 21, 22, 23, 25, 26–29, 30–31, 32, 42, 62–63, 75, 80, 84–85, 88, 106, 115–19, 122–25, 151, 153–54, 159, 160, 178, 179, 180, *180,* 201, 205, 223, 252–53, 255, 265, 274, 277, 311; *see also* upward mobility
  wages of, 21, 74, 77, 79, 84, 112, 246
  see also middle managers; office workers
Whitman, Walt, 16
Whyte, William H., 160–62, 163, 164, 165, 167, 171, 190, 198, 272
Wiener, Norbert, 187
Wiesel, Elie, 265
Wilde, Frazer B., 150, 151
Wilder, Billy, 154
Wilkinson, Clive, 284, 285, 288
Will & Grace, 271
Willis, Carol, 111
Willson, Paul, 280
Wilson, Sloan, 154, 156, 167
window washers, 135
Wired, 266, 276, 277
Witthoft, Scott, 307
wives, corporate, 170–72
Wolverine Worldwide, 306
Womb chair, 148
women, 72–95, 125
  business education for, 78–79, 93–95
  "marriage bar" against, 81, 92
  "Metropolitan Belles," 89
  mid-twentieth-century restrictions on, 172, 176, 177, 179, 181–82
  in office population, 36, 74, 76–78, 90, 240

women *(continued)*:
  office protests by, 249–55, *251*
  office work's appeal to, 78
  in post–World War II corporate
    workforce, 145, 149–50
  sexual harassment of, 6, 83–84, 86,
    249, 250, 252
  in temp industry, 293
  traditional office roles of, 6, 74–76,
    77, 79, 80
  wage discrimination against, 74,
    77, 79
  white-collar labor organizing of,
    112
  see also office(s), sexual politics in;
    wives, corporate
women's suffrage movement, 81
Women Working, 254
Woolworth tower, 101
Wooton desk, *24*, 42
work:
  American attitudes toward, 14, 34,
    70
  "piece-rate" approach to, 49, 55
  Taylor's ideas about, 47–49, 54; *see*
    also Taylorism
  twenty-first-century arrangements
    for, 298–300, 301–3, 305–7, 311
  see also office(s); office workers

Work and the City (Duffy), 305
Work in America (report), 245
Working (Terkel), 227
working class:
  female office workers from, 78
  see also blue-collar workers
Working Girl, 237–38, 248, 254–55
workstations, 187, 189, 206–10, 211,
  269, 270
World Design Congress, 239
World Trade Center, 204, 228
World War I, 112, 115, 116
World War II, 143
Wozniak, Steve, 261, 262
Wright, Frank Lloyd, 5, 64, 65, 66,
  67, 68, 69
Wright, Richard, 120

Yahoo!, 290–92, 303
Yamasaki, Minoru, 228
Yates, Richard, 154
YouTube, 2
yuppies, 247–48

Zappos, 306
Zola, Émile, 91
Zunz, Olivier, 88

ABOUT THE AUTHOR

Nikil Saval is an editor of *n+1*. He lives in Philadelphia.
This is his first book.